ABOUT ISLAND PRESS

Island Press is the only nonprofit organization in the United States whose principal purpose is the publication of books on environmental issues and natural resource management. We provide solutions-oriented information to professionals, public officials, business and community leaders, and concerned citizens who are shaping responses to environmental problems.

In 1999, Island Press celebrates its fifteenth anniversary as the leading provider of timely and practical books that take a multidisciplinary approach to critical environmental concerns. Our growing list of titles reflects our commitment to bringing the best of an expanding body of literature to the environmental community throughout North America and the world.

Support for Island Press is provided by The Jenifer Altman Foundation, The Bullitt Foundation, The Mary Flagler Cary Charitable Trust, The Nathan Cummings Foundation, The Geraldine R. Dodge Foundation, The Charles Engelhard Foundation, The Ford Foundation, The Vira I. Heinz Endowment, The W. Alton Jones Foundation, The John D. and Catherine T. MacArthur Foundation, The Andrew W. Mellon Foundation, The Charles Stewart Mott Foundation, The Curtis and Edith Munson Foundation, The National Fish and Wildlife Foundation, The National Science Foundation, The New-Land Foundation, The David and Lucile Packard Foundation, The Pew Charitable Trusts, The Surdna Foundation, The Winslow Foundation, and individual donors.

Cool Companies

To Patricia

Cool
COMPANIES

How the Best Businesses
Boost Profits and Productivity
by
Cutting Greenhouse Gas
Emissions

Joseph J. Romm

ISLAND PRESS
Washington, D.C. • Covelo, California

Library of Congress Cataloging-in-Publication Data

Romm, Joseph J.
    Cool companies : how the best businesses boost profits and
productivity by cutting greenhouse gas emissions / Joseph J. Romm.
        p.   cm.
    Includes bibliographical references and index.
    ISBN 1–55963–709–9 (cloth : alk. paper)
    1. Industrial productivity.   2. Just-in-time systems.
3. Industrial efficiency.   I. Title.
    HD56.R64   1999   99–18911
    658.5—dc21   CIP

Printed on recycled, acid-free paper ✪

Manufactured in the United States of America
10 9 8 7 6 5 4 3 2 1

Cool COMPANIES

How the Best Businesses
Boost Profits and Productivity
by
Cutting Greenhouse Gas
Emissions

Joseph J. Romm

ISLAND PRESS
Washington, D.C. • Covelo, California

Library of Congress Cataloging-in-Publication Data

Romm, Joseph J.
   Cool companies : how the best businesses boost profits and
productivity by cutting greenhouse gas emissions / Joseph J. Romm.
      p.   cm.
   Includes bibliographical references and index.
   ISBN 1–55963–709–9 (cloth : alk. paper)
   1. Industrial productivity.   2. Just-in-time systems.
3. Industrial efficiency.   I. Title.
   HD56.R64   1999   99–18911
   658.5—dc21   CIP

Printed on recycled, acid-free paper ♲

Manufactured in the United States of America
10 9 8 7 6 5 4 3 2 1

Contents

Preface   ix

Introduction
How to Be a Cool Company   1

1
Strategic Planning in the Greenhouse   16

2
Henry Ford and Toyota   28

3
Buildings   46

4
Design for Workplace Productivity   77

5
Computers and Clean Rooms   100

6
Cool Power   113

7
Factories—Part I: Motor Systems   140

8
Factories—Part II: Steam and Industrial Processes   157

9
Beyond Benchmarking   180

10
What Price Carbon Dioxide?   205

Conclusion
Carbon Dioxide and Productivity   216

Appendix
There Is No Such Thing as the "Hawthorne Effect"   219

Notes   244

Company Index   265

General Index   267

Preface

This is first and foremost a benchmarking book. I wanted to tell the stories of how the best businesses are leading the way in confronting the new challenges of global warming. With more and more companies making commitments to reduce greenhouse gas emissions, there is a clear need for a book that brings together the best strategies for reducing the emission of such heat-trapping gases as carbon dioxide. Using these strategies as a base, I have laid out a coherent approach for boosting your company's profits and productivity.

But more than gauging what companies can do to reduce emissions from their factories and buildings, this book provides a yardstick for what the entire country can do. For when a significant fraction of businesses adopt these strategies, the country as a whole will not only easily meet its international obligations to reduce greenhouse gas emissions, it will also accelerate economic growth and job creation.

This is a strong claim, particularly given the popular misconception that responding to the threat of global warming will be difficult and costly for businesses and for the nation. That is why I have included detailed case studies from many different types of companies that have boosted profits and productivity by cutting greenhouse gas emissions: to demonstrate that any company can do this and that every company should do this.

❖

I am indebted to the more than one hundred managers, engineers, designers, and line employees who shared their experiences with me. I have named them throughout the book, both in the text and in the endnotes, for it is in the case studies that their remarkable contributions come to life. I thank all of them for their candor and willingness to share their strategies for success.

I am very grateful to all of those who gave me the chance to work at the Department of Energy for five years. It was at the DOE that I was able to study the cutting edge technologies and financial strategies—and able to meet the practitioners—that are the focus of this book. I owe the most thanks to Amory Lovins, who first recommended me for a position at the DOE. He is the most original thinker in this field, and it was working with him that instilled in me the essential idea of this book: that businesses can make money by reducing pollution.

A number of people supported me in my original position as special assistant to the deputy secretary and in my subsequent positions as principal deputy assistant secretary and acting assistant secretary in the Office of Energy Efficiency and Renewable Energy: Bill White, Hazel O'Leary, Charles Curtis, Federico Peña, Kyle Simpson, Dirk Forrister, Christine Ervin, Peter Fox-Penner, Brian Castelli, Elgie Holstein, and Dan Reicher. These are among the finest public servants the country has ever had in the energy field, and they made the DOE a place where the best ideas flourished.

Many colleagues at the DOE and its national laboratories shared their expertise and experience with me over the years. I would particularly like to thank Bob San Martin, Eric Petersen, Darrell Beschen, Dave Bassett, Kim Kendall, Richard Bradshaw, Jessie Ulin, John Archibald, Mark Ginsberg, Ron Fiskum, Mike Myers, Denise Swink, Bill Parks, Lou Divone, Kurt Sisson, Marsha Quinn, Paul Scheihing, Bruce Cranford, Dan Wiley, Tom Gross, Richard Moorer, Pandit Patil, Allan Hoffman, Jim Rannels, Paul Kondis, Marc Chupka, Pat Godley, Bob Kripowicz, Marilyn Brown, Tony Schaffhauser, Michael Simonovitch, and Mark Levine.

Particular thanks go to Art Rosenfeld and John Atcheson for reading multiple drafts and sharing their extensive knowledge with me. I would also like to thank Howard Geller, Neil Elliot, and Gregory Kats for reading through early drafts.

Chris Robertson's unique expertise on energy efficiency in the semiconductor industry proved invaluable for my discussion in Chapter 5. I am indebted to Andrew Jones and Linda Baynham for their assistance in researching some of the case studies. A number of other people provided help that was invaluable to the book, including Tina Kaarsberg, Daniel McQuillen, Michael Muller, Sanjay Agrawal, and Julie Vickers. The appendix on the Hawthorne Effect would not have been possible without the help of Richard Franke, Karen Smith, Doug Tarr, and Carla Moore.

My mother—a designer, a writer, a building manager, and chief executive officer—has always shared her extraordinary wisdom with me. I am very grateful to her for applying her world-class language and management skills to countless drafts.

Todd Baldwin, my editor at Island Press, improved the book immeasurably. He is the best book editor I have had the privilege of dealing with. I would also like to thank Chuck Savitt and the rest of the staff of Island Press for their enthusiastic support of this book from the very beginning.

I owe a permanent debt to Peter Matson, my agent, for his unwavering efforts on behalf of my work and my writing.

Finally, special thanks go to Patricia Sinicropi, whose idealism and support provide me unlimited inspiration every day.

Introduction

HOW TO BE A COOL COMPANY

The most remarkable manager I met during my years working with businesses at the Department of Energy was Aaron Feuerstein, CEO of Malden Mills. His Lawrence, Massachusetts, textile factory makes the popular Polartec and Polarfleece high-tech fabrics. After the plant burned down in December 1995, Feuerstein received national attention because he pledged to keep paying all 3,000 of his employees while he rebuilt the factory, rather than relocate.

At the time, I was helping to run the Office of Energy Efficiency and Renewable Energy, the largest program in the country for developing low-polluting technologies and helping businesses use them. In early 1996, I asked my industrial experts to assist Feuerstein.

Two years later, I attended the groundbreaking for the technology we helped Malden Mills with—a high-efficiency, natural-gas turbine that provides both electricity and steam at low cost, so-called "cogeneration" (see Chapter 6). I was elated to see how well Feuerstein had made use of almost every other strategy discussed in this book to reduce greenhouse gas emissions, including flooding his factory with daylight.

I asked him why he had focused on seemingly secondary issues—reducing energy use, air pollution, and greenhouse gas emissions—even as he was fighting to save the company. Feuerstein answered, *"Over the long-term, it is more profitable to do the right thing for the environment than to pollute it."*

In this book, you will see again and again just how right Feuerstein was. You will meet the best managers, architects, and engineers that I know, to learn their secrets, to benchmark against their astonishing results.

I

> "Global warming is here to stay as a hot button for policymakers, a wild card for business, and a disturbing prospect for us all."
> —*Fortune*[1]

Every company can *significantly* reduce its emissions of gases that contribute to global warming. A "cool" company will cut its emissions by 50 percent or more while *reducing* its energy bill and *increasing* productivity, with a return on investment that can exceed 50 percent and in many cases 100 percent. This book explains how.

Most firms today do not qualify as completely "cool," but many have gone a long way, from the largest companies, such as DuPont, 3M, Toyota, Compaq, and Xerox, to the smallest companies, from the service sector to light manufacturing to heavy industry. The result is a surprising number of "cool" buildings and "cool" factories, of which more than fifty are profiled in this book.

Cool Companies is for three kinds of companies: those who have already made a decision to reduce their emissions, those who are considering whether to do so, and those who are indifferent to global warming but are looking for a major source of competitive advantage.

Since the science of global warming has been the subject of dozens of books, I will not discuss it here, other than to make these points. First, the industrialized nations of the world agreed in December 1997 at Kyoto, Japan, to reduce greenhouse gas emissions below 1990 levels by 2008 to 2012, and, second, the principal greenhouse gas emitted by human activity is carbon dioxide. Your company—every company—should have a strategy to reduce carbon dioxide emissions, for one or more of the following reasons:

- You become convinced by the abundance of case studies in this book that you can vastly improve your profits and productivity with this strategy.
- You believe that the price of carbon dioxide will rise because governments will inevitably do it to restrict emissions. Some states have already put a price on carbon dioxide.
- You want to be known as a green company, a cool company, especially in a world where the foreign competition is becoming greener and more efficient.
- You care about the environment you are leaving your children.

You may believe that your carbon dioxide emissions have nothing to do with your company's competitiveness. If so, you have missed recent

advances in technology and design that have created high-performance work-places and factories where the carbon dioxide reductions pay for themselves rapidly, often in under a year. *This book allows you to benchmark yourself against the remarkable achievements of the very best companies.* You will learn the specifics of how your company can achieve the new standard for excellence.

Corporate carbon dioxide emissions come almost entirely from using energy generated from the burning of fossil fuels. About *one-sixth* of the nation's carbon dioxide emissions come from energy used in commercial buildings. About *one-third* comes from energy used in manufacturing. Your company can reduce its emissions in two ways:

1. *Energy efficiency:* achieving the same output of goods and services while reducing total energy consumption, and
2. *Decarbonization:* using energy that has lower emissions of carbon dioxide (what I call "cool" power).

Combining these two approaches will sharply reduce not only your carbon dioxide emissions. It will also drastically cut your emissions of sulfur dioxide, oxides of nitrogen (NOx), and particulates—*primary components of urban air pollution, which inflict serious harm on human health and the environment.* These pollutant emissions have a market value (about \$100/ton for sulfur, and, in some places, more than \$1,000/ton for NOx). So, here is another good reason to become a "cool" company: You may be able to make money reducing these harmful air pollutants.

This book provides you with the strategies you need to boost profits and productivity while reducing greenhouse gas emissions. Each chapter begins with a discussion of the key components of the strategies and at least one representative case study.

Chapter 1 focuses on how strategic planning has begun to transform the practices of a company whose product is a major source of greenhouse gases—Royal Dutch/Shell. Shell is the world's most profitable oil company and a benchmark for corporate strategic planning. It has two scenarios—one based on energy efficiency, the other on cool power—that have convinced it that the world can respond to global warming while maintaining historical levels of economic growth. The scenarios have helped lead Shell to invest a half billion dollars in its new core renewable energy business. Shell is also reducing its own emissions of greenhouse gases. *Shell projects that it will have reduced its total greenhouse gas emissions in 2002 to more than 25 percent below 1990 levels.*

Chapter 2 presents the case of Toyota Motors, a company that is obsessed with reducing waste and increasing productivity:

- One Toyota plant in California cut its total energy consumption by one-third while more than doubling its output with technology that helped *reduce its defect rate from three per hundred to zero.*

Defects were once accepted as inevitable and quality was viewed as expensive, but that changed in the 1980s and 1990s as U.S. manufacturers responded to the Japanese manufacturing challenge. Defects are now seen as a measure of *inefficiency,* and the goal is to prevent them from occurring in the first place. So, too, *pollution is seen by our coolest companies as a measure of their inefficiency,* rather than an inevitable by-product of production. The goal is to prevent pollution from occurring in the first place.

What is perhaps most striking about Toyota's remarkable strategy for eliminating waste is that it has its origins with Henry Ford, who pioneered many of the best practices in both lean production and pollution prevention. I discuss Ford's and Toyota's thinking about lean production to explain why systematic efforts to reduce greenhouse gas emissions so often lead to productivity gains.

> Lean thinking focuses on process improvement and prevention-oriented design strategies to reduce waste systematically. In this book, you will learn how to apply lean thinking to offices, buildings, and factories to minimize wasted energy. With this "cool and lean" strategy, your company will increase productivity at the same time it reduces greenhouse gas emissions.

Chapter 3 begins the step-by-step "How To" for becoming cool. Since every company—service sector or manufacturing—has buildings, we begin with the proven strategies for making any building energy efficient. Cutting energy use by a quarter has been achieved in thousands of buildings. Hundreds of buildings have broken through the "25 percent savings" barrier. Cool buildings that cut energy use—and hence greenhouse gas emissions—*in half* are increasingly commonplace, as many of the examples in this chapter demonstrate:

- Centerplex, a small business in Seattle, reduced the energy consumption in its two office buildings *by 55 percent with a 1.5-year payback,* and expects to raise that to 65 percent.
- The Ridgehaven office building in San Diego cut its energy consumption *by 70 percent,* saving $80,000 a year, using a "low-bid" contractor. Utility financing of the efficiency improvements turned a three-year payback into an *instantaneous payback.*

- BlueCross BlueShield of Oregon cut energy use *by 61 percent* at its Portland headquarters. BlueCross *did not have to put up any money* for the project, which was financed by the local utility, but instead is paying for it entirely from the monthly energy savings.

A good rule-of-thumb for what a comprehensive efficiency upgrade can achieve today is an annual energy savings of $1 per square foot with a simple payback of two to three years—a return on investment (ROI) of 33 to 50 percent. (In this book, a one-year simple payback means a $1 investment that generates $1 in savings each year, which equates to a 100 percent ROI. If it generated $0.50 in savings each year, that would be a two-year simple payback or a 50 percent ROI.)

> By following the strategies in this book, you may be able *to finance some or all of the cost of your upgrade off-balance-sheet—letting you achieve savings without adding to your overall debt.*

Stop thinking of energy efficiency as mundane. Whether you are a service sector or manufacturing firm, your employees work in buildings designed by people who probably had little understanding of the work that would be done in the building, and even less understanding of how to design a building to maximize performance. We now know how to design a new building or upgrade an old one to reduce energy use and other operating costs, while at the same time reducing absenteeism and increasing worker productivity.

Chapter 4 examines more than a dozen office and building designs that have boosted productivity from 5 to 15 percent, providing measurable benefits that can dwarf reductions in operating costs. While an upgrade that cuts energy use in half can save $1 per square foot in annual energy costs, it can generate more than $10 a square foot in new profits every year if it boosts productivity even 5 percent. Productivity gains have made it possible to achieve deep energy savings with paybacks of under two years—ROIs exceeding 50 percent:

- VeriFone, a California manufacturer, renovated and daylit one of its buildings. The improvements that saved 60 percent of the energy would have paid for themselves in 7.5 years. The *productivity rise of more than 5 percent* and absenteeism drop of 45 percent brought the payback to under a year—an ROI of more than 100 percent.
- A Georgia carpet manufacturer moved into an extensively daylit building and *workers' compensation cases dropped from twenty per year to under one per year.*

Researchers at Carnegie Mellon University's "Intelligent Workplace"—a must-see building for anyone designing a new or upgraded office—have begun to quantify these productivity improvements. They have systematically analyzed a large post-occupancy database of new buildings and retrofits. The researchers then estimated the benefits of design improvements for a 100,000-square-foot workspace with 500 employees. They concluded, for instance, that while improved lighting design would add $370,000 to the initial cost of the workplace, it would add $680,000 in value in energy savings and other reduced operating costs. Far more important, Carnegie Mellon has calculated that *efficient lighting could provide a productivity benefit of up to $14.6 million.*

Productivity-enhancing design requires a shift in your corporate thinking. Companies underinvest in their workplaces in part because they tend to see efficiency improvements as simple cost-cutting, which rarely motivates much management attention or capital spending. A key purpose of Chapter 4 is to help managers see these investments as strategic productivity-enhancing investments crucial to their company's long-term survival.

Many, if not most, managers believe that physical changes in the workplace, such as improved lighting, are irrelevant to the productivity of its workers. Their error is due in large part to a powerful myth created at Western Electric's Hawthorne Works in the 1920s and 1930s. The so-called Hawthorne Effect, discussed in the Appendix, has not been supported by subsequent research. Even more shocking, the original experiments not only failed to demonstrate the effect, but actually *proved the reverse,* that work conditions can have the dominant impact on productivity.

Chapter 5 examines the work of two of the best energy-efficiency experts in the business: Ron Perkins and Lee Eng Lock. It explores how Perkins, facilities manager for Compaq in the 1980s, helped break down the traditional corporate barriers to strategic investment in buildings, and, with Lee, helped Compaq become one of the coolest of companies. The chapter then follows Perkins' move to Supersymmetry, an energy consulting company founded by Lee in Singapore, the benchmark for reducing energy consumption in semiconductor manufacturing.

The chapter discusses the strategy of one of the industry leaders in cool semiconductor manufacturing, STMicroelectronics. The company measures its energy inefficiency in terms of electricity consumed per million dollars of production cost. With Supersymmetry's help, the company has exceeded its remarkable goal of *reducing its energy inefficiency 5 percent per year for three years running.* The chapter concludes with two more of Supersymmetry's best upgrades, which have wide application throughout the semiconductor industry:

- An integrated circuit factory outside of Manila upgraded its lighting, heating, and cooling system and *cut the electricity usage per chip by 60 percent*.
- In Malaysia, Western Digital built what is now considered the most efficient disk drive factory in the world, *cutting energy consumption 44 percent with a one-year payback*. These cuts were achieved even though plant floor space increased by more than 10 percent and air filtration requirements increased 1,000-fold!

Chapter 6 looks at "cool" power. Just as every business from the service sector to manufacturing can improve the energy efficiency of its workplaces, so too can everyone choose energy sources that have lower emissions of greenhouse gases.

Your opportunities for cool power, rare just a few years ago, are booming, sparked by recent advances in technology as well as the accelerating trend toward deregulation of the electric utility sector. For the first time in decades, your company will in all likelihood have considerable choice in how you get your electricity. When you choose wisely, you can lower both costs and emissions at the same time.

The average fossil-fuel electric power plant converts *only one-third* of the primary energy it burns—coal, oil, or gas—into electricity. More energy is lost distributing it from the power plant to the end user. *The energy lost by U.S. electric power generators equals all of the energy that the entire country of Japan uses for all purposes: buildings, industry, and transportation.* Most of this lost energy is in the form of waste heat that is literally thrown away by electric utilities. Thus, more fossil fuels must be burned in your company's furnaces and boilers to generate the heat and steam needed to run your business.

Today, off-the-shelf natural gas technologies can simultaneously generate electricity and steam with *80 to 90 percent efficiency right at a factory or building*. This power deserves the label "cool" not merely because it has lower emissions of greenhouse gases but also because it is not wasteful of heat. Chapter 6 examines companies big and small that have reduced emissions of carbon dioxide by one-quarter to one-half while lowering their energy bill simply through the use of cogeneration, also known as combined heat and power:

- One small fiber processor in New York City installed a cogeneration system that cuts its energy costs by more than half and its carbon dioxide emissions by one-third, all with a *two-year payback*.
- A 90 percent efficient cogeneration system at the Chicago Convention Center *saves $1 million a year* in energy costs and cuts carbon dioxide emissions in half.

We'll also examine the remarkable advances in renewable energy, including solar, wind, and geothermal, that will allow a company to get some of its power from these coolest of energy sources:

- Some Phillips 66 gas stations are using geothermal energy to cut energy costs and carbon dioxide emissions from heating, cooling, and refrigeration by 40 percent.
- Toyota has chosen to purchase electricity from purely renewable sources for virtually all of its California facilities. This choice, made possible by California's utility deregulation, instantly cut Toyota's carbon dioxide emissions in California by more than half.

A few companies have combined energy efficiency in their buildings with cool power, to achieve large reductions in greenhouse gas emissions:

- McDonald's is using both geothermal energy and energy efficiency in a new restaurant near Detroit to reduce greenhouse gas emissions 40 to 50 percent while cutting energy costs by 20 percent.
- The first cool U.S. skyscraper—the forty-eight-story office tower, Four Times Square, in Manhattan—has cut greenhouse gas emissions 40 percent. The design combined energy efficiency with two fuel cells for cogeneration as well as photovoltaics for clean electricity from the sun.

> "Only a third of U.S. manufacturers are seriously scrutinizing energy usage, where savings in five areas can move billions to the bottom line."
> —*Fortune*[2]

Chapters 7 and 8 focus on energy efficiency in manufacturing. The five areas on *Fortune*'s list are energy-efficient lighting and efficient HVAC (heating, ventilation, and air conditioning), covered earlier, and motors, compressed air, and steam. (These are the five easiest gold mines. Two others that I discuss on these pages—cogeneration and process improvement—add billions more to the bottom line.) Large savings are available. General Motors audited ten of their manufacturing plants and found opportunities for cutting energy used in compressed air and steam systems by 30 to 60 percent.

Chapter 7 examines motors and motor systems (including compressed air). These are probably the best opportunities for most companies because electricity production generates so much carbon dioxide and motors consume *nearly three-fourths* of industrial electricity. At one research, development, and manufacturing facility, *Lucent Technologies examined fifty-four motors and found that 87 percent were oversized.* Some motors were operating at only 16 percent of full load. The Department of Energy audited a dozen industrial motor retrofits around the country and found an average energy savings of one-third with a payback of a year and a half. What was rare even five years ago is off-the-shelf today. You can reduce the energy use of motor systems *by one-quarter to one-half* with increases in productivity and decreases in maintenance and scrap:

- An Arkansas steel tube manufacturer replaced a key motor and drive. The 34 percent energy savings would have paid for the new system in five years, but the improvement in productivity and reduction in scrap paid for it in five months—*a 200 percent return on investment.*
- A California textile plant cut the energy consumption of its ventilation system 59 percent by installing motor controls, *saving $101,000 a year.* An energy services firm paid for the system, turning a 1.3-year payback into an *instantaneous* one. By reducing the plant's airborne lint, the new system increased product quality.

What happens to that sharp manufacturer who pursues the comprehensive approach I describe—making its motors, compressed air systems, and buildings *all* more energy efficient? You become a cool company like Perkin-Elmer, maker of analytical instruments.

- Perkin-Elmer *cut energy consumption per dollar of sales by 60 percent from 1991 to 1997.* Its Norwalk, Connecticut, plant cut the electric-power bill 26 percent, despite an increase in rates and expansion in square footage.

Chapter 8 examines the large opportunities for saving steam and process energy. These strategies are of most value to heavy manufacturing and the process industries, such as chemicals, pulp and paper, and steelmaking, which are the industries responsible for most manufacturing energy usage. Steam accounts for $20 billion a year of U.S manufacturing energy costs and over one-third of U.S. industrial carbon dioxide emissions. To be cool, your industrial company needs to improve the efficiency with which you generate and use steam, as these companies have:

- At a multi-factory complex in Flint, Michigan, General Motors combined efficiency with cool power to cut carbon dioxide emissions from steam use by more than 60 percent. Annual savings came to $4 million with a two-year payback.
- Simply by insulating its steam lines, Georgia-Pacific reduced fuel costs by

one-third with a six-month payback at its Madison, Georgia, plywood plant. The project saved 18 tons of fuel per day, lowered emissions, made the workplace safer, and improved process efficiency.

Even the most energy-intensive industries, such as chemical manufacturing, can achieve remarkable results when they take a systematic approach that combines all seven cool strategies: energy efficiency in lighting, HVAC, motors, compressed air, and steam systems with improved cogeneration and process redesign.

- From 1993 to 1997, DuPont's 1,450-acre Chambers Works in New Jersey reduced energy use per pound of product by one-third and carbon dioxide emissions per pound of product by nearly one-half. Even as production rose 9 percent, the total energy bill fell by more than $17 million a year. By 2000, the company as a whole has committed to cut greenhouse gas emissions by 40 percent compared to 1990 levels.

Chapter 9 examines how you can help your employees and your community lower their energy bill while reducing their carbon dioxide emissions.

- Chicago-based A. Finkl & Sons has cut energy consumed per ton of forged steel shipped by 36 percent and has planted more than 1,600,000 trees, which capture carbon dioxide. As a result, *the company's net manufacturing emissions of greenhouse gases are zero.*
- A shade tree planted near a city building saves ten times as much carbon dioxide as a tree planted in the forest because it reduces the energy used for air conditioning and helps to cool the city. Such tree-planting, coupled with use of lighter colored roofs and road material, could *cool a city like Los Angeles by five degrees,* cutting annual air-conditioning bills by $150 million, while reducing smog by 10 percent, which is comparable to removing three-quarters of the cars on L.A.'s roads.

Perhaps you are a manufacturer whose raw materials require more energy to create than the energy you buy to run the company. Reducing the so-called embodied energy in your products could become part of your new cool strategy. Consider the case of Interface Flooring Systems, a leading manufacturer of carpet and carpet fiber:

- *The embodied energy in the material that Interface uses to make 25 million square meters of carpet tile a year exceeds the process energy needed to manufacture that carpet tile by a factor of twelve.* Interface Flooring Systems made process improvements that saved 2.5 million pounds of nylon from being purchased. The embodied energy of the unneeded nylon equaled the energy used by their manufacturing and administrative facilities.

"The temperature is really rising. . . . It's time to act. . . . Let's also experiment with a carbon-trading system for CO_2 emissions that emulates the current market for pollution credits."
—*Business Week*[3]

Chapter 10 explores a key issue for your company's planning: What is the future price of carbon dioxide likely to be as the world's nations move to restrict greenhouse gas emissions? My answer to this question is shaped by the experiences of two companies, SYCOM and British Petroleum (BP).

SYCOM is an energy services company based in New Jersey that helps companies adopt the cool strategies described in this book to reduce their emissions of sulfur dioxide and oxides of nitrogen (NOx), which at the same time reduces their carbon dioxide emissions. Some economic models suggest that the price of carbon dioxide needed to meet the Kyoto target may be as high as $30 to $60 a ton (which would raise energy prices substantially). SYCOM's experience suggests the price for carbon dioxide will ultimately be far less, well below $15 a ton.

BP is the world's third largest oil company and a major source of greenhouse gases. It has begun cutting its emissions:

- At one Australian refinery, BP has reduced unit carbon dioxide emissions 19 percent since 1995 and expects to achieve an overall 45 percent reduction through efficiency and cogeneration. Ultimately, the company expects to offset all the rest of the refinery's emissions by improved land-use practices and forestry sequestration.

Based on its experience, *BP has voluntarily committed to reduce its greenhouse gas emissions to 10 percent below 1990 levels by 2010.* This is a deeper cut than the industrialized nations as a whole agreed to at Kyoto. The more companies make such commitments and reduce emissions using the strategies in this book, the lower the future price of carbon dioxide will be. Already some entire industrial sectors have made major climate commitments:

- The steel industry has put forth a voluntary plan to reduce greenhouse gas emissions by 10 percent below 1990 levels by the year 2010.

COOL *CONTINUOUS* IMPROVEMENT

You may believe that your company "did energy conservation" in the late 1970s or early 1980s, or that you've captured all the "low-hanging fruit," the "obvious" energy-saving investments with the quickest payback or highest rate of return. As we'll see, today's energy efficiency is to yesterday's energy conservation as the personal computer is to the typewriter. Advances in combined heat-and-power and renewable energy are just as amazing.

The entire notion that low-hanging fruit is easily exhausted turns out to be a myth. Environmental improvement is continuous. Consider Dow Chemical's Louisiana Division.[4] With some 2,000 employees in more than twenty plants making chemicals such as ethylene, the division was incredibly successful at continuously increasing productivity through pollution prevention. You might have predicted that by 1982, after two major energy shocks, if any company in the country had captured the low-hanging fruit of energy savings, it would be one as energy intensive as a world-class chemical manufacturer. Nonetheless, the division's energy manager, Ken Nelson, began a yearly contest in 1982 to find energy-saving projects that paid for themselves in less than one year (an ROI of over 100 percent). His success was nothing short of astonishing. Here are the numbers:

The first year had twenty-seven winners requiring a total capital investment of $1.7 million with an average ROI of 173 percent. After those projects, many in Dow felt there couldn't be others with such high returns. The skeptics were wrong. The 1983 contest had thirty-two winners requiring a total capital investment of $2.2 million and a 340 percent return—a savings for the company of $7.5 million in the first year, and every year after that. Even as fuel prices declined in the mid-1980s, the savings kept growing. Contest winners increasingly achieved their economic gains through process redesign to improve production yield and capacity. By 1988, these productivity gains exceeded the energy and environmental gains. The average return for the 1989 contest was the highest ever, an astounding 470 percent. In 1989, sixty-four projects costing $7.5 million saved the company $37 million a year—*a payback of eleven weeks.*

Certainly anyone would predict that after ten years, and nearly 700 projects, the 2,000 employees would be tapped out of ideas. Yet the contests in 1991, 1992, and 1993 each had in excess of one hundred winners with an *average ROI of 300 percent.* Total savings to Dow from the projects of just those three years exceed $75 million a year.

➡️   **If Dow, with all its well-trained engineers and a systematic process for identifying opportunities, hasn't finished capturing all its energy-savings opportunities, how likely is it that your company has?**

The only question is whether or not Ken Nelson's approach can be transferred to other enterprises in completely different lines of business.

I was able to answer that question when I came to the Department of

Energy in 1993 as special assistant to the department's chief operating officer, the deputy secretary. After I had benchmarked a number of the best companies, it was obvious that Dow's approach was one of the most successful. Could the department duplicate Dow's results?

As a $15 billion agency, the Department of Energy is involved in a variety of activities that consume energy and generate waste, from basic research to the production of electronic equipment. Although our various divisions had robust pollution prevention programs, I was certain that some of the largest opportunities were being missed. To find and fund the projects with the highest return on investment, we reorganized our Waste Minimization and Pollution Prevention Executive Board, with the department's chief operating officer as the chair and myself as the executive director. We hired Ken Nelson, who had recently retired from Dow, to train several of our facility staffs around the country on Dow's program. We held a "Return-On-Investment" contest.

As at Dow, many in the department were skeptical that such opportunities existed. Yet, *the first two rounds of the contest identified and funded eighteen projects that cost $4.6 million and provided the department with $10.0 million in savings every year,* while avoiding more than 100 tons of low-level radioactive pollution and other kinds of waste.[5] Many of the projects increased worker productivity or achieved other benefits not included in ROI calculations, such as freeing up valuable laboratory space for other activities. In addition, one special project identified by the contest but funded separately cost $4.2 million to implement but provided the department a one-time savings of $37.6 million, a stunning 1,300 percent ROI.

Finally, on the basis of the success of this headquarters-based program, many of the regional operating offices decided to run their own contests. They funded 260 projects *at a cost of $20 million that have been estimated to achieve annual savings of $90 million a year.* No wonder the department's director of waste minimization, who was originally one of the biggest skeptics, recently called the return-on-investment contest "one of the most successful programs in government I've ever been associated with."

If an organization as diverse, far-flung, and bureaucratic as the U.S. Department of Energy can adopt Dow's approach of *continuous* environmental improvement, any company can. Yours can. Chapter 8 details how you will maximize profits by minimizing waste.

After a few years, I was put in charge of the Office of Energy Efficiency and Renewable Energy. This is the largest program in the world aimed at working with companies to speed the development and adoption of energy-saving, pollution-preventing, productivity-enhancing technologies, products, and processes. With its billion-dollar budget and 500 employees, the office has developed many of the energy-efficient and low-carbon-dioxide technologies discussed in this book, from advanced lighting and high-tech windows to clean industrial technologies and advanced cogeneration to renewable energy.

The office has helped tens of thousands of families and building owners reduce their energy consumption. It has funded audits of more than 7,000 small and medium-sized manufacturers of every sort, providing them 50,000 energy-saving and waste-reducing recommendations, information now available on-line. The office has worked with the major motor suppliers and users to validate a systems approach to reduce motor energy use and to develop a software package that any company can obtain for free. And it has formed partnerships with all of the major process industries—chemical, pulp and paper, steel, aluminum, metal casting, and glass—to develop technologies to reduce their energy use and pollution while increasing their competitiveness.

In 1998, I left the Department of Energy to work with companies to identify best practices and develop customized strategies. I am constantly amazed at how many major companies are unaware of how much money and energy they are wasting and how many are misinformed about cogeneration and other opportunities for lowering emissions while increasing profits. That is why I have written this book and established the nonprofit Center for Energy and Climate Solutions. The center is a one-stop shop for businesses seeking to reduce greenhouse gas emissions and is helping companies to adopt the cool strategies discussed in this book.

No law says that your company has to rush out tomorrow and reduce its greenhouse gas emissions, although every day lost is money lost. The Kyoto Agreement does not require reductions to begin until 2008, but since the goal is to reduce emissions *below* 1990 levels, starting sooner will inevitably lower your costs. Emissions are rising every year for most companies. The longer your company waits to act, the less time there will be for you to achieve reductions and the deeper those reductions will ultimately have to be.

Most energy-efficiency improvements result in such higher profits and productivity that you will want to begin them immediately. On the other hand, some of the cool power opportunities will be influenced by the age of your equipment or the peculiarity of your state's utility regulations; these improvements may make sense now—or five years from now. A key point of this book is that *every company should have a multi-year strategy* for capturing the largest possible benefits of becoming cool with the least investment and the fastest payback.

Every kind of company faces different opportunities and challenges. If you are a service sector company, you should be able to cut your total carbon dioxide emissions *in half* over a five-year period, with energy efficiency playing the biggest role. If you are a manufacturer, you could do the same, with at least half of the savings coming from energy efficiency and the rest from cogeneration and fuel switching. If yours is a process industry, your equipment costs the most and turns over the most slowly, but you also gain the most from the new cogeneration technology; you may require ten years to become cool.

The biggest energy users—as well as companies that are growing very fast—may need to set their 50 percent goal in terms of greenhouse gas emissions per unit of product. If yours is a fast-growing company, you have a chance to incorporate cool features into the design phase of *new* buildings or *new* factories, where huge gains are possible at much lower cost than in retrofits.

The 50 percent reduction goal is neither easy nor impossible. Many companies have already achieved it. *Xerox's "Waste-Free Office" program requires offices across Europe and North America (including forty-five buildings in New York) to reduce energy consumption 50 percent.* It has already achieved that goal at its Palo Alto Research Center in California (see Chapter 9).

The 50 percent goal is a target that your company publicly announces, which then drives you to take a longer term perspective than you normally do, but, which, paradoxically, will lead you to fast payback, low-risk investments you never knew you were missing—process-improving investments that decrease waste while increasing productivity. You will have transformed yourself into a richer company because you have become a cool company.

STRATEGIC PLANNING IN THE GREENHOUSE

Imagine a world in which fossil-fuel use has begun a slow, steady decline. More than a third of the market for new electricity generation is supplied from renewable sources. The renewables industry has *annual* sales of $150 billion, and the fastest growing new source of power is solar energy. An environmentalist's fantasy? No, that's one of two planning scenarios for three to four decades from now, developed by Royal Dutch/Shell Group, the world's largest publicly traded oil company, widely viewed as a benchmark for strategic planning. In this future, average per capita energy consumption nearly doubles by 2060.

Imagine "a rather different world in which new technologies, systems and lifestyles would deliver continuing improvements in energy efficiency so that average per capita consumption rises by only some 15 percent by 2060."[1] A techno-fantasy? No, this is Shell's other energy scenario as described in 1997 by John Jennings, former chairman of the Shell Transport & Trading Group. "Technological advances are enabling increasing energy efficiency in many areas from industrial processes to building construction," *cutting primary energy use by up to 60 percent in the transportation, industrial, and commercial sector.* Shell bases this "dematerialization" scenario on emerging advances ranging from highly fuel-efficient "supercars" to advances in materials, miniaturization, and information technology.

Whether through cool power or energy efficiency, Royal Dutch/Shell Group, the best predictor in the energy business, anticipates a cool future for the world. It is betting hundreds of millions of dollars on its scenarios by expanding its renewable energy division. At the same time, the company is dramatically reducing its own greenhouse gas emissions. Shell projects it will reduce its total greenhouse gas emissions from the equivalent of 140 million tons of carbon dioxide in 1990 to 100 million tons or less in 2002.[2]

The key strategic planning question for any company is: How can we thrive in an uncertain future? The version of that question considered on these pages: What should we do if our core business is likely to be affected by growing concern over global warming? We will learn how big companies like Toyota, DuPont, Interface, and General Motors, as well as small ones, are changing their products and processes because of environmental considerations, including global warming. I begin with a company whose primary product—oil—is a leading cause of global warming: Royal Dutch/Shell. Shell is reinventing itself using its much admired approach to strategic planning. As you seek to help your own company change, you will find few better models than the process pioneered by Shell.

If a major producer of fossil fuels, such as Royal Dutch/Shell, can embrace the change that global warming requires, your company can, too. The key is scenario planning aimed at changing the decision-making assumptions of your managers.

All that is needed for either of Shell's remarkable scenarios to come true is for companies to adopt the cool strategies described in this book.

THE PLANNERS OF ROYAL DUTCH/SHELL

Throughout the 1990s, Royal Dutch/Shell has found itself leading the list of the world's most profitable companies, thanks in large part to its excellence in strategic planning. In 1997, the company had sales of $128 billion, net income of $7.8 billion, and more than 100,000 employees in 132 countries.

Yet, just as the company has reached the top, its future is in jeopardy. On the one hand, the company believes that both global warming and limited supplies of fossil fuels, particularly oil, merit serious attention. On the other hand, the company has been shaken by the public response to its practices in Nigeria and to its plans to dispose of its forty-story Brent Spar oil storage tank. These factors have driven the company's latest efforts at planning, inspiring its top managers to pursue transforming Shell into a "sustainable energy company." While it is easy to be skeptical of such a difficult goal for the world's largest oil company, Shell's track record on turning planning into reality is matched by very, very few companies.

According to the *Economist* magazine, "The only oil company to anticipate both 1973's oil-price boom and 1986's bust was Royal Dutch/Shell."[3] Correctly anticipating the future was not the hard part for the Planning Group. One of the developers of Shell's planning process, Pierre Wack, has written, "Surprises in the business environment almost never emerge without warning." Many others foresaw the oil crisis. *The hard part was getting Shell's managers to rethink their mental models.* Wack saw the same mind-set problems that scientists, for example, must overcome before they break through to novel insights. Wack came to realize that providing new information was not enough, because "novel information, outside the span of managerial expectations, may not penetrate the core of decision makers' minds, where possible futures are rehearsed and judgment exercised."[4]

Wack compares that time to the days prior to the attack on Pearl Harbor, when there was a massive volume of intelligence signals ("noise") coming in. He quotes Roberta Wohlstetter writing in 1962: "To discriminate significant sounds against this background of noise, one has to be listening for something or for one of several things. . . . One needs not only an ear but a variety of hypotheses that guide observation." The Japanese commander of the attack, Mitsuo Fuchida, was quite surprised that the attack on Pearl Harbor was a surprise. Prior to the Russo-Japanese War of 1904, the Japanese Navy used a surprise attack to destroy the Russian Pacific fleet at anchor in Port Arthur. Fuchida asked, "Had these Americans never heard of Port Arthur?"[5]

The approach Wack developed at Shell was "scenario planning," but a type of scenario planning entirely different from that of most companies. Wack did not merely want to quantify uncertainties—i.e., the price of oil may be $20 or $40 per barrel in 2005—because this offers little help to decision makers. Wack wanted to offer managers two or more complete worldviews or scenarios—grounded in a sound analysis of reality. One of these scenarios might be business as usual, while at least one would be a radically different, though plausible, view of the world.

Even though Wack foresaw the energy crisis and presented the results to Shell's management, "no more than a third of Shell's critical decision centers" were acting on the insights gained from the energy crisis scenario. Wack came to realize that although all managers had the new information, most were still processing it through their old paradigm or mental model, what Wack called their "microcosm."

> I cannot overemphasize this point: unless the corporate microcosm changes, managerial behavior will not change; the internal compass must be recalibrated. . . .

> Our real target was the microcosms of our decision makers: unless we influenced the mental image, the picture of reality held by critical decision makers, our scenarios would be like water on stone. . . .

Wack and his fellow planners realized they "needed to design scenarios so that managers would question their own model of reality and change it when necessary, so as to come up with strategic insights beyond their minds' previous reach." The Planning Group designed a set of scenarios early in 1973 that would force a paradigm shift. Shell managers were presented a business-as-usual scenario. They were also presented the underlying assumptions required for that scenario to hold. Those assumptions were shown to be wholly unrealistic, requiring several "miracles"—each of which was highly improbable—to occur simultaneously. The only way to delay the energy crisis would be the discovery of "new Middle East–sized oil reserves in an area that would have no problem in absorbing revenues" or "seizure and control of producers by consuming countries."

Once managers saw that their faith in the status quo was built on miracles, they were more receptive to new thinking. Wack and his fellow planners led the Shell managers through the process of building a new paradigm, showing them what was likely to happen in the future and what the implications were for the managers' own decisions and actions.

Since oil price increases were inevitable, oil demand would drop. Demand would no longer outpace GNP. Using this scenario, Wack told the refining managers to prepare to become "a low-growth industry."

The planners made clear that the energy shock would have dramatic effects worldwide, but it would affect individual nations differently. The effect would depend on whether a given country was an oil exporter or importer, whether it was free market or centrally planned, and, for importers, how much they relied on imports and how easily they could find alternatives. Therefore, one basic, rigid strategy would not be useful for operating different companies in different parts of the world. Each region would have to respond independently. As a result, Shell would "need to further decentralize the decision-making and strategic process."

Even those managers who remained skeptical at least understood the flaws in their old paradigm and the powerful implications of the new one. When the OPEC oil embargo did occur, and the underlying assumptions of the energy crisis scenario were proven correct, Shell managers were far quicker to shift their behavior accordingly. They slowed down investments in refineries. Their projections of energy demand were consistently lower and more accurate than those of their competitors. They decentralized, while their competitors were becoming more centralized—and hence more inflexible—in a world of rapidly changing events.

Shell rose rapidly from its position as the weakest of the seven largest oil companies in 1970 to one of the two strongest *only ten years later.* Anticipating the oil bust of the mid-1980s was apparently even more lucrative, helping to put the company atop *Fortune* magazine's list of the world's most profitable companies in the 1990s.

Shell developed the two scenarios described in this chapter in the mid-1990s. Predicting our energy future over the next few decades is risky, but Shell's track record on predictions is hard to beat. When such a company predicts a fundamental transition from fossil fuels to renewable energy and other advanced energy technologies—one that will have a significant impact on every aspect of our lives—smart executives pay attention.[6]

SCENARIO ONE: SUSTAINED GROWTH (WITH COOL POWER)

The first scenario, which Shell labels "Sustained Growth," entails rapid growth in renewable energy. Here is what Chris Fay, Chairman and CEO of Shell UK Ltd., said in a 1995 speech:

> There is clearly a limit to fossil fuel. I showed how Shell analysis suggests that resources and supplies are likely to peak around 2030 before declining slowly. . . . But what about the growing gap between demand and fossil fuel supplies? Some will obviously be filled by hydroelectric and nuclear power. Far more important will be the contribution of alternative, renewable energy supplies.

Fay presented a detailed analysis of future trends in oil supply and demand, noting that the fossil fuel peak in 2030 would occur at a usage level 50 percent higher than today. Shell's analysis does not rely exclusively on supply limits. After all, people have been worried about such limits for decades. What's significant is that the analysis incorporates the tremendous technological advances that have been made in renewables over the past two decades and that are projected to be made over the next two decades.

These advances in wind power, solar energy, and biomass power (discussed in Chapter 6) have been receiving only modest press attention. They have, however, been sufficient to convince Shell planners that renewables may take over the market for electricity generation in a few decades *even if electricity from fossil fuels continues to decline in costs.* Their analysis does not assume price hikes in fossil fuels. Nor does Shell assume any attempt by governments to incorporate environmental costs into the price of energy, even though every single independent analysis has found much higher environmental costs for fossil fuel generation than for non-fossil fuel generation. Indeed, the growing consensus on the dangers of global warming, as reflected in the work of the Intergovernmental Panel on Climate Change and in the Kyoto agreement, makes it almost inevitable that carbon dioxide will have a price in most industrialized countries within several years (see Chapter 10).

This scenario is called Sustained Growth because "abundant energy supply is provided at competitive prices, as productivity in supply keeps improving in an open market context." In this scenario, energy consumed per capita worldwide rises steadily, so much so that by 2060 the global average reaches the level Japan has today. Worldwide economic growth of 3 percent per year is achieved through a 1 percent per year improvement in energy intensity (energy per unit GDP) and a 2 percent per year increase in energy production, which increasingly comes from renewable sources.

According to Shell's strategic planning group, the Sustained Growth scenario "can claim to be a genuine 'Business as Usual' scenario, since its energy demand is a continuation of a long historical trend, and the energy is supplied in the way which continues the pattern [of the last 100 years] in which energy forms rise and fall over periods of decades."

Shell's analysis projects the steady and large drops in the price of renewables of the last two decades into the next two decades, as further advances in technology combine with economies of scale as market share grows. For instance, Shell believes that by 2010 commercial energy from biomass (plant matter) could provide 5 percent of the world's power. The value of that power generation would exceed $20 billion. By the mid-2020s, annual sales of wind power plants could exceed $50 billion.

Shell expects photovoltaics (which converts sunlight into electricity), along with emerging highly efficient, low-polluting natural-gas-driven technologies, such as fuel cells (see Chapter 6), to be key drivers of the growth of distributed power systems. Such systems may increasingly be the power source of choice as opposed to the large, expensive, polluting power plants of the past. Just as smaller, more versatile personal computers trumped large mainframe computers or as cellular phones are making the grid of telephone lines obsolescent, distributed sources can obviate the need for huge power lines and other costly elements of a large electric-power grid in developing nations (aside from having superior environmental performance.) The Sustained Growth scenario projects that photovoltaics and other direct conversion of sunlight will be the most rapidly growing form of commercial energy after 2020. Annual sales in 2030 could exceed $100 billion.[7]

This is a "cool power" scenario because it anticipates greatly expanded use of both renewable energy and advanced natural gas technologies. This scenario is tantalizing not only because of Shell's reputation but because it offers the serious possibility that the world could soon realize the dream of nearly pollution-free energy. As we will see, Shell is betting a considerable amount of money on this scenario.

SCENARIO TWO: DEMATERIALIZATION (WITH ENERGY EFFICIENCY)

Shell's second, "Dematerialization," scenario is "driven by convergent and mutually enhancing developments in information technology, telecommunications, materials and biotechnology which in turn could have considerable potential to change social values and with them lifestyles. If this indeed happened, we would experience a transition phenomenon as profound as that brought about by the invention of the automobile and subsequent developments in individual mobility during this century."

Shell planners, for instance, see converging technological developments having a revolutionary impact on transportation. Advances in engines (such as fuel cells), batteries, control system electronics, alternative fuels, and super-strong, light-weight materials lead to the emergence of a super-efficient car. This supercar, together with advances in information technologies that make possible extensive telecommuting, internet shopping, and the like, reduce primary energy use in transportation by 60 percent. New technologies, processes, and materials make possible similarly large savings—60 percent—in the industrial and commercial sectors. *To achieve this level of savings would require most companies in the developed world and then in the developing world to adopt the energy-efficiency strategies described in this book.*

In this scenario, average per capita energy consumption rises by only some 15 percent by 2060. Primary energy use grows at only 1.3 percent per year until 2030 and then slows to "below one percent as greater energy productivity spreads from the more advanced regions of the OECD to the industrialized and developing countries elsewhere," says Jennings. "To support a three percent growth in GDP, improvements in energy intensity will have to reach a sustained two percent per annum—a rate which admittedly has only been seen for limited periods in the past." Indeed, the historical average of energy intensity improvements in the United States for the last 100 years has been 1 percent per year.

❖

Scenarios are not, however, predictions. The Royal Dutch/Shell planners are not saying how the world *will* be or even how the world *should* be, only how the world *may* be. What is particularly interesting about these scenarios is the extent to which Shell believes in them and is willing to act on them. Perhaps this is in part because these scenarios emerged at a time when the company was, in several respects, under siege.

DRIVING STRATEGIC CHANGE AT SHELL

In the mid-1990s, Shell was trying to decide what to do with a forty-story North Sea oil storage tank, named Brent Spar, that it no longer needed. Its giant carcass extended more than 90 feet above the surface and 370 feet below. When Shell and the British government agreed to allow the company to scuttle the platform and let it sink to the bottom of the ocean, Greenpeace organized a boycott against Shell gasoline in Europe and even landed protesters on the platform itself. Ultimately, the public outcry drove Shell to get independent scientific help to decide what to do with Brent Spar. It chose an innovative reuse proposal for the tank. Slices of the Spar's hull will be cleaned and then used to help complete a planned extension of a Norwegian landing dock. This agreement saved both money and energy that would otherwise have been spent in new steel construction.

At the same time, Shell has been criticized for its operations in Nigeria, where it has been a major oil producer for decades. Nigeria has had a history of political repression. When members of the Ogoni people began attacking the company's oil fields in the early 1990s, "Shell gave Nigeria an important pretext for violence when it specifically asked the government to send the mobile police—known locally as the 'kill-and-go mob,' " *The New York Times* explained in 1996. "Shell paid for the transportation and salary bonuses of some troops—ostensibly oilfield guards—who committed the abuses."[8]

There was more. Growing concern over climate change has led to increased criticisms of Shell, both because of its emissions and for its membership in the Global Climate Coalition, an organization that opposes strong action on global warming. Far more so than in America, Europeans view strong action on global warming as essential and have been critical of companies that appear to endorse inaction.

In response to all of these issues, Shell launched a major effort to rethink its purpose and long-term goals. In the mid-1990s, the company interviewed 7,500 members of the general public in ten countries; 1,300 opinion leaders in twenty-five countries, including experts on energy and the environment; and 600 Shell people in fifty-five countries "to understand society's expectations of multinational companies" and "to explore the reputation, image, and overall standing of the Group." In a remarkable 1998 report, "Profits and Principles—Does There Have to Be a Choice?" the company reported some of the questions in sobering terms: *We had looked in the mirror and we neither recognized nor liked what we saw.*

The result has been a series of actions to reinvent the company. For instance, in the report Shell committed to begin reporting a "triple bottom line" of economic, social, and environmental performance. Shell will continue reporting basic economic measures, such as "return on average capital employed" and economic value added. In addition, Shell will report on "environmental value added," acknowledging "we must adjust our measurements of wealth creation and profit with a charge for natural capital employed," taking into account the impact of their actions on the ecosystem and the depletion of raw materials. The third bottom line Shell will report on is "social value added," which includes benchmarks on social and ethical accountability.

Other reinvention actions involve Shell's business investments. In October 1997, the company established a fifth core business, Shell Solar, which will sit alongside its other core businesses: exploration and production, oil products, chemicals, plus gas and oil. Shell Solar brings together the company's activities in solar, biomass, and forestry. Shell says it will pump more than $500 million into renewable energy technology over the next five years, splitting the money between photovoltaics and biomass. *Shell already owns two photovoltaic companies,* one in Japan and one in the Netherlands. It plans to increase solar cell manufacturing worldwide, with the goal of capturing a 10 percent share of the photovoltaics market by 2005. It is exploring the possibility of entering the wind power business.

The company also plans to expand its existing tree plantation business, much of which is located in South America. It intends to apply its expertise in this area to development of biomass power generation, which, as noted earlier, it expects to be a rapidly growing business.

This move "underscores the Group's strategic direction," said Jeroen van der Veer, the group managing director responsible for renewables, "which is to provide energy and develop resources efficiently, responsibly, and profitably in order to help meet the world's growing needs and to do so in a way that contributes to sustainable development." Commenting on van der Veer's statement, *Oil & Gas Journal* noted in November 1997, "Two years ago, no oil company would have risked a statement stressing sustainable development— at least in the context generally favored by environmental activists—but Shell has learned some hard lessons."[9]

Shell's vision of sustainable development is perhaps best exemplified by its idea of a "Sun Station" for self-sustaining communities:

> In operation, a Sun Station can be owned and managed by Shell Solar or by a local consortium of investors. A station manager with a small local team will operate a tree nursery, a managed wood plantation of high-yield tree varieties, tree harvesting and delivery, and power generation equipment based on a small wood gasifier-engine system. A local grid will be installed to distribute electricity to homes, health clinics, schools, and commercial activities such as small workshops. Photovoltaic power will also provide backup resources for essential uses such as vaccine refrigeration. Co-generated heat supplies will be available for grain-drying, laundry, etc. Where connection to the grid is impracticable, photovoltaic panels with dedicated battery storage will provide basic lighting and

other low-power applications including radio and television. A rural shop located at the power generation sites would stock goods for basic energy needs such as high-efficiency/low-energy consuming lamps or appliances, solar home systems, batteries, gas cylinders, and perhaps fuel and lubricants for two-stroke engines.

That's Royal Dutch/Shell talking—not Arthur C. Clarke or any other science fiction visionary.

Shell is also beginning to invest in the core element of its Dematerialization scenario—the hydrogen fuel cell at the heart of the supercar. Fuel cells are pollution-free electric "engines" that run on hydrogen (see Chapter 6). At the July 1998 launch of London's new Zevco hydrogen-powered taxi, Chris Fay said "we believe that hydrogen fuel-cell powered cars are likely to make a major entrance into the vehicle market throughout Europe and the U.S. by 2005."

In August 1998, Shell signed an agreement to work with a fuel cell engine company owned by DaimlerChrysler, Ballard Power Systems in Canada, and Ford Motor Company. Initially, fuel cell cars are likely to run on liquid fuels such as gasoline, if those fuels can be converted to hydrogen cost-effectively. Shell has proprietary technology for making such conversions. Running on gasoline, fuel cell cars would still have half the carbon dioxide emissions of a regular car.

In the long term, Shell believes cars will run on hydrogen that is generated from renewable energy sources. Those would truly be cool cars, since they would have no carbon dioxide emissions at all. Shell has launched a new company, Shell Hydrogen, to control all activities related to fuel cells and hydrogen research. Fay noted that "at Shell, we are convinced that hydrogen . . . represents one of the fuels of tomorrow. For us, the long-term decarbonization of fuel represents an exciting challenge. *Hydrogen could be the next logical step in the long but steady march from high carbon to low carbon to no carbon fuels.*"

On global warming, Shell's thinking extends back a decade or more. In 1989, Ged Davis, head of scenario planning for Shell International, wrote a paper for Shell titled, "Global Warming: The Role of Energy-efficient Technologies." Today, the company's public expression of concern spans the breadth of their senior management. Shell's senior managing director, Cor Herkstroter, has said, "Despite the many remaining uncertainties about the nature and the risks of the process, I believe that there is now sufficient evidence to support prudent precautionary action." Jennings has said, "given the risks and uncertainties, it is clearly prudent to develop alternative ways of generating energy, learn to use energy more efficiently, and reduce the environmental impact of producing and burning fossil fuels."

In a February 1998 speech, Mark Moody-Stuart, Shell's chief executive, said, "For my own part, I find myself increasingly persuaded that a climate effect may be occurring. . . . We believe that the nature of this risk is such that prudent precautionary measures should be taken. We favored agreement at Kyoto—provided targets were consistent with a flexible long-term global approach. And we believe the outcome was reasonable." He noted that charting a careful course of action on climate change "means not allowing real concern for economic costs and practicalities to prompt shrill opposition to any action—or even a tobacco-industry-like reluctance to admit the possibility of any problem."

In April 1998, Shell decided to leave the Global Climate Coalition.[10] It has also started a new "Sustainable Energy Solutions" fund to support projects outside the company, which will ultimately grow to $25 million a year. At the same time, it has made a high-level internal commitment to reinvent itself as a "sustainable energy company." Whether the world's most profitable oil company can, in fact, achieve as seemingly a contradictory a goal as being a sustainable energy company remains to be seen; but given their past successes, Shell should never be underestimated.

The company has also begun to address its own greenhouse gas (GHG) emissions, which include carbon dioxide as well as methane and chlorofluorocarbons. The company expects to cut its emissions sharply by curtailing the flaring of natural gas in its oil production, by making its operations more energy efficient, and by factoring in a "carbon price penalty in our investment calculations for new projects, and existing major assets, with major GHG emissions." In August 1998 Jeroen van der Veer told an International Energy Agency conference that Shell had already reduced its total GHG emissions 13 percent below 1990 levels and that emissions per unit of production had dropped by nearly 30 percent. In 2002, Shell projects its total emissions will be more than 25 percent below 1990 levels, a drop from 140 million tons of carbon dioxide equivalent to 100 million tons or less.

Shell has, as we have seen, already begun to devote considerable resources to bringing about the two scenarios described earlier, "Sustained Growth" and "Dematerialization." Both of these are, in some sense, sustainable energy scenarios because they stabilize carbon dioxide concentrations at twice the preindustrial levels. This is still likely to result in serious climate change worldwide. Yet, it would stave off the far more brutal impacts that the models suggest the planet would experience if we triple or quadruple carbon dioxide concentrations, which is likely without strong action from both the public and private sector. Either of the goals at the heart of the scenarios—50 percent renewable power by 2050 or decades of 2 percent per year improvement in energy intensity—will require a significant number of the companies in this country and around the world to become cool.

This book is, in one sense, a guide for how to make Shell's scenarios a reality. Indeed, I suspect the ultimate way the planet will stabilize carbon dioxide concentrations is by combining Shell's scenarios, by combining cool power *and* energy efficiency.

Now let's examine the guiding principle behind creating a cool company—the application of lean thinking to reducing your company's greenhouse gas emissions. That will explain why such reductions can be achieved together with the kind of rise in profits and productivity needed to sustain economic growth throughout the twenty-first century.

HENRY FORD AND TOYOTA

Toyota is a triple threat as a cool company. It pioneered the lean production system that minimizes wasted time and wasted resources. It has become a world leader in making and selling highly fuel-efficient cars. And all of Toyota's operations in Southern California are now cool since the company buys 100 percent renewable electricity (see Chapter 6).

Here I examine the lean production system and its origins with Henry Ford. You will learn why process improvement and prevention-oriented design strategies aimed at reducing greenhouse gas emissions lead to productivity gains. Let's start with the story of one of the most energy-efficient manufacturing plants in the country.

TOYOTA AUTO BODY OF CALIFORNIA

In Long Beach, Toyota Auto Body of California (TABC) manufactures and paints the rear deck of Toyota pickup trucks.[1] In 1991, TABC consumed 2.5 million kilowatt-hours (kWh) of electricity. By 1996, TABC had doubled production, was winning special awards for quality, and yet dropped its electricity consumption to 1.7 million kWh. TABC achieved these incredible results with a comprehensive set of energy-efficiency improvements. These included improvements in motors, compressed air, and lighting.

The most striking upgrade turned out to be variable-speed motor drives for controlling the air in the paint booths. Variable- or adjustable-speed drives are electronic controls that let motors run more efficiently at partial loads. *These drives not only save a great deal of energy but also improve control over the entire production process,* as we will see in a number of other factories (Chapter 7). Microprocessors keep these drives at precise flow rates. Moreover, when the production process must be redesigned, adjustable drives run the motor at any required new speed without losing significant energy efficiency.

The company's primary goal in this retrofit was not to save energy but rather to improve the quality of the paint application. Applying paint properly to truck beds requires control over the temperature, airflow/balance, and humidity in the paint booths. Before the upgrade, manually positioned dampers regulated airflow into the booths. Since the upgrade, the dampers are left wide open, while the fan motor speed changes automatically and precisely with touch screen controls, which also provide continuous monitoring of the airflow.

The improvements to the motor systems reduced the energy consumed in painting truck beds *by 50 percent.* More important, the energy-efficient drives had a fantastic effect on product quality. Before the upgrade, TABC had a production defect ratio of 3 out of every 100 units. After the upgrade, the ratio dropped to 0.1 per 100. The value of the improvement in quality is hard to quantify, but TABC's senior electrical engineer Petar Reskusic says, "In terms of customer satisfaction, it's worth even more than the energy savings."

Moreover, as is usually the case with variable-speed drives, the new system gives workers greater control over their process, with even more energy benefits. The old system limited the motors controlling the air into the paint booths to two modes—production and nonproduction. The new system added a third mode (maintenance), thereby saving more energy. Reskusic notes, "As we used it, we learned how to improve its performance." The remarkable success of this upgrade led the company to do more motor upgrades.

TABC also comprehensively upgraded its air compressor system, which consumed 22 to 25 percent of the company's electrical energy. Compressed air is used in all kinds of factories for all kinds of work, such as cleaning, mixing, running machine tools and looms, and moving products around on conveyor belts. The motors that run the air compressors consume a lot of energy.

Originally, Toyota had two 150-horsepower (hp) air compressors in each of five different departments. Following the advice of PlantAir Technology, a consulting firm, the company moved these ten scattered compressors to a centralized area. Now, instead of running six or seven compressors at any one time, TABC uses at most three and only one on weekends. The energy consumed by their compressors was reduced by *more than half*—a typical level of savings for compressed air upgrades (see Chapter 7).

In 1997, the plant received a special award for achieving zero defects. At the same time, the company had reduced total energy consumption by almost one-third in five years, and consumption per unit output by two-thirds. TABC was truly cool and lean.

Why did TABC go to much greater lengths than most companies in reducing energy consumption? As Reskusic explained to me, TABC is "part of the Toyota family," which sees reducing *"muda"* (the Japanese word for "waste") as a key means of increasing profits. Management is very supportive of all efforts to reduce wasted energy, far more than most other companies. Improving motor systems and other energy-efficiency upgrades achieved two key Toyota goals simultaneously: process improvement and waste reduction. To repeat the key point discussed in the Introduction:

> Lean thinking focuses on process improvement and prevention-oriented design strategies to reduce waste systematically. Lean thinking can also be applied to offices, buildings, and factories to minimize wasted energy. This cool and lean approach ensures that your company will *simultaneously* increase productivity and reduce greenhouse gas emissions.

The history of Toyota's lean production system illuminates the intimate connections among reducing waste, improving processes, and increasing productivity. To minimize energy use and greenhouse gas emissions while maximizing profits, your company must become both cool and lean. You must understand not only, as many companies have, that "time is money" but also that "time is energy" and that both time and energy are easy to waste. You must become as obsessed with reducing all kinds of waste as Toyota. And to understand Toyota's obsession with waste first requires understanding Henry Ford's.

FORD'S OBSESSION WITH WASTED RESOURCES AND WASTED TIME

The twentieth century began with Henry Ford's introduction in 1908 of the Model T, coupled with the discovery of huge pools of oil in Oklahoma and Texas. Ford's manufacturing breakthroughs made the Model T affordable to the average worker. The car itself was durable and easy to repair, even by the typical owner. In 1914, Ford had 48 percent of the U.S. auto market and was able to make almost as many cars as the other 300 U.S. car companies combined, using only one-fifth of their total labor.[2]

Ford's Model T came at a time when America was the leading producer of the natural resources needed for an automobile revolution: coal, iron ore, and petroleum. Yet while Ford led the nation to greater wealth by exploiting our seemingly unlimited supplies, he was obsessed with using them efficiently by reducing waste. Here's a typical description in his 1926 book *Today and Tomorrow,* from a chapter titled "Saving the Timber":

> We treat each tree as wood until nothing remains which is ser-vicable as wood, and then we treat what remains as a chemical compound to be broken down into other chemical compounds which we can use in our business. . . . Why should not crating be done with the smallest instead of the largest amount of lum-ber? . . . Why should a crate or a packing box once used be con-sidered only as so much waste to be smashed and burned? . . . We are cutting farther into wood by using wherever possible burlap bags and cardboard boxes—the latter made from waste and in our own paper mill. . . . All scrap wood eventually gets back to the wood salvage department.[3]

These were five standard Ford techniques: (1) using every bit of a raw material, (2) replacing raw material with reusable or recycled products, (3) minimizing packaging, (4) reusing packaging, and (5) recycling as much waste as possible. They would not become standard waste minimization prac-tices for sixty long years. Terms like "clean technology" and "clean produc-tion" would not come into widespread usage until the 1980s, after more than a decade of environmental regulations helped reveal the true cost of pollution and hazardous waste.

With his techniques, *Ford was able to reduce his use of wood by two-thirds even as he doubled production.* Ford distilled all of the wood waste, including sawdust, shavings, chips, and bark: "Each ton of waste wood yields 135 pounds of acetate of lime; 61 gallons of 82 percent methyl alcohol; 610 pounds of charcoal; 15 gallons of tar, heavy oil, light oils, and creosote; and 600 cubic feet of fuel gas."

Ford understood the hierarchy of clean production. Avoiding waste or scrap is most desirable. Next best is reusing waste or scrap, which finds value in the waste and eliminates disposal costs. Ford wrote: "It is not possible to repeat too often that waste is not something which comes after the fact. Restoring an ill body to health is an achievement, but preventing illness is a much higher achievement. *Picking up and reclaiming the scrap left over after production is a public service, but planning so that there will be no scrap is a higher public service.*"

He was equally obsessed with reducing wasted metal. In a chapter titled "Learning From Waste," Ford writes, "Our studies and investigations up to

date have resulted in the saving of 80 million pounds of steel a year that formerly went into scrap and had to be reworked with the expenditure of
labour." Ford saved 80 million pounds seventy-five years ago. Can you do the
same in your plants today?

No change was too small if it reduced waste. Ford saved nearly 300,000
pounds of steel a year by cutting the fan-drive pulley out of the scrap from
the hand door stock rather than out of new stock. He originally made eighteen pieces of one part from a metal bar 143 inches long but was able to save
"more than two inches per bar" when he found he could get the same number of pieces out of a bar 140 and 9/32 inches long. Two inches saved out of
143—again, for Ford, no change that reduced waste was too small.

Ford understood the importance of squeezing every last drop of useful
work out of energy. Every ton of iron leaving the blast furnace came with
more than five tons of hot gas, 200,000 cubic feet. The hot gas is "cleaned and
filtered to remove blast furnace dust and *part of it used in the stoves to pre-heat
the blast.* The balance is piped to the power house, where it forms the principal fuel." The blast furnace dust was nearly half-pure iron—once regarded as
waste, it too was reclaimed. Ford also cogenerated:

> Steam is required for heating the wood-drying kilns at five
> pounds per square inch pressure. Steam at 225 pounds pres-
> sure suitable for operating turbines can be produced at only 10
> percent greater cost than that for the heating pressure. Thus, by
> developing steam in the power-house boilers at 225 pounds per
> square inch, passing it through turbines and "bleeding" low
> pressure heating steam from the turbines after a part of its
> available energy has been obtained, *the steam is practically serv-
> ing a double duty—supplying both power and heat.*

Though Ford pioneered the reduction of wasted resources, he is better
known for reducing wasted time. His two great achievements—interchangeable parts and the moving assembly line—were incredible time savers. In
1908, Ford workers had to gather the needed parts, file them down and adjust
them so they would fit, and then put them all together. Each assembler would
work on a large part of the car, perhaps spending all day on the mechanical
system. The task cycle for a typical assembler—the time worked before
repeating the same operation—was 514 minutes, or 8-1/2 hours. Ford
changed the standard for efficiency by delivering parts to each work station,
minutely dividing the labor to individual tasks, and making the parts per-
fectly interchangeable (so they didn't need adjustment each time). Workers
became surpassingly more efficient at their more specialized tasks. Cycle time
plummeted from 514 to 2.3 minutes![4]

Ford's greatest leap came in 1913: the moving assembly line. No longer would workers move from assembly stand to assembly stand. This cut cycle time in half—from 2.3 minutes to 1.19 minutes. In less than a year, Ford reduced the effort needed to build major components by 60 to 80 percent. The time needed to assemble the major components into a complete vehicle dropped nearly 90 percent. The modern industrial factory had arrived.

Ford's obsession with reducing wasted time went far beyond interchangeable parts and a moving assembly line. He wrote, "Time waste differs from material waste in that there can be no salvage." It is "the easiest of all wastes, and the hardest to correct" because "wasted time does not litter the floor like wasted material." At the Ford Motor Company, "we think of time as human energy. If we buy more material than we need for production, then we are storing human energy—and probably depreciating its value." Indeed, he believed that "time . . . is a method of saving and serving which ranks with the application of power and the division of labor."

No price was too high for saving time: "We have spent many millions of dollars just to save a few hours' time here and there." Ford's approach was *systematic:* Improving the cycle time for the entire production process was as important as improving the cycle time for individual workers:

> Our aim is always to arrange the material and the machinery and to simplify the operation so that practically no orders are necessary. . . . Our finished inventory is all in transit. So is most of our raw material inventory. . . .
>
> Our production cycle is about eighty-one hours from the mine to the finished machine in the freight car, or three days and nine hours instead of the fourteen days which we used to think was record breaking. . . .
>
> Let us say one of our ore boats docks at Fordson at 8:00 a.m. on Monday. . . . By noon Tuesday, the ore had been reduced to iron, mixed with other iron in the foundry cupolas, and cast. . . . By 3 o'clock in the afternoon the motor has been finished and tested and started off in a freight car to a branch for assembly into a finished car. Say that it reaches the branch plant so that it may be put into the assembly line at 8 o'clock Wednesday morning. By noon the car will be on the road in the possession of its owner.

The man who wrote "our finished inventory is all in transit" and "having a stock of raw materials or finished goods in excess of requirements is waste" is rightly called the true father of just-in-time. Taiichi Ohno, co-founder of the Toyota Production System, once said that "if [the young] Henry Ford were alive today, I am positive that he would have done what we did."[5]

I would go further.

If Henry Ford were alive today, he would without doubt still be minimizing wasted time *and* resources. He understood profoundly that a focus on the end result demanded an integrated approach: "All men do not see the wisdom of fitting means to ends, of conserving material (which is sacred as the result of other's labours), of saving that most precious commodity—time; they must be taught." A contemporary British historian, J. A. Spender, wrote of the production systems at Ford's marvelous River Rouge industrial complex, "If absolute completeness and perfect adaptation of means to end justify the word, they are in their own way works of art."[6]

As I noted in my 1994 book, *Lean and Clean Management,* Ford wrote in 1924 what might today be the credo of companies that are both lean and environmentally responsible:

> "You must get the most out of the power, out of the material, and out of the time."

Above and beyond his philosophy of eliminating wasted time and wasted resources, Ford was committed to constant improvement. His most important lesson may well have been to never rest on one's successes: "If we reach a stage in production which seems remarkable as compared with what has gone before, then that is just a stage of production and nothing more." The only lesson to be drawn from successful change is that more change is possible: "We know from the changes that have already been brought about that far greater changes are to come, and that therefore we are not performing a single operation as well as it ought to be performed."

Ford was, however, far from the perfect manager. He understood processes but not people. Ford's specialization of tasks turned what had been skilled work for artisans into repetitive and unsatisfying labor done at an ever-increasing pace. His workers called him "the speed-up king." In the year Ford mechanized the assembly line, 1913, turnover in the highly paid labor force hit 380 percent! Soon, in order to keep a hundred men working, Ford was hiring almost a thousand.[7] Top wages were needed to attract good men but were never enough to keep them.

A key reason Ford was able to focus so much effort on improving the efficiency of the production process was that he built only one product—the Model T. It remained amazingly popular for many years, and he rigidly stuck with the basic design for two decades. Ford could embrace change in process but not in product.

In 1921, his dealers asked him if he would vary the color of the Model T. Ford's famous answer: "You can have them any color you want, boys, as long as they're black." Ford's competitors, however, had begun to adopt his production techniques and were more responsive to customers. They gained ground steadily as sales of the Model T dropped. In May 1927, Ford announced that he would at last build a new car, the Model A. The Model T was dead, as was Ford's domination of the automobile market.

SHIGEO SHINGO AND TAIICHI OHNO

Ford's competitors realized the obvious benefits of interchangeable parts and a moving assembly line, but they never grasped the power of the hidden paradigm—his systematic approach to time, as well as his systematic efforts to reduce resource use. For decades, Ford's lessons were lost on American industry—particularly his own beloved auto industry. They would have to be rediscovered, and refined, by the Japanese.

The Japanese have always been generous about giving credit to Henry Ford. In 1982, Toyota President Eiji Toyoda told a visiting Philip Caldwell, then head of Ford: "There is no secret to how we learned to do what we do, Mr. Caldwell. We learned it at the Rouge"—Ford's industrial complex.[8]

Why were so many American businesses so reluctant to embrace a systematic approach to production? Why were Japanese businesses eager? First, Japan was open to change when W. Edwards Deming, Joseph Juran, and Armand Feigenbaum began preaching a revolutionary message about quality in the 1950s. Japan had been devastated, both physically and psychologically, by the American triumph in World War II. Their products were notoriously shoddy. "Made in Japan" was a joke.

In 1950, Deming first presented to top Japanese managers a "systematic approach to solving quality problems." He introduced rigorous consumer research and urged top managers to become intimately engrossed in quality improvement. Eventually Deming became a national hero in Japan. Juran arrived in 1954, focusing on management, planning, and organizational approaches to improve quality. At the same time, the work of Feigenbaum, head of quality at General Electric, became widely disseminated in Japan. Feigenbaum argued for "a systemic or total approach to quality (which) required the involvement of all functions in the quality process, and not simply manufacturing."[9]

American companies were exposed to these very same ideas. But America had triumphed in World War II. What need was there for us to improve? In the two decades that followed the war, American companies had little serious competition from foreign firms only slowly recovering from the war. Again, where was the motivation to change?

A dramatic paradigm shift requires dramatic evidence of failure. That would be some time coming for most American companies.

The second reason Japanese companies were able to embrace systems thinking is more fundamental. It is best told by Shigeo Shingo and Taiichi Ohno, who developed the Toyota production system in the 1950s and 1960s. Their views are worth noting not merely because they were the first to perfect fast-cycle manufacturing in Japan but also because the system they developed has had such enduring success. According to a *Fortune* magazine headline from December 1997, Toyota's *"secret is its legendary production system. Though competitors have been trying to copy it for years, nobody makes it work as well as Toyota."* Michael Cusumano, a professor at MIT's Sloan School of Management and a member of the International Motor Vehicle Program, has said, "I don't know of a company that better combines superior skills in all the critical areas: manufacturing, engineering, and perhaps marketing. If they wanted to blow away GM, they could."[10]

According to Shingo, although "many people have thought about improvement . . . it was [Frederick] Taylor and the Gilbreths—F.B. Gilbreth and his wife, Lillian—who in the 1890s, developed a clearly-defined notion of improvement and established techniques to achieve it." Shingo notes that both Taylor and the Gilbreths focused their attention on "time." He summarizes their work as follows:

- *Taylor:* "Define the status quo analytically and temporally, and improve it through scientific reasoning—these activities are known as *time-study techniques.*"
- *The Gilbreths:* "Carry out motion analysis by breaking up the status quo into elemental units of motion called therbligs. Identify the purpose of each therblig, and find the one best way (in which work is broken down, purposes are tracked down, and better methods are devised) using techniques that accord with those purposes."[11]

Shingo and Ohno were heavily influenced by the American focus on time. Shingo, however, is very critical of how American companies applied the teachings of their own management experts. He wrote in the mid-1980s:

> Although Taylor argued for the establishment of standard times based on time analysis, many U.S. producers, in response to pressure to establish standards, set times without actually studying time. They simply accept the status quo (the times required for current operations) and then set mean standard times. . . . Conceptual approaches and activities basic to work improvement are often forgotten. . . . It seems that American management has lost sight of the original goal of doing away with waste.[12]

Means and ends had become disconnected in the United States.

The American authors of *Dynamic Manufacturing* noted in 1988 that Taylor "assumed that learning about production (through staff analysis) and the actual making of things (by the line organization) were separable activities: both could and should be done by specialists." The disconnection between learning by staff people and making by line people, between thinking and doing, had serious results: It "increased the likelihood that learning only took place as a result of analysis that was divorced from hands-on experience, performed by people who were both physically and psychologically removed from the workplace."[13] But to Americans it all seemed so much more efficient, and everyone was making so much money, that few noticed the fault lines.

Shingo offers an even deeper explanation for why the Japanese, but not the Americans, took a systems approach to production.[14] He begins by retelling the story of the British industrial revolution as related by Adam Smith in his 1776 book, *The Wealth of Nations*. Before the industrial revolution began in England in the mid-eighteenth century, the individual artisan made an entire product. The most skilled and diligent craftsperson could, for instance, make only twenty pins a day. Pin production increased 200-fold when labor was divided into eighteen separate tasks (such as cutting the material, sharpening the tip, attaching the head). The price of pins dropped considerably. At the same time, unskilled laborers previously unable to participate in industry could now be paid for performing useful tasks. Demand exploded because far more people could now buy pins. This spread to other products and led to the rapid growth of British industry.

The "secret of the high productivity" gained through division of labor, Shingo writes, is that "simplified tasks made individual judgments unnecessary," and "the elimination of intermediate motions enabled work to be performed reflexively." *Thinking was disconnected from doing.*

> Until the industrial revolution, process (the flow from raw material to finished product) and operation (the flow of tasks performed by human workers on products) had been fused in the work of single individuals. One consequence of the division of labor was to separate processes from operations.[15]

PROCESS AND OPERATIONS

To understand the systems approach, we must first understand the distinction between *process* and *operations*. Process refers to the "stages through which raw materials gradually move to become finished products": Worker A cutting a piece of raw material, Worker B sharpening it, and Worker C attaching the head. Operations refers to the discrete actions of an individual laborer working on different products. Worker B sharpening the first pin, then sharpening the second pin, and so on.[16]

To Shingo, process represents the primary view of production, while operations are secondary. But even though operations are of lesser importance, they may seem more important because they are easier to see and control. Each operation is performed in one spot and involves actually shaping the product, and as a result, people "inevitably became captivated by directly observable human motion—that is, operational movements." It's not so easy to understand that our huge warehouse is part of the production process, which, if we made it truly efficient, might let us get rid of the whole building. Process phenomena, though far more important, end up escaping our attention. The result of our misunderstanding has been "the delusion that production is synonymous with operations."[17]

The effects of this error were, to Shingo, enormous. Many in the West ended up thinking wrongly that overall production would improve whenever operations were improved. The West was not seeing the forest for the trees, a major flaw that can be seen in three examples from a 1990 collection of Shingo's writing:

- An automated warehouse is an *operations* improvement: It speeds up and makes the operation of storing items more efficient. Eliminating all or part of the need for the warehouse by better tuning production to the market is a *process* improvement.
- Conveyor belts, cranes, and forklift trucks are *operations* improvements: They speed and aid the act of transporting goods. Elimination of the need for transport in the first place is a *process* improvement.
- Finding faster and easier ways to remove glue, paint, oil, burrs, and other undesirables from products are operations improvements; finding ways not to put them there in the first place is a process improvement.[18]

These examples show that when you improve the process, you do not merely cut out unnecessary operations, critical though that is; you *invariably reduce energy consumption* as well as environmental impact. Reducing your warehouse space reduces the need for energy to heat, cool, and light it. Reducing your transportation reduces fuel use and exhaust fumes. Eliminating your "undesirables" means no glue, paint, oil or scrap; it also avoids the resulting cleanup and disposal. *Process improvements are cool.*

Streamlining an unnecessary operation is not very different from downsizing a flawed company. The flaws remain and no systemic problems are solved. Getting rid of your unnecessary operations is the only way to get rid of the flaws. Harvard Business School professors Robert Hayes and Kim Clark noted in 1985 that in a highly complex factory environment two approaches are possible: "One can either attempt to develop a highly sophisticated . . .

information and control system to manage all this complexity, or one can set about reducing the complexity."[19] Process is more than an incoherent collection of operations; the whole is greater than the sum of its parts, points which may now seem obvious. Shingo himself considered them self-evident. Since 1955 he has "emphasized a theory of production management rooted in the assertion that production is a network of processes and functions. It is probably fair to say that this is the basis of Taiichi Ohno's Toyota Production System, a system that arguably is the first in the world to place major emphasis on process functions."[20]

TAIICHI OHNO AND THE FIVE WHYS

The man credited with inventing—or reinventing—the just-in-time production system is Taiichi Ohno. In the Toyota production system he developed after World War II with Shigeo Shingo, he could manufacture a variety of cars in small batches with the same manufacturing processes. Their system used close supplier relations, total quality control, simplified production flows, and a scheduling strategy that allowed employees to make decisions on the factory floor. The just-in-time production system allowed Toyota assembly lines to stock only about two hours' worth of parts inventory, compared to two weeks' worth of expensive inventory for a typical General Motors plant in the 1980s.

Ohno studied Henry Ford's work and quoted his writings at length.[21] Like Ford, Ohno was obsessed with eliminating waste. The authors of the 1996 book, *Lean Thinking: Banish Waste and Create Wealth in Your Corporation,* identify Ohno as "the Toyota executive who was the most ferocious foe of waste human history has produced."[22]

Just as Ford devoted a whole chapter to learning from waste, Ohno wrote, "To implement the Toyota production system in your own business, there must be a total understanding of waste. Unless all sources of waste are detected and crushed, success will always be just a dream." Ohno reduced his formula for success to one line, which defines waste as the difference between current capacity and the actual output of work:

$$PRESENT\ CAPACITY = WORK + WASTE$$

Ohno was not talking about wasted resources. For Ohno, waste meant such customary practices as overproduction, waiting, making defective products, and excess inventory ("the greatest waste of all")—all of which were (and often still are) accepted as unavoidable business procedures, not as waste. Rooting out such waste was by no means easy, he warned: "Underneath the 'cause' of a problem, the *real cause* is hidden. In every case, we must dig up the real cause by asking *why, why, why, why, why.*"

REPEATING *WHY* FIVE TIMES

(1) *Why* did the machine stop?
There was an overload and the fuse blew.

(2) *Why* was there an overload?
The bearing was not sufficiently lubricated.

(3) *Why* was it not lubricated sufficiently?
The lubrication pump was not pumping sufficiently.

(4) *Why* was it not pumping sufficiently?
The shaft of the pump was worn and rattling.

(5) *Why* was the shaft worn out?
There was no strainer attached and metal scrap got in.

Failing to ask *why* five times would no doubt lead one to simply replace the fuse or the pump shaft, in which case the problem would recur within a few months. Ohno writes, "The Toyota production system has been built on the practice and evolution of this scientific approach. By asking *why* five times and answering it each time, we can get to the real cause of the problem."

Once again, this essential idea came from America. It was Frank Gilbreth, at the turn of the century, who argued for tracking down the goals of work by repeatedly asking, *Why?*

Asking the specific questions and ferreting out the answers require participation by everyone, especially the production line worker. Few managers are likely to know the right question to ask, and they're even less likely to know the answer. Even the best company can improve. In a typical year, Toyota's employee suggestion system has received over a million suggestions (more than thirty per worker), of which 95 percent were implemented.[23] The commitment to improve the way things are done must be constant and must include everyone.

WHY CLEAN PRODUCTION AND COOL DESIGN IMPROVE PRODUCTIVITY

The Japanese achieved their dramatic productivity gains by eliminating waste through improving the production process. Focusing on individual operations, what is called industrial engineering in this country, rarely achieves significant or enduring productivity gains. A narrow focus on operations misses your main targets, the root causes of systemic problems, such as long cycle time, large inventories, high waste, poor communications, flawed strategy, poor design, and low quality. These systemic problems are the obstacles to productivity growth in most companies.

The productivity gain from pollution prevention is well documented, if not yet well known. This book discusses countless cases. All of the cool strategies in this book both prevent pollution and save energy. Chapter 4 covers the huge productivity benefits from a systems approach to cool workplace design. Chapters 7 and 8 include a discussion of the same huge benefits achieved from a systems approach to motor and process redesign.

Consider a 1992 study of chemical manufacturing examining source reduction measures, which focus only on those actions that reduce or eliminate waste at the source. (It does not include waste treatment, recycling, or any other measures to address wastes once they are created.) The report concluded: "More than 95 percent of the source-reduction activities affecting product yield at 19 of the study plants increased production output. Ten plants reported an average increase in product yield of about 7 percent."[24]

At a Ciba-Geigy plant in New Jersey, the study found that two improvements in its dye-making *process* "made possible a 40 percent increase in yield, reduced iron waste by 100 percent and total organic carbon waste by 80 percent for the process, and resulted in annual cost savings of $740,000." A second look showed that process improvement could increase the yield *another 15 percent.*

A stunning example of increasing productivity by decreasing waste comes from the authors of the book *Dynamic Manufacturing.* They found that "reducing materials waste often improves productivity far beyond what one might expect from the material saving alone." Their study looked at Total Factor Productivity (TFP), which is not merely the output per unit of labor but also a calculation of the product output as a function of all labor, capital, energy, and materials consumed in its production. TFP examines the overall efficiency of a process, as opposed to the efficiency with which it uses any single factor, such as labor. The "waste rate" is the ratio of wasted material (scrap and rejects) to total cost. The table summarizes their findings in one plant:[25]

Plant	Average Waste Rate (percentage)	Effect on TFP of a 10 Percent Reduction in Waste Rate
C-1	11.2	+1.2
C-2	12.4	+1.8
C-3	12.7	+2.0
C-4	9.3	+3.1
C-5	8.2	+0.8

The authors note that "reducing waste . . . by 10 percent from its mean value (which by itself would reduce total manufacturing costs by only half of 1 percent) appears to have been accompanied by a 3 percent improvement in total factor productivity." This reveals the "powerful impact that reducing waste has on overall productivity."

Reducing waste leads a company to rid itself of many types of inefficiencies, as Harvard Business School professor Michael Porter wrote in a 1995 article, "Green *and* Competitive," in *Harvard Business Review:*

> When scrap, harmful substances, or energy forms are discharged into the environment as pollution, it is a sign that resources have been used incompletely, inefficiently, or ineffectively. Moreover, companies then have to perform additional activities that add cost but create no value for customers: for example, handling, storage, and disposal of discharges.[26]

Getting rid of inefficiency and improving productivity by such pollution prevention doubtless explains the profit-making results found by business professor Stuart Hart.[27] He examined the relationship between emission reduction and firm performance for a sample of 127 Standard & Poor's 500 firms. Hart used an "Emissions Efficiency Index"—a ratio of reported emissions (in pounds) to the company's revenues (in thousands of dollars), tabulated by the Investor Responsibility Research Center. He first looked at emissions reductions, using the change in the Index from 1988 to 1989. He compared that to operating and financial performance from the Compustat data base, including return on sales, return on assets, and return on equity for the years 1989 to 1992 (under the hypothesis that pollution prevention in the first year will have economic benefits in later years). Hart also controlled for other variables that might affect the comparison among firms, including R&D intensity, advertising intensity, capital intensity, and industry-average performance.

Hart concludes "reducing emissions has an effect on operating and financial performance net of the control variables." Emissions reduction in a given year "significantly benefited" operating and financial performance over the next few years. The dozens of case studies in this book make clear that *reducing greenhouse gas emissions will have the same significant benefit for your company's operating and financial performance.*

Pollution prevention is an unexpected key that unlocks the solutions to many of your systemic problems. Clean production and cool process design are classic pollution prevention methods. These strategies force a manufacturer to look at the whole production process rather than at operations alone. Your company is driven to use many of the same techniques for minimizing wasted resources that Shingo and Ohno used to minimize wasted time, including cross-functional teams. Similarly, cool office design (which is also pollution prevention) forces a service company to look systematically at what it does. This strategic approach also requires a team-based design. It leads that team to focus on the end users—office workers—and to improve control over their work environment. These are all essential elements of lean thinking.

> Clean production and cool design lead companies to eliminate waste systematically by improving processes. That approach invariably increases productivity and so is both cool and lean.

THE OPPORTUNITY FOR AMERICAN COMPANIES

American companies have a unique opportunity to benefit from a cool and lean approach. The United States became a major industrial power at the turn of the twentieth century, when it was the world's leading producer of copper, phosphate, coal, molybdenum, zinc, iron ore, lead, silver, salt, tungsten, petroleum, and natural gas; and the number two producer of bauxite and gold.

One study of the origins of American industrial success concluded: "The most distinctive characteristic of U.S. manufacturing exports was intensity in nonreproducible natural resources; furthermore, this relative intensity was increasing between 1880 and 1920." By the late 1920s, iron and steel products, machinery, automobiles and parts, and petroleum products accounted for more than half of all American manufacturing exports. Automobiles contained roughly half their value in iron and steel, nonferrous metals, and other fabricated metal products.[28]

Our country's prosperity was thus built on a foundation of natural resource abundance. Even as late as the 1950s, America was still the world's largest producer of oil, extracting twice as much as the Middle East and North Africa combined. *It is not surprising, then, that so many American companies overuse resources. We require 50 percent more energy to produce a dollar of goods than Japanese companies, and we produce roughly five times the waste per dollar of goods sold as Japanese companies and more than twice that of German companies.*[29]

A heavy reliance on energy and resources—and the resulting pollution—is built into the basic paradigm or world view of most American companies. This is beginning to change.

For decades, most U.S. companies dealt with defects in quality *after* they had been made. The focus was not on preventing defects; rather it was on inspection and rework: an expensive, inadequate "end-of-pipe" approach to quality. Similarly, our paradigm of waste and resource abundance led most companies in the 1970s and 1980s to focus on dealing with pollution *after* it had been created—with landfills, treatment, incineration, and the like—an expensive, inadequate end-of-pipe approach to waste.

This approach to waste has created many institutional barriers that limit the adoption of profit-making pollution prevention techniques. The old Congressional Office of Technology Assessment noted many of these barriers in their comprehensive 1994 report, *Industry, Technology, and the Environment:*

> Many firms are unaware of pollution prevention opportunities or their relative merits over end-of-pipe solutions . . . responsibility for finding pollution prevention solutions may not rest with those most capable of doing so [line workers, engineers]. . . . Most environmental managers have been trained in end-of-pipe practices and thus may overlook opportunities for prevention . . . most environmental consulting focuses on end-of-pipe treatment, while most environmental equipment vendors sell end-of-pipe equipment . . . capital accounting practices and capital availability may limit the adoption of even profitable prevention projects."[30]

Many if not most companies have viewed environmental projects simply as a means to satisfy a certain regulatory requirement and fail to perform even simple financial analyses on alternative prevention projects. Regulators, too, have traditionally emphasized end-of-pipe controls, thereby creating de facto standards, though that is starting to change as U.S. environmental regulations are beginning to be rewritten to encourage innovation and prevention.

The 1997 Kyoto Treaty and the rising concern over global warming can only increase the opportunities and competitive advantage created by a cool and lean strategy, a conclusion reached by many, many companies, including Toyota.

TOYOTA: TODAY AND TOMORROW

Where is Toyota today? Toyota's "product fecundity has been unrivaled" and "Toyota has been dazzling on the technology front," noted *Fortune* in 1997.[31] In December 1997, Toyota became the first car company in the world to introduce a mass production hybrid electric vehicle—the Prius—that has both a gasoline engine and electric motor and gets 66 miles per gallon (mpg), producing half the carbon dioxide of a normal car. By July 1998, Toyota had sold over 7,700 Prius and initial demand far exceeded expectations. The company has announced it will introduce the car to the U.S. market in late 2000.

Toyota understands that its products are major contributors to global warming, and it sees both the challenge and the opportunity that this presents. "Consumers are smart," says Toyota president Hiroshi Okuda. "They recognize the threat that pollution and global warming present to them and their children."[32] Highly fuel-efficient vehicles are likely to be one of the biggest selling cool products in the twenty-first century. Toyota is estimated to be losing money on each Prius they sell today, but they are committed to becoming the world leader in the manufacture of green automobiles and are willing to lose some money now in order to make a great deal of money in the future.

FORD MOTORS: TODAY AND TOMORROW

Ford Motors is also developing super-efficient fuel cell vehicles and hybrid vehicles, in collaboration with the other automakers and the federal government. The target is an 80-mpg car.

On January 1, 1999, William Clay Ford, Jr. became Chairman of the Board of Ford Motor Company. The great-grandson of Henry Ford is widely seen as an environmentalist. He has said that his "vision for the company is product leadership, the highest quality and customer satisfaction, and environmental leadership. If we get these right, we will lead in shareholder value." He believes that environmental leadership "will create an image for Ford in the marketplace that is different from others, and in a cluttered and crowded marketplace in which differentiation is hard to obtain, particularly in image. If we achieve this, we will attract better employees and the highest caliber people out of universities."[33]

If William Clay Ford, Jr. can re-infuse the company with his great-grandfather's obsession with minimizing wasted resources, he may well succeed in making Ford a cool company and environmental leader.

Indeed, the best companies have begun the transition toward a systematic approach to pollution prevention, toward cool and lean thinking. In his 1995 *Harvard Business Review* article, Michael Porter wrote:

> We are now in a transitional phase of industrial history in which companies are still inexperienced in handling environmental issues creatively. . . . The early movers—the companies that can see the opportunity first and embrace innovation-based solutions—will reap major competitive benefits, just as the German and Japanese car makers did [with fuel-efficient cars in the early 1970s].[34]

Chapter

BUILDINGS

Suppose you could boost your profits and productivity and significantly cut your greenhouse gas emissions—all while risking very little of your company's own money. That's now possible by combining innovative new financing and technology strategies for making your buildings and offices more energy efficient. Using the approach discussed in this chapter, you may be able to finance some or all of the cost of your upgrade off-balance-sheet.

A building upgrade was once exceptional if it achieved a 25 to 35 percent reduction in energy consumption with a three- to five-year simple payback—a 20 to 35 percent return on investment. Now that is the minimum for a whole-building retrofit. You can achieve a 35 to 50 percent reduction with a similar or faster payback. You'll see even deeper reductions in the energy used by certain building components, such as lighting.

- Centerplex, a small Seattle business, cut energy use in its office buildings *55 percent* with a 1.5-year payback and expects to reduce that further to 65 percent.
- The Ridgehaven building in San Diego lowered energy consumption *70 percent,* saving $80,000 a year, using a "low-bid" contractor. Utility financing of the efficiency improvements turned a three-year payback into an instantaneous one.
- BlueCross BlueShield of Oregon cut energy use *61 percent* at its Portland headquarters. BlueCross did not have to put up any money for the project but instead is paying for it entirely from the monthly energy savings.

- A number of new buildings have beaten state energy codes by *50 to 65 percent,* including the Way Station in Maryland and a Wal-Mart in California.
- Boeing reduced the lighting electricity used in its buildings by up to *90 percent* with a two-year payback—a 53 percent return on investment. The new, higher quality lighting cuts down glare and helps workers reduce defects.

The Energy Cost Savings Council, a partnership of electrotechnology manufacturers and trade associations says that *businesses can expect to achieve a savings of $1 per square foot of floor space* with the kinds of whole-building upgrades discussed in this chapter.[1] Since the United States has 4 to 5 *million* commercial buildings with *tens of billions* of square feet of floorspace, the potential savings are vast.

If your building or office has avoided a comprehensive upgrade in the last five years, you are throwing away a great deal of money. The bottom line is:

> You can cut workplace energy use, costs, and greenhouse gas emissions in half with rapid payback by a systematic energy upgrade.

Xerox, for instance, launched its "Waste-Free Office" program in 1995, which requires offices across Europe and North America (including forty-five buildings in New York) to reduce energy consumption 50 percent. They have already achieved that goal at their Palo Alto Research Center in California (see Chapter 9).

Hundreds of case histories attest to the do-ability of a 50 percent reduction. The trade journal *Energy User News* examined 1,000 energy-efficient upgrades involving one or more of the following components: lighting, motors, drives, heating and cooling, and building control systems. *They found an average reduction in energy use of 39 percent, with an average return on investment of 32 percent—a 3.1-year payback.*

Your company should do *better* overall than a 39 percent average energy savings from individual components. Here are three reasons. First, a complete upgrade can achieve super-efficient synergies. For instance, better lighting, windows, and insulation will allow you to use a smaller, less-expensive heating and cooling system. Second, a cool company looks at investments with a payback longer than two or three years, although as we will see in the next chapter, this systems approach to upgrading a building will often provide more rapid paybacks from large *productivity* gains. Third, a computerized

Energy Management Control System (EMCS) will allow you to capture large, low-cost operations and maintenance savings. An EMCS has many other benefits. It ensures that projected savings become actual savings and that savings persist over time. It helps you obtain lower-cost capital for building upgrades, since efficiency improvements are a *lower risk than virtually any other high-return investments your company can make.*

Coupling an energy management control system with a new financial instrument—the International Performance Measurement and Verification Protocol—may allow your company to finance some or all of the cost of your upgrade off-balance-sheet.

In the Introduction, I proposed this goal for a company that wants to be "cool": a 50 percent reduction in greenhouse gas emissions. If your company is a typical service sector company, you can become cool with a cost-effective building upgrade alone, since most of your energy use is in your buildings. Let's start with the case of a small business that has done this.

SMALL BUSINESS, BIG SAVINGS IN SEATTLE

In the early 1990s, Jonathan Pool began noticing publicity from a variety of sources—the EPA, the local utility, and contractors—that claimed he could significantly lower his energy bill with new technology. He owns Centerplex, a small business in Seattle that leases commercial office space in its two small buildings totaling 26,500 square feet with an energy bill approaching $50,000 a year. Pool was intrigued and pursued the savings.[2]

By 1998, Centerplex had reduced the electricity consumption in its all-electric buildings by 55 percent through efficient lighting and better windows, occupancy sensors, insulation, and programmable thermostats. The upgrade had a 1.5-year payback because the local utility, Puget Power, picked up about two-thirds of the cost of the new equipment. The new system had many nonenergy benefits. Tenant complaints about erratic temperatures dropped. Longer lasting bulbs meant lower replacement and maintenance costs. New windows with low-emissivity coatings (that let light in but keep heat out) replaced the original bronze-tinted windows, *tripling* the amount of daylight admitted. Besides reducing utility bills, the new lights and windows "turned into a selling point—something that makes the office more attractive to a customer," says Pool.

Why did Pool make the investment in efficiency when so many others hadn't? He offers two reasons. "First, it was economical. Even here in the Northwest electricity is expensive." To Pool's credit, his electricity rate is only about 6 cents per kilowatt-hour, less than the national average and half the price in many parts of the country. He adds that, at the time, "conservation was a subsidized public policy. The local utility was offering to pay for two-thirds of the upgrade." Yet he notes that even without the help of the utility, the payback would have been 4.5 years and that commercial real estate is usually bought on the basis of a 10-year return on investment, so the efficiency upgrade still would have made sense.

Second, Pool says he has "a personal taste for conservation. It is something that I grew up liking to do. Some people are savers, some are spenders. I'm a saver." As a result, "I was attuned to and watchful for conservation measures. So when they came along, I noticed."

The best efficiency projects occur only when there is an "energy champion." Whether it is Ken Nelson at Dow Chemical, Petar Reskusic at Toyota, Ron Perkins at Compaq, or Jonathan Pool at Centerplex, energy champions are needed to break down the barriers both inside and outside a company that block efficiency projects.

For Centerplex, Pool notes that "there were serious obstacles that made it a lot more difficult than it might have been." For instance, to get the utility incentive, he had to comply with utility rules demanding an elaborate bidding process. That approach failed because even the best contractors submitted bids that were unresponsive to the utility's rules. Pool was then permitted to try an approach in which he worked closely with two contractors (one for lighting and the other for heating and cooling), and the utility based its subsidy on the contractors' calculations of the energy to be saved by its design.

Even with this new approach, the contractors often had poor information and made mistakes specifying equipment. For instance, the programmable thermostats chosen were not fully compatible with the building's heating system. The efficient fluorescent lights were not fully compatible with the occupancy sensors. In both cases, the utility failed to catch the mistakes, and so the wrong technologies were installed, although hardware existed that would have avoided all the problems.

Because of Pool's twin desires to save money and support conservation, he persisted. He is still persisting. He is pursuing even deeper reductions in energy use and emissions. He has prohibited his tenants from using halogen torchieres (those tall, stylish floor lamps that run very hot—*1,000 degrees Fahrenheit*—and are exceedingly inefficient). He has collected information from the U.S. Environmental Protection Agency (EPA) and insurance companies that the lamps' extreme heat can start a fire. Other than the halogen lamps, however, Pool has not required a tenant to use energy-saving office equipment, though, as we will see, such equipment can provide large savings at low cost. He installed occupancy sensors to control lights only in common areas, such as hallways and bathrooms, not in his tenants' offices.

Currently, his tenants' rent bills do not break out electricity as a separate cost because their offices are not individually metered; the whole building has a single meter. This is, unfortunately, common practice around the country and a major barrier to energy efficiency (except for cases like Centerplex where the building owner is the energy champion). Pool notes, "Since we don't know how much they are using, we can't bill them separately." Because his tenants aren't billed separately for energy, they have little incentive to reduce their consumption.

To solve that problem, Pool has been investigating the most cost-effective technology needed to "submeter" the building, to track the electricity use for individual tenants so they can be billed for their electricity use. Then they will have a direct incentive to reduce their own energy bills, perhaps by installing occupancy sensors plus energy-efficient copiers and computers.

Pool expects that these measures will ultimately boost energy savings to a whopping 65 percent. For achieving such remarkable reductions in energy use and greenhouse gas emissions, and for continuing to pursue even more reductions, Centerplex deserves the label "cool company."

If a small business owner like Jonathan Pool can achieve better than 50 percent savings, most companies, which have far more resources and in-house expertise, should be able to match him. Also, as will be discussed in Chapter 6, your company should consider including in any building upgrade a small natural-gas cogeneration system to meet part of the building's need for electricity and heating (and possibly even cooling). This system can significantly increase the energy and emissions savings, thereby making the 50 percent target easier to meet.

Larger companies will see another advantage of an energy-saving retrofit if they still have a chiller using chlorofluorocarbon (CFC) refrigerants. Although CFCs are being phased out, only 30 percent of CFC-based chillers had been converted or replaced by January 1, 1998, and fewer than half are expected to be by 2001.[3] By first *reducing* the cooling load with lighting retrofits, insulation, and other basic measures, you can upgrade your old chiller to a *smaller,* more efficient CFC-free system. The capital savings from *downsizing* the cooling equipment can offset much of the cost of the whole-building retrofit. As we will see in Chapter 6, you will achieve even bigger carbon dioxide and dollar savings by installing a cogeneration unit coupled with a replacement chiller that runs on hot water instead of electricity. Here's the general rule:

If you are about to replace a major piece of heating and cooling equipment, *first* do a systematic energy retrofit. That will *reduce* the heating and cooling load, which then allows you to buy *smaller* and hence *less expensive* equipment.

Retrofits are extremely profitable, but designing buildings right the first time is far more profitable. New buildings with *half* the energy consumption and *under a one-year payback* are increasingly common. A number of cases will be discussed here. Perhaps you doubt that little Centerplex's fantastic success has any application for your own buildings. Let's look at other recent well-documented examples of large savings and rapid paybacks.

DEEP SAVINGS IN SAN DIEGO

One of the best upgrades is the award-winning Ridgehaven office building. In the mid-1990s, the City of San Diego Environmental Services Department (ESD) renovated an existing three-story, 73,000-square-foot office building. They set three goals: healthy indoor air quality, increased energy efficiency, and resource efficiency (recycled material and reduction of construction waste).[4]

The indoor air quality was greatly improved. ESD used products that minimize the emissions of noxious volatile organic compounds. They increased the flow of outdoor air to 20 cubic feet per meter (cfm), compared to 5 cfm when the building was originally built.

The energy-efficiency measures began by replacing the entire HVAC (heating, ventilation, and air conditioning) system with a high-efficiency system, which included a new cooling tower, adjustable speed pumps, and a computerized energy management control system. High-efficiency window films reduced heat gain. Efficient fluorescent lamps and fixtures were installed, as were daylight sensors and occupancy sensors.

The energy consumption of the Ridgehaven building was monitored and found to be *70 percent lower* than before. This is particularly amazing considering that the original building was built in 1981—at the height of the second energy crisis. The building surpasses California's strict Title 24 building code by more than 50 percent. *It is 60 percent more efficient than an identical city office building next door.* The building had been operating at 21 to 22 kilowatt-hours (kWh) per square foot but is now operating at 7 to 8 kWh/square foot. Annual savings equal about $80,000 per year or $1.10 per square feet.

What is most striking about Ridgehaven is that "all of this was achieved for a city government building, with local government budgetary constraints and City Council requisite approval, open 'low bid' approach, and a [tight] construction schedule," in the words of David A. Gottfried, who worked on the project. He points out that "since the project qualified for SDG&E [San Diego Gas & Electric] financing, all high performance, 'state-of-the-shelf' measures (13 in total) were financed by the utility." So the return on the energy-saving measures was "infinite." Gottfried notes that "even if the City had paid for these measures, the internal rate of return would have been over 30 percent."

A SYSTEMS APPROACH: PORTLAND'S 100 MARKET BUILDING

One of the most comprehensive commercial retrofits was done in Portland.[5] In 1993, BlueCross BlueShield of Oregon upgraded its 106,000-square-foot corporate headquarters to boost employee productivity while cutting energy costs. MicroGrid, Inc., an engineering design and management firm specializing in energy efficiency, and the Hartman Company, HVAC specialists, systematically upgraded the building envelope, plus its electrical and mechanical systems in the following ways:

- Incandescent down-lights were replaced with compact fluorescents, and standard fluorescents were upgraded to efficient ones. Daylighting systems were installed in perimeter offices, combined with dimming controls. Lighting energy was cut in half while computer screen glare was reduced.
- Building envelope improvements included extra roof insulation and replacing the existing single-pane windows with high-performance double-glazed windows.
- Indoor air quality in the building had been a problem, in part because of an on-site printing shop and minimal intake of outside air. The upgrade included new outside air intakes to give the building more fresh outside air. The project team isolated the print shop with its own air intakes and exhaust system.
- A new high-efficiency HVAC system with variable speed drives and an advanced digital control system uses real-time information to deliver just the right temperature and amount of air to different zones in the building. Energy is no longer wasted conditioning unoccupied areas or over-conditioning occupied areas.

Does all that add up to a lot or a little? Here's a number that will astound you: Fan load was *reduced 79 percent* during the daytime.

Overall energy consumption was *reduced a remarkable 61 percent,* saving nearly 4.0 million kWh. The project team tracked energy use for a year and found that energy costs savings came to $130,000 a year, 57 percent lower than pre-retrofit energy costs. The $1.5-million project was funded by Pacific Power and Light; the utility's investment is repaid through an add-on to the monthly utility bill. Once the loan is paid off, using the savings for payment, BlueCross BlueShield of Oregon will retain all of the savings.

The project has other benefits. Maintenance costs are reduced, as the new equipment is easier to maintain and the old equipment was used more optimally, reducing wear and tear. Finally, as Paul David of MicroGrid told me, "We feel very strongly from talking to workers and managers that these changes did improve productivity."

HOW TO MAKE YOUR BUILDING AN ENERGY STAR

EPA has developed a five-stage process for reducing energy consumption in buildings. As part of their voluntary "Energy Star" Buildings program, EPA helps companies reduce energy consumption in their buildings. This standardized comprehensive approach has been documented in two dozen showcase buildings to save an average of 30 percent of building energy with an *average internal rate of return of 22 percent.* Typically, the people in these buildings enjoyed higher quality lighting, improved indoor air quality, and increased worker comfort—benefits whose value is not added into the overall payback (though in other buildings where these benefits have been valued, these savings can *exceed* the energy savings, as we will see in the next chapter). Here are EPA's five stages.

- *Stage One:* Upgrade the *lighting* through the approach EPA pioneered in its Green Lights program, which will be discussed later in this chapter.
- *Stage Two:* Tune-up the building. Check, monitor, and adjust *building equipment* to maximize efficiency and occupant comfort. This will probably require an energy management control system.
- *Stage Three:* Further reduce the heating and cooling loads on the building through improvements to the facility *exterior,* such as windows and roofs.

Once you have optimized the building and reduced loads, you can reduce the size and cost of mechanical equipment upgrades in the last two stages.

- *Stage Four:* Examine closely the building's *fan systems* to see which are oversized and thus good candidates for a motor downsizing or for motor controls (such as variable speed drives that allow efficient operation of the fan motors at reduced speeds).
- *Stage Five:* Upgrade the *heating and cooling plant equipment* to a lower capacity, properly sized, energy-efficient system.

You may want to do Stage Two (especially the control system) before Stage One for a number of reasons, as I will explain shortly. But in any case, what is most important about these five stages is that you do the first three *before* the last two. And you can do all five at nearly the same time *if* you figure out in advance the reduced loads on the upgrade to the fans and HVAC system.

While the average Energy Star Building achieved 30 percent savings, some of the buildings had lower savings because the upgraded buildings had been relatively efficient to begin with. A number of the buildings realized closer to 40 percent savings.[6]

In 1991, the Lausche State Office Building in Cleveland, Ohio, started a comprehensive energy management program.[7] The staff upgraded the lighting, retrofitted the HVAC controls, weatherized the building shell, downsized the air handler motors, and added motor controls. This Energy Star Showcase building has *cut energy use and costs by over 40 percent already,* and savings are projected to grow. This is particularly impressive because the Ohio State Lottery's computer facility housed in the building has been expanded and two major new tenants moved in during the measurement period.

The 350,000-square-foot Community Towers Complex in downtown San Jose, California, *reduced energy consumption 37 percent* using the Energy Star strategy.[8] At the same time, the two office towers ended up with brighter lighting, digital HVAC controls, a CFC-free chiller, and a replacement for troublesome pneumatic temperature controls. The owners financed the $1.4 million project over a seven-year period with positive cash flow (the project's annual energy savings exceeded the loan payments).

Building comfort has improved. "Hot and cold calls have been cut on average from about ten a day to two or three," says John Falvey, chief engineer. Falvey "used to spend three hours a day calibrating and adjusting" the old pneumatic system. "Now I can monitor and make temperature and airflow adjustments at a PC in my office. Finally, I have time to handle the important maintenance needs of the buildings."

The building's owners saw far-reaching benefits. "I considered the energy savings as fuel for improvements to our business," says Taylor Clayton, Vice President of Boccardo Properties. "The new systems, including chillers, comprehensive temperature controls and lighting, have greatly benefited our customers. In the long and short haul, this investment will help us renew our leases and bring new customers to our buildings. Would I do it again? Let me answer briefly: Absolutely!"

EFFICIENCY: A LOW-RISK, HIGH-RETURN INVESTMENT

The growing number of buildings taking advantage of these savings has instigated a revolution in the way businesses and lenders think about energy efficiency. Aspen Systems, an Oak Ridge, Tennessee, consulting company, looked at the financial risk and return from "14 whole-building energy-efficiency upgrade projects from firms that chose to become showcase projects of the U.S. EPA Energy Star Buildings program." As showcases, the firms provided detailed information about their building, pre-upgrade energy use, investment cost, and post-upgrade energy performance.[9]

Aspen Systems calculated the internal rate of return (IRR) of the efficiency investment using a ten-year project lifetime. The investment *risk* was defined as "the risk that the energy-efficiency upgrade will produce more or less than the expected return on investment." In other words, risk was measured as the variability in the expected investment return. Aspen Systems looked at the distribution of investment returns from the Energy Star projects and calculated the average return (i.e., the mean) and the variability (i.e., the standard deviation). Risk was calculated as the standard deviation divided by the mean. Either high variability or low return increase risk.[10]

Here are their results, compared with the risk and return for a number of common investments:

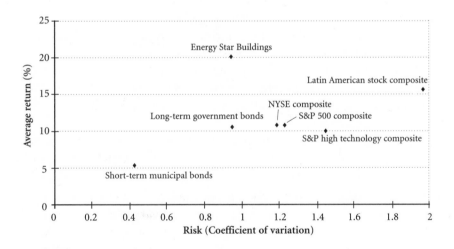

So a whole building upgrade is an astonishingly good financial investment—not even counting any productivity gains that might result.

You might ask, if energy efficiency is such a high-return, low-risk investment, why hasn't every company already upgraded all of its buildings? One answer is that, as I document, many of the best companies, such as Xerox and Interface, as well as countless smaller ones, such as Centerplex, are finally beginning to upgrade their buildings. Even a few years ago, however, most of the case studies in this book did not exist, so it was not possible to do the kind of risk-return analysis Aspen System has done. But there is a more complete answer, one that lies at the heart of the new efficiency revolution.

THE INTERNATIONAL MONITORING AND VERIFICATION PROTOCOL

One of the biggest barriers to energy-efficiency upgrades has been the difficulty in financing the upgrades. We have seen that efficiency upgrades can be low risk, but that requires the kind of standard approach developed in the past few years by EPA's Energy Star program and others, coupled with rigorous monitoring and verification of savings. The problem is that until recently, there has been no mechanism to ensure that projected savings are realized and persist over time. Absent such a mechanism, lenders and a company's internal decisionmakers would naturally be wary of any promise that an investment today would realize large savings in the future.

The International Performance Measurement and Verification Protocol (IPMVP) addresses these financial concerns. Gregory Kats and Arthur Rosenfeld of the Department of Energy (DOE) organized the development of the IPMVP. Kats, a Stanford MBA who is director of finance at DOE's Office of Energy Efficiency and Renewable Energy, notes that efficiency investments have traditionally been inconsistently implemented and have lacked substantiated savings. The IPMVP is a voluntary consensus document written for technical, procurement, and financial experts in government, commerce, and industry. It spells out a standard methodology for upgrading a building and—most importantly—for measuring and verifying the savings.[11]

Kats and Rosenfeld have compiled data on well-monitored and verified upgrades, such as the IPMVP requires. These upgrades achieve a number of desirable benefits:

- *High initial savings level:* Traditional upgrades often fail to achieve the projected level of savings. In contrast, upgrades made with a protocol like IPMVP *generally come in above the projected level of savings.* I will explain this unexpected outcome shortly when I discuss the energy wizards of Texas A&M.

- *Persistence of savings:* Traditional upgrades often experience drops in energy savings, often within a few years. Upgrades made with a protocol tend to maintain their savings because they have real-time metering of equipment energy use or an energy management control system.

- *Less variability:* If a company performs traditional upgrades at a number of buildings, the results may vary widely. The protocol ensures consistency through its standardized approach to upgrades.

These three measures of performance reliability help explain why the old-style efficiency upgrades have been viewed with suspicion by finance firms and why these same finance firms so strongly endorse the IPMVP.

As Kats explains, the IPMVP, by ensuring high initial savings and persistence of savings over time, significantly reduces the risk associated with efficiency upgrades. It allows a company to have confidence that projected savings will be achieved, which in turn means that a lender can have confidence that there will be a continuous stream of energy savings. Because of the high confidence in the stream of savings, those savings can be used as collateral to finance the upgrade *partly or completely off of a company's balance sheet* (thereby not adding to a company's overall debt). Such deals are rare today, but they have been considered for government buildings. Companies are more likely to get this deal from a bank if they have many buildings over which the risk can be spread.

GETTING IT DONE OFF THE BALANCE SHEET

(1) Get one of the lenders or financial institutions you do business with regularly to join you in testing the efficiency approach.

(2) Do a comprehensive upgrade using the International Performance Measurement and Verification Protocol and finance part of the cost off the balance sheet.

(3) If it works, put together a large off-balance-sheet deal to retrofit all of your buildings.

The key to making the protocol work is the energy management control system (EMCS). Once an expensive and complicated technology, the EMCS has emerged today as one of the most crucial energy-saving technologies, benefiting from the advances in computers and micro-electronics. In the right hands, like those of the energy wizards of Texas A&M, an EMCS can seem to work magic.

THE ENERGY WIZARDS OF TEXAS A&M

I first met David Claridge and Jeff Haberl of the Energy Systems Laboratory at Texas A&M University in the summer of 1994. I was attending a conference at which they described their efforts to capture savings in an area that had widely been seen as mundane, operations and maintenance (O&M)—maintaining equipment in good working order and operating it correctly. Their results were nothing short of unbelievable: "As of April 1994, this approach has identified over $3.5 million in annual savings opportunity in *buildings that have already been retrofitted."* Indeed, one of the papers they presented was boldly titled, "Can You Achieve 150 Percent of Predicted Retrofit Savings?" It turns out that you can—and with an average payback of eighteen months.[12]

Consider what they achieved in the Basic Research Building of the M.D. Anderson Cancer Center in hot and humid Houston. Built in 1986, the eight-floor, 120,000-square-foot medical research facility is used continuously, needs a great deal of outside air, and has stringent temperature and humidity requirements. It has had an aggressive energy management program in place for many years. Indeed, prior to Claridge and Haberl showing up, the building had been successfully upgraded with all measures identified as cost-effective in an audit performed by consulting engineers. For instance, all fluorescent lamps had been converted to high-efficiency fixtures, and incandescent lights had been replaced with compact fluorescents in 1991. In 1992 and 1993, the facility staff installed an EMCS and optimized the HVAC system—or so they thought. These measures reduced energy consumption by 31 percent, lowering their energy bill from $1,228,000 a year to $845,000 a year.

You might think such large savings meant that most of the opportunities had been wrung out. They had not. This building is part of the Texas Loan-STAR program, a $100-million revolving state loan program that retrofits state and local buildings. So it was examined by Claridge, Haberl, and the other energy management wizards of Texas A&M, who use hourly monitoring of energy consumption and then follow up with fine-tuning for the buildings that have been retrofitted.

When the wizards of Texas A&M visited the Houston medical research building they found three major opportunities for savings that had been overlooked. First, a temperature sensor calibration problem was costing over $111,000 a year. Second, changing the winter and summer HVAC settings to optimize efficiency would save another $143,000 a year. Finally, they noted that the air exchange rates in much of the building were higher than those required by the standard for laboratory spaces set in 1991 by ASHRAE (American Society of Heating, Refrigeration and Air Conditioning Engineers), offering another potential savings of $121,000 a year. These three changes would produce an additional 44 percent reduction in energy costs, which would have dropped the energy bill to $470,000 a year—*a 60 percent overall reduction.*

In practice, however, the facility staff made all of these improvements except lowering the air exchange rates. The extra energy O&M savings came to $196,000 a year—a 23 percent additional reduction—bringing the total reduction in energy consumption to 47 percent, instead of the potential 60 percent.

When I spoke to Claridge in 1998 about his approach, he was quick to tell me that it works even with a brand-new state-of-the-art building, such as the 1992 Capitol Extension Building. The 590,000-square-foot building was designed to be energy efficient, and in 1993 it averaged about *one-third less energy per square foot* than the other buildings in the Texas Capitol Complex.

Nonetheless, Claridge and the Texas A&M staff were still able to find large O&M savings. They suggested a number of measures to optimize heating and cooling, improve comfort, and reduce occupant complaints, including simple things like shutting off the steam during the summer. These measures together saved about $140,000 a year in energy costs with a payback of under three months. The energy wizards of Texas A&M had *reduced energy consumption further by a remarkable 27 percent.*

   If this degree of savings is possible in new and well-managed buildings with modern energy management control systems, how much savings are possible in your old buildings?

Claridge's Approach

Claridge's approach is methodical. He starts with long-term hourly whole-building *measurements* (and sometimes submetered hourly measurements at each piece of equipment). He does an engineering analysis. He visits the site often. He works closely with the local facility personnel. He figures out whether HVAC systems are operating as efficiently as possible.

One of the keys to the Texas A&M approach to O&M savings is careful and continuous monitoring of energy use, what Claridge calls "continuous commissioning." With it you will identify the true low-hanging fruit of building energy savings—O&M improvements. Combining it with a comprehensive upgrade and the IPMVP will allow you to achieve large, enduring energy savings—and to obtain low-cost financing.

Installing the monitoring equipment and paying for the recording of the data, analysis, and reporting typically add 5 to 10 percent to the retrofit cost. For simple retrofits, this may mean nothing more than continuous tracking of electricity and thermal loads, costing only a few thousand dollars. For retrofits costing more than $300,000, you might also be tracking several pieces of equipment as well as weather-related data (such as temperature), and the cost will be a few tens of thousands of dollars.

This seems like a lot of money until you consider that, in the LoanSTAR buildings we are looking at here, the total measured savings are *150 percent of the audit-estimated savings. That is, commissioning finds energy savings greater than those identified by professional engineering audits designed to identify all cost-effective opportunities.*

   The O&M savings achieved through continuous commissioning equal a remarkable 25 percent of the total building energy consumption. For twenty-eight buildings commissioned using Texas A&M guidelines, measured savings average $90,000 a year ($0.54 per square foot per year) with a payback less than eighteen months.

The installation of an EMCS and the continuous monitoring and analysis of the building must be part of any cool building upgrade. Such continuous commissioning will not only irrefutably demonstrate to everyone in your company that large, cost-effective savings are possible, but it will also, as we have seen over and over again, actually help make such savings possible. And, as noted earlier, it allows the use of a protocol like the IPMVP that can reduce the cost of financing a whole-building upgrade.

Most of the measures Claridge identifies are straightforward—turn-off lights and equipment when the building is unoccupied, use efficient temperature settings, use efficient system operations strategies and settings. I would add, "Make sure your equipment is working as intended," which is the most obvious energy-saving measure but perversely is the most neglected.

Basic Science Building

Here's a classic example of neglecting to ensure that equipment is working as intended: The 138,000-square-foot, seven-story Basic Science Building at the University of Texas Medical Branch at Galveston consists of offices, classrooms, labs, and storage. The main chiller plant provides both steam and chilled water. The building gets 75 percent of its outside air from two 150-horsepower fans. The HVAC system is operated twenty-four hours a day, all year long. From mid-1992 through mid-1993 the daily steam and chilled water use was measured as a function of the outside temperature. The study revealed that the building, like a monster run amok, was consuming a substantial amount of *steam during the torrid summer days*. The HVAC system was *simultaneously heating and cooling the building*.

It was easy to optimize the HVAC system, which reduced annual chilled water consumption nearly 30 percent and reduced annual steam consumption more than 30 percent. Total savings from this one O&M improvement exceeded $150,000 a year, a decrease of 23 percent of the building's annual energy cost.

North Texas Schools

In 1991, the LoanSTAR program funded a lighting upgrade in forty-five schools in North Texas. Since the LoanSTAR guidelines call for energy monitoring for expensive upgrades, two of the schools had equipment installed to meter the gas and electricity consumption and submeter the lighting circuits. When Texas A&M staff visited the two schools and examined the data, they found ways to save $57,000 a year—33 percent of the 1992 energy bill—mostly by having the controls turn off the HVAC system at night.

Both schools were already supposed to have night shut-off of the HVAC systems. After the operator for the EMCS checked their programming, consumption data showed no change at one of the schools. What had gone wrong? Over thirty of the forty-seven roof-top HVAC units were discovered to be operating at 5:00 P.M. in mid-April, long after the kids had gone home. The EMCS had been turned off at three different points. Some thirty other schools were found to have turned off EMCS systems. The potential electricity savings alone at the 104 schools in the district equal $1.5 million, corresponding to a 27 percent savings.

Sadly, the school system decided these sure-fire low-cost savings were not a high priority, and they failed to pursue most of the opportunities. A cool company with EMCS expertise might offer to work with local schools to make sure they have working EMCS systems or to help finance installation of new systems.

❖

During the 1980s, a 150,000-square-foot Student Recreation Center installed several energy-saving improvements, such as better insulation, improved lighting, and a pool cover. Heat reclaimed from the ice rink compressors was used to heat the shower water. These measures cost $100,000 and reduced energy consumption by 30 percent, saving $60,000 a year.

By continuously monitoring and analyzing the *smallest* tasks making up the building's energy consumption, Claridge and Haberl were able to identify much waste. For instance, the sloped ramp that leads to the building's garbage containers had been heated from September to May, whenever the outside temperature fell below 35 degrees Fahrenheit, to prevent icing from snowstorms. Yet the ramp needed to be heated only when it was snowing. Similarly, heating tapes in the rain gutters were turned on from September to May, even though they were needed only when large ice dams had formed. The lights in the men's locker room had somehow been cross-wired and could not be switched off. When this was fixed, they were turned off at night.

Claridge and Haberl also discovered that the system for reclaiming shower water heat had been turned off. Daily monitoring of pool water usage quickly uncovered a *20,000 gallon a day water leak,* a monstrous waste of energy, water, and chemicals. (Moreover, had the leak gone undetected, it would have led to massive and expensive structural damage.) The ice rink refrigeration system had a partially closed valve that reduced efficiency. The ice resurfacing machine had been routinely spraying hot water. Using hot water only before figure skating and competitive events, and cold water at all other times, reduced hot water consumption by 2,000 gallons per day.

These few simple measures required less than $1,000, but they added up to another $30,000/year reduction in energy consumption—resulting in an *overall cut in energy use of 45 percent.* You will find these budget-busting energy wasters by analyzing every single task that consumes energy (and thus generates greenhouse gases) in your buildings and by asking all employees to join in the chase to save energy and reduce the emission of greenhouse gases.

Learning from Texas A&M

The Texas A&M staff has good advice for dealing with change: Go slow. The facility operators at one building ignored initial recommendations to turn off the air handling units for seven hours each night. The agency had operated on a "zero complaints" priority for many years, and the facilities manager was worried that the temperature swings would generate complaints.

So Texas A&M staff convinced the facility operators at one building to try a gradual approach: Shut down more and more air handling units for longer and longer periods of time. They started by shutting off five of the twenty-five air handlers for four hours a night and ended up shutting off sixteen units for six hours per night. No discomfort complaints were heard. Savings of electricity, gas, and chilled water consumption were a whopping *$300 a night* in a single building.

Despite this success practically next door, the facilities personnel in a neighboring building also "expressed a fear of temperature excursions and occupant complaints and did not want to initiate any turn-offs." They changed their minds only after Texas A&M staff gave another presentation proving the success of the shutdowns in the nearby building as well as other state facilities. Later, these manual decisions were discontinued after a retrofit with EMCS-controlled shutdowns achieved the same level of savings.

Since Texas A&M is the benchmark for capturing Operations and Maintenance savings, let's learn from their lessons:

(1) There is so much variation in the O&M opportunities at different sites that a cookbook approach is of limited value.

(2) Measured energy consumption data is extremely valuable as a diagnostic tool—annual data can be used to identify promising candidates for [continuous commissioning]. Hourly and sub-metered data are extremely valuable when used with site measurements and data in diagnosing specific opportunities for improved efficiency. They also provide immediate feedback on whether system changes have made a difference.

(3) *The facilities engineers/operators are crucial participants in an O&M improvement effort.* An O&M consultant will be most

effective if they can build trust and a good working relationship with the facilities personnel. Their knowledge of a facility is crucial, and some sort of incentive should be established for their participation before the project begins.

(4) Identification of O&M opportunities is necessary but is often insufficient to achieve implementation. While some facility staffs will take a verbal recommendation and implement it immediately, others require written reports followed by continued consultation on specific steps. In some cases, trial tests of the O&M may be needed to assure the staff that it can work.

IMPROVED LIGHTING

More efficient lighting is probably the fastest way to save energy and reduce costs, *while increasing productivity.* Such upgrades are at the heart of cool building design since lighting consumes about 40 percent of the electricity used in commercial buildings, and another 10 percent of building electricity goes to cool the heat generated from lighting. Lighting improvements thus afford one of the lowest-cost, lowest-risk investments for reducing electricity use—and hence greenhouse gas emissions—in a building.

Upgrades that improve lighting quality while reducing lighting electricity consumption 50 to 70 percent are now commonplace.

Equally important, most lighting systems were designed for people writing on horizontal surfaces or using typewriters. Thus, your buildings are most likely to be both overlit and mislit for computers and word processors. A 1991 Worldwide Office Environment Index Survey found that eyestrain was perceived as a hazard by 47 percent of office workers—a greater hazard than quality of air, radiation from video display terminals, repetitive strain injuries, or hazardous materials.[13] Conditions have not improved since. For that reason, when you improve lighting, you will often boost productivity. In particular, daylight, whose use results in no pollution, is also the most natural and the most associated with productivity gains (see Chapter 4).

Your company—any company—can achieve large savings with a straightforward lighting upgrade, as the EPA has repeatedly demonstrated with its "Green Lights" program to help businesses reduce energy use and air pollution. This voluntary pollution-prevention program, which has now been incorporated into EPA's Energy Star Building program, helps you get the most current information about which energy-efficient lighting technologies work best for your particular application. It also provides guidance on how upgrades can be financed.

Electricity used for lighting *can be reduced up to 90 percent*, with a 30 to 60 percent rate of return. Consider the following:

- Ortho-McNeil Pharmaceuticals *reduced lighting energy by 63 percent* using the Green Lights approach. In their manufacturing, research, and administration facility in Raritan, New Jersey, which covers more than 1 million square feet, they saved almost 4 million kWh and $320,000 annually, with a 2.5-year payback.

- Elkhart General Hospital in Indiana *reduced lighting electricity by more than 70 percent* over 430,000 square feet for a total annual savings of $102,000. The upgrade cost only $85,000 and prevented emissions of 1,500 tons of carbon dioxide, 13 tons of sulfur dioxide, and 6 tons of nitrogen oxides.

- The St. Francis Hotel in San Francisco *reduced lighting electricity 82 percent* over 1 million square feet. An investment of $76,000 produced annual savings of $85,000.[14]

BENCHMARKING BOEING

Boeing made one of the most successful Green Lights upgrades. *Boeing reduced lighting electricity use by up to 90 percent* in several million square feet of its facilities, with a 50 percent return on investment. Boeing's upgrades saved 270 million kWh, reducing its contribution to air pollution by more than 100,000 tons of carbon dioxide, 8,000 tons of sulfur dioxide, and 4,000 tons of nitrogen oxides—*per year*. Lawrence Friedman, Boeing's former conservation manager, estimated that if every company adopted the lighting Boeing is installing, "it would reduce air pollution as much as if one-third of the cars on the road today never left the garage."[15]

Renton, Washington, is called the aircraft capital of the world because Boeing produces up to fifty jets a month there in huge 500,000-square-foot plants. Some of those plants were in the middle of a lighting upgrade when I visited them in the spring of 1993. In some cases, half the building had new lighting, half old. The difference between these areas was like day and night: Crystal clear vision, with excellent color rendition on one side; fuzzy, distracting lighting on the other.

With the new lighting, employees had more control, glare was reduced, and the overall appearance of the plant was improved. Friedman says that after the new lighting was put in, the feedback was "almost mind-boggling."

One woman, who put rivets in thirty-foot wing supports, said that she had previously been unable to see inside one part she had been working on and had been relying on touch alone. Now, for the first time in twelve years, she could actually see inside the part. Another riveter reported that with the old lighting a rivet head would occasionally break off, fly through the air, and smash one of the old fluorescent light tubes, scattering glass everywhere. The new high-efficiency metal-halide lamps with hard plastic covers don't break when a flying rivet head hits them. Workers are safer.

Improved lighting also resulted in better quality in the shipping and receiving area. The number of packages sent to the wrong destination declined. No wonder engineers in other places came up to Friedman to demand, "When are you going to upgrade our building?" Steve Cassens, a lighting engineer for Boeing, says that the first thing machinists under the new lighting tell him is that they can now easily read the calipers on their lathes and measurement tools.

One of the shops that was moved to an area with improved lighting attaches the jets' interior side-wall panel to a stiffening member using numerous fasteners that leave a very small indentation in the panel. The old fluorescent lighting provided poor contrast and made it difficult to tell if a fastener had been properly attached. The new high-efficiency metal-halide lamps make it far easier to detect imperfections, far easier to see whether there are indentations—and hence fasteners—everywhere there should be. The new lighting improved by 20 percent the worker's ability to detect imperfections *in the shop.*

When you catch errors as they happen, the cost savings are enormous. Friedman explained that most errors that used to slip through "weren't being picked up until installed in the airplane, where it is much more expensive to fix." Even worse, "some imperfections were found during customer walk-throughs, which is embarrassing." Embarrassing *and* costly, because "the customer says, 'I don't like the way this panel looks,' and then you have to do a special order to match the interior of the customer's plane." Although it is difficult to calculate the savings from catching errors early, Friedman estimated that those cost savings alone exceed the energy savings.

Energy-efficient lighting doesn't just save money and reduce pollution. It lets people see better. It reduces defects, increases quality, and boosts productivity.

BASIC HARDWARE IN A LIGHTING UPGRADE

For an upgrade to more energy-efficient lighting, you will need to:

- Reduce the number of existing fixtures (most offices are overlit)
- Replace remaining four-foot fluorescent lighting fixtures with more efficient lamps and more efficient control ballasts and optical reflectors
- Replace incandescent bulbs with compact fluorescent bulbs
- Install sensors to turn off lights when rooms are vacant and photocells to adjust light to changing outside conditions

The ballast is the transformer of the fluorescent light, providing the current and voltage to run it. The new electronic ballasts are much more energy efficient than the old electromagnetic ballasts they replace. Also, they operate the lights at a much higher frequency, which gets rid of the annoying flicker and hum that give so many people headaches and eyestrain. The color rendition of the best new bulbs is much better—far closer to sunlight than the old bluish bulbs that give everything a sickly pale tinge.

A typical upgrade replaces inefficient "T12" fluorescent lamps (usually four to a fixture) running on magnetic ballasts with more efficient "T8" lamps (often only two to a fixture with a reflector) running on an electronic ballast. The T-measure for a fluorescent lamp is a measure of the diameter of the tube in eighths of an inch. A T12 lamp is a tubular lamp with a diameter of twelve-eighths of an inch (or 1-1/2 inches). A T8 lamp has a diameter of 1 inch. Even more efficient T5 lamps have begun entering the market.

Compact fluorescent bulbs last considerably longer than incandescents do, and even though they cost more, the savings in replacement labor more than make up for the price. That particular change is profitable for a business without even counting the savings in electricity. An article written jointly by Amory Lovins and researchers at the Electric Power Research Institute noted that switching to compact fluorescents "is not a free lunch; it is a lunch you are paid to eat."[16]

Occupancy sensors automatically turn off the lights in an unoccupied room. Early versions of the sensors would also turn off the lights in a room when the occupant remained fairly motionless for a few minutes. Today, there are heat-sensitive occupancy sensors, which eliminate the problem (and even "dual sensors" that use both ultra-sound and heat to detect occupants).

The Department of Energy (DOE) followed this basic lighting upgrade strategy in 1993 and *reduced lighting electricity use by 60 percent* in its Forrestal Building headquarters in Washington, D.C. The DOE put no money up-front. The project received a $1.1 million rebate from the local utility,

Potomac Electric and Power Company, and the rest was financed by EUA Cogenex (an energy service company) over seven years through a shared savings program. Of the $400,000 in annual savings, the DOE retains 27 percent for the first three years, 85 percent for the final four years, and 100 percent thereafter.

DOE surveyed the employees on lighting quality before and after the upgrade. Workers thought the upgrade significantly improved lighting conditions. Physical data supported their answers, with measured improvement in office illumination. Overall light levels were raised from 30 foot-candles at the desk level to 50 foot-candles, which is probably too high for general lighting. It would have made more sense to follow an end-use approach: Provide less general lighting and use task lights (such as desk lamps) tailored to each worker.

FOCUS ON THE END USER

Never lose sight of the basic systems principle: Focus on the end user. Focusing on the end user of the lighting will open the biggest opportunities to increase savings and productivity.

It is easy to become caught up in the excitement of installing the latest energy-efficient lighting and miss what may well be the main benefit of the changes. One major manufacturer has recently installed state-of-the-art fluorescent lamps and electronic ballasts in a 15,000-square-foot facility where the workers do a great deal of detail work, including wiring. The company cut the electricity used for lighting in the facility by 50 percent with a payback of about two years.

But as I walked through the area with the energy manager, it quickly became clear that the most cost-effective improvements, the end-use ones, had been ignored. On one side of the area, about three-fourths of the lights were on, even though not a single person was working there. On the other side, all of the lights were on, even though only two supervisors were working in one corner of the area. In other words, hundreds of lights, albeit energy-efficient ones, were providing illumination for two workers.

The supervisors explained that, because of the recession, the company had recently gone from two shifts to one. They assured me, however, that the lights were on a timer set to turn off at 5:30 P.M. Since it was nearly 6:00 P.M., we were not reassured. Those lights may well have been on twenty-four hours a day, and no one in the company would have known of the money they were burning up. The supervisors also pointed out that their half of the area was controlled by only three switches, so they could have turned off only two-thirds of the lights, in any case.

No one had actually measured the rate of errors, defects, or rework, so nobody could give a quantitative answer when I asked whether or not the new lighting had reduced errors or defects. The workers didn't think quality had risen, however, because they did mainly detail work, and the super-efficient replacement lights were exactly where the old ones were, about six feet above the work area—too high to be of much help. Many of the workers had bought small desk or task lamps at Wal-Mart for $6.

Instead of a one-size-fits-all lighting upgrade, the company should have taken the end-use approach. It should have interviewed its workers to find out what kind of illumination they needed. It should then have mocked up several areas with different combinations of overhead lighting and task lamps and allowed workers to pick the lighting they liked best.

An end-use approach adds the following:

- Task lights tailored for the work in each area
- More individual light switches, to allow workers direct control of the over-head lighting above their own small work area
- Fewer overhead lights
- Occupancy sensors to turn the lights off when no one is there

These simple improvements would have cut lighting electricity use not by just 50 percent but by 80 to 95 percent, depending on whether the lights were on just for the second shift (i.e., sixteen hours a day), or if they were, in fact, on all night. Most of these changes are inexpensive, and some, like reducing the number of overheads, are virtually cost-free.[17] The payback period would have dropped to under one year—*a return on investment exceeding 100 percent.* Moreover, quality would certainly have increased with the improved lighting from the task lamps. Workers would have lamps they themselves had chosen, and they wouldn't have to waste their own money buying desk lights. Pro-ductivity would no doubt have improved measurably (when, that is, the com-pany started measuring it), and the return on investment would probably have *doubled* or *tripled.* The next chapter discusses how one utility took the end-use approach and achieved *a return on investment in excess of 500 percent.*

❖

One of the most successful software companies in the country did a similar one-size-fits-all upgrade with new bulbs and ballasts, cutting lighting elec-tricity by over one-third with rapid payback. Unfortunately, this company also never bothered to ask its workers what troubled them most about the old lighting. The answer would have been glare, since every office worker uses a computer. The new lighting also produced glare, and many of the workers simply shut the lights off and either worked in the dark or bought a desk lamp or a special task lamp that attached to the computer. An end-use, worker-

focused approach would have used anti-glare fixtures, far fewer overhead lights, and new task lamps. It would have cut electricity use even more with a faster payback. Again, productivity would probably have risen.

The lesson is clear: *The end-use approach is always the least-cost approach.* Don't do a "one-size-fits-all" lighting retrofit. Don't adopt the checklist mentality: "We did fluorescent lamps with electronic ballasts, so we've done energy-efficient lighting. Now we can move on to something else."

Talk to employees. See what their needs are. They may prefer pale-blue fluorescent lamps, which give sharper contrast to the black-and-white drawings of modern blueprints; buy them high-efficiency versions of those lamps. The maintenance people who clean and replace lamps should also understand the changes, so they don't replace a burnt-out efficient bulb with some old inefficient bulb in storage. Get rid of those old bulbs. In fact, better maintenance schedules can also be a source of energy savings. In one office building, the building manager saved $17,000 per year at no cost whatsoever. He changed the cleaning schedule to overlap normal business hours, which avoided over half the building's lights being left on between 5:00 P.M. and when the cleaning crew normally started.[18]

EXIT SIGNS

Exit signs burn twenty-four hours a day—little items that escape your notice until you learn their large potential for energy savings. Buy low-wattage units to get huge savings with a quick payback. A University of Illinois at Chicago retrofit project to replace 4,000 exit signs will reduce energy consumption by *more than 1 million kWh per year,* saving the institution $76,000 in energy costs. More important, the $80,000 investment in new longer-lasting exit lamps will save more than *$400,000* in lower labor and equipment costs, yielding a *two-month payback* for the system.[19]

LARGE SAVINGS FROM IMPROVED OFFICE EQUIPMENT

Computers and related equipment use as much as one-fifth of the total building electric load in some buildings. Electricity also goes to air conditioning to cool the excess heat produced by the equipment. Up to 70 percent of office equipment is left on all the time, even though it is used infrequently. *Turning off computers and other equipment when not needed does not hurt the hard drive or other components and will save considerable energy.*

A mid-sized copier might directly consume $350 worth of electricity a year if left on 24 hours a day, a personal computer about one-third that amount.[20] A typical company could save about $50 per year per computer in energy costs. If your company is in a region with high electricity rates, you will save far more, perhaps $75 per computer.

➡️   **Take a moment and count the number of computers on your floor and then your entire building. How many dollars are you throwing away?**

Get specifications from several dealers before buying a new copier. Many copiers have standby features that save a great deal of energy yet allow warm up in a matter of seconds. Consider buying smaller tabletop copiers for small jobs. They use far less energy and can warm up very quickly. Similarly, save the laser printer for important work and use ink-jet printers for most work. *Ink jet printers are far cheaper than laser printers and use up to 90 percent less energy when printing.*

The EPA's Energy Star computers program certifies computers and related equipment as energy-efficient. The EPA has worked with the major manufacturers, including Apple, Compaq, DEC, Hewlett Packard, IBM, NCR, Smith Corona, and Zenith, to develop computers that run on less energy and either go on standby or shut off when not being used.

Buy only equipment with good power management features. And be sure they are properly enabled. A case study from the California utility Pacific Gas and Electric Company (PG&E) reveals why.

In the early 1990s, PG&E wanted to verify that large and cost-effective energy savings were possible, both in new building construction and retrofits.[21] One of the retrofits was done at the 7,329-square-foot VeriFone office building in Auburn, California. VeriFone is an international company that manufactures the electronic verification equipment used in verifying credit card purchases.

The comprehensive retrofit covered all aspects of the building, including extensive daylighting, dimmable ballasts, occupancy sensors, task lights, improved insulation, and a more efficient heating system. To lower the squandering of air-conditioning energy, an uninterruptible power supply (UPS) for the minicomputer was moved from the air-conditioned computer room to the unconditioned attic. A standard refrigerator located in the lunch room was replaced with a new efficient one, which was cleverly modified so that the refrigerant passes through a heat exchanger to preheat the building's hot water.

One year of pre-upgrade energy-use data was compared with one year of post-upgrade energy-use data, revealing that the retrofit cut electricity and gas use by 42 percent. The retrofit had been expected to reduce electricity consumption by over 60 percent.

What's remarkable about this case is that the single biggest improvement

was essentially not even used: Power management controls had been installed on the computers to duplicate the efficiency of Energy Star computers without having to buy a new set of computers. The new controls shut off power to each old monitor when the computer is inactive for 15 minutes. But computer operators disabled all but three of the new power controllers, mainly because the time delay was not adjustable. The result was an improvement that could have saved 18,000 kWh/year actually saved only about 1,000 kWh/year. Had these controls and computers been installed properly and used, electricity savings would have hit 50 percent and overall energy savings would have exceeded 48 percent.

The problem of disabled Energy Star computers is very significant. One 1996 study of power management features for several dozen Energy Star machines found "only 11 percent of CPUs fully enabled and about two-thirds of monitors were successfully power managed." The study recommended that monitors rather than CPUs be the first priority. Monitors are "generally easier to configure, less likely to interfere with system operation, and have greater savings."[22]

CPU energy-saving features are often not turned on when they are delivered, or they are disabled because they interfere with people's work or with the local area network, or at least people think they do.

New flat-panel monitors use half the energy of traditional monitors. You should consider them for your next purchase.

One of the first things a company seeking to save energy should do is examine the power management features of its existing equipment. If the energy-saving features cause problems, find equipment that avoids those problems before your next major equipment purchase.

Finally, *laptop computers use up to 90 percent less energy than desktop computers,* and the best new ones consume almost no standby power. Laptops often have a higher initial cost but a much lower life-cycle cost. Rocky Mountain Institute's Rick Heede and Amory Lovins have found that "the extra cost of the laptop machine can often be repaid by just its energy savings, especially in new buildings."

Laptops are cool. They increase your company's flexibility, making it easy for employees to work at home. (Chapter 9 covers telecommuting.) As computers get even smaller, with flat-panel displays and built-in energy management systems, your energy savings will grow and grow. The benefit of energy-efficient equipment is considerable. As Heede and Lovins note, reducing the electricity load can avoid "costly expansions" of air conditioning and ventilation.

IMPROVED HEATING AND COOLING

Like most efforts to reduce waste, saving the energy used in heating, ventilation, and air-conditioning (HVAC) requires a *systematic* approach. Do not upgrade your HVAC until the lighting, office equipment, and building envelope have been upgraded because *so much of the load the HVAC system must cool is the excess heat* from inefficient lights, computers, and the like.

Poorly insulated windows are responsible for about 25 percent of all heating and cooling requirements. They let excess solar radiation into a building during the summer and lose heat during the winter. A modern high-efficiency window (with so-called "selective glazing") lets in the visible light but blocks much of the infrared radiation (heat), which avoids most of that loss. Advanced window films that let in the light but block the heat are now available. These "retrofit films" can turn normal windows into superwindows. Many utilities offer rebates for such films.

> *Upgrades that improve comfort and air quality while reducing HVAC energy consumption 40 percent or more are now commonplace.*

Lockheed Martin wanted to improve the performance of the ventilation system at its Burlington, Vermont, industrial plating plant.[23] The company assembled a team from the local utility, Johnson Controls, General Electric, and the Department of Energy. The team upgraded the plant's twenty-five-year-old ventilation system by adding adjustable speed drives, which make the ventilation supplied by the fans automatically match the levels needed by the plant—a significant improvement over the continuous twenty-four-hour operation of the old system. The company also installed a new energy management system to control the fan motors as a system. Now when the plant is idle, airflow is reduced to 55 to 65 percent of full speed.

These upgrades have reduced electricity and gas costs by 38 percent, improved ventilation control, and reduced plant emissions. The upgrade cost $99,000 and saves more than $68,000 a year for a simple payback of 1.5 years. Other facilities have had similar results:

- Parker Chiropractic College in Dallas, Texas, upgraded its chiller plant and control system in 1996. It reduced annual electricity consumption by 43 percent with a 3.5-year payback while eliminating use of a refrigerant that depletes the earth's ozone layer.[24]

- The Capitol Square Building in Edmonton, Alberta, reduced its annual HVAC-related electricity use by 44 percent and reduced natural gas consumption 41 percent with a three-year payback.[25]

- Magnetic Metals Corp. of Camden, New Jersey, which makes components for motors, installed gas-fired infrared heating devices that cut heating expenses 47 percent with a two-year payback. Perhaps more important, "People have more comfort and a more healthy environment," says Norm Thornton, the company's manager for manufacturing engineering and facilities.[26]

- The City of Long Beach, California, together with Southland Industries, an energy services company, significantly reduced energy at a number of facilities, particularly the fourteen-story, 764,000-square-foot Civic Center. The upgrade reduced energy consumption 44 percent in lighting, 43 percent in the chiller plant, and 69 percent in ventilation with a seven-year payback.[27]

Perhaps you are a building owner who has yet to figure out how to eliminate chlorofluorocarbon (CFC) refrigerants from your cooling system. The best strategy is to reduce the cooling load first, using the previously described strategies, such as advanced lighting and windows. Then you can buy a new, smaller, efficient chiller, or perhaps convert the existing system to a smaller, more efficient chiller with a new motor and compressor.

The Bank of America building in San Francisco did such a conversion with its CFC-based chiller. It reduced the cooling load so that the converted chiller was 40 percent smaller. At the same time, the chiller's full-load efficiency was increased by more than 25 percent. Overall, at full load, *the converted chiller uses 56 percent less electricity.*[28]

Reducing the building's cooling load *before* upgrading the HVAC system makes the whole retrofit more successful.

NEW BUILDINGS

We have seen that many, many building upgrades have reduced energy consumption 35 to 50 percent or more with rapid payback. As might be expected, if upgrading an old design can achieve such remarkable results, then designing a building correctly the first time will achieve those savings or higher, with an even faster payback.

New building design can optimize the use of daylight and take advantage of all the latest technologies. When the design team is truly a team, it can adopt a genuine systems approach. The number of new green buildings that use *half the energy of existing buildings or less* is growing rapidly. Here are a few of the best.

The Way Station, a private, nonprofit health-care facility in Frederick, Maryland, completed its new 30,000-square-foot building in 1991.[29] Greg Franta, a principal architect of the Boulder, Colorado, ENSAR Group, used *a whole systems design that resulted in about one-third the energy consumption of a typical building.* That is, he uses 67 percent less energy than you do. The lighting electricity use is one-quarter that of the average building, thanks to a design that maximizes natural daylighting through a combination of light shelves, skylights, and high-performance windows. The building has a sun-tracking skylight system, which is linked to the indoor automatically dimmable electric lights that adjust their light levels according to outside conditions. The building envelope is highly insulated and the high-efficiency variable air volume HVAC system makes use of passive heating and cooling from outside air whenever possible. The hot water system makes use of solar preheat tanks in the greenhouse and a heat recovery system on the chiller (with gas-fired boilers as a backup). The return on investment for the added cost of the energy-efficient features was 22 percent, a 4.5-year payback.

Henningsen Cold Storage Company's 50,000-square-foot refrigeration facility in Gresham, Oregon, *uses 58 percent less energy than a conventional facility.*[30] Opened in June 1996, the award-winning structure stores and freezes all types of food products. The facility is highly insulated and uses high-efficiency evaporators and condensers. The refrigeration has a state-of-the-art control system that monitors and operates each refrigeration unit separately, allowing operators to make rapid modifications and generate accurate operational records for the company and its customers. Fast-acting doors in the loading docks minimize energy losses. Bilevel lighting in individual rooms provides automatic dimming when a room is unoccupied. The warehouse uses nearly 1.15 million kWh per year less than a typical facility. The improvements also extend equipment life and improve service quality. "This project reduces our power bill and improves our bottom line," according to Paul Henningsen, manager of the company's engineering services and great-grandson of its founder. "And since we know more about what's going on in our facility, we make better decisions."

Other recent green buildings include:

- Utah's 105,000-square-foot Department of Natural Resources building in Salt Lake City beat the energy requirements of the standard building code by 42 percent with a six-year payback. The various efficiency measures, including extensive daylighting, reduced cooling loads by about 90 percent compared with a conventional building.[31]

- The National Renewable Energy Laboratory's 10,000-square-foot Thermal Test Facility in Golden, Colorado, uses 63 percent less energy than conventional construction.[32]
- The 15,700-square-foot California State Automobile Association building in Antioch, California, adopted a comprehensive energy-efficiency package that cut energy use 64 percent compared to other new office buildings.[33]

A SYSTEMS APPROACH: THE COMSTOCK BUILDING

It is worth taking a closer look at one case to see what design process is needed to achieve a cool building. The ten-story, 175,000-square-foot Comstock building *cost $500,000 less to build and has half the normal energy costs of other large Pittsburgh office buildings.*[34]

The architects, Burt Hill Kosar Rittelman Associates, used a variety of measures to save energy. Good insulation plus careful placement and design of windows allowed the architects to make the HVAC system smaller than what would typically be needed. The efficient heat pump system used to provide heating and cooling cost half as much as a conventional system. The Comstock building achieves high efficiency in lighting even though very high light levels were used in the 30 percent of the building that housed an engineering firm's drafting department. An energy management system controls the building.

The Comstock building was also built on a very tight schedule: eighteen months for design and construction. How did architects achieve a design that was both fast-cycle and green? First, the building owner was "open to doing things differently," in the words of Paul Scanlon, the director of engineering at Burt Hill and the engineering project manager on Comstock. The "very enlightened owner" gave the architects the freedom to experiment. Second, "We did a lot of life-cycle analyses," says Scanlon. The life-cycle analyses did not just cover operations and maintenance, as is often the case, but also included construction costs and leasing income. *Only such comprehensive analyses can minimize overall costs.*

Finally, and most important, the architects used a cross-functional team with an unusually high degree of coordination among all design team members. The functional disciplines on the team included everyone: architects; engineers for HVAC, electrical, communications, and structural systems; space planners; and interior designers. Scanlon himself had graduated from a special five-year program that included both architectural and engineering training, so he was particularly suited to manage interdisciplinary work.

The fast pace drove the interdisciplinary process. "We had such a tight time schedule that there was no other way to go," says Scanlon. "Representatives from each discipline locked themselves in a room from day one." Thus, a systematic, integrated approach to building design can lower both inital costs and life-cycle costs, while reducing pollution and meeting a very tight schedule. *This is cool and lean building design.*

WHY ISN'T EVERYONE DOING IT RIGHT?

If the benefits of getting the design right the first time are so large, why isn't every new building cool and lean? The forces working against you are large, and they are hidden. First, there is a general lack of awareness of the opportunities among developers, architects, and engineers. Most American buildings of the past few decades fail to take advantage of daylight and passive heating and cooling measures. Just choosing the best orientation, building shape, and envelope can often save one-third of the building's energy at no extra cost.[35]

The barriers to cool design go far deeper. Scanlon notes that "we put in a lot of work to save the owner $500,000, *which cut into our design fee.*" Architects are typically paid at a percentage of the construction cost. If they do energy efficiency in the traditional way, they don't have to spend much of their time on it, and their fee may actually be higher. In the words of Paul Scanlon, the engineering project manager on Comstock, "It's a lot easier to put out a standard system. You don't do a lot of research. You don't interact with the client." In other words, the system is a strong *disincentive* to efficiency.[36] To avoid this disincentive, you could include in the fee for your design team a bonus for any energy savings achieved beyond the average building in the area (or the state building code).

Another serious problem is that in most buildings, the developer, architects, and engineers are not the ones who will be using the building. They rarely talk to those people—the employees of whatever company leases space—to find out what their specific needs are. They rarely perform customer surveys after everyone moves in to find out what employees did or did not like about the building. Without talking to customers, how can any good product be built? Without talking to employees, how can a building be designed to maximize their productivity?

Cool and lean design is a true customer-driven end-use approach, and failing to use it is definitely a missed opportunity. As the next chapter shows, cool building and office designs have benefits that far exceed the energy savings: higher productivity, higher quality work, higher employee morale, and lower absenteeism.

Chapter

DESIGN FOR WORKPLACE PRODUCTIVITY

The best architects and engineers now understand very well how to increase worker productivity through the design of an office, building, or factory. However, the techniques have not received widespread attention, partly due to a lack of well-documented case studies. Although there are many workplaces where these practices are delivering awesome results, their productivity gains have rarely been quantified. In some cases, the savings have been so huge that owners have been reluctant to give away the "secret" of their new competitive advantage.

Without the help of an extraordinary group of managers, architects, engineers, professors, and builders, I could not have compiled this chapter, which explores some of the best case studies in order to understand productivity-enhancing design:

- VeriFone, a California manufacturer, renovated and daylit one of its buildings. The improvements that saved 60 percent of the energy would have paid for themselves in 7.5 years. The increase in productivity of more than 5 percent and drop in absenteeism of 45 percent brought the payback to under a year—*a return on investment of more than 100 percent.*
- A Georgia carpet manufacturer moved into an extensively daylit building and *workers' compensation cases dropped from twenty per year to under one per year.*

- North Carolina schools built with daylighting cut energy consumption by 22 to 64 percent with a payback of less than three years. Students outperformed those in nondaylit schools on standardized tests by *as much as 14 percent.*
- A Wisconsin insurance company moved into a new building with 40 percent lower energy costs and work stations that give employees personal control over their lighting, heating, and cooling. *Productivity rose 7 percent.*
- Lockheed built a daylit, energy-efficient engineering development-and-design facility in Sunnyvale, California, that saves $300,000 to $400,000 a year on energy bills—and *productivity rose 15 percent.*

Why doesn't everyone insist on such productivity-enhancing design? Because, as you began to see in the last chapter, there are formidable barriers built into the very system of making buildings. Almost everyone involved in building construction—such as the developer, architects, and engineers—is rewarded by their ability to *minimize the initial cost of a building,* as opposed to its *life-cycle cost.* Moreover, they are rarely the ones who will be paying the energy bill or the salaries of the people working in the building. The owners and renters who do pay the bills must learn to ask the right questions. The total life-cycle costs are the numbers you should evaluate. Here is how the costs break down over thirty years:[1]

Thirty-Year Life-Cycle Costs of a Building	
Initial cost (including land and construction)	2 percent
Operation and maintenance	6 percent
People costs	92 percent

In a typical building, energy costs average $1.50–$2.50 per square foot, while salaries exceed $200 per square foot. That's why *productivity savings dwarf energy savings.* Cutting energy use (and hence greenhouse gas emissions) by a whopping 50 percent can typically save $1 per square foot per year. Boosting productivity a mere 5 percent will generate more than $10 per square foot in new profits every year. Failing to design buildings to increase worker productivity means ignoring 92 percent of its life-cycle cost. Yet most developers, architects, and engineers have been doing just that.

Researchers at Carnegie Mellon University's "Intelligent Workplace" have begun to quantify the benefits of these productivity gains.[2] For lighting, they found that while improved design would *add* $370,000 to the first cost of a typical workplace, it would *save* $680,000 in energy and other reduced operating costs, and more important, *could provide a productivity benefit of up to $14.6 million.* Carnegie Mellon's analysis, and a description of their own benchmark, "must see," Intelligent Workplace facility, are discussed in greater detail later in this chapter.

The key lessons of this chapter are that any manager who wants to maximize productivity should:

(1) Give workers the best lighting, which means daylight wherever possible.
(2) Improve heating, cooling, and air quality.
(3) Give workers more control over their environment—their lighting, temperature, and air flow.

The benefits are large and quantifiable.

Let's start with the case of VeriFone and see how their management, who were initially skeptical about environmental design, came to insist on productivity-enhancing design for all new as well as existing VeriFone buildings.

VALUING EMPLOYEES AT VERIFONE

VeriFone, a wholly owned subsidiary of Hewlett-Packard, manufactures the electronic verification equipment that you swipe your credit cards through. In Costa Mesa, California, VeriFone achieved an astonishing result when it renovated a 76,000-square-foot building containing offices, a warehouse, and light manufacturing.[3]

William R. Pape is cofounder of VeriFone, its first chief information officer, and a former senior vice president. How has his company ended up with one of the coolest buildings in the country? He says that in the "virtual environment" of a high-tech, information-based business like VeriFone's, "We encounter most of our colleagues only as voices on a wire or words on a screen. . . . Lacking face-to-face contact, we risk forgetting that those voices and words belong to real people who labor in real places and are vulnerable to the many environmental ills that flesh is heir to. Though most of our company's operations are virtual, we still have manufacturing plants and office buildings."

VeriFone's "first big push into environmentally sound construction" came in 1992 as the company planned its Costa Mesa renovation. "As was usual with projects like this, we consulted first with our environmental planner," Louise Pape, who made "a startling suggestion. Since we planned to build from scratch, why not create a facility that would actually enhance the health of its occupants?"

At first, VeriFone's executives were skeptical: "Back then the case for investing in healthy buildings was not obvious to senior management, and our environmental planner got what might generously be described as a lukewarm reception. Undeterred, she went away and came back armed with hard numbers." Her numbers showed that the proposed environmental modifications would save $110,000 annually in energy costs with an estimated payback of a few years. The numbers also showed that the productivity gains would be many times the energy savings.

The environmental planner also brought in an outside expert in designing healthy buildings, Randolph Croxton, president of the New York architectural firm Croxton Collaborative. "Standing before a group of VeriFone executives, the native North Carolinian patiently explained his philosophy." Croxton believes that good buildings "not only stave off illness but actually promote their inhabitants' well-being and productivity." He promised VeriFone he could build them such a building. "After reviewing Croxton's figures and plans, we told him to do it."

Croxton used a multidisciplinary team that "paid close attention to integration, while using fairly simple materials but sophisticated design measures" to maximize productivity while minimizing wasted resources. For example, an industrial hygienist focused on how materials and building systems affect worker health and productivity. Croxton told me that his firm has a "continuous improvement strategy" with a "self-critical design process," so that unhealthy and flawed designs are avoided in the first place. His team includes a "forensic mechanical engineer" who is an expert in how systems fail.

The upgrade included energy-efficient air handlers, high-performance windows, 60 percent more insulation than is required by code, a natural-gas-fired cooling system, occupancy sensors, and a comprehensive daylighting strategy, including a series of skylights. Croxton strongly believes that "the eye is hungry for full spectrum light." He says that "lighting systems are so bad today, you can do a lot to boost productivity just with better lighting." His goal is not merely "to bring daylight deep into buildings" though that is important. He believes that "the key to productivity" is "understanding how to blend artificial and natural systems."

On sunny days, workers in the remanufacturing area construct circuit boards with *only natural light and small task lighting*. In the office area, on the other hand, Croxton's design minimizes direct solar glare on computers, while providing enough daylight to allow workers there to connect to the natural world and see changes associated with the sun's daily and seasonal variation.

His design uses low-toxic and nontoxic paints, carpeting, and other toxic furnishings. The building has three to five times more air recirculation than required by code. Croxton also employed a system that automatically flushes out old air and brings in fresh air every morning.

The building beat California's strict Title 24 building code by 60 percent with a 7.5-year payback on energy-efficient technologies. But far more exciting was the impact on absenteeism and worker productivity. Here's how cofounder Pape describes it:

> We started using the building in June 1993. Eighteen months later the absentee rate for employees working in the new facility was *40 percent lower* than for those performing the same jobs in an older VeriFone building next door, and *productivity was up more than 5 percent.* Workers in the new building proclaimed the demise of end-of-the day headaches and end-of-the-week sluggishness. They loved the natural light and said the air was so fresh they felt as if they were working in a forest (no mean feat when you consider that the building sits practically in the lap of Interstate 405 and the John Wayne Airport).

The bottom line is one that we will meet again and again:

➡ **The productivity gains reduced the payback time to under one year—more than a 100 percent return on investment.**

"Those results were enough to sell senior management," says Pape. "Every VeriFone facility built since 1992 has replicated the Costa Mesa experiment; we have retrofitted many of our older facilities as well." Pape puts the results in terms any information-age company would envy: "While this program is the rare instance in which our tools have been largely low-tech, I believe it has done more to boost productivity than all the bandwidth in the world."

Finally, Pape notes that savings are not the only financial benefit of productivity-enhancing design: "It's also a nice way to show employees that you care, which can only help nurture loyalty and improve retention."

THE PRODUCTIVITY CHALLENGE

Most managers are as VeriFone's were in the beginning—skeptical that improved office and building design can increase productivity. Managers are taught that physical changes in the workplace, such as improved lighting, are irrelevant to the productivity of workers. This is perhaps the single greatest myth in the long history of worker productivity studies.

This pervasive myth has its origins in research done at Western Electric's

Hawthorne Works plant in the 1920s and 1930s. You will find a typical restatement of the myth in the book *In Search of Excellence:* "For us, the very important message of the [Hawthorne] research . . . is that it is *attention to employees,* not work conditions per se, that has the dominant impact on productivity."[4] Remarkably, as we will see, if the research actually proved anything, it proved the reverse, that *work conditions, not attention to employees, have the dominant impact on productivity.*

I asked Vivian Loftness, head of Carnegie Mellon's School of Architecture, to describe just how pernicious the myth is:

> Executives consistently cite the Hawthorne effect as clear disproof of any real linkage of productivity to the physical workplace—all that matters is management method. *This allows workers to be put into increasingly poorer work environments, smaller workstations, cheaper furniture, less work surface, less storage, no daylight or view, no control of air, temperature, or light.* It is time to put the Hawthorne study away, and to teach business students the mountain of international evidence that links physical and environmental quality to great gains in individual and organizational productivity.[5]

Because the Hawthorne myth continues to have such an appalling effect on workplace design, it is discussed in the Appendix.

Here in this chapter you will read some of the "mountain of evidence" that Loftness refers to—a dozen case studies covering the spectrum of businesses—an insurance company, a large retail store, an engineering company, a school, a post office, an electric utility, and several manufacturers.

This chapter demonstrates how a great many companies have increased worker productivity with improved workplace design. These techniques involve designing workspaces for the end user—the worker. They deserve the label cool not just because they are aesthetically superior but because they invariably save energy, thereby reducing emissions of greenhouse gases.

At the heart of cool design is cool lighting, giving workers just the light they need, no more and no less. As shown in the previous chapter, this not only can reduce by 50 to 70 percent what is the single largest source of carbon dioxide emissions for a building—the electricity used for lighting, but it can also reduce the electricity used for cooling the heat generated by inefficient lighting. The coolest lighting is daylight, since it is the most natural and the least polluting. As we will see, it is also the lighting best documented to enhance productivity.

Interface

Interface, a leading carpet manufacturer, is one of the foremost practitioners of environmental sustainability in the corporate world (more in Chapter 9).

They consider the environmental impact of every major investment decision. So, when one of their subsidiaries, Prince Street Technologies, built a new 160,000-square-foot factory in Cartersville, Georgia, they made extensive use of daylighting.[6] The building has thirty-two skylights, and, as architect Frank P. Boardman, manager of creative services for Prince Street brags, it is the "only carpet factory with a sixty-foot picture window."

Daylight streams into the factory, which is a big help for employees making carpets that are richly colored. "The workers love it. They love the light," says Boardman. "It's made an immense difference in attitude."

In the old factory, worker's compensation cases averaged twenty a year. In the first three years in the new daylit facility, the company has had only two cases, representing an estimated savings of $100,000 to $200,000 a year, which *exceeds the energy savings*. Boardman says that a large part of the reason is "most definitely" the superior lighting, and that the "building has made this company a safer place."

North Carolina Schools

Daylight also improves the performance of students, as documented in a groundbreaking series of studies in Johnston County, North Carolina.[7] The Raleigh, North Carolina, firm Innovative Design used extensive daylighting in three schools. The design incorporates extensive south-facing roof monitors or skylights, with translucent fabric baffles suspended in the lightwells, which keep direct sunlight from entering the classrooms. Light sensors control the backup electric lighting to maintain the correct lighting level. Each classroom also has shades to darken the room as well as override switches to increase light levels—total control.

The daylit schools had energy costs 22 to 64 percent below typical schools, with paybacks of less than three years. An independent construction cost-estimating firm calculated the extra cost of daylighting one of the schools to be $230,000. The reduced cooling and lighting loads that resulted from the daylighting, however, allowed downsizing of the mechanical equipment and electrical system, which reduced the added cost to under 1 percent of the school's total construction budget. The school was actually built *5 percent under budget* and the daylighting system will *pay for itself in less than one year*.

A research study then compared student performance on standardized tests in Johnston County from both daylit and nondaylit schools. The study's conclusion:

> The students who attended daylit schools outperformed the students who were attending nondaylit schools by 5 to 14 percent, depending upon whether you consider short- or long-term impacts. When analyzing the improvement experienced by all the reference classes at Four Oaks, Clayton, and Selma,

the average improvement was 4.7 percent. When you consider the impact on student performance resulting from being within a daylit facility for multiple years, the impact is even greater. During the same timeframe, Clayton's 8th graders showed a 21 percent improvement versus the norm improvement of 10 percent. The Selma Middle School 7th graders showed a 32 percent gain versus the norm of 15 percent. This equates to an average increase of *14 percent better performance* by the students in daylit schools.[8]

These improvements were not simply the result of moving students into a new school. As the study noted, "the new, non-daylit North Johnston Middle School actually showed a *negative* impact on the students' performance." Other studies have shown similar results. A Canadian study compared students attending elementary schools with full-spectrum light versus those attending similar schools with standard lighting during a two-year timeframe.[9] It concluded that the students in full-spectrum light were healthier and attended school three to four days more per year.

Wal-Mart and Target

Daylighting can also improve the performance of retail stores. Gregg Ander, the chief architect for Southern California Edison, says, "Our data show that over a six-month period, stores in the same districts with daylighting, selling the same products, showed a 25 percent increase in sales. The numbers are pretty impressive." Ander has been working with both Wal-Mart and Target daylit stores.[10]

Target has an Energy Star showcase building in Fullerton, California. The 102,000-square-foot store combined the standard five-step Energy Star upgrade (Chapter 3) with extensive daylighting to achieve a 24 percent energy reduction with a five-year payback. Prior to the upgrade, energy costs per square foot at the store had already been 9 percent below the average for buildings in the Los Angeles area, even though the store had virtually no natural lighting. Daylighting included forty sun-tracking skylights (made by Natural Lighting Company of Phoenix, Arizona), with diffusing lenses that look like normal electric light fixtures for the sales area. The checkout counter has four fixed skylights. The center of the store and the jewelry counter have Fresnel or prismatic lenses (by Anderson Windows), which diffuse incoming light and prevent harsh direct sun rays from entering the store. Interior electric lights have dimmable ballasts to gain maximum benefit from the skylights.

Wal-Mart's store in City of Industry, California, uses *half the energy of a typical new California store*. It has advanced lighting with dimming controls. The store uses an efficient and downsized HVAC system. In place of opaque roofing material, the store has an 18-kilowatt photovoltaic canopy. Annual energy savings are estimated at $75,000 to $80,000, which would have meant a three-year payback for the incremental cost of the energy-efficient equipment. Southern California Edison, the local utility, provided a $170,000 incentive that will *shorten the payback to under one year.*

The store is extensively daylit. Wal-Mart installed 180 skylights, taking up about 5 percent of the roof's 120,000-square-foot surface. There are 142 traditional 4-by-8-foot fiberglass diffusing skylights for most of the store, and 12 tracking skylights (manufactured by So-Luminaire, of Los Angeles) installed above the lawn and garden departments. The rest of the skylights (Anderson Window Lighthouse models with Fresnel lenses) are positioned above the apparel department. Ander notes that "the color rendition is a little bit better and the store seems to be brighter." That leads to increased sales.

Wal-Mart used skylights in California because of the stunning success of its prototype "Eco-Mart" that had opened June 1993 in Lawrence, Kansas. This was the first foray into sustainable design by the nation's largest retailer. The design team was led by Wal-Mart's own Environment Committee and BSW Architects of Tulsa, Oklahoma, and included the Rocky Mountain Institute. The team introduced a series of environmentally savvy design strategies and technologies.[11]

The building has a glazed arch at the entrance for daylighting, an efficient lighting system, and a new type of light monitor (skylights) developed specifically for this project. To save money, Wal-Mart decided to cut the number of these light monitors in half. Rather than scatter the monitors across the roof, they were placed on only half the roof, leaving the other half without daylighting.

These conditions created an unintentional experiment whose results caught management's attention. Each of Wal-Mart's cash registers is connected in real time back to the headquarters in Arkansas as part of the company's highly effective "just-in-time" retail stocking and distribution system, which allows them to respond rapidly to changing customer demands. According to Tom Seay, Wal-Mart's vice president for real estate, the data revealed "that the sales pressure [sales per square foot] was significantly higher for those departments located in the daylit half of the store." This sales rate was also higher than the same departments in other stores. That's the key reason many of the "Eco-Mart" measures have been put into other Wal-Mart stores, such as the one in City of Industry.

DESIGNING FOR THE END-USER

Daylighting is far from the only way to increase your company's productivity while reducing lighting energy use. With new lighting technologies, as well as good design techniques, you can achieve terrific results in spaces where daylighting is hard to achieve. Here is the key: Adopt the cool design practice of "end-use/least cost." Design so as to give your employees the lighting and the comfort that they want, which usually means giving workers more control over lighting, heating, and cooling.

> Top managers have always been rewarded with corner offices and thermostats—daylight and control. With cool design, you can reward everyone else.

One particularly powerful new technology gives workers' remote dimming control over their light levels. Most offices are populated with people of various ages and visual acuity, who neither need nor desire the same lighting level. They are working at different or multiple tasks, which themselves can best be performed with different lighting levels. One light level for the entire room wastes energy and hurts productivity. Give people individual control and you will save energy while increasing individual productivity.

California Steel Industries

The power of individual control was demonstrated when California Steel Industries in Fontana upgraded the lighting over eleven workstations in its Drafting Engineering Department.[12] The department has workers ranging in age from twenty-eight to sixty-nine who divide their time between blueprint drawing on drafting boards and computer-assisted design on computers. Traditional practice typically suggests 100 foot-candles on the drafting board and 50 foot-candles at the computer. The original lighting system provided about 75 to 80 foot-candles at every workstation. Not surprisingly, some engineers complained about glare on their computer screens while others complained about poor lighting for drafting. (The office has no significant amount of daylighting.)

Energy Controls and Concepts, a Redlands, California, energy services company, designed a new lighting system with half the fixtures using efficient T8 fluorescent lamps, which cut lighting electricity use in half. In addition, the fixtures over the workstations were fitted with electronic dimming ballasts and an infrared wireless remote dimming control that can be set from 0 to 100 foot-candles at each workstation.

➡️ **After the upgrade, California Steel measured light levels at every engineer's workstation over a six-day period. Light levels varied by task, age, and personal preference. They averaged 36 to 38 foot-candles for computers and 55 to 57 foot-candles for drafting—much lower than standard design practice would suggest. Many engineers** used as little as 20 foot-candles for computer work and 30 foot-candles for drafting work. The personal lighting controls brought overall energy savings to more than 60 percent.

According to Bill Rehm, a California Steel engineer, "We feel we have something special. Group morale is improved, and our area is the envy of the company. People are more settled and tend to stay at their workstations, rather than congregating and chatting in the aisles." A second engineer said, "It's great. Too much light gives me a headache. I find a comfortable level and leave the lighting set. I need lights dimmed for computer work." A third engineer said, "I stopped using my [desk] task light. I need more light for drafting, less for computer work." A fourth engineer said, "I got rid of the cardboard shield over my screen. There's no more glare. I change light levels throughout the day." Stephen Guthrie of Energy Controls and Concepts summarized the results: "Productivity is improved by an environment that is more conducive to work."

❖

Cool office design requires a systems-oriented focus on the specific workplace environment. It requires "more engineering," as Frank Lloyd Wright pleaded for so long ago in a 1909 reply to a critic's evaluation of his daylit Larkin Building:

> There is a common chord in all this that will be heard; and it is not a plea for ugliness. It is a plea for first principles—for less heat and parasitism, and more light and pragmatic integrity; for less architecture in quotation marks and more engineering. I feel that the sceptre has all but passed from the hands of the architect to the hands of the engineer, and if it is ever to be the architect's again, he must take it from the engineer by force of superior virtue.[13]

Designers must come to see any workplace as a "production system," in the words of architect Lee Windheim, who designed the Reno post office upgrade as well as the heavily daylit Lockheed building, both of which will be discussed shortly. As discussed in Chapter 2, designing systematically and giving workers more control over their work environment are techniques that Toyota pioneered with its lean production system to boost productivity in manufacturing. No surprise that these measures boost productivity in the office as well.

The Reno Post Office

In 1986 the mail sorters at the Reno, Nevada, main post office became the most productive—and the most error free—of all the sorters in the western half of the United States. Was this remarkable result made possible by the introduction of a new quality-oriented management initiative? Did some of the operators of the mail sorting machines receive special training? Were they part of an experiment designed to boost productivity?[14]

None of the above. In fact, Robert McLean, who was director of mail processing at the time, denies any personal responsibility for the improvement. McLean, now postmaster for Carson City, says, "We had the same people, the same supervisor, and I don't believe I was doing any motivational work." Yet he says that the data on the productivity and quality increase were solid: "It was irrefutable."

What happened? It had begun a few years earlier when the Reno Post Office was selected to receive a renovation that would make it a "minimum energy user." An architectural firm, Leo J. Daly, was hired to design changes aimed at doing everything necessary to reduce energy use.

The post office was a modern warehouse with high ceilings and a coal black floor. It was quite noisy in the areas where the two sorting machines were run. The chief architect, Lee Windheim, proposed a lowered ceiling and improved lighting, among other energy-saving measures. With the new ceiling, the room would be easier to both heat and cool and it would have better acoustics. The ceiling would be sloped to enhance the new indirect lighting, which would replace the old, harsh, direct downlighting with softer, more efficient, and longer-lasting bulbs. The energy-efficient room would be a far more pleasant place to work.

Before starting the complete renovation, which would cost about $300,000, Windheim did a mock-up of the lighting and new ceiling. The idea was to let it run for a few months to see how it worked and how people liked it. The mock-up was installed over only one of the two sorting machines.

In the twenty weeks following the renovation, productivity shot up more than 8 percent, while the machine in the area with the old ceiling and lighting showed no change in productivity. A year later productivity had stabilized at an increase of about 6 percent. A postal worker operating the machine was now sorting about 1,060 pieces of mail in the time it had taken to sort 1,000.[15]

After the mock-up, the rate of sorting errors by machine operators dropped to 0.1 percent—only one mistake in every 1,000 letters—the lowest error rate in the entire western region. As McLean tells it, "No one could poke holes in the story." The data were "solid enough to get $300,000 to do the whole building." After the renovation, "People used to hang out there after work. It wasn't just the lighting, it was the whole impact on the work environment. But the lighting was the main thing."

The energy savings projected for the whole building came to about $22,400 a year. The new ceiling would bring additional savings of $30,000 a year by reducing the recurring maintenance cost of repainting the underside of the exposed roof structure. Combined, the energy and maintenance savings came to about $50,000 a year—a six-year payback.

The productivity gains, however, were worth $400,000 to $500,000 a year. In other words, *the productivity gains alone would pay for the entire renovation in less than a year.* The annual savings in energy use and maintenance and the reduced air pollution were a free bonus. Working in a quieter and more naturally lit area, postal employees did their jobs better and faster.

> Designing for the end-user costs the least and invariably increases productivity.

The Reno Post Office became not only the most energy-efficient, environmentally benign post office in the western region, as intended, but also the most productive and error free.[16]

Pennsylvania Power and Lighting

In the early 1980s, Pennsylvania Power & Lighting Company had been increasingly concerned about its lighting system, especially in a 12,775-square-foot room for its drafting engineers. According to Allen Russell, superintendent of the office complex, "The single most serious problem was veiling reflections, a form of indirect glare that occurs when light from a source bounces off the task surface and into a worker's eyes." These veiling reflections wash out the contrast between the foreground and background of a task surface—such as the lines on a drawing and the film on which they're drawn. This in turn increases the time required to perform a task and the number of errors likely to be made. Russell adds:

> Low quality seeing conditions were also causing morale problems among employees. In addition to the veiling reflections, workers were experiencing eyestrain and headaches that resulted in sick leave.[17]

After considering many suggestions, the utility decided to upgrade the lighting in a small 2,275-square-foot area with high-efficiency bulbs and ballasts. Perhaps more important, while the old fixtures ran perpendicular (north/south) to the workstations (east/west), the new fixtures were installed parallel (east/west) to reduce veiling reflections. To improve lighting quality even further, the fixtures also were fitted with eight-cell parabolic louvers—metal grids that help reduce glare. Russell notes:

> Generally speaking, it can be said that we converted from gen-
> eral lighting to task lighting. As a result, more of the light is
> directed specifically to work areas and less is applied to circu-
> lation areas, creating more variance in lighting levels which
> upgrades the appearance of the space.[18]

With veiling reflections reduced, less light was needed to provide better
seeing conditions. Russell believes this is a general principle: "As lighting quality is improved, lighting quantity often can be reduced, resulting in more task
visibility and less energy consumption."

Finally, local controls were installed, according to Russell, "to permit more
selective use of lighting during cleanup and occasional overtime hours."
Previously, all the lighting was controlled by one switch, and every fixture had
to be on during cleanup. With multiple circuits, maintenance crews can now
turn the lights on and off as they move from one area to the next.

Allen performed a detailed cost analysis, comparing the initial capital and
labor costs of purchasing and installing the new lighting with the total annual
operating costs, including energy consumption, replacement lamps and ballasts, and fixture cleaning and lamp replacement labor. He found that the
total net cost of the changes amounted to $8,362; lighting energy use dropped
69 percent. Total annual operating costs fell 73 percent, from $2,800 to $765.
The $2,035 a year savings would have paid for the improvement in 4.1 years,
a 24 percent return on investment.

Under the improved lighting, however, productivity jumped 13.2 percent.
In the prior year, it had taken a drafter 6.93 hours to complete one drawing—
a productivity rate of 0.144 drawings per hour. After the upgrade, "the time
required to produce a drawing dropped to an average of 6.15 hours, boosting
the productivity rate to 0.163 drawings per hour." *The productivity gain was
worth $42,240 a year to the utility.*

The annual saving from the lighting system upgrade increased from a
modest $2,035 per year to a magnificent $44,275 per year with energy savings,
maintenance savings, and productivity improvement benefits all carefully
documented. Simple payback dropped from 4.1 years to 69 days. *The productivity gain turned a 24 percent return on investment into a 540 percent return
on investment.*

"Not only is this an amazing benefit," comments Russell, but "it is only one
of several." Before the upgrade, drafters in the area had used about 72 hours
of sick leave a year. After the upgrade, the rate dropped 25 percent to 54 hours
a year. "Improved employee morale also is noticeable." The better appearance
of the space, reduced eye fatigue and headaches, and the overall improvement
in working conditions all helped boost morale. Finally, supervisors reported
that the new lighting has reduced the number of errors. Better lighting means

better quality work. Russell says of the reduced error rate, "We are unable to gather any meaningful data on the value of these savings because any given error could result in a needless expense of thousands of dollars. Personally, I would have no qualms in indicating that the value of reduced errors is at least $50,000 per year."

If this estimate were included in the calculation, the return on investment would exceed 1,000 percent. The new lighting slashed operating costs, reduced energy use and pollution, raised productivity, raised morale, reduced sick leave, and cut errors. Drafters did higher quality work in less time. The lighting improvement was truly cool and lean.

Moreover, other companies have replicated the result:

- The Superior Die Set Corporation of Oak Creek, Wisconsin, upgraded lighting for $3,000, providing annual energy and maintenance savings of $1,750, a payback of twenty months. Reduced veiling reflections allowed drafters to produce one drawing in 6.3 hours, down from 7.1 hours, an 11.3 percent reduction, which was worth $37,500 a year, *reducing the payback to under one month.*[19]

- Control Data's Operations Group in Sunnyvale, California, upgraded their lighting for $15,000. Energy use dropped 65 percent, saving $7,000 a year. The reduced glare cut the number of input errors, raising productivity by an estimated 6 percent, which was worth $28,000 a year.[20]

Hyde Tools

Hyde Tools is a manufacturer of cutting blades with 300 employees and an active Total Quality Environmental Management program. Doug DeVries, purchasing manager from 1972 to 1992, notes that no amount of money saved will compensate for unhappy workers. He did a lighting upgrade from old fluorescents to new high-pressure sodium-vapor and metal-halide fixtures in the Hyde Tools building. The cost was $98,000, with $48,000 covered by the local utility. He estimated that annual energy savings would also come to $48,000 (for a payback of about one year), but he still insisted on trying the upgrade in only one area to start. He left the original fixtures up in case workers wanted to change back after an agreed-upon six-month trial period.[21]

"For the first three weeks, a lot of people complained because the new lights cast an orange hue," said DeVries. "But when we experimented by turning the old fluorescent lights back on after six months, there was a near riot of disapproval." Why? For one thing, the new lights now made it possible to see tiny specs of dirt on the equipment that holds the blades while they're being worked on. That dirt creates tiny indentations on a blade, called "mud holes." The mud holes make the blade defective or difficult to plate, which can lead a customer to reject it.

DeVries told me that with the new lighting, "the quality of work improved significantly because we could see things we couldn't see before." *DeVries estimates that the improved quality was worth another $25,000 a year.* Those bottom-line savings are critical to a small company. DeVries explained that every dollar saved on the shop floor is worth $10 in direct sales. In other words, the value of the improved quality alone was the equivalent of a $250,000 increase in sales. Add in the energy savings, and DeVries achieved the equivalent of $730,000 annual increase in sales.

DeVries's upgrade is far from the first time the company has used lighting to improve quality. I was delighted to learn that Isaac P. Hyde, who founded the company in 1875, built his first shop in the form of an "H" so that all of his workers could examine the edges of the finished blades in natural light.

Lockheed Building 157

One of the most successful examples of daylighting in a large commercial office building is Lockheed's Building 157 in Sunnyvale, California. In 1979, Lockheed Missiles and Space Company commissioned the architectural firm Leo J. Daly (the firm that designed the Reno post office) to design a new 600,000-square-foot office building for 2,700 engineers and support staff.[22]

The architects posed a question to Lockheed: "If we could design a building for you that would use half as much energy as the one you're planning to build, would you be interested?" Lockheed said yes, and Daly's architects responded with a design for energy-conscious daylighting that was completed in 1983 for $50 million.

Daly used fifteen-foot-high window walls with sloped ceilings to bring daylight deep into the building. "High windows were the secret to deep daylighting success," says the project architect, Lee Windheim. "The sloped ceiling directs additional daylight to the center of each floor and decreases the perception of crowded space in a very densely populated building." Daylighting is also enhanced by a central atrium, or litetrium, as the architects call it. The litetrium runs top to bottom and has a glazed roof. Workers love it. They consider it the building's most attractive feature.

Other light-enhancing features include exterior "light shelves" on the south facade. These "operate as sunshades as well as reflectors for bouncing light onto the interior ceiling from the high summer sun," in the words of two researchers from Lawrence Berkeley Laboratory. "In the winter, the interior light shelves diffuse reflected light and reduce glare during lower winter sun angles." The overall design "separates ambient and task lighting, with daylight supplying most of the ambient lighting and task lighting fixtures supplementing each workstation." Finally, continuously dimmable fluorescents with photocells were installed to maintain a constant level of light automatically and save even more energy.

The daylighting has *saved Lockheed about 75 percent on its lighting bill.* Since daylight generates less heat than office lights, the peak air conditioning load is also reduced. Overall, the building runs with about *half of the energy costs* of a typical building constructed at that time. Though Daly's energy-efficient improvements added roughly $2 million to the cost of the building, the energy savings alone were worth nearly $500,000 a year. The improvements paid for themselves in a little over four years—a high return on investment.

But the daylighting was part of a larger plan to boost worker productivity. The open office layout and a large cafeteria were designed to foster interaction among the engineers. At the same time, workstations were tailored for employee needs, including acoustical panels and chambers to block out ambient noise. When a worker moves forward into a chamber, the annoying sound of telephones becomes practically inaudible. Ambient noise was further controlled by sound-absorbing ceilings and speakers that introduced background white noise on each floor.

EMPLOYEE REACTION TO BUILDING 157

"I love my workstation. It's very comfortable, quiet, pleasant, with good lighting, air conditioning—it's great. . . . I think the daylighting is a major contributor to the pleasantness of the surroundings—it's a very comfortable place to work."

—Jacques Avedissian, design engineer

"My workspace is fifteen feet from the litetrium and the lighting is great. The office decor, arrangement, and temperature are ideal. There are many people working on this floor, but the feeling is not one of crowding, but of spaciousness. Interface with other departments is greatly facilitated because we're finally all in one building. By nature I'm very cynical, but the conditions in this building are far superior to any I've experienced in thirty years in the aerospace industry."

—Ben Kimura, staff engineer

"I love my work space. I think the building itself is very pretty; my own workstation is very functional. I am five workstations from the window and the light is fine. I use my task light and could order an additional desk lamp if I felt the need to. I like the daylight."

—Joanne Navarini, financial controller

The workstations were also designed to be flexible and fast cycle, allowing varying configurations as well as rapid reconfigurations. The floor is raised 10 inches, which provides for unlimited under-floor wire-way systems. According to Russell Robinson, manager of facility interior development, *70 percent of Lockheed's employees are moved every year.* In older buildings, reconfiguring each work area costs up to $600 per change. Moves at Building 157 involve unplugging equipment, placing two dollies under the workstation and then relocating it. The whole process takes about half an hour and costs $60 per station.

Employees love the building. Robinson reported that "productivity is up" because absenteeism was down. Lockheed never published the figures about improvements in absenteeism and productivity, but according to Don Aitken, then chairman of the Department of Environmental Studies at San Jose State, "Lockheed moved a known population of workers into the building and absenteeism dropped 15 percent." Aitken led numerous tours of Building 157 after it opened and was told by Lockheed officials that the reduced absenteeism "paid 100 percent of the extra cost of the building in the first year."

The numbers get better. The architect, Lee Windheim, also reports that *productivity rose 15 percent* for the first major contract done in the building, compared to previous contracts done by those same Lockheed engineers. Aitken reports an even more wonderful story: Top Lockheed officials told him that they believe they won a very competitive $1.5 billion defense contract on the basis of their improved productivity—and that the profits from that contract *paid for the entire building.*

West Bend Mutual Insurance

One of the most thoroughly documented increases in productivity from cool and lean design is West Bend Mutual Insurance Company's new 150,000-square-foot building headquarters in West Bend, Wisconsin. The award-winning design uses a host of energy-saving design features, including efficient lighting, windows, shell insulation, and HVAC, all with a $90 per-square-foot budget.[23]

In the West Bend Mutual building, all enclosed offices have individual temperature control. But the most high-tech features of the building are the environmentally responsive workstations (ERWs). Workers in open-office areas have direct, individual control over both the temperature and airflow. Radiant heaters and vents are built directly into their furniture and are controlled by a panel on their desks, which also provides direct control of task lighting and of white noise levels (to mask out nearby noises). A motion sensor in each ERW turns it off when the worker leaves the space and brings it back on when he or she returns. The specific ERWs used at West Bend were personal environment modules manufactured by Johnson Controls.

The ERWs give workers direct control over their environment, so that individuals working near each other can and do have very different temperatures in their spaces. No longer is the entire HVAC system driven by a manager, or by a few vocal employees who want it hotter or colder than everyone else. The motion sensors save even more energy.

You may want to follow West Bend's way of introducing change. Before moving into the new building, employees were given the chance to try out and comment on a full-scale mock-up of the ERWs. Those who had expressed the greatest doubts about the ERWs were allowed to test them at their own desks.

The lighting in the old building had been provided by overhead fluorescent lamps, not task lamps. The workers in the new building all had task lights and they could adjust them with controls according to their preference for brightness. The annual electricity costs in the old building were $2.16 per square foot. The annual electricity costs in the new building are $1.32 per square foot. The $0.84 per square foot savings represent a 40 percent reduction.

The Center for Architectural Research and the Center for Services Research and Education at the Rensselaer Polytechnic Institute (RPI) in Troy, New York, conducted a detailed study of productivity in the old building in the twenty-six weeks before the move and in the new building for twenty-four weeks after the move. The RPI study used the same productivity assessment system West Bend Mutual had used for many years, which basically tracked the number of insurance files processed by each employee per week. Researchers also conducted a detailed survey of workers' perceived levels of comfort, air quality, noise control, privacy, and lighting both before and after the move. The RPI study concluded, "After the move, *productivity increased by about 7.1 percent* when the ERWs were fully functional."

To learn just how much of the productivity gain was due to the ERWs, the units were turned off randomly during a two-week period for a fraction of the workers. The researchers concluded, "Our best estimate is that ERWs were responsible for an increase in productivity of about 2.8 percent relative to productivity levels in the old building." The 2.8 percent figure almost certainly underestimates the actual benefit of the ERWs, according to Ronald W. Lauret, West Bend Mutual's senior vice president. Lauret observes that many workers demanded that their units be turned back on immediately. Some even threatened to go home (they were eliminated from the study). He estimates that if those employees were factored back in, the productivity gain from the ERWs alone would have been 4 to 6 percent.

The company's annual salary base is $13 million, so even a 2.8 percent gain in productivity is worth about $364,000. With the higher estimate of Lauret's, the ERWs paid for themselves in under one year, and, in Lauret's words, "That's a substantial return on investment."

PUTTING IT ALL TOGETHER: THE INTELLIGENT WORKPLACE

Your company will one day start thinking about an energy-efficient retrofit or new building and you will insist on maximizing productivity. Begin your effort by visiting the "Intelligent Workplace" at Carnegie Mellon University in Pittsburgh.[24] This 7,000-square-foot, one-floor extension of an existing campus building is a living laboratory of the latest cool technologies and design techniques. It consumes just *one-third the energy* of a comparable workspace, while giving the occupants maximum daylight, windows that open, nearly complete control over their workspace conditions, and the ability to quickly reconfigure offices—the keys to maximizing productivity.

A multidisciplinary team led by Volker Hartkopf, director of the University's Center for Building Performance and Diagnostics, created the Intelligent Workplace. Although payback is difficult to calculate because it was designed to be a technology showcase, laboratory, and workspace, Vivian Loftness, head of Carnegie Mellon's School of Architecture, estimates that most of the higher performance technologies would have individual paybacks of three to five years.

The shell of the Intelligent Workplace is made of recycled aluminum and includes a heavily insulated roof pierced by many skylights. A three-layer daylighting system begins with external "light-shelves," which redirect light to provide optimum daylight while minimizing both glare and the internal cooling load. Layer Two is the high-efficiency glass windows, which have excellent transmission of visible light and low thermal conduction. Layer Three is the motorized shades located on the inside.

The interior uses high-efficiency T5 fluorescent lamps with advanced controls including daylight dimming and occupancy sensors. The ambient lighting of 25 foot-candles is supplemented by high-efficiency task lighting.

With operable windows, the HVAC system takes advantage of natural ventilation. Rooftop ventilators make use of the natural stack effect, which automatically draws the outside air in through open windows, then up and out ventilation tubes in the roof peaks, creating a gentle breeze inside. Excess heat from the lights and equipment is ingeniously pumped through vertical bars running between the windowpanes, *eliminating the need for perimeter heating.* For most of the year, these natural systems provide the vast majority of the heating and cooling.

Among the more intriguing innovations is that the mechanical ventilation—as well as all electrical, telephone, and computer wiring—is handled under a raised floor (rather than in the ceiling). This is the wave of the future for several reasons. First, it allows the use of systems such as personal environment modules, which give your individual workers direct control of their task lighting and ventilation, including air speed and temperature. These systems not only save energy but also increase productivity, as shown at West Bend. Second, the underfloor system allows you to rapidly reconfigure office space, as at Lockheed Building 157, a necessity in the modern workplace. Third, as Carnegie-Mellon researchers noted, "Numerous studies have shown that floor-based ventilation is much more effective at dissipating pollution and ensuring adequate thermal comfort."[25]

❖

Researchers at the Intelligent Workplace shared with me an early version of an analysis that goes far beyond simply surveying studies. They have systematically analyzed a large post-occupancy database of new buildings and retrofits, including many of the cases detailed here. They estimated the benefits of various design improvements for a hypothetical 100,000-square-foot workspace with 500 employees using the business yardstick of economic value added (essentially the extra net operating profit after taxes created by the upgrade, minus the capital cost of the upgrade).

In particular, they examined design options that improve the seven key features of a workplace: employee privacy and interaction, ergonomics, lighting, air, heating and cooling, access to the natural environment (such as being near a window), and network access (computers and telecommunications). They then considered the first cost of each design option (such as better lighting or ergonomics) and compared that to a variety of benefits: operations and maintenance costs (including energy costs), individual productivity, health costs and workers compensation, worker retention, salvage value (when the equipment has reached the end of its lifetime), and renewal (organization churn or the cost of reconfiguring workspaces).

What did they find? Improved lighting—including combinations of daylighting, energy-efficient fluorescent lighting, and individual lighting control (what I have been calling cool lighting design)—adds $370,000 to the initial cost of the 100,000-square-foot workplace. But, on the positive side of the balance sheet, the new lighting adds $680,000 in value in terms of energy savings and other reduced operating costs (over a fifteen-year period assuming a 10 percent cost of capital). Far more important, Carnegie Mellon calculated that *cool lighting provides a productivity benefit of up to $14.6 million.*

The Carnegie Mellon researchers have made similar calculations for each of the other design features, creating a powerful tool to allow your company to maximize economic value added and minimize environmental harm.[26]

DESIGN FOR PRODUCTIVITY

Let us draw some general conclusions from all these diverse case studies. First, energy-efficient design can have a significant impact on productivity. You can achieve improvements of 7 to 15 percent. At the same time, sick leave and absenteeism may drop significantly.

Second, productivity gains are typically accompanied by far fewer errors and defects. Many errors are the result of visual problems that good lighting can resolve. *Quality work requires quality lighting.* Similarly, defect prevention and pollution prevention go hand in hand.

Third, people like daylight. This was as true for Georgia carpet workers as for students in North Carolina and employees of Lockheed and Compaq. Top managers typically command a corner office with lots of windows, and now it is easier to daylight far more of your people.

The greater the connection to the natural environment, the better. Socio-biologist Edward O. Wilson coined the term "biophilia" to describe what he believes is our innate affinity for the natural world. A 1993 book, *The Biophilia Hypothesis,* examines the evidence in detail and cites studies of hospitals and prisons that "suggest that prolonged exposure to window views of nature can have important health-related influences." As Roger Ulrich, an expert in behavioral geography and environmental psychology at Texas A&M University's College of Architecture, notes:

> Research on biophilia is at a relatively early stage of development, and no findings have yet appeared that constitute convincing support for the proposition that positive responding to nature has a partly genetic basis. Perhaps the most persuasive findings currently available are the striking patterns across diverse groups and cultures revealing a preference for every day natural scenes over urban scenes lacking nature.[27]

Biophilia or not, daylight is the most cost-effective and least polluting way to both light and heat a building.

Fourth, the two elements of cool and lean design that most improve productivity and quality are (1) focusing on the end-user and (2) giving workers more control over their environment. Focusing on the end-user—a basic systems principle—here means you are designing lighting with the worker's specific task in mind. This invariably saves energy, and its impact on worker performance can be substantial. Give workers more control over their workplace environment—control of lighting, heating, and cooling—and they are more comfortable and more effective.

Fifth, a systems approach to new building design achieves the most cost-effective improvements in energy use and productivity. Designing a building right the first time is obviously cheaper than retrofitting an inadequate design. For one thing, you don't have to buy equipment twice. The very best gains are achieved when green design principles are coupled with other techniques aimed at boosting productivity, such as improved acoustics. A variety of measures were taken by Lockheed Building 157, Wal-Mart and Target, and West Bend Mutual. We can never measure the precise contributions of each separate cool design principle—indeed, the point of a systems approach is that the whole is greater than the sum of its parts. But a systems approach to cool design is the major reason for the productivity jump.

Sixth, while designing an office right the first time is obviously best, upgrades can be extremely effective. This is good news because the vast majority of businesses will not be moving anytime soon, and when they do, most will not be commissioning a whole new building. The cases of VeriFone, the Reno post office, Boeing, and the two drafting areas show that even simple improvements in lighting can create tremendous savings.

Seventh, and finally, the savings from the gain in productivity can dwarf the savings in energy, in some cases by a factor of ten. Paybacks of a few years become paybacks in less than one year. Return on investment can jump from 25 percent to 500 percent.

Chapter

COMPUTERS AND CLEAN ROOMS

We have seen many instances of how energy efficiency has increased productivity and saved companies money. Behind the best cases is an energy champion, like Petar Reskusic at Toyota, who breaks down the barriers that block efficiency projects. Often, too, the champion brings in an outside expert, such as the Papes did with architect Randy Croxton.

This chapter examines one of the best such duos I have come across, Ron Perkins and Lee Eng Lock. They have much to teach about busting barriers and making your company cool. Perkins, the facilities manager for Compaq in the 1980s, helped break down the traditional corporate barriers to strategic investment in buildings and, with Lee, helped Compaq become one of the coolest of companies. Perkins then went to Supersymmetry, an energy consulting company founded by Lee in Singapore. Supersymmetry is the benchmark for reducing energy consumption in semiconductor manufacturing.

> Lee Eng Lock's motto: *Efficiency is Free. Ask for More.*

Worldwide, some $170 *billion* in new semiconductor plants are on the drawing boards, a commitment of almost $30 billion in present value electricity costs. The energy bills of semiconductor fabrication plants often exceed the cost of salaries and benefits. They reach levels of $1 million to $2 million a month, in large part because of the need to make chips in extremely clean rooms, with high levels of ventilation. So it is worth exploring some of the best energy-savings practices for the industry.

I'll discuss the strategy of one of the industry leaders in cool semiconductor manufacturing, STMicroelectronics. The company measures its energy inefficiency in terms of electricity consumed per million dollars of production cost. With Supersymmetry's help, STMicroelectronics has exceeded its remarkable goal of *reducing its energy inefficiency 5 percent per year for three years running.* This chapter concludes with two more of Supersymmetry's best cases, which have wide application throughout the industry:

- An integrated circuit factory outside of Manila upgraded its lighting, heating, ventilation, and cooling system and *cut the energy usage per chip by 60 percent.*

- In Malaysia, Western Digital built what is now considered the most efficient disk drive factory in the world, *cutting energy consumption 44 percent with a one-year payback.* These cuts were achieved even though plant floor space increased by more than 10 percent and air filtration requirements increased 1000-fold!

Whoever best uses energy efficiency and pollution prevention to lower costs and increase productivity—whoever is the most proactive—will achieve a unique competitive advantage and dramatically lower greenhouse gas emissions as well.

THE COMPAQ STORY

The Perkins–Lee story begins with the story of Compaq, which is a leader in making both itself *and* its products more efficient. In accepting the World Environment Center Gold Medal in May 1997, Compaq's President and CEO Eckhard Pfeiffer said, "We view business and the environment as parts of the same total system—the Earth's ecosystem. And therefore we think through the environmental consequences of every aspect of our business." Pfeiffer committed Compaq to "continuous environmental improvement" saying "we can and will get even better at product design, work processes, materials use, recycling, waste minimization, and energy conservation." He said Compaq's ultimate goal is "zero emissions" and "zero impact."[1]

Compaq's environmental strategy has made good business sense for the company. Not only has this approach lowered operating costs and increased quality, productivity, and profits, it has also improved Compaq's international competitiveness. With their superior environmental performance, many Compaq products carry Germany's Blue Angel eco-label, which identifies products that are environmentally friendly, recyclable, and easily serviced, and Sweden's TCO '95 designation, which recognizes personal computers and monitors that are recyclable, upgradable, and manufactured without CFCs.

These labels have given Compaq a competitive advantage in entering the European market.

I find it impressive that Compaq has been cool from day one. Unlike many companies, which come to energy efficiency after they are big and profitable, Compaq was efficient from the start.

Compaq is one of the great American success stories. Founded in 1982, it achieved the highest first-year sales in the history of U.S. business, $111 million, with its first product, the Compaq portable. By 1985, it had become the world's second largest manufacturer of personal computers (after IBM). In 1987, after a mere five years, Compaq surpassed $1 billion in sales—faster than any other company in history. In 1997, the company had worldwide sales of $24.6 billion. Today, it is the largest supplier of PCs in the world.

While everyone knows the story of Compaq's financial success, their enduring efforts in energy efficiency and emissions reduction are less well known. Compaq's long experience shows that being energy efficient is not merely compatible with success in the business world, it is a key contributor to that success. Few companies growing as fast as Compaq grew would take notice of the electricity bill, which equaled only 1 percent of the cost of business.

❖

Does your company view your facilities as a *source* of moneymaking investments? Most companies don't. Ron Perkins, buildings manager for Compaq Computers in the 1980s, saved Compaq about $1 million a year by reducing energy use and hence pollution. To do it, however, he had to overcome a major obstacle: In the buildings and facilities division of Compaq, as in most companies, projects had traditionally required a payback period of two years or less. If an investment took more than two years to pay for itself, forget it.

Ron had been a facilities engineer at Texas Instruments but didn't like the constraints and short-term focus of traditional corporate facilities management. "What attracted me to Compaq was that everyone was in over their heads," says Perkins. "There were no experts. . . . There was an open, casual, 'organized frenzy.' The chain of command was simple. My boss Karen Walker and I reported directly to [then] Chief Financial Officer, John Gribi."

In his desire to move to longer paybacks, Perkins went to Gribi, who was well known to have a long-term view. Gribi's philosophy was simple: *Apply capital dollars to reduce future expense.* In other words, "Spend money to save money." With that proactive mission in mind, Perkins went to the treasurer to get capital for his money-saving projects. The treasurer had come from a top accounting firm. He told Perkins that he didn't do payback calculations: "I do Return on Investment. I compare the ROI with the company's cost-of-money [the interest rate the company pays to borrow money], which ranges from 7 percent to 11 percent. Give us our cost-of-money plus 3 percent. If we don't have the money, we'll borrow."

In other words, Compaq would make almost any investment *in itself* with an ROI of 14 percent or more. From that moment on, the company would invariably pursue efficiency investments in the 15 to 20 percent range—a five- to seven-year payback.

To the facilities people, "the concept of borrowing money to pay for a change was completely foreign." But to the treasurer, it made a lot of sense—when the change had a higher ROI than the interest rate on the borrowed money. Another fact Perkins understood is that energy-efficiency investments are much lower risk—and hence much safer—than most investments a company makes.

THINK LIFE-CYCLE

By connecting the finance people with the facilities people for the first time at Compaq, Perkins had shattered the traditional mindset of the two-year payback, which demands a 50 percent return on investment. The new goal was a five- to seven-year payback.

As Perkins explained to me, "That's how we were able to do life-cycle costing, to figure out the effect of any change on the ability of the company to make a profit." Perkins now knew that in judging any proposed capital improvement, he could look five to seven years out and make money for his company. A great deal of money.

Perkins had uncovered the connection between the company's capital spending on its buildings and its *future* operating costs. A life-cycle analysis of any purchase considers its total costs over many years, including the money needed for energy use, operations, and maintenance. Compaq could spend a little more now to save a lot more later. Initial costs might be a bit higher, but life-cycle costs would be far lower. Most of Perkins' improvements, such as daylighting Compaq's buildings, were also aimed at improving worker productivity, or, as Perkins described it to me, "systematically removing the barriers to productivity." Productivity growth at Compaq was so rapid—55 percent in 1985 alone—that it is not possible to trace it to any one cause.

Ron Perkins succeeded at Compaq by using systems thinking, which requires making new connections in space and time. In his search for money to reduce energy use, pollution, and long-term operating costs, he helped break down not only the barrier between facilities and finance but also the barrier between the company's present purchases and its future costs. The company's people became *more physically interconnected* and *more forward thinking*—two hallmarks of systems thinking.

Life-cycle analysis lies at the heart of a systems approach to becoming cool and lean. It leads to energy efficiency and high-productivity workplaces. It is crucial to designing cool products and cool production processes. Overuse of resources in the beginning of the production process leads to excess pollution and waste at the end. A company can achieve huge savings at both ends by reducing resource use and pollution when a product is manufactured, when it is used, and when it is ready to be discarded. Again, a life-cycle approach is needed to minimize overall costs, not merely initial costs. This in turn requires a systematic approach to production: The people who research, design, manufacture, and market must work together at the same time in cross-functional teams.

> Becoming a cool and lean company through systems thinking requires making connections in time (through life-cycle analysis) and in space (through teamwork). Systems thinking is the only way to achieve process improvements, which is the only way to raise productivity significantly, which is the only enduring way to achieve success in business.

Perkins has said, "The role of facilities managers is to embody the corporate culture in brick and mortar." At Compaq, "Every effort was made to create a setting that stimulates creativity and enhances individual effort and productivity," whether it was a heavily wooded landscape or sophisticated manufacturing systems. Designing the work environment to increase productivity requires first asking employees what they want. Compaq repeatedly surveyed and interviewed its workers to find out how they felt about their current workplaces and what they would like to see in a new facility.

The single most common response concerned daylighting. People want as much natural light as possible in their office and would like to be able to see outside. Perkins "tried to maximize the amount of natural light to people who didn't have outside windows in their offices by putting in sidelights, a window beside each door. This allows a person with an interior office to look outside through the windows of the person across the hall." Other design measures include top-floor skylights, lobby-level atriums, and glass-enclosed walkways. Coffee break areas were moved to the atrium to increase interactions between manufacturing and office workers. People were given a fair amount of individual control over their temperature. Every exterior office had thermostats. Clusters of three or four interior offices also had thermostats.

Compaq made no attempt to measure the effect of these and other efforts on productivity, but as we saw in Chapter 4, similar changes in other companies have led to significant productivity increases. No doubt these measures contributed to the high growth in productivity and profits that Compaq achieved in the 1980s. Perkins notes that "*rather than building buildings for the sake of the buildings, Compaq was building buildings for people and productivity.*"

LEE ENG LOCK JOINS THE COMPAQ TEAM

Perkins visited an AT&T plant in Singapore and was struck by the EMCS (energy management control system) and the level of data collection he saw. As we saw in Chapter 3, monitoring and verification of a building with an EMCS can achieve huge energy savings. Lee Eng Lock, a Singapore-born British-educated engineer, has raised systems-oriented HVAC (heating, ventilation, and air conditioning) design to a high art through his pioneering work with EMCSs.

In 1986, Perkins hired Lee to improve Compaq's HVAC systems. It's worth repeating Lee's motto: *Efficiency is Free. Ask for More.* Lee believes that most engineers approach energy like salesmen: Selling more is better. Indeed, he complains that in Asia, it is particularly common to waste electricity because companies model themselves on standard U.S. practice.

With Compaq, Lee took the Gilbreth-Ohno approach of repeatedly asking questions. On his first visit to the Houston-based firm, he asked, "How big is the [cooling] load?" "Why are you using 3,000 tons of refrigeration?" "How do you know your peak load?" More often than not, Perkins could not give immediate answers.

Lee examined Compaq's central cooling plant, which circulated a "river of water" through a 24-inch pipe to all of Compaq's buildings. He concluded that the primary pumps were oversized, as well as the secondary pumps feeding each building. He recommended turning the secondary pumps off, thereby shutting down eight pumps using a total of 240 horsepower. This simple but "radical" change not only improved overall system performance, it saved Compaq $100,000 a year. It took only four hours to get done. When Compaq was taking bids for replacement cooling towers, Lee recommended units that were *ten times as efficient.* The payback was *only eight months.*

Fans and pumps move air or water against friction. Lee relentlessly pursues the causes of that friction. In the 1997 book, *Factor Four: Doubling Wealth, Halving Resource Use,* Amory Lovins, Hunter Lovins, and Ernst von Weizsacker provide a good example of Lee's thinking process:

- The pipe in the original design has too much friction because it's too long and has too many bends. That happened because the engineer laid out the equipment first, then connected it with pipes that had to run through all sorts of twists and turns to get from A to B. (The pipefitters didn't mind, they're paid by the hour.) Instead, let's lay out the pipes first, then the equipment.
- The pipe has so much friction because it's rough inside when it should be smooth. Choosing the right material and surface finish can cut friction 40-fold or more.

- The pipe is also too small. How easily the water flows varies as nearly the fifth power of diameter. If the pipe's diameter were increased by only 10 percent, its friction would drop by 37 percent; if 20 percent, then by 59 percent; if 50 percent, then by 86 percent. So, fatter pipe can almost eliminate friction. It does cost a bit more, but the first designer balanced that extra cost only against the value of the saved energy. . . . He forgot by using fatter pipe we can make all the expensive parts—pump, motor, inverter, electricals—at least twofold smaller and hence cheaper. That's a better buy than too-slender pipe.[2]

Perkins work with Lee taught him a number of valuable lessons. He learned the importance of gathering as much information as possible "before the design period." He notes that "at Compaq this approach led to lower overall costs, totally inclusive of the costs of design, architecture, consultants, and buying the land and building the spaces."

Another lesson Perkins learned was the need to teach everyone involved in running a building "the value of collecting data and making operational changes as necessary." He points out that "monitoring and evaluation allow for greater energy efficiency and smoother running facilities as problems are caught in very early stages." In other words, Lee's approach allows a building manager to *prevent* problems from occurring in the first place.

VALUE AND TRAIN SUPPORT STAFF

The need to closely monitor and evaluate a building's performance led to one of the most important lessons Perkins learned at Compaq: *No enduring gains in energy efficiency are possible if building managers and maintenance people are ignored.* Perkins concluded:

> One of the biggest problems is the high turnover of facilities managers and building operators. The employees assigned to the task of operating buildings tend to be treated like very well paid pump managers. They are not fully trained in the particulars of the systems they are running. Thus, tools at hand—computer software and hardware as well as the energy-saving technologies—are often not used. Companies should create primers for new building managers and operators and introduce them with four days of training in building operations and a tune-up training course every six months.

All of your employees need to be imbued with cool thinking. You should listen to them for valuable, money-saving advice. We have seen over and over that good building managers turn the company's vision into reality. If building managers and staff are not brought into the decision-making process when a company decides to become cool, your company may win the battle but lose the war. They may undermine the improvements, either intentionally or out of ignorance. Or they may simply leave shortly after a major retrofit, taking with them irreplaceable experience with the idiosyncrasies of your building and its HVAC systems.

Building managers control so much of the workplace environment. If they are left out of the picture, the chances of improving worker productivity drop dramatically. They deserve to be properly recognized and rewarded for making such a contribution to the bottom line.

Compaq has gone further than just reducing its own energy consumption. Compaq was one of the charter members of EPA's "Energy Star Computer" program, to reduce the energy consumed by the computers it sells. It has been so successful at developing energy-efficient products and educating customers and employees on the benefits of reducing energy consumption that it was recognized by the EPA as Energy Star PC Partner of the Year in 1996 and 1997. In 1998, the EPA presented to Compaq a Climate Protection Award for Corporate Leadership in Energy-Efficient Electronic Products.

In April 1993, Compaq eliminated CFC use in all of its manufacturing processes. Since 1993, Compaq has increased recycling per unit production by 125 percent. It has dramatically decreased its emissions of volatile organic compounds (VOCs), by 73 percent since 1993, and anticipates being able to reduce them another 50 percent or more.

As usual, process redesign aimed at preventing pollution achieves other benefits. The equipment that eliminated CFCs from their processes was smaller and faster. It allowed Compaq to shorten the production line, and it ultimately allowed the company to save space on the manufacturing floor and thus to add more production lines in the free space (which in turn saved the energy that would have been used constructing and operating a new building to house those lines). It also shortened cycle time, increasing production. In also eliminating alcohol-based fluxes used in soldering components to printed circuit boards, Compaq reduced VOCs and cleaned the boards better, reducing poor solder connections and improving quality.

Compaq continues to reduce the energy used to make each PC. Some of this reduction is the result of the process redesign made possible by eliminating CFCs, and some comes from adopting vertically integrated manufacturing, which has allowed Compaq to eliminate redundancy, shut down conveyor lines, and improve overall efficiency. Also, much of Compaq's energy use is in its buildings, so when the company went from one or two shifts to round-the-clock operations, it was able to save the energy associated with setting up equipment and cooling it down. In addition, Compaq's new buildings use half the energy of typical buildings. As a result of these actions, energy consumption has remained flat while production has soared. In 1998, the U.S. EPA named the company the "1998 Green Lights Corporate Partner of the Year" for its outstanding efforts in energy conservation and environmental awareness.

In his acceptance speech, President Pfeiffer explained the reason for Compaq's success in both business and environmental performance:

> We insist on being anticipatory and proactive. If there's a single reason Compaq remains the global PC leader four years running, it's because we stay ahead of change by anticipating what we'll need to do and then doing it early, while we have maximum control over the what, where, and how.

Compaq thrives as a genuinely cool and lean company.

COOL CLEAN ROOMS

The most energy-intensive part of the computer industry lies not in the final assembly of the components, as performed by companies like Compaq and Dell. Rather, it lies in the manufacture of the chips and the hardware that go inside the computer. As noted earlier, semiconductor manufacturing is one of the fastest growing energy-intensive industries in the world. The typical plant has an electricity bill of $1 to $2 million *a month*. Globally, some $170 billion in new plants are on the drawing boards, more than 36 million square feet of clean-room floor space. This represents a commitment of almost $30 billion in present value electricity costs (18 percent of total capital investment). These plants' combined electric load bill totals more than 5,000 megawatts and 40 billion kWh, consuming more energy than five Chernobyl-sized powerplants. The Pacific Northwest alone, which is home to about half of all U.S. semiconductor production, may see some $20 billion in new facilities over the next several years, with a combined electric load in excess of 500 megawatts.[3]

Yet as with every other industry, energy consumption of the standard chip factory can be cut by 40 percent or more—and greenhouse gas emissions by more than that. In particular, HVAC typically represents 30 to 50 percent of the electricity costs because the huge clean rooms require tremendous amounts of filtered air, and, as we have seen, there are large opportunities for HVAC energy savings.

The benchmark engineering-design firm in this area is Singapore-based Supersymmetry, founded in 1988 by Lee Eng Lock. Lee wanted to create a team of top engineers, research scientists, and energy consultants who would design HVAC systems and buildings that emphasized frugality and elegance using a "back to basics" approach of "measure accurately, measure often." In 1991, Lee hired Ron Perkins to head Supersymmetry USA, in Houston. In recent years, they have brought their HVAC expertise to the design of clean rooms.

❖

In 1995, Supersymmetry helped design and build perhaps the most energy-efficient disk drive factory in the world. Western Digital, a U.S.-based hard disk drive manufacturer, asked Supersymmetry to help it renovate an existing semiconductor factory located outside Kuala Lumpur, the capital of Malaysia. Floor area increased from 80,000 to 90,000 square feet. More importantly, the filtration needed to improve dramatically to get the clean room from class 10,000 to class 10. (The class number refers to the maximum number of particles per cubic foot in the air, which meant that the new clean room required 1,000 times fewer particles per cubic foot.)

Supersymmetry designed a high-efficiency air filtration system using advanced filters, coils, and ducts, combined with efficient fans coupled to variable speed drives. Supersymmetry monitored the chiller load and found that the maximum cooling load was 210 to 220 tons, whereas the existing cooling plant had two (inefficient) 300-ton chillers. Instead of replacing the chillers, they retrofitted them with a conversion kit, which reduced the capacity to 250 tons, with higher efficiency, at *one-quarter the cost of a new chiller.* They also improved the lighting, compressed air system, pumping system, cooling towers, and vacuum pumps.

Perhaps most important, the Western Digital plant uses a state-of-the-art energy management control system designed by Supersymmetry that operates on powerful Silicon Graphics workstations. The system has high-accuracy sensing, including 0.01 degrees Celsius temperature sensors. It stores measured, real-time data that can be retrieved at one-minute intervals. It generates performance curves of all major mechanical and electrical equipment, in 3-D format, with the ability to compare measurements against vendor's curves. Interactive modeling of variable speed drive effects on pumps and fans allows optimum settings to be chosen.

Even with a larger plant area and 1,000 times the filtration, the new factory uses 44 percent less energy than the original building. The total cost of the efficient design was similar to costs of other bidders who proposed standard (i.e., inefficient) designs. Indeed, the efficient filtration system design lowered some equipment costs, because it required fewer, smaller pumps and fans. Other efficiency-related costs paid for themselves in the first year. This cool factory won the Association of Energy Engineers "1996 Energy Project of the Year."

❖

In 1996, Amkor/Anan Pilipinas asked Supersymmetry to help reduce the electric bill in its 689,000-square-foot chip packaging plant in Muntinlupa City, outside Manila, which has more than 6,000 employees. Amkor/Anan is part of a group that comprises the world's largest independent packager of integrated circuits. Their job is to test wafers manufactured by plants around the world, cut them into individual chips, and package them in plastic. Amkor's customers include IBM, Lucent, and Intel. Lee upgraded the lighting, put in a high-efficiency chiller, and tuned the system within an advanced control system, *cutting more than $2 million from the annual energy bill.* While chip output *doubled* from 1995 to 1997, the electricity bill *declined.* Adjusting for chip size, the power cost per chip fell 60 percent.

"ECOLOGY IS COST-FREE" AT STMICROELECTRONICS

Supersymmetry helped STMicroelectronics (formerly SGS-Thomson Microelectronics) make its Singapore chip fabrication plant more than twice as efficient as the typical fabrication plant.[4] From 1994 to 1997, the plant cut energy use by 24 million kWh a year, saving $2.2 million with a 0.95 year payback and reducing carbon dioxide emissions by 21,000 tons.

The $4 billion company has 26,000 employees and fabrication plants in Europe, Asia, and the United States. A leading manufacturer of integrated circuits, its revenues doubled from 1993 to 1997, and it is ranked among the top ten worldwide semiconductor suppliers. The company is a leader in quality, winning the 1997 European Quality Award for Business Excellence. *President and CEO Pasquale Pistorio has committed the company to be "best-in-class" in environmental protection,* as part of the company's "Vision 2000" Initiative. It is one of the first companies to receive the European Eco-Audit and Management System and ISO-14001 environmental accreditations in the countries where it operates. It won the 1998 Business Environment Trophy in Europe for large corporations.

STMicroelectronics has concluded that meeting environmental targets has meant economic savings and that "environmentally friendly technologies and processes are more efficient, less costly, more reliable and safer." The company believes that improved environmental performance also increases their ability to attract investment capital, reduces insurance costs, makes it easier to win government contracts in countries like Sweden, and makes them more attractive to "young capable human resources" who prefer to work for an environmentally responsible company.

Pistorio explained the company's environmental strategy in a 1998 speech:

> We are convinced that a company which is wholly and truly committed to protecting the environment will be financially more competitive than those which are not. We believe that *"ecology is cost-free,"* just as it was said several years ago that quality is cost-free. *Prevention is better than a cure and these processes which are intrinsically ecological are also far more economical, therefore ensuring greater profitability.*

STMicroelectronics has decided to be a leader in mitigating global warming because they are worried that, by generating so many greenhouse gases, humankind is engaging in "a giant unplanned, uncontrolled, blind experiment," with potentially catastrophic results. The company believes that the price of carbon dioxide will rise as governments create an international trading system for carbon dioxide permits (see Chapter 10) to meet the goals of the Kyoto Treaty. That poses a risk to the semiconductor fabrication industry because it is both fast growing and energy intensive.

The company measures its energy inefficiency in terms of electricity consumed per million dollars of production cost. In 1994, the company set a goal of *reducing its energy inefficiency by 5 percent per year* every year through 2000. It has so far beaten the goal every year.

To help it to continue beating the goal and to achieve even bigger savings in carbon dioxide, the company has created a team of experts to work with them and Supersymmetry, including Amory Lovins (of Rocky Mountain Institute in Snowmass, Colorado), perhaps the world's leading authority on energy efficiency; Gil Friend, an expert on industrial ecology and environmental management; and Chris Robertson, a Portland, Oregon, consultant who is an expert on systems, design integration, and process technology. I have provided the company assistance in its analysis of cogeneration and carbon dioxide mitigation.

➤ **STMicroelectronics and its sustainability team have put together a design for a next-generation fabrication plant that *reduces carbon dioxide emissions per chip by 75 percent* compared to their average plant in 1990 *at a lower initial cost*. And that is for a company whose plants are already much more efficient than the industry average.**

One key reason the company is pursuing energy efficiency so relentlessly is that they have found it brings them a number of benefits beyond reduced operating costs and reduced emissions. Supersymmetry's strategy of systems-oriented design increases productivity. Energy-efficient systems have a higher reliability because of reduced vibration and wear and tear. They also provide greater control over air filtration, exhaust, and air quality, which can improve yield as well as employee health and safety.

Indeed, the company understands better than most the link between lean thinking and cool design. That's why they have a corporate Vice President for Total Quality *and* Environmental Management, Murray Duffin. I asked Duffin what he saw as the link. He answered, "The principles and practices that change a company from business-as-usual to a culture of Total Quality Management apply equally and as effectively in developing the culture of environmental responsibility. In both cases it's an easy sell, because even as people want to do good work, they also want to protect their children's future."

The fast product cycles for semiconductors also make them a good candidate for new process technology, since new plants are being built at a much faster rate than in most other energy-intensive industries. Siemens Solar Industries, the largest maker of solar-electric cells in the world, grows silicon ingots in their Vancouver, Washington, plant. Because of the rapid growth in the solar industry (discussed in Chapters 1 and 6), Siemens expects to triple its crystal-growing capacity every few years. It has been working on improvements to the electric resistance-heated furnaces used to grow single-crystal silicon ingots. Siemens believes it will be able to cut its energy use 60 to 75 percent and reduce the use of expensive argon gas 90 percent while shortening the crystal growth cycle time by 33 to 50 percent. Company executives believe these improvements could be applied to all the furnaces now used to make ingots, which would represent a huge energy savings.

Another breakthrough technology for use in these plants is light guides or light pipes with external sources. Ultimately, central lighting may be as common in your buildings as central cooling, with concentrated daylight used when it is available and super-high-efficiency lighting, such as the recently developed sulfur lamp, when it isn't. The advantage for a semiconductor maker is that the light pipes, made by companies like 3M, do not require regular replacement, as lightbulbs do, which can be highly intrusive in a clean room environment, requiring expensive interruption of production.

Semiconductor manufacturing is also a good candidate for cogeneration because of the need to maximize the availability, reliability, and premium quality of electricity. Semiconductor makers designing plants today should be looking to combine efficiency with cool power to achieve carbon dioxide reductions approaching 75 percent, as STMicroelectronics is.

For a semiconductor manufacturer—or any company—to achieve such savings, it will need to embrace the key strategy for becoming cool perfected by Lee and Perkins: *Measure energy use accurately and often.*

Chapter

6

COOL POWER

So far, we have been looking only at how to reduce greenhouse gas emissions through the more efficient use of energy. You can also lower your emissions by choosing energy sources that generate reduced levels of greenhouse gases. I call these low-carbon energy sources "cool power."

Two types of cool power yield the biggest carbon dioxide savings. First is the simultaneous generation of heat and electricity—called cogeneration or combined heat and power, which can cut carbon dioxide emissions by one-third to two-thirds. Second is renewable energy—solar energy, wind power, biomass (energy from plants), and geothermal (energy from the Earth's heat), which can eliminate carbon dioxide emissions entirely. Opportunities for cost-effective cool power, rare just a few years ago, are booming, sparked by recent advances in technology as well as the accelerating trend toward deregulation of the electric utility sector. For the first time in decades, your company may have considerable choice in how you get your electricity. When you choose wisely, you can lower both costs and emissions at the same time. Here are a few of the many who have already made that smart choice:

- A 90 percent efficient cogeneration system at the Chicago Convention Center saves *$1 million a year* in energy costs and *cuts carbon dioxide emissions in half.*
- Coors Brewing Company has a 60 percent efficient cogeneration system at its Golden, Colorado, plant, which is the largest single brewing site in the world. The system, run by Trigen, *saves 250,000 tons of carbon dioxide annually.*
- Superior Fibers in Brooklyn installed a cogeneration system that will *cut its*

energy costs by more than half and its carbon dioxide emissions by one-third, all with a two-year payback.

- The First National Bank of Omaha is installing a system of four fuel cells because the bank believes it gives them the most reliable electrical power available at the lowest life-cycle cost. The new system also cuts back the bank's carbon dioxide emissions by more than one-third compared to a traditional uninterruptible power supply system.

- Anheuser-Busch's wastewater treatment system *cuts electricity use and green-house gas emissions by 80 percent* compared with a conventional system. At the same time, it *produces a renewable source of energy that supplies up to 15 percent of a brewery's fuel needs.*

- The new forty-eight-story, 1.6-million-square-foot office tower at Four Times Square in Manhattan has *reduced emissions of greenhouse gases by 40 percent.* The design combined energy efficiency with a variety of cool power measures, including fuel cells for cogeneration and rooftop photo-voltaics for clean electricity from the sun.

What really makes cool power—renewable energy and cogeneration—worth a new look is a number of recent advances in technology. On the renewable side, the cost of both solar energy and wind power have dropped dramatically in the past two decades. More and more utilities are offering electricity from these *zero-carbon* energy sources. And advances in on-site renewable technologies—especially geothermal heat pumps and photo-voltaics integrated directly into your building—give you even more options for lowering emissions.

On the cogeneration side, you can now buy a variety of technologies that are more than 80 percent efficient in converting clean, natural gas to heat and electricity at low cost. These include advanced gas turbines for industrial uses and microturbines for commercial use.

Your cost-benefit analysis of cogeneration will be affected by utility and environmental regulations (which vary by state) as well as the timing of the turnover of your energy equipment (such as your boilers).

The primary lessons from this chapter are:

(1) Every company should have a cool power strategy to maximize emissions reductions and payback. The strategy will allow you to take the best advantage over the next few years of new technology, changing regulations, and the natural turnover of your company's energy equipment.

(2) Combining cool power with energy efficiency achieves deep reductions in carbon dioxide emissions.

Let's start with two cases—one a factory, the other a building—that each demonstrate the challenge and the opportunity of cogeneration.

MALDEN MILLS

One of the coolest factories in the country is Malden Mills in Lawrence, Massachusetts, which produces textiles, including the popular Polartec and Polarfleece fabrics.[1] The privately owned company received national attention in December 1995 when a fire devastated its main factory buildings. The CEO, Aaron Feuerstein, pledged to keep paying all 3,000 of his employees while he rebuilt the textile factory rather than relocating. Local and national political leaders offered help. The company has since exceeded its pre-fire levels of production and employment, with $300 million in sales in 1997.

At the time, I was helping to run the Department of Energy's Office of Energy Efficiency and Renewable Energy. So I asked our Office of Industrial Technologies (OIT), which develops cogeneration and energy-efficient technologies, to provide assistance. As it turns out, the company had been thinking since 1987 about how to generate its own electricity, steam, and heat. By 1992, years before the fire, Malden Mills had created a plan for a 12-megawatt (MW) combined heat and power system based on a natural-gas-fired combustion turbine.

The process of meeting the state's new air pollution standards, however, took endless time and threatened to make the project uneconomical. Although the system would have avoided the use of both boilers and grid electricity and *cut emissions in half,* the state's new standards for the emission of NOx (oxides of nitrogen) required an expensive ammonia-based, exhaust-gas, after-treatment technology. While the project was stalled, the company's pressing need led it to buy four boilers, and it also started to purchase electricity from the local utility, Massachusetts Electric Company.

At the same time, however, OIT had been developing a new ultra-low-NOx cogeneration system with Solar Turbines, a California company. After the fire, OIT advised Malden Mills that the new cogeneration system would meet the state's new environmental requirements, and it helped the company negotiate an agreement with Massachusetts. In 1997, the state's Department of Environmental Protection issued a permit allowing Malden Mills to demonstrate the new technology and install three 4-MW gas turbines. Since some of the technology was still in development, that combined heat and power system would have to be installed in three phases.

First, in late 1998, Malden Mills installed two 4.3-MW low-NOx commercial turbines made by Solar Turbines. After the first year, the turbines will be retrofitted with an advanced liner that reduces NOx by another 40 percent. The system will be monitored for two years to determine if it meets the state's emissions requirements and if the liner is durable. During this time, the first commercial Advanced Turbine System, a 4.2- to 4.8-MW engine, will become available and could be installed as part of the third phase.

Compared with the pre-1995 system, this super-efficient, three-turbine system is projected to *almost completely eliminate SO₂ emissions, cut NOx emissions by three-quarters, and cut carbon dioxide emissions 25 percent.* Yet cogeneration is only part of the story.

With a rebate from Massachusetts Electric, the new 500,000-square-foot textile manufacturing plant will also be using more energy-efficient manufacturing processes, lighting systems, and air handling systems than the mills it replaced. Massachusetts Electric estimates these improvements will *save more than 4 million kilowatt-hours (kWh) a year.* "We are proud to take these energy-saving steps in what we consider the most advanced textile manufacturing facility of its kind in the world," Feuerstein has said. "These efforts are in line with our corporate philosophy of sustainable growth in the inner city."

The plant has many other energy-saving features. For instance, the jets that dye the fabric heat up to temperatures as high as 160°F. The plant recovers the heat from the wastewater and uses it to preheat the fluid going into the dyeing system.

The daylighting at the new factory is quite wonderful, as I saw at a spring 1998 visit to Malden Mills for the groundbreaking on the cogeneration unit. Louise Feuerstein, Aaron's wife, who helped oversee the rebuilding, insisted on daylighting. "Factory buildings built today are very miserable looking. No windows. Metal siding. Whatever is cheapest." Mrs. Feuerstein runs Glenn Street Studio, a division of Malden Mills that designs and manufactures upholstery fabric.

The new factory has a space-age curtainwall made by Kalwall Corporation of Manchester, New Hampshire. The Kalwall system is a unique translucent material that is both an insulating wall and a source of diffuse light. Whether under bright sunlight or cloudy skies, the Kalwall system bathes the factory in a warm, evenly balanced glow. At the same time, the system insulates up to four times more efficiently than double-glazed windows. Kalwall curtainwall is composed of a sandwich made by permanently bonding fiberglass-reinforced translucent faces to a core of interlocked, extruded structural aluminum or composite I-beams. The panels are then filled with various densities of translucent spun glass insulation.

With the Kalwall system, the factory building looks modern, even as the material blends in with the brick that comprises much of the exterior, including the one part of the original structure that was saved from the fire, a multi-story stair tower in the southwest corner of the building at the main entrance. The visual effect inside the building is stunning. As Louise Feuerstein says, "The daylight creates an uplifting, positive atmosphere for everyone."

When the cogeneration systems are fully up and running, they, combined with the energy-efficiency measures, will make Malden Mills one of the coolest textile plants in the world. The company has had equally astonishing success at other facilities. For instance, by combining more efficient lighting with occupancy sensors at its warehouse, *the company cut lighting energy consumption 96 percent.* A $350,000 energy bill is now under $35,000, an annual savings of more than $300,000 with a one-year payback. Overall, Malden Mills has reduced annual carbon dioxide emissions by 30,000 tons.

And this is only part of Malden's environmental achievement. Malden's Glenn Street Studio division has developed "EcoSpun Velvet," a luxurious upholstery fabric that is made completely out of 100 percent recycled PET (polyethylene terephthalate) from post-consumer soda bottles. This diminishes landfill burdens and reduces the embodied energy of upholstery compared with the processing of raw materials into fabric (for a discussion of embodied energy, see Chapter 9).

When I asked him how he came to do so many uncommon things all at once, Mr. Feuerstein said, "First, we wanted to do the right thing. Then we used our heads to do what was needed to make money. And then we used our heads to do what was environmentally correct." Fundamentally, the company is focused on "doing something long term for the profitability of Malden Mills." Being privately owned, they "don't look at what will increase share price next month."

This exact same perspective has focused Malden Mills on reducing energy use, air pollution, and greenhouse gas emissions, even as they were fighting to save the company. As noted in the Introduction, CEO Feuerstein's philosophy is what distinguishes Malden Mills: *"Over the long term, it is more profitable to do the right thing for the environment than to pollute it."*

LEARNING HOW TO CUT CARBON DIOXIDE IN WAVERLY

One of the coolest buildings in the country is the Waverly Junior-Senior High School in New York, 40 miles west of Binghamton. About 900 students and 100 support staff occupy the 200,000-square-foot all-electric building. This school building can teach us a lot about how to combine cogeneration and efficiency to cut carbon dioxide emissions in buildings.[2]

Built in 1967, the school had used conservation measures to cut its electricity use from its original design projection of 4 million kWh to 2.5 million kWh when prices skyrocketed during the energy shocks of the 1970s. Still, by the mid-1980s, the two-story building had power costs approaching $200,000 per year and they wanted to achieve further reductions.

In 1986, the school superintendent looked into self-generation and commissioned a study that confirmed a payback of less than three years for a 375-kW cogeneration system that would also supply most of the school's winter thermal needs. The school board, however, was hesitant to invest, even though manufacturers had sold hundreds of the units that had operated reliably since they were introduced in the early 1980s. Representatives of the local utility came to school board meetings and opposed the proposal. Convincing the board and the county's taxpayers to make the investment required an external technical assessment, several internal studies, traveling to other cogeneration sites, additional administration studies and a $365,000 Energy Conservation grant from the New York State Energy Office.

The school finally installed five 75-kW Tecogen cogeneration units in 1990, and the project was almost an instant success. It paid itself off in twenty-seven months and won the 1993 Governor's Award for Energy Excellence, given each year by the New York State Energy Office and the New York Power Authority for energy efficiency, innovation, and education. Energy cost savings and energy use reduction have exceeded the projections of the initial technical study. In 1998, after eight years of operation, the school had *saved more than $800,000—a 60 percent reduction in energy use and green-house gases.*

The energy savings are partly due to the fact that the Tecogen on-site pack-aged cogeneration units generate electricity at 35 percent efficiency compared to 30 percent for the electricity delivered from the grid. But the savings are mainly due to the fact that "free" waste heat from electricity generation replaces the expensive and inefficient use of electricity for hot water and space heating. Instead of electric heaters, the school is now heated by hot water piped from the cogeneration system to hydronic heaters in each room. In addition, the waste heat is also used to heat the school's swimming pool. Finally, during the cooling season, the system makes use of an absorption chiller that runs on hot water (discussed below). Because hot water, heating, and cooling are now provided from the unit's thermal output, electricity self-generated by the cogeneration unit is needed only for lighting, motors, computer, and other office equipment. The amount of electricity now purchased by the school has dropped sharply.

In addition to saving energy, the system provides many other benefits. It is simple to maintain and requires no additional people to operate it. The 1,000 students and staff in the Junior-Senior High School each day are also more comfortable because the temperature is more consistent and the system provides more cooling, air exchange, and hot water.

Finally, the design includes a large control room with viewing windows overlooking the cogeneration power operation to allow the area to be used as a teaching facility. More than 500 representatives of schools, institutions, commercial buildings, and other energy users have visited the site to learn about cogeneration.

Cogeneration reduced primary energy use and net emissions at Waverly by 60 percent. When that is coupled with the energy conservation measures applied in the 1970s and 1980s, *the overall energy and carbon dioxide reductions achieved at Waverly come to a remarkable 75 percent.* Many buildings, and certainly the majority of the millions and millions of all-electric buildings in this country, could achieve comparable results from combining cool power with efficiency.

❖

The examples of Malden Mills and Waverly demonstrate that, although cogenerating can require persistence, it can produce significant rewards. Let's look at cogeneration more closely.

COMBINED HEAT AND POWER

Cogeneration provides great opportunities to save energy and carbon dioxide. Right now, fossil fuels burned at large central station power plants generate most of the electricity used by U.S. companies. These plants are, on average, relatively inefficient, converting *only about one-third* of the energy in fossil fuels into electricity. The waste heat generated by that combustion is thrown away, and then more energy is lost transmitting the electricity from the power plant to the factory or building. As noted in the Introduction, the total energy "wasted" by U.S. electric power generators equals all of the energy that Japan uses for all purposes: buildings, industry, and transportation. To provide heat, hot water, and steam, more fossil fuels are then burned in our buildings and factories. The average building boiler converts only two-thirds of the fossil fuels to useful heat or steam.

By generating electricity and capturing the waste heat in a cogeneration system, much energy and pollution can be saved. *Overall system efficiencies can exceed 80 percent.* Also, when the cogeneration system uses natural gas (replacing electricity or steam generated from coal or oil), further environmental benefits result. Natural gas generates fewer greenhouse gases and other pollutants per unit of energy produced than either coal or oil. From the point of view of greenhouse gas emissions, then, cogeneration has two benefits: The system is more efficient and it uses a cleaner fuel.

Cogeneration is not, however, simple, as we have already seen with the Malden Mills and Waverly cases. A key issue is whether or not a company has use for the cogenerated heat. Opportunities tend to be larger for manufacturers than for most commercial buildings, though technologies such as steam-driven chillers are changing even that equation. Cost-effectiveness will improve when the purchase of a cogeneration unit is timed to coincide with a major overhaul or replacement of your chiller or boiler. Also, the array of state-based utility regulations—and utility deregulation efforts—complicates any calculation of cost-effectiveness. While some states have laws to encourage or at least not to discourage cogeneration, others have introduced penalties on companies that unhook from the electricity grid and self-generate. Typically, however, these short-sighted laws sunset after a few years.

The environmental benefits of cogeneration vary by region of the country. Cogeneration saves the most carbon dioxide in regions where electricity mainly comes from coal. It could hypothetically increase emissions if your utility generates most of its electricity from zero-carbon sources such as hydroelectric or nuclear power. Nonetheless, in most parts of the country, *a cogeneration system can save significant carbon dioxide,* and, when the system is well designed and its installation well timed, *it can save significant money.* In some cases, when the local utility learns a company is considering cogeneration, it offers a lower electric rate in return for an agreement not to cogenerate for a specified period of time. This can be a seductive offer because it saves the company the expense of making a major capital investment and the effort to figure out how to integrate the heat and power into their processes. Cool companies, however, will take a longer-term perspective to make sure they choose the approach that minimizes costs *and* emissions.

Finally, technologies just coming on the market now will significantly expand options for both commercial and industrial users. So, while some cool companies may decide not to cogenerate immediately, *every company that wants to become cool will need to develop a cogeneration strategy.*

A SHORT HISTORY OF AN OLD IDEA

The combined generation of heat and power is a very old idea. It can be traced to the smokejack, which powered a turbine with the hot air that rose through a chimney. The smokejack was introduced into Europe in the 1300s and was used widely to turn spits. Da Vinci sketched one in the fifteenth century, and Benjamin Franklin wrote about them in 1758. As James Watt's steam engine increased the popularity of that form of power, one of his salesmen advised him in 1776:

> Some attempt has been made to apply the Fire Engine to the purpose of turning mills for squeezing the Sugar Cane in the West Indies, & that it is supposed that the same fire which is used to boil the sugar, will be sufficient to produce steam to work the mill. If this should be practicable, it would be a matter of infinite consequence to the Islands & to the Public & would occasion a very great demand for your Invention.[3]

Watt soon expanded his business to providing power and hot water heating in his customers' factories.

Thomas Edison's first commercial electric generating plant in Manhattan in 1881 produced both heat and power.[4] By the turn of the century, cogeneration was increasingly common. Many cities had district heating plants that piped hot water to dozens of buildings. And most buildings that used steam engines to power pumps, elevators, and other machinery also used the exhaust steam for heating. Henry Ford described a typical cogeneration application in his factory:

> Steam is required for heating the wood-drying kilns at five pounds per square inch pressure. Steam at 225 pounds pressure suitable for operating turbines can be produced at only 10 percent greater cost than that for the heating pressure. Thus, by developing steam in the power-house boilers at 225 pounds per square inch, passing it through turbines and "bleeding" low pressure heating steam from the turbines after a part of its available energy has been obtained, the steam is practically serving a double duty—supplying both power and heat.[5]

By World War I, more than 400 U.S. companies were selling heat and power from cogeneration plants, not counting industrial and other self-cogenerators.

Nonetheless, the rise of the large central station power plant led to a decline in cogeneration by electric utilities after World War I. For much of the twentieth century, economies of scale and government regulations made it difficult for most companies to compete with the electricity offered by utilities, and so cogeneration did not flourish in this country as it did in Europe. An excellent discussion of all the myriad ways that regulations have undermined cogeneration can be found in the 1998 book, *Turning Off the Heat*, by Thomas R. Casten, the CEO of Trigen.[6]

One of the purposes of the Public Utility Regulatory Policy Act of 1978 (PURPA) was to promote cogeneration. The 1980s did see the expanded use of cogeneration by certain large industrial users, such as chemical plants and paper mills, as well as institutions that had a need for huge quantities of hot water, such as hospitals and universities.

Only recently, however, has the right combination of new technology and new regulations (or deregulation) opened the door for most companies to benefit from combined heat and power. Let's look at some other case studies of existing and emerging systems.

Trigen Energy Corporation

Trigen Energy Corporation of White Plains, New York, operates a number of high-efficiency combined heat and power systems around the country. I have visited their plants in Tulsa, Oklahoma, and Philadelphia, Pennsylvania. In Tulsa, they provide district heating and cooling for thirty-one buildings, including government offices, hotels, and residential and office buildings. The system can achieve conversion efficiencies of 89 percent, saving $660,000 a year in fuel costs and more than 16,000 tons of carbon dioxide.

In 1993, Trigen formed a partnership with the local Philadelphia utility, PECO Energy, after purchasing a large steam district heating system that served 375 users at the Gray's Ferry site in downtown Philadelphia. The city had been producing steam for its heating system from old oil-fired boilers. In the new system, a large gas turbine generates 118 MW of electricity, and its exhaust gas is used by a heat recovery system to generate high-pressure steam, which then is run through a condensing steam turbine to generate another 54 MW of electricity as well as low-pressure steam for use in the district heating system. PECO will purchase up to 150 MW of the plant's electricity. The entire system has a fuel conversion efficiency exceeding 70 percent. Replacing an old oil-fired system with a new gas-fired system that was more efficient had significant environmental advantages. *Carbon dioxide emissions were reduced by more than 50 percent,* saving more than 1 million tons per year, and NOx emissions were cut 90 percent, helping to reduce smog and other pollution problems in the Philadelphia area.

Large cogeneration projects of this kind do face some problems in this era of deregulation. Recent changes in the regional power markets, for instance, have reduced the short-run cost of purchased power. In March 1998, PECO announced that it wants to negotiate a lower price for the electricity it purchases from the Gray's Ferry plant.

Chicago Convention Center

In 1992, Chicago's 2.8-million-square-foot McCormick Place Exhibition and Convention Center was planning to nearly double its size with a 2.2-million-square-foot expansion.[7] Because that would have required a $27 million capital investment in new heating and cooling facilities, the Center decided to outsource the operations of the existing energy facility and any future energy needs. Trigen Energy Corporation formed a partnership with the local gas utility to provide heating and cooling to the Convention Center through a twenty-nine-year contract.

They installed a trigeneration system that simultaneously provides heating, cooling, and electricity. This system combines a gas turbine, a motor/generator, a heat recovery steam generator, and chillers that run on steam and natural gas. It can produce any combination of electricity, steam, or chilled water. *It is able to achieve an overall fuel conversion efficiency of 91 percent.* Trigen also installed the largest chilled water storage tank in North America (8.5 million gallons) to store cold water produced at night to meet peak daytime cooling loads.

The economic savings of the project were considerable. By outsourcing the energy plant, the center avoided a $27 million up-front capital outlay. Also, because the system is so efficient, energy and other operating cost savings of $1 million in a year are projected over the life of the project.

Finally, the system produces about half the carbon dioxide emissions that would be generated if the electricity, steam, and chilled water all had to be produced separately. It saves 24,000 tons of carbon dioxide and 59 tons of NOx a year.

Trigen and Coors Brewery

In 1873, Coors Brewing Company began producing beer in the foothills of the Rocky Mountains in Golden, Colorado, 20 miles west of Denver.[8] Soon thereafter, they were taking advantage of combining on-site energy and cooling processes to maintain the quality of their products. Since 1967, Coors has operated a coal-fired cogeneration plant for on-site electricity and steam at the largest single brewing site in the world.

In 1995, Coors decided to outsource their energy assets. This type of outsourcing is increasingly common, as it allows a company like Coors to focus on their core business of brewing and marketing beer, while allowing a company with energy expertise to maximize the performance of the energy system.

Trigen was selected from a bidding process with over forty competitors. In the system Trigen runs, three coal-fired boilers and two gas-fired boilers produce super-heated steam that is directly piped to three turbine generators that produce a total of 40 MW of power. The turbines also exhaust medium-pressure steam and low-pressure steam. The medium-pressure steam mainly drives refrigeration equipment and also is exhausted into the low-pressure steam system. Low-pressure steam is condensed in Coors' processes such as brewing, malting, and container manufacturing; it is also used for domestic heating at the Colorado School of Mines.

This sequential use of steam (or any resource) is called *cascading*. Here, it doubles the energy efficiency of typical utility power plants by avoiding waste-heat losses. Trigen has upgraded the control systems to further increase efficiencies. The overall energy conversion efficiency of the system exceeds 60 percent. It saves 260,000 tons of carbon dioxide annually as well as 125 tons of NOx and 900 tons of SO_2.

Trigen's original plan for Coors' energy system called for adding a s team turbine, a gas turbine, and a heat recovery system, which would have doubled electricity production while reducing emissions by an additional 10 percent. Overall system efficiency would have approached 90 percent. That would have provided Coors with virtually all of their electricity and allowed them to disconnect from the electric utility grid. As is all too common, however, the local utility offered Coors a better short-term deal and they have turned Trigen down. Though this is no environmental benefit, the reduced utility rate does represent another economic benefit provided to Coors from the cogeneration system. And once the electric utility system in Colorado is fully deregulated, Trigen will be able to upgrade the system and sell its low-carbon, low-cost electricity on the open market.

Brewing is an energy-intensive process, and Trigen facilities around the country provide steam to a number of micro-breweries, such as River Market Brewing Company in Kansas City, and Commonwealth Brewery and Brew Moon Restaurant & Brewery in Boston.

Superior Fibers

Superior Fibers, Inc., of Brooklyn, New York, produces more than 1 million pounds of polyester fiberfill insulation a year for garments, comforters, and bedspreads.[9] The plant takes virgin polyester fibers, combs them, layers them with adhesive, and then dries and cures them in an oven. Then the product is trimmed to desired dimensions. The 24,000-square-foot plant employs sixteen to twenty people and has annual sales of $2 million.

Energy for the motors and curing oven had been a very large expense. Natural gas cost $45,000 and electricity cost $60,000. The energy bill is thus about 5 percent of total sales.

The Department of Energy has an Industrial Assessment Center (IAC) program that performs assessments for small and medium-sized businesses seeking to reduce their energy costs. In the summer of 1996, a team of students and faculty from Hofstra University performed an IAC Assessment for Superior Fibers.

The principal recommendation made by the IAC team was that the company should install a small cogeneration unit. The unit, a 250-kW natural gas engine generator set, would provide most of the electricity for manufacturing, but the lights and computers would still get electricity provided by Con Edison. The unit would cost $140,000 to install, but the total annual cost savings came to $74,000—a two-year payback. Not only were there savings from dramatically lowering the electricity bill, but the gas utility offered a very favorable rate. Also, the local government offered a rebate for such capital improvement projects.

Superior Fibers also made clear that a key part of the attraction of the system was the heat recovery. During the winter, the hot air from the cogeneration unit's radiator will be exhausted into the plant, which will save energy by reducing heating requirements. In the summer, the company will reverse the process—i.e., intake air for the cogeneration unit from inside the plant will be exhausted outside, thus cooling the building. Finally, the company can recover the high-temperature (1,200°F) exhaust gas from the cogeneration unit's engine and use it to preheat the air going into the oven (which maintains 325°F).

Preliminary estimates indicate that the system when fully implemented will reduce greenhouse gas emissions by about one-third. The overall efficiency of the engine in providing electricity and heat will approach 70 percent.

When I visited the plant with a member of the IAC team in April 1998, the company had only installed part of the heat recovery system. It turned out that the contractor suggested by the local utility company was not competent to do all of the ductwork or to install the necessary heat exchanger. As a result, the contractor started a job it couldn't finish, costing Superior Fibers both time and money.

A key lesson for any small business considering cogeneration is to get everything clearly laid out on paper before agreeing to allow a contractor to start work on such a system.

Using the electricity from a cogeneration unit is straightforward and might even be described as turnkey. Taking advantage of all of the opportunities for heat recovery, however, is much more complicated, particularly for a manufacturer, as it depends on the types of activities taking place in the factory where the unit is installed as well as the unique geometry of the factory building.

In talking to the company, however, it also became clear that the unit could provide economic and other benefits that had not been factored into the cost-benefit analysis. The local electric utility, Con Edison, has had a number of brownouts that have cost the company as much as two days worth of business. Also, poor power quality from the utility had been repeatedly interrupting production. Each time, the production run had to be restarted, which cost time, and all of the partially created material had to be either recycled or thrown away. The ability to supply reliable, high-quality power is yet another benefit of on-site cogeneration.

ADVANCED TURBINE SYSTEM

A number of emerging technologies are likely to transform the market for combined heat and power.[10] In the Malden Mills case, we have already seen one, the Advanced Turbine System, which can be ordered today. It has an overall efficiency exceeding 80 percent with considerable flexibility over how much electricity and how much steam is produced. It will have a relatively low installed cost ($500 to 1,000 per kW), low maintenance, and low emissions of oxides of nitrogen (NOx). For those who can use the steam, it can potentially deliver electricity at *under 3 cents/kWh*. It will reduce carbon dioxide emissions by as much as two-thirds compared to traditional separate generation of off-site electricity and on-site steam. Its primary application will be industrial, though it could be used by some very large commercial users or district heating and cooling systems, such as the ones that Trigen runs in a few major cities.

In December 1997, Solar Turbines (which is owned by Caterpillar) unveiled the first Advanced Turbine System, its 4.2- to 4.8-MW "Mercury 50" gas turbine.[11] It has already begun installing these turbines. The first one will be operated by Rochelle Municipal Utilities about 75 miles west of Chicago. Other early orders, which were announced in December 1998, have gone to Clemson University in South Carolina, New Energy Ventures in California, and Solar Turbines' own Harbor Drive manufacturing plant in San Diego. Its relatively small size makes the Mercury 50 ideal for a number of small to medium-sized industrial applications, such as Malden Mills.

TWO OTHER EMERGING TECHNOLOGIES

So far I have focused on cogeneration by industrial users or from centralized district heating and cooling systems. That's because technology and economics have made those the biggest cogeneration users. Only a few kinds of large commercial users, such as hotels and hospitals, or universities, have a use for the cogenerated heat sufficient to justify the kind of systems that have typically been available for buildings.

Two other types of emerging technologies deserve special attention because they are likely to significantly expand the cogeneration market into the general commercial (and residential) building sector in the coming years: microturbines and fuel cells.

Microturbines
Until recently, natural gas turbines derived from jet engines—the kind used by Trigen in Chicago and Philadelphia—have not been cost-effective much below 1,000 kW, the size needed for a small to medium-sized manufacturing plant or a medium-sized to large building. Companies that wanted less on-site power or cogeneration had to resort to reciprocating engines derived from diesel engines (usually running on natural gas). These tend to be quite efficient systems but relatively complicated, noisy, high maintenance, and dirty in terms of air pollution. Such systems dominate emergency power and power backup systems. Cummins and Caterpillar now make systems down to 25 kW, suitable for a fast-food restaurant or small office building. While new and better reciprocating engines are likely to be introduced into the marketplace, the new fast-growing entrant to on-site power is likely to be the microturbine.

A number of manufacturers are introducing small, natural gas turbines in the 50-kW to 250-kW range, including AlliedSignal, Allison Engine, Capstone, Elliott Energy Systems, and Northern Research and Engineering Corporation. AlliedSignal, for instance, has already sold several thousand units of its "TurboGenerator," a 75-kW gas turbine. The turbines will be far less polluting and quieter than comparably sized reciprocating engines. They will also be more fuel flexible (accommodating natural gas, diesel, gasoline, and methane) and potentially require no maintenance. The system has only one moving part, minimizing mechanical losses and maximizing efficiency by mounting the turbine, compressor, and permanent magnet generator on a single shaft. An inverter reduces the generator frequency from 1,200 Hz to 50 or 60 Hz. It also features "air-bearings" that need no oil, water, or other maintenance.

For generating electricity alone, however, these turbines are currently less than 25 percent efficient, which means that they will not save carbon dioxide in most regions of the country. They are expected to reach electric-only efficiencies of 30 percent or higher in a few years. More important, many of these microturbine units, including AlliedSignal's, will be able to cogenerate and achieve overall efficiencies exceeding 70 percent.

The key, then, will be applications that take advantage of the waste heat, such as hotels, hospitals, restaurants, and health clubs with swimming pools. Of course, all buildings have a need for heat and, usually to a lesser extent, hot water. The problem is that it is rarely enough to justify adding the heat recovery system needed to cogenerate. In part, that is because the need for heat is seasonal in most parts of the country, with a great deal of hot water needed in the winter months and very little needed in the summer months.

If your company wants to cogenerate but lacks a sufficient thermal load, two approaches should be considered. First, buy a small cogeneration unit sized for the thermal load and purchase the remaining electricity from the grid. This will provide some carbon dioxide reductions, give you a good uninterruptible power supply, reduce demand charges if you have them, and probably be quite cost-effective—a two- or three-year payback in many locations. It will also give you early experience with cogeneration so that as the systems improve (and as state exit fees for leaving the grid completely disappear), you can quickly expand your use of cogeneration.

Second, as noted, the key problem for most commercial buildings that want to cogenerate is insufficient need for the waste heat, especially in the summer. The solution is *a technology that can run your air conditioning system on hot water, an absorption chiller.* Instead of using an electric motor to compress the refrigerant, as conventional electric chillers do, absorption coolers use what is essentially a thermochemical compressor running on hot water. The key point is that an absorption chiller simultaneously reduces peak electric use and increases demand for hot water in the summertime.

Therefore, you should seriously consider an absorption chiller coupled with a cogeneration unit when you replace your chiller for whatever reason—because it is reaching the end of its life, because you need a non-CFC chiller, or because you are doing a whole-building retrofit (such as those described in Chapters 3 and 4).

 Combining energy efficiency, cogeneration, and an absorption chiller can reduce a building's greenhouse gas emissions by 75 percent or more, as in the Waverly case.

Fuel Cells
Fuel cells are one of the holy grails of energy technology.[12] Unlike the previous technologies discussed in this section, fuel cells do not rely on combus-

tion. Hence, they produce no combustion by-products, such as NOx, SO_2, or particulates—the air pollutants that cause smog and acid rain and that have been most clearly documented to harm human health. Fuel cells are small, modular, electrochemical devices that convert hydrogen and oxygen directly into electricity and water. Typically, for stationary applications, such as in buildings or power plants, the hydrogen is derived from natural gas, which means that the only significant emissions are water and carbon dioxide.

Because they can achieve efficiencies of 40 percent running on natural gas, fuel cells that merely provide on-site electricity in a building can achieve significant carbon dioxide savings in most parts of the country. The fuel cell process, however, also releases heat that can be used for cogeneration, which can significantly improve the carbon dioxide savings by reducing some of the need for on-site heating from fossil fuel sources. In a cogeneration application, the overall efficiency of the natural gas fuel cell *can exceed 80 percent.*

The National Aeronautics and Space Administration developed early versions of fuel cells for space missions, and they are used today on the space shuttle. However, until recently, the only fuel cell commercially available in the United States was a 200-kW phosphoric acid fuel cell, the PC25, from International Fuel Cells, a subsidiary of United Technologies, the company that makes fuel cells for the space shuttle. More than one hundred of these fuel cells have been sold.

The PC25 fuel cell has a relatively high price—$3,000 per kilowatt—although it has benefited from a government subsidy that lowers that price by about $1,000 per kilowatt. One important growing use for the PC25 is as part of an uninterruptible, high-quality power supply for companies that would suffer significant business loss from a power outage or disruption.

Consider the case of the new 200,000-square-foot technology center of the First National Bank of Omaha, which processes credit card orders from around the country 24 hours a day, 365 days a year. It has been estimated "that a single major retail client can lose as much as $6 million an hour if the center's power fails and orders are not processed," according to Thomas Ditoro, the project's electrical engineer, writing in the fall of 1998. That is why the First National Bank installed the most reliable electrical power source they could find, a fuel cell system developed by Sure Power Corporation of Danbury, Connecticut.

"To protect existing clients and attract new ones," the bank needed to maximize the availability of the computer system. Ditoro writes, "The average uninterruptible power supply system (UPS)/generator/utility systems has an availability of about 3-nines [99.9 percent]. The most redundant UPS can achieve an availability of 4-nines. The fuel cell system at First National Bank of Omaha has a calculated availability of 6- to 7-nines."

The difference is striking. With only 4-nines of availability, downtime would be about an hour a year, while 6-nines translates to only 32 seconds. Thus, the difference between the best UPS system and the Sure Power fuel-cell system is an hour of availability a year, which could mean millions and millions of dollars of lost business as well as higher insurance rates. Equally important, even a disruption of a few seconds could shut a computer system down and take hours to recover. And a 4-nine system might allow far more of these costly interruptions.

While the initial cost of the fuel-cell system is higher than that of the UPS system, "the life-cycle costs, however, prove the fuel cell to be less expensive than UPSs," which, Ditoro notes, is "remarkable since electricity costs in Omaha are some of the lowest in the nation."

The system Sure Power designed for the bank uses four PC25 fuel cells (combined with fly wheels and other components to eliminate the possibility of disruptions) to provide 320 kW of critical power. Since each fuel cell provides 200 kW, the system has redundancy built in, which is part of the reason it achieves such high availability. This also means the system generates significant excess electricity—as well as free cogenerated heat—all of which it provides to the bank, and that is what gives it a lower life-cycle cost. Moreover, the fuel cell requires no conditioned space, while the traditional UPS system would have required $28,000 in annual cooling costs: more wasted energy.

It is particularly satisfying to me that the system with the lowest life-cycle cost for the bank and the best availability performance also has the best environmental performance: more than one-third lower emissions of carbon dioxide and under one one-thousandth the emissions of other air pollutants. In every way it is a cool system.

A number of manufacturers will soon introduce the proton exchange membrane (PEM) fuel cell in sizes ranging from a few kilowatts to 250 kW. The PEM fuel cell may well be one of those energy technologies that revolutionize the energy marketplace. Several of the world's largest automakers, including Ford, General Motors, DaimlerChrysler, and Toyota, are spending hundreds of millions of dollars pursuing PEM fuel cells for use in their vehicles. Most of these companies have said they will have a fuel-cell vehicle on the road by 2005. If a 50-kW PEM fuel cell can be made small enough and affordable enough, it could be used in a highly efficient, nearly pollution-free car. Because of all the money being spent on their development, PEM fuel cells are likely to come down steadily in price both as the technology improves and as manufacturing economies of scale are achieved.

One of the first companies to sell PEMs is Plug Power in Latham, New York, a sister company of Detroit Edison. The company demonstrated the first prototype fuel cell system for use in a home in June 1998. This 7-kW system will be sold, installed, and serviced by General Electric Fuel Systems by the year 2000.

Ballard Power Systems of Canada expects to start selling a 250-kW PEM fuel cell by 2002. The goal for this product is 40 percent electrical efficiency, cogenerated water hot enough to run an absorption chiller, an overall efficiency in excess of 80 percent, and a price of $1,500 per kilowatt. This would make it a very attractive technology for larger buildings. Ballard is also developing a smaller unit, under 10 kW, for sale by 2002.

Because PEM fuel cells have such low emissions, your company should consider using them early on in limited applications, so that when they become very cost-effective in broad applications, you will have the experience needed to take full advantage quickly.

The best early uses for fuel cells are when:

- Natural gas costs are low and electricity and demand costs are high;
- The thermal energy can be recovered and used;
- Compliance with stringent environmental air-quality regulations is limiting the options available to meet electric power requirements;
- Critical electric loads are currently being supplied by high-cost uninterruptible power supplies, motor-generator sets, or backup generators running on fossil fuels; and
- Computers, telecommunications equipment, electronic security, or other electronic control systems demand a noise-free, highly reliable, high-quality electric energy source.

PEM fuel cells are likely to be a crucial element of the transition to a very low carbon dioxide economy because they may ultimately be using hydrogen created from renewable sources, virtually eliminating the greenhouse gas emissions from the buildings and cars that run on them.

RENEWABLE ENERGY

The coolest power is derived from renewable sources—the sun, wind, plants (biomass), and the Earth's heat (geothermal). Renewable energy has no carbon dioxide emissions at all, and companies have two ways of utilizing it. First, increasingly, companies will have the choice to purchase some or all of their electricity from renewable sources as more and more utilities offer renewable electricity products to their customers. Toyota Motors in Southern California has chosen to purchase *all* of its electricity from 100 percent renewable sources (see the accompanying boxed text). Second, companies can use renewable energy technologies directly in their own buildings, especially solar and geothermal technologies, for the on-site production of electricity or for specific end uses, such as heating and cooling.

Tremendous advances in technology over the past two decades have significantly brought down the cost of most forms of renewable energy. Royal Dutch/Shell Group, the world's most profitable oil company and a benchmark for corporate strategic planning, believes renewable energy may provide

Toyota U.S.A. and Cool Power

Toyota Motors is a cool and lean company, as discussed in Chapter 2. In April 1998, Toyota announced that it will purchase 100 percent renewable electricity for virtually all of its Southern California operations, including its U.S headquarters in Torrance as well as facilities in Irvine and Ontario. Toyota estimates an annual usage of 38 million kWh, making them the largest single user worldwide of 100 percent renewable power.[13]

Yoshi Ishizaka, Toyota Motor Sales chief executive, stated, "Toyota has a responsibility to the environment that runs beyond designing, building and selling clean, efficient and high quality trucks and cars. We also must re-evaluate every part of our operations from recycling waste paper to purchasing renewable-resource electricity."

Toyota's cool power purchase was made possible by California's deregulation of its electric utility industry, which has begun to give businesses and consumers some choice in how they purchase their power. A number of companies have introduced retail and wholesale electricity products that are at least 50 percent renewable. Toyota chose electricity that is derived exclusively from renewable sources.

Toyota's switch to purely renewable electricity represents a 10 to 15 percent increase in price, according to Jeremy Barnes, a Toyota spokesperson. The company views the decision as part of their corporate environmental responsibility. "We think it is the right choice even though it costs a bit more," says Barnes. "The more people who use renewable energy, the more the price will go down." Barnes adds, "We stand behind the accord that came out of Kyoto."

That Toyota is willing to pay a bit more for energy to reduce emissions is the strongest signal of the seriousness with which it takes global warming. Toyota retains a competitive edge even with higher-cost power. Since the company is obsessed with eliminating every kind of waste, its employees are driven to use energy more efficiently—no doubt in part because industrial electricity rates in Japan are three times what they are in the United States. The company will easily be able to keep their total energy bill low and remain competitive.

half the world's power within a few decades, as discussed in Chapter 1. They have bought two photovoltaics companies, invested heavily in biomass power, and launched a major solar energy subsidiary to coordinate all of their renewable energy work.

WIND POWER

The fastest growing form of renewable power—indeed, the fastest growing of all forms of power in the 1990s—is wind. Like combined heat and power, wind energy has a long history. More than 2,000 years ago, simple windmills were used in China to pump water and were used in Persia and the Middle East to grind grain. Merchants and returning veterans of the Crusades introduced windmills to Europe in the eleventh century, where first the Dutch and then the English improved on the design. By the eighteenth century, there were more than 10,000 windmills in the Netherlands alone, where they were used to grind grain, pump water, and saw wood. Ultimately the mills were replaced by steam engines because they could not compete with the low cost, convenience, and reliability of fossil fuels. In America, windmills were widely used in the West by the end of the 1800s; applications included providing water for irrigation and electricity for isolated farmers.[14]

While wind has not been able to compete with large central station electric power plants for most of this century, it began to see a resurgence in the 1970s because of the energy crises. Those wind turbines, however, were crude derivatives from airplane propellers and were noisy and inefficient. Over the past 15 years, significant aerodynamic improvements in blade design have largely solved those problems and have brought down the cost of electricity from wind power by 10 percent per year. Wind energy can now be captured efficiently over a broad range of wind speeds and direction. Utilities have been receiving long-term bids for electricity from wind at 4 cents per kilowatt-hour in the best wind sites. The next generation wind turbine is projected to bring costs down to 3 cents per kilowatt-hour by 2002.

Such advances have helped give wind energy an annual growth rate averaging more than 25 percent. Wind power has been growing particularly rapidly in Europe, which has higher electricity prices than the United States. Even in America, the declining cost for wind is helping green power producers to deliver zero-carbon electricity at near-market rates. In Colorado, a number of companies, including Coors and IBM, have begun purchasing a small portion of their electricity from a new wind farm built by the local utility.

GEOTHERMAL ENERGY AND HEAT PUMPS

The Earth's heat was first used in prehistoric times for bathing. Hot spring water was popular in ancient Rome, where it was used not only for bathing but also to heat bathhouses. In 1923, the first geothermal wells at the Geysers, California, were drilled and a 250-kW generator was installed. Today, geothermal electricity provides only a tiny portion of the nation's total electric generation capacity.[15]

New technology, however, has brought a resurgence of the original direct

use of geothermal energy for heating—and, in addition today, cooling.[16] It goes by a variety of names, including geothermal heat pumps, ground-source heat pumps, and, most recently, GeoExchange systems. The names are used to distinguish the systems from conventional water-source or air-source heat pumps. For the purposes of this discussion, I will use the term *geothermal heat pumps.*

The first patent on the technology dates back to 1912 Switzerland, and systems such as the one at United Illuminating in New Haven, Connecticut, have been operating since the 1930s. But only recently has technology advanced to a stage where the market for geothermal heat pumps is rapidly expanding. In 1985, only some 14,000 were installed in the United States in residential and commercial applications. By 1990, about 100,000 units were operating. By the late 1990s annual sales of geothermal heat pumps had reached 50,000 units.

Geothermal heat pumps provide both heating and cooling. They typically run piping a few hundred feet below the Earth's surface (or occasionally connect to a nearby body of water). Here, the temperature stays relatively constant throughout the year. Since the ground is warmer than the outside air in the winter, the geothermal system has to expend less energy than conventional systems to heat up a building. Similarly, since the ground is colder than the outside air during the summer, the geothermal system has to expend less energy than conventional systems to cool down a building. Thus, geothermal heat pumps maintain high efficiency all of the time in virtually any climate. Indeed, when it is very hot outside or very cold outside, that is exactly when there is the largest temperature difference between the outside and underground, and so geothermal heat pumps are ideal in severe climates or in climates characterized by high daily temperature swings.

Compared to conventional systems, geothermal heat pumps typically have higher initial costs but lower maintenance and energy costs. They require less floor space than conventional heating and cooling systems because the exterior system is underground. They are very quiet and long lasting. Also, they can provide simultaneous heating and cooling. For example, in the summertime they can provide both air conditioning and hot water.

The EPA compared a variety of different heat pumps and found that advanced geothermal heat pumps can reduce energy consumption and, correspondingly, emissions of greenhouse gases and other pollutants by 23 to 44 percent compared to advanced air source heat pumps, and by 63 to 72 percent compared to more standard heating and cooling equipment. Geothermal heat pumps had superior environmental performance in virtually all locations except where the local electricity was very coal-intensive, in which case gas-fired heat pumps were superior. Of course, geothermal heat pumps are best suited for new construction or major retrofits where digging up the ground is viable.

A number of companies are starting to use geothermal heat pumps to cut costs and emissions. For instance, Phillips 66 installed a geothermal heat pump in its new Prairie Village, Kansas, gas station and convenience store.[17] By connecting the coolers, freezers, and ice maker of the convenience store into the system, Phillips cut the overall energy use of their heating, cooling, and freezing systems *40 percent with a two-year payback.* The company has made geothermal heat pumps the standard for new construction. Other large chains, Texaco and Conoco, also have stations with these systems.

McDonald's

In the suburbs of Detroit, McDonald's has integrated a geothermal heat pump with energy efficiency to achieve a restaurant with *40 to 50 percent less greenhouse gases* than a typical restaurant.[18] The 2,700-square-foot restaurant in Westland, Michigan, has a 1,500-square-foot kitchen/dining area and a 1,200-square-foot play area for children. Three heat pumps are connected to a ground-loop heat exchanger composed of thirty-two boreholes drilled 200 feet deep into the ground. With three units, the restaurant can simultaneously cool the kitchen and heat the dining room. The restaurant uses a large volume of outside air from early morning to late in the evening. The geothermal heat pump produces far lower greenhouse gas emissions than a conventional heating and cooling unit and has 20 percent lower energy costs.

Working with Detroit Edison, the local utility, McDonald's also integrated a number of advanced energy-efficiency technologies into the restaurant. The kitchen, dining room, and play area use efficient lighting, occupancy sensors, and photoelectric sensors to dim the lights when daylight is available. The windows are triple-glazed, the motors that run the cooking fans are energy-efficient, and the building shell has improved insulation.

The Largest Geothermal Heat Pump System in the World

The Galt House East Hotel in Louisville, Kentucky, was built in 1984.[19] Its geothermal heat pump has annual energy costs that are $300,000 below that of the adjacent Galt House Hotel, which has the same amount of space but a conventional HVAC system. The system saves 5.6 million kWh/year, and reduces peak electrical demand in August by 1,100 kW, a *50 percent reduction* over the original hotel constructed in 1970. Carbon dioxide savings total 3,000 tons a year. Chemical emissions from the cooling tower and boiler are eliminated by the system. Maintenance and personnel requirements for the system have been minimal since it does not require the scale or experience required of large HVAC systems.

Al Schneider, the owner of the Galt House East Hotel, decided to expand and extend the system to include the Waterfront Office Buildings, completed in 1994. The combined 4,700-ton system provides heating and cooling for more than 1.5 million square feet of hotel and office space, making it the largest geothermal heat pump system in the world. Compared to centrifugal

chillers and boilers for the hotel and office complex, the geothermal system actually had a *lower initial cost* of $2,250,000. By eliminating the need for maintenance rooms and a 4,000-ton cooling tower, the system provided *25,000 more square feet of rentable space* in the office building.

For the hotel, groundwater at 58°F is pumped into a 140,000-gallon reservoir under the mechanical room. It is circulated through heat exchangers that separate the groundwater from the closed-loop circulation system in the buildings. The geothermal heat pump system can provide any area heating or cooling at any time.

Because of the high occupancy and resulting high internal load, using geothermal heat pumps and thermal storage is very efficient. The energy stored in the reservoir during the day from air conditioning can be used to heat the building at night. The HVAC designer and construction manager for the project, Marion Pinckley, notes that it is "a very friendly system to the owner, occupants, and to maintenance personnel," with "lower initial cost, lower operating cost." Tom O'Hearn of the Galt House says that complaints about the HVAC system "have virtually been nonexistent, whereas before we had frequent comments about lack of adequate comfort."

BIOMASS ENERGY

Human beings have used plant matter for cooking and heating since the discovery of fire. In many rural parts of the developing world, fuelwood is still the main source of energy for cooking and heating. Many companies have low-cost biomass waste streams that they use to generate cool power.[20] Pulp and paper mills, for instance, use one of their by-products, black liquor, to cogenerate. An emerging technology, the gasification of biomass, allows the black liquor to be used together with high-efficiency natural-gas cogeneration technologies. This black-liquor gasification combined-cycle system will greatly increase the cool power available to pulp and paper mills.

One of the most remarkable systems for bio-energy recovery was developed by Anheuser-Busch to treat the wastewater from its brewing operations.[21] Bacteria consume organic compounds in a tank of water, releasing bio-gas (mostly methane) that bubbles to the top. The system simultaneously reduces solid waste and generates fuel. Moreover, this system has both a lower capital cost and lower operating expenses than building and running another conventional treatment facility.

This bio-energy recovery system uses 80 percent less electricity—and hence it generates 80 percent less greenhouse gases—than a conventional system. At the same time, it produces a renewable source of energy that supplies up to 15 percent of a brewery's fuel needs. In addition, solid waste is reduced 50 percent, which frees up capacity at municipal treatment plants and increases brewery capacity. By the year 2000, Anheuser-Busch plans to use the bio-energy recovery system in eight of its facilities, saving *more than $40 million annually and 20,000 tons of carbon dioxide.* No wonder that Anheuser-Busch Chairman and President August A. Busch III has said: "Environmental responsibility is good corporate citizenship; it's also good business."

SOLAR ENERGY

The best-known form of renewable energy is direct solar energy.[22] I have already discussed the most cost-effective type of solar energy in earlier chapters: daylighting. And, of course, the sun provides any building with passive heating. There is far more to the story. With intelligent design and new technology, your company can cost-effectively tap solar energy more actively.

Photovoltaic (PV) cells, which convert sunlight directly into electricity, have come down in price *by a factor of ten* since 1980. The promise of PV has been a long time coming. Bell Laboratories invented the first practical PV cell in 1954. Investments by NASA, the Pentagon, the National Science Foundation, and ultimately the Department of Energy helped to sustain the industry. Today, we have paper-thin PV cells that take advantage of the tremendous advances of the past two decades in semiconductor manufacturing and are the key to making PV affordable for widespread use.

By 1997 the Sacramento Municipal Utility District (SMUD) had installed more than 5 MW of distributed PV systems on its customers' buildings. SMUD has contracted to more than triple that PV capacity by 2002, by which time the PVs are projected to be providing electricity at under 10 cents a kilowatt-hour. Worldwide PV production, which was at 3 MW in 1980 and 24 MW in 1985, reached 120 MW in 1997 and continues to grow at over 15 percent a year.[23]

In places where there is no electricity grid, as in much of the developing world, PVs are cost-effective today as an alternative to building large central station power plants and stringing up hundreds of miles of power lines. That is why 70 percent of U.S. PV sales are overseas. Recent advances will allow your company to directly integrate low-cost PV cells into window glass or roofing shingles.

> Photovoltaics should be a part of any cool building design.

Photovoltaics reduce peak summer electricity loads and provide backup for uninterruptible power supplies. They have been incorporated into a number of the buildings already discussed in this book, as well as many others, such as the following:

- Interface, Inc., with Solarex and AC Battery, is installing a 109-kW solar array that will generate the electricity needed to manufacture tufted carpet at its Bentley Mills plant in City of Industry, California.

- The Austin Convention Center has a 20-kW PV system. It is roof-mounted on a motorized east–west tracking system to follow the sun throughout the day for maximum efficiency.

- One of the country's first large arrays of thin-film PV modules is a 17-kW system on top of a warehouse operated by the New York City Transit Authority, in Queens, New York.

- The Okotec office building in Berlin has 4.2 kW of customized PV panels that are partially reflective to match the building's architectural glass. This investment had a fast payback because the building received a great deal of attention, becoming the first new speculative office building in Berlin to be fully rented.

- A New York City Department of Sanitation building on Riker's Island makes use of 216 translucent building-integrated PV modules for its roof. Besides providing electricity, the modules have a 17 percent light transmittance that provides daylight for the facility.

- An Applebee's Restaurant in Charlotte, North Carolina, has a 1.7-kW photovoltaic array that replaces part of the roof. Integrated into it is a heat-recovery system that uses the array's waste heat to preheat water. The project had a payback of under two months with state tax credits.[24]

The Amtrak passenger station at Normal/Bloomington, Illinois, combines photovoltaics with energy efficiency.[25] A 2.4-kW rooftop array provides energy for part of the building's electricity requirements, including two vending machines and much of the lighting. The use of daylighting and efficient lighting technologies has reduced the energy needed for lighting by more than 70 percent. Passive solar heating, increased insulation and shading, and a gas-fired air conditioning system help reduce the HVAC energy. The station also has a computerized energy management control system. *Overall, this station requires 75 percent less energy—and thus generates one-quarter the greenhouse gases—than a typical station of similar size located in a similar climate.* The energy savings of $20,000 a year over standard design paid for the extra cost of the energy-saving measures *in about five years.*

❖

There are other solar technologies besides PVs, some of them quite well tested. Early on, humans learned to concentrate the sun's rays to create intense heat. In ancient Syracuse, Archimedes is said to have used a great number of polished shields to reflect and concentrate the sunlight to set fire to the sails of attacking Roman ships. Today, so-called "solar thermal" heating systems are used in a wide variety of applications. Solar water heating can be used cost-effectively to provide up to 80 percent of the hot water needs of many buildings around the country, especially those in the Southwest, without any carbon dioxide emissions and with minimal operation and maintenance expense. Solar heating in the form of a transparent swimming pool cover is particularly cost-effective.

An emerging solar heating technology is the unglazed transpired collector, which uses solar energy to heat outside air, which is then pulled into a ventilation system. In parts of the country and the world with a great deal of sunlight and a long heating season, such systems can warm outside air by as much as 50°F, significantly reducing energy consumption with paybacks under five years.

Ford Motor Company's stamping plant in Buffalo, New York, uses such exterior solar ventilation walls to preheat air for the plant. The 50,000-square-foot Solarwall system, made by Conserval Systems of Buffalo, covers plant walls with a southern exposure. The heated air is distributed throughout the plant by more than a mile of flexible ducting. The system saves Ford nearly $200,000 a year.[26]

FOUR TIMES SQUARE: A COOL SKYSCRAPER

Few buildings combine all of the energy-efficient and cool power opportunities. One recent building that has done more than most is Four Times Square, the beautiful skyscraper at the intersection of Broadway and 42nd Street, built by the Durst Organization. The first speculative (not built for a specific tenant) office tower to be built in Manhattan since 1988, Four Times Square is also the first project of its size—forty-eight stories and 1.6 million square feet—to adopt a cool design strategy.[27]

The building is between 35 and 40 percent more efficient than New York State code requires. The annual energy savings of $500,000 will pay for the incremental cost of these measures within five years. On the efficiency side, the building has energy-efficient lighting and windows, as well as increased insulation and an automated energy management system with efficient heating and cooling, individual fan units, and variable air volume. Some 25 percent of the floor area is daylit. Savings from using daylight dimming on the lighting system will payback in fourteen months.

On the cool power side, the building has two 200-kW phosphoric acid fuel cells (to provide electricity and hot water), an extremely efficient natural-gas-fired chiller, and a 15-kW photovoltaic system integrated into the building. Thin film panels were placed at the center of the southern and eastern sides of the building on the upper nineteen floors in the spandrels (the area of a façade between the top of one window and the bottom of the one above). The efficiency and cool power measures together bring total greenhouse gas emissions *down by 40 percent.*

The payoff: Four Times Square has completely rented out its space. Many organizations are eager to work in an environmentally superior building with reduced operating costs. To see if productivity gains occur, the Department of Energy is partnering with the Durst Organization on a productivity study. Jonathan Durst, executive vice president of the Durst Organization, has said, "We believe that productivity studies will be the most effective tools to convince others of the advantages of green buildings. To that end, we are awaiting … an in-depth scientific investigation of these issues at Four Times Square. But, we're not waiting. The Durst Organization is already convinced."

The building was also a great learning experience. Bruce Fowle, principal-in-charge of design at Fox & Fowle Architects, has said, "What would we do next time? If we had known who the Four Times Square tenants were from the beginning, we might have been able to utilize an under-floor air distribution system. I think this is, without question, the way of the future. Under-floor air allows you to eliminate ductwork, give individualized air supply, reduce floor-to-floor heights, and increase layout flexibility, thereby reducing energy, material, and waste."

On the cool power side, Jonathan Durst recommends, "Start early. . . . Fuel cells are a very clean and attractive technology, but we did not learn about them until fairly late. We were at one time considering spending $1.5 million to build the infrastructure necessary to put eight on the roof. We could have avoided that expense entirely, if we had initially contemplated siting them next to the switch gear in the sub-cellar." With eight fuel cells integrated into the design from the beginning, a steam-driven absorption chiller could have been used for cooling the building, rather than a gas-fired unit.

All of these improvements added to the actual design would have delivered a building with under half the greenhouse gas emissions of a typical skyscraper. "Now that we've been through it once," says Durst, "we're ready for the next building and committed to improving upon the accomplishments of Four Times Square."

As the country's first cool skyscraper, *Four Times Square stands as both a benchmark and a challenge to all cool designers who follow.*

THE COOL POWER STRATEGY

The opportunities for taking advantage of cool power are growing rapidly. The key point to remember: You do not need to reduce your company's greenhouse gas emissions tomorrow. What you need is a strategy that takes the best advantage over the next several years of new technology and changing government regulations to achieve the deepest reductions at the lowest cost and the maximum benefit to your bottom-line. Your strategy will vary by state and type of facility and the age of key pieces of your equipment. You must factor in a comprehensive efficiency upgrade so that you do not spend more money on a cogeneration system or purchase more renewable energy than you really need. Combining the two strategies of efficiency and cool power can achieve greenhouse gas reductions of 75 percent or more.

Chapter

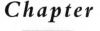

FACTORIES—PART I: MOTOR SYSTEMS

As *Fortune* magazine wrote in May 1998, "Only a third of U.S. manufacturers are seriously scrutinizing energy usage, where savings in five areas can move *billions* to the bottom line."[1] Two of these areas—lighting and HVAC (heating, ventilation, and air conditioning)—have already been covered in this book. This chapter focuses on motors and compressed air. The fifth, steam systems, will be addressed in Chapter 8.

If you are a manufacturer, motors are your muscles. They do the most work and burn the most energy. Yet the majority of them are inefficient and oversized. Lucent Technologies examined fifty-four motors for efficiency and size at its 1.3-million-square-foot Colorado research, development, and manufacturing facility. *Of the fifty-four motors, 87 percent were oversized and some were operating at only 16 percent of full load.*[2]

Worse still, motors are often part of systems that further waste energy and impede production. The Department of Energy audited a dozen industrial retrofits of motor systems around the country and found an *average energy savings of one-third with a payback of a year and a half.* When you take a systems approach to analyzing motor-based production, you will uncover unexpected opportunities for boosting profits and productivity, especially with the advanced motors and computer-controlled drives now available. Here are some examples:

- An Arkansas steel tube manufacturer replaced a key motor and drive. The 34 percent energy savings would have paid for the new system in five years, but the improvement in productivity and reduction in scrap paid for it in *five months.*

- A Washington State fruit storage company found that by shutting their fan motors down 75 percent of the time and installing computer controls they could achieve productivity gains that exceeded the energy savings by a factor of *ten.*

- A South Carolina aluminum refiner analyzed its dust collection system and found that a few simple operational changes would save it $104,000 per year, reduce system energy consumption 12 percent a year, and reduce carbon dioxide emissions by over 2,500 tons a year *with no capital outlay whatsoever.*

- A California textile plant reduced the energy consumption of its ventilation system 59 percent by installing motor controls, saving $101,000 a year in energy costs. An energy services firm paid for the $130,000 system (a *1.3-year payback*) and took its payment from the energy savings. The new system reduced maintenance costs and, by reducing the plant's airborne lint, increased product quality.

- Using a simple, free software package, seven audits of compressed air systems identified measures to reduce electricity used to run compressed air systems *in half* with an average return on investment of 150 percent. Available airflow increased up to 51 percent, providing additional benefits that *doubled the return on investment.* Companies ranged from a bakery, to foundries, to electronics.

For most manufacturers, electricity consumption by motors is their biggest source of carbon dioxide emissions (the exceptions are companies whose electric utility does not get most of its power from fossil fuels or those in the major process industries, such as chemicals, pulp and paper, and metals). In the United States, motors consume about half of all electricity and almost 70 percent of industrial electricity. Motors tend to be energy hogs. An inefficient motor can use *five times its capital cost in electricity each year.* A typical 75-hp motor costs $4,000 and running at full load for 6,000 hours a year consumes $18,000 worth of electricity (at $0.05 per kWh). Thus high-efficiency motors, new control systems, and systematic process redesign will give you tremendous opportunities for energy savings.

Motors are so crucial to a company's operations that when one burns out, it is immediately replaced with whatever is available. Therefore, it's worth taking the time to *survey all of your motors now.* You need to know which motors are cost-effective to replace or upgrade today. More important, you need a plan. What do you intend to do with a burnt-out motor? Will you replace it with a smaller motor? Or replace it with an efficient motor of the same size? Or redesign the system to avoid the need for the motor entirely? You will need to locate a supplier today who can quickly provide you with that new system when it is needed. If there is no plan, when a motor burns out, your people are likely to use whatever motor they can get fastest, which is probably the same, inefficient motor that you are using now.

The primary lessons from this chapter are:

(1) All companies need a proactive motor policy to identify the largest immediate savings and to maximize savings as motors burn out.

(2) Motor and compressed air electricity usage—and hence their greenhouse gas emissions—can typically be cut 30 to 60 percent with a payback of under three years.

(3) A focus on improving motor systems can capture productivity gains that cut the payback time *in half or more.*

Let's start with two companies that have integrated motor efficiency into their overall strategy for energy efficiency and pollution prevention.

3M: HARVESTING THE FRUIT OF POLLUTION PREVENTION

A multi-billion dollar company perhaps best known to the public for Post-It Notes and Scotch Tape, 3M is famous in the business and environmental communities for its pollution prevention programs, among the oldest in corporate America. Livio DeSimone, chair and CEO of 3M, is one of the world's leading proponents of resource efficiency. In a 1997 book he co-authored, *Eco-Efficiency: The Business Link to Sustainable Development,* DeSimone writes:

> If companies respond to [environmental] pressures only when forced to do so, they will miss important opportunities to gain the competitive advantage that accrues to early movers. Introducing new technology ahead of regulatory requirements can avoid delays and higher costs later. Similarly, *firms that give priority to resource productivity, process change, and product innovation will achieve significant performance gains at lower cost.* And there will also be huge new business opportunities from meeting the continuing need for added-value products and services.[3]

This strategic thinking drives 3M's Energy Policy: "Improve energy consumption efficiency, reduce cost, decrease capital investment, reduce environmental emissions, and conserve natural resources."[4]

In 1994, 3M established a cross-functional team to examine the motor efficiency opportunities in the 7.5-million-square-foot corporate headquarters located in the St. Paul suburb of Maplewood, which houses corporate research and development facilities, pilot plants, and corporate offices. The team included 3M employees from facilities engineering and plant engineering (a mechanical engineer, an electrician, and an air conditioning and refrigeration specialist), an engineer from the local utility specializing in demand-side management, a motor specialist from a GE subsidiary, and an engineering consultant who designed, managed, and commissioned the control systems that were installed. As we have seen over and over, cross-functional teams using a systems approach are the way to go when you want to capture large savings quickly.

The team developed a systematic building-by-building methodology to identify the best energy-saving, productivity-enhancing opportunities:

1. Locate and identify equipment.
2. Document the type of motor systems, operational requirements and use (including field measurements), type of system and motor controls, and nameplate information.
3. Analyze efficiency of the existing system, operational use vs. operational need, and present energy consumption.
4. Develop technical options, evaluate alternatives, calculate savings, estimate cost to implement, and determine financial and operational feasibility.
5. Develop proposals and reports, including system description, opportunities for improvement, and recommendations.
6. Present feasible proposals to management for funding approval, follow up, and obtain authority for expenditure.
7. Implement the projects.
8. Follow up with measurements and monitoring, compare actual savings to calculated savings, and report the results.
9. Communicate activities and progress to steering committee and building energy teams.

The team also used the U.S. Department of Energy's MotorMaster software, which helps users select motors and controls that meet specific performance and economic criteria.[5] The DOE also independently validated the results achieved in 3M's Building 123, a 530,000-square-foot building that houses research pilot plants, mechanical and electrical maintenance shops, laboratories, and support functions. There were four key improvements.

First, the air supply system for the research pilot plant was upgraded. Rather than running the fans twenty-four hours a day at full speed, a direct digital control system allows for variations in ventilation. One of the key fan motors was also retrofitted with a variable speed drive, which is an electronic control that permits the motor to operate more efficiently at partial loads.

Second, the team upgraded the building's reheat water supply system, which pumps hot water to the building's supply-air reheat coils. The old system operated the pumps at full flow continuously. It controlled temperature by regulating the flow of hot water, *diverting the unneeded flow through a bypass valve,* a classic inefficiency. The team optimized the system with energy-efficient motors and variable speed drives, which better match the amount of water pumped with the system requirements.

Third, much of the air to Building 123 is supplied by two 50-hp fans. The air requirements were variable, depending on building occupancy and activity, but, as usual, the fans ran constantly and dampers controlled flow. The team optimized the system with variable speed drives. Also, the team put an energy-efficient motor on the one fan that did not already have one.

Finally, a comprehensive survey of all electric motors in the building larger than 1.5 hp found fifty older, standard-efficiency motors that operated more than 6,000 hours a year and hence would save big money if replaced by energy-efficient motors.

Together, these four improvements reduced electricity consumption 41 percent, yielding total savings of electricity (and steam and chilled water) of $77,600. The net cost to 3M, after including demand-side management incentives from Northern States Power, was $79,500 for a simple payback of only 1.03 years, *nearly a 100 percent return on investment.* These are retrofits that most companies, both manufacturing and service sector, might be able to make.

➡ **What I find particularly telling about this case study is that 3M has for two decades been a leader in pollution prevention and energy efficiency, and yet it still was able to find huge and very cost-effective energy savings. If one of the most environmentally proactive companies in the world can find such large energy savings in its motor systems, every company can. Your company can.**

From 1975 to 1996, 3M's Pollution Prevention Pays program has prevented 750,000 tons of pollutants and *saved $790 million.* During that same time period, the company achieved *an energy-efficiency improvement of 58 percent per unit of production* or per square foot of office and warehouse space in the United States. The company has won awards from the President's Council on Sustainable Development, the National Wildlife Federation's Corporate Conservation Council, the World Environment Center, and the Alliance to Save Energy.

Process improvement is a high priority for 3M. In December 1996, the company announced *a breakthrough in the process for making medical adhesive tapes that reduces energy consumption by 77 percent.* The new process also cuts solvent use by 2.4 million pounds, lowers manufacturing costs, and cuts manufacturing cycle time by 25 percent. The proprietary process (five patents) took researchers nine years from conception through final implementation. Six different 3M divisions are planning to use the method for making a variety of adhesive products.

After twenty-three years of achieving *annual improvements* in energy efficiency exceeding 3 percent, 3M still expects to cut motor energy consumption by some $7 million using its systems approach. It has committed to continue 3 percent per year improvements for the foreseeable future. Its carbon dioxide intensity will improve even more as 3M uses more and more cool power. For instance, at one Illinois plant, 40 percent of the hot exhaust from air pollution control equipment is recirculated in product dryers and another 40 percent is burned to make steam for plant use; the process improvement cost $690,000 but saves $460,000 a year in energy costs. Also, *3M has been phasing out coal boilers and increasingly adopting natural gas cogeneration technologies.*

In June 1998, I asked Robert L. Renz, a senior environmental engineer at 3M, what his response was to those who say that after more than two decades of remarkable achievements in efficiency, 3M must have captured all of the low-hanging fruit. His response: "Fruit grow back."

SYSTEMATIC ENERGY SAVINGS: PERKIN-ELMER

Perkin-Elmer is a billion-dollar manufacturer of analytical instruments headquartered in Connecticut.[6] In 1991, facilities manager Jim Oberndorfer began focusing on energy efficiency at the company's headquarters building in Wilton and its nearby factory in Norwalk. He needed a new air compressor, and the local utility had a rebate program that bought him a better machine.

Then, with the help of RPM Systems in New Haven, an environmental services company, he did a comprehensive energy audit and upgrade. High-efficiency lighting was followed by an energy management control system and an upgrade to the HVAC equipment. Energy-efficient motors and improvements to compressed air followed. In one case, a new low-pressure air system replaced a system that had put out 125 pounds per square inch (psi) but had been throttled down to 7 psi, wasting virtually all of the energy. The upgrade didn't qualify for a rebate, but Oberndorfer went forward because the system paid for itself in a year anyway.

Oberndorfer explained, "We've always achieved what we set out to do in savings, and usually a bit more," because of synergies such as reduced lighting use lowering the cooling demand. Since 1992, the Connecticut plant has achieved a 26 percent cut in its electric-power bill, despite a rate increase, expansion in square footage, and an increase in sales.

I asked Oberndorfer how he achieved savings so much greater than most other companies do. His answer: "Awareness is probably the biggest key to energy savings. If people don't think you care about it, they won't do anything about it. Workers have no idea what energy costs."

Perkin-Elmer set up an innovative chargeback mechanism so that managers, for instance, who brought workers in on the weekend for work not only had to budget for overtime but for energy costs too. "We tell a manager that it costs $300 an hour to run the air conditioning for his area," says Oberndorfer. A manager bringing in three people on a Saturday now knows it costs $2,400 to cool those three workers for eight hours. "So now the managers make better decisions. If they have to work Saturdays, they'll bring in more people for fewer hours."

The combination of all these efforts has achieved an impressive cumulative effect. Company-wide, Perkin-Elmer *cut energy consumption per dollar of sales by 60 percent from 1991 to 1997.*

According to the company's Environmental Mission Statement: "Perkin-Elmer believes that a long-term commitment to protect and improve the environment is synonymous with sound business practice. This commitment is among our highest corporate priorities. The continued improvement of environmental quality is not a temporary issue but an essential activity for sustaining corporate viability and, indeed, the quality of life on Earth." If Perkin-Elmer is able to sustain its environmental mission through continuing energy-efficiency improvements, it will continue to be a very cool company indeed, one of the world's benchmarks.

INCREASING MOTOR EFFICIENCY SYSTEMATICALLY

The simplest thing for your company to do: As your old, inefficient motors burn out, replace them with more efficient ones. New high-efficiency motors alone can save $25 per horsepower per year compared to standard motors. Since factories are likely to have dozens of motors, the cumulative savings can be considerable. Nevertheless, because of their higher initial cost (often 10 to 30 percent more than standard motors, though, as we will see, that can be negotiable), such motors still comprise well under half of motor sales. Most companies are not thinking about life-cycle costs.[7]

A 1998 survey by Xenergy of 250 manufacturing plants found that for companies with fewer than 500 employees, only 16 to 24 percent of the motors purchased in the previous two years were efficient. That rose to only 33 to 38 percent for large companies. Yet, when included as part of an entire motor system changeover, *paybacks are often under two years.* The payback is even faster when the local utility provides a rebate for energy efficiency. About two dozen North American utilities offer such rebates, averaging about $10 per horsepower for high-efficiency motors.

While replacing inefficient motors with efficient ones is vital, it is an "operations" improvement, as opposed to a "process" improvement, which is where the biggest savings are (as described in Chapter 2). As a result, I am more concerned in this chapter with how to take a *systematic approach* to improving the efficiency of motor systems and related equipment, such as compressed air. By systems approach, I mean a way to look at the big picture, not merely making the motor itself more efficient, but examining motor controls plus the downstream parts of the process.

Motors are part of a system that includes the equipment the motor runs, such as a fan or pump, and the transmission or drivetrain, which transfers the motor's mechanical power to the equipment. The strategy of focusing on the entire motor system is the one most likely to achieve the large gains in productivity, quality, scrap rates, and other nonenergy benefits that can *more than double* returns on investment.

The first step in any systems analysis of a production process is to look for bottlenecks. If you are a manufacturer, that is where you will probably find an old, inefficient motor. A new motor and control system here will not merely save energy but will inevitably increase productivity. And when you find a motor system upgrade with multiple benefits, you help reduce the natural resistance to changing anything as fundamental to a plant's operation as one of its key motors. Consider the case of Greenville Tube Company.

Productivity Gain at Greenville Tube

The 200 workers at the 100,000-square-foot Greenville Tube plant in Clarksville, Arkansas, produce 1 million feet of customized stainless steel tubing per month for automotive, aerospace, and other high-tech businesses. One of the company's competitive advantages is the ability to rapidly supply customized tubes for a business experiencing costly downtime due to equipment failure.[8]

Greenville's production process involves pulling or "drawing" stainless steel tubing through dies to reduce their diameter and/or wall thickness. Tubes first go through "breaking" draws to bring the tube close to its final size before a few final finishing draws. The Number 6 drawbench is where all these breaking draws occur and as such was the main production bottleneck. An analysis of the motor system by the plant engineer found that the 150-hp motor was *undersized*. The power distribution system and motor drive were inefficient and antiquated, leading to overheating, overloading, and poor control of the motor at low speed.

A larger, but more efficient motor (200 hp) was installed along with a computerized control system (enclosed, with an air conditioner) for $37,000. Electricity consumption (including the air conditioning) dropped 34 percent, saving $7,000 a year, which would have meant slightly more than a five-year payback. More important, however, the greater horsepower meant that many of the tubes needed *fewer* breaking draws: On average, one draw was *eliminated* from half the tubes processed. Each draw has a number of costly ancillary operations, including degreasing, cutting off the piece that the motor system latches on to, and annealing. Reducing the number of draws provided total labor cost savings of $24,000 a year, savings in stainless steel scrap of $41,000, and additional direct savings of $5,000. Thus, total annual savings from this single motor system upgrade was $77,000, yielding a simple *payback of just over five months* or a return on investment in excess of *200 percent.*

There's more: The new system provided better process control for the operator, resulting in improved product quality. Finally, the company learned that a number of other drawbenches might benefit from motor system upgrades. A systems approach invariably surprises you with the breathtaking gains you achieve from what start off as modest improvements.

With Motors, Smaller Can Be Better

Undersized motors are the exception. Far more common is the situation where motors are oversized or even completely unnecessary. When motors are excessively large, you will uncover big savings simply by replacing them. Most motors achieve maximum efficiency at around 75 percent of maximum load, and they start to lose significant efficiency below 40 percent. The 1998 Xenergy study, one of the most comprehensive surveys ever done, which performed measurements on 35,000 motors in 254 manufacturing plants, found that *one-third of motors are running at below 40 percent of rated load.* Such oversized motors waste considerable energy and should be replaced for three reasons:

1. A smaller motor is less expensive.
2. Operating a more efficient motor at a more efficient load saves energy.
3. High-efficiency motors tend to maintain high efficiency over a broader range: While a standard motor might begin losing efficiency rapidly at 48 percent of full load, a high-efficiency motor might not drop off until 42 percent.

For pumping fluids and gases, the savings from motor system redesign can be disproportionately huge. For example, when you need only half of the flow from a pump, you can theoretically *save seven-eighths of its power.* Motors are usually sized for peak requirements—a common sense solution. But peaks rarely occur. A pump might operate at 40 percent of its rated power 90 percent of the time and at 80 percent of its power 10 percent of the time. What is the solution? A smaller pump in parallel with the first will cover peak loads, saving considerable energy while providing additional reliability because both sets of pumps are unlikely to break down at the same time.

It is equally important to investigate the 10 percent of the time the motor operates at 80 percent of load. One principle of energy saving: *Reduce peak loads.* Utilities try to reduce peak power demands to avoid costly excess generating capacity. For the same reason, your company should reduce surge requirements. Ask the "five whys" (see Chapter 2): Why is there a power surge at that time? Is the surge caused by poor system design that creates the bottleneck? Can process redesign eliminate the bottleneck? What is the cost of the redesign compared with the savings in energy use? Would the redesign capture other benefits, such as productivity gains?

When you have many motors working together on the same function, such as fans or pumps, an option simpler than downsizing may turn out to be running the motors less often or shutting some of them down entirely. Do a comprehensive analysis of your motor systems. What is each one used for? Are they underused or oversized? Let's look at two cases of motors providing unneeded work.

The Fruits of Systematic Process Redesign

Consider the Regal Fruit Co-op in Tonasket, Washington, which stores more than 1 million bushels of fruit for farmers in the north-central part of the state. Apples and pears have traditionally been stored at 31 to 32°F in an atmosphere of almost pure nitrogen, the facility's fans running twenty-four hours a day. In 1989, Bonneville Power Administration approached Regal Fruit with a proposal to save energy and prevent pollution. Researchers at Washington State University had found that an astonishing *60 percent of the heat* in an apple-storage facility came from the fans. Waste had been designed into the process—a classic systems problem. Researchers found that with a computer-controlled monitoring system, the fans needed to be on only about six hours a day, in a repeated cycle of two hours on and six hours off. In other words, the motors that run the fans can be turned off three-fourths of the time.[9]

The new equipment cost $104,000, more than half of which was covered by Bonneville. Yearly electricity savings were estimated at $13,000. Actual energy savings exceeded estimates by $2,000 to $5,000 a year. Regal Fruit's investment would pay for itself in three to four years. A good move, but it gets much better. Productivity went up, as is usually the case when a company reexamines and redesigns a process that has been used for many years. The researchers had found that by reducing the oxygen content further, they could not only increase the temperature a few degrees (saving more energy), but they could also improve the quality of the fruit.

Fruit is typically stored five to nine months before being taken to market. "We used to factor in a shrinkage rate of up to 20 percent," says Ron Gonsalves, refrigeration supervisor for Regal Fruit. "With our Golden Delicious, we raised the temperature to 33 degrees, from 31, eliminating the defrost cycles, which contributed to dehydration. Now our shrinkage is only 1 percent." Where Regal once might have sold one hundred partially dehydrated apples in every bushel, now they can sell eighty-five plump, juicy apples.

The savings from reduced shrinkage "far exceeds anything we make back from energy savings," says Gonsalves, "*probably tenfold*." In other words, while the energy savings would have paid for the new system in three to four years, the productivity rise paid for the new system in *less than one year.* The goal of reducing energy use (and pollution) led to systematic process redesign that increased productivity. That is environmental reengineering.

Instant Paybacks at Alumax

Aluminum refining is one of the most energy-intensive processes in the world. Alumax is the third largest producer of aluminum in the United States. Their Mount Holly plant in South Carolina produces 200,000 tons of aluminum a year from alumina (aluminum oxide). They wanted to improve the efficiency of the fan system that removed dust and other airborne impurities created in the process of converting alumina to aluminum.[10]

The conversion takes place in 360 pots of molten cryolite (sodium aluminum fluoride). Every 90 pots have their own system of four fans that pull the dirty air through a dry scrubber and exhaust the air into a stack. The fans, which run continuously, were designed to provide each system with 360,000 cubic feet per minute of airflow. Years of experience taught the staff that the fans could do the job at reduced flow. They reduced the flow by partially closing the inlet vane controls, although that meant that the fans were operating at an efficiency of only 68 percent.

Working with an energy consulting firm, the staff analyzed in detail several different options, including using variable frequency drives to control the fans. As it turns out, the option that saved the most energy and money was simply turning off one of the fans and opening the intake valves wider. This saved 12 percent of the system energy, a total of 3.35 million kWh (and over 2,500 tons of carbon dioxide) for *an annual energy savings of $104,000 with no capital outlay whatsoever.*

As always, the change had a number of other benefits. A spare fan is available for each of the systems. Maintenance is reduced. Noise levels are lower from running only three fans. The fans are under more accurate control. The value of these benefits has not been quantified.

This case has a useful lesson. A lot of fan systems have inlet vanes or outlet dampers to control the flow of air (similarly, many pumping systems use valves to control flow rates). Both approaches waste energy. As Alumax showed, for a system with a *constant* flow, opening the vanes or dampers and using a smaller fan is probably the best and simplest approach to save energy.

A great many systems have a need for *variable* flow, which can benefit from variable frequency drives, as the next case illustrates.

Improving a Textile Plant's Ventilation

Nisshinbo California's Fresno facility is a spinning and weaving textile plant.[11] Every day, it processes 45,000 pounds of raw cotton into about 60,000 yards of fabric. Monitoring the temperature and humidity levels is essential.

If the air is too wet, cotton fibers can stick to equipment, become difficult to process, and cause equipment breakdown. If too dry, the fibers fly away. Moreover, the ten different steps of textile manufacturing are performed in separate areas and have different ideal ranges for temperature and relative humidity. As if that were not enough, many different types of fabric are manufactured, and each can have different heat and ventilation requirements.

For all these reasons, the ventilation system, composed of nine supply fans and nine return fans, is critical. Plant personnel had been controlling the system *manually* through the use of dampers and variable valves, which is always both inefficient and imprecise. Following an analysis by ADI Control Techniques Drives of Hayward, California, the company retrofitted fifteen of the fans with variable frequency drives. The dampers can open up completely. The engineering analysis, new equipment, and installation cost $130,000. An energy services company provided the entire up-front cost and is paid back with a share of the energy savings, which comes to $101,000 a year. The company got new equipment and a share of the savings—*all for free.*

It's an old story on these pages: The project has had a number of extra benefits to the company. The variable frequency drives have given the plant greater control over its airflow and hence air quality. They have saved forty-eight hours of labor per year that had been used to manually control the system. Perhaps more important, *airborne lint has decreased, which has improved product quality and reduced the number of equipment breakdowns.* Finally, as a result of the project, more opportunities for energy savings were identified.

The Importance of Control

As we have seen, sometimes it is better to put controls on the old motor instead of replacing it with a new one. Electronic speed controls (variable-frequency or adjustable-speed drives) permit large motors to operate more efficiently at partial loads. These adjustable drives not only save energy, but they improve control over the entire production process. Microprocessors allow these drives to maintain more precise and accurate flow rates. When the production process needs to be redesigned, adjustable drives provide the flexibility to operate the motor at any different speed without losing significant energy efficiency.

A load that changes is best handled by adjustable speed drives. Yet, Xenergy found in its comprehensive 1998 survey that while 24 percent of motors between 100 and 200 hp used in the primary metals and paper manufacturing sectors had fluctuating loads, only 0 to 5 percent of these motors are equipped with adjustable speed drives. Xenergy found that 43 percent of the motors between 200 and 500 hp used by paper manufacturers had fluctuating loads, but only 4 percent of those motors were equipped with adjustable speed drives. Large opportunities remain untapped even in this most energy-conscious of industries.

> Variable-speed drives are at the core of any cool motor upgrade. They save energy, which reduces greenhouse gas emissions, and improve process control, which is the best way to improve productivity and quality.

MOTOR CASE STUDIES FROM AROUND THE WORLD

While the previous stories are remarkable, they are by no means unique. Consider this sampling of cases from other countries.[12]

- Royal Darwin Hospital in Australia installed variable speed drives (VSDs) on its air-handling units. With the improved air control of the VSDs, room setpoints could be increased by 1°C. The result: *fan power was cut by 71 percent with a payback of three months.* An investment of $120,000 (Australian dollars) yielded savings of $450,000 a year.

- The Scott Paper Company Mill in Westminster, British Columbia, eliminated the control valve regulating the flow of their pulp stock and installed a VSD. Energy was cut in half, saving 300,000 kWh with a simple payback of under two years.

- Suntory's Musashino Brewery in Japan upgraded five motors with VSDs. Overall energy consumption dropped 47 percent, saving more than 700,000 kWh a year with *a simple payback of 1.9 years.*

- A British Steel plant upgraded its system for pumping the water that cools the steel plates during manufacturing. The systematic combination of new motors, VSDs, and the control regime made possible by the VSDs resulted in *a 76 percent energy savings with a payback of 3.3 years.* The process improvement also seems to have improved product quality, with a slight increase in the percentage of steel plates successfully cooled.

The bottom line is that anywhere in the world, in any kind of business, a systems approach to motor retrofits will result in deep reductions in electricity use—and hence carbon dioxide emissions—with rapid payback.

Compressed Air

One motor-driven system that is often overlooked yet affords large opportunities for savings is compressed air.[13] Many companies use compressed air for cleaning, running machine tools, running looms, mixing, and moving products around on conveyor belts. Some 200,000 plants use compressed air, and the electricity it consumes could power the state of Connecticut. One study of 125 small and medium-sized factories found that motor-driven air compressors account for an average of 10 percent of total plant energy use. In some textile mills, more than half the electricity is used by compressed air systems. Compressed air is called industry's "fourth" utility (after electricity, natural gas, and water) and it is the most expensive. Yet it is generally viewed as "free" by plant staff.

Boeing Commercial Airplane Group *reduced air-compressor energy use 50 percent* at its three-building campus in northeast Portland, Oregon. A $180,000 upgrade cut energy use from 4.5 million kWh down to just 2.2 million kWh, saving $92,000 a year, a two-year payback. In addition to these energy savings, the company saves $9,500 in equipment depreciation and $8,500 on maintenance, parts, and labor each year. Also, the local utility provided a $40,000 incentive.

This kind of savings opportunity is not unique. General Motors audited ten of their own manufacturing plants and found opportunities for cutting energy used in compressed air by 30 to 60 percent.

Begin your own analysis by understanding that your air compression systems are among the most inefficient motor systems, with as much as *90 percent* of compressor power dissipated as heat. Relatively simple improvements, such as reducing air pressure and eliminating leaks, can achieve large energy savings with a high return on investment. You will also gain substantial nonenergy benefits.

First, improving air compression systems dramatically increases airflow to existing equipment and tools, allowing a manufacturer to avoid or delay the capital costs of purchasing a new compressor as demand for air grows; this factor alone can *double the return on investment.*

Second, some system upgrades improve product quality and increase productivity.

Third, since virtually all of the energy used for compressing air is electricity, upgrades achieve significant carbon dioxide savings.

Oregon State University (OSU) is one of the nation's Industrial Assessment Centers funded by the Department of Energy. Working with Bonneville Power Administration, a major electricity provider in the Pacific Northwest, OSU developed a spreadsheet-based software tool called AIRMaster, together with a method for auditing air systems. They demonstrated the power of their software at audits of seven northwest plants, including a bakery, a sawmill, a metal fabrication plant, a foundry, and an electronics plant. Compressors account for an average of 15 percent of electricity use at these plants (33 percent at the metal fabricator and 2.7 million kWh at the sawmill).

The results were astonishing. The average savings in air compressor energy use was 49 percent, a total energy savings of 4.1 million kWh, yielding an annual cost savings of $152,000. The total cost to achieve these savings was $95,000, a simple payback of 0.6 years (or a *return on investment exceeding 150 percent*). But in addition to saving energy and money, the improvements increased available airflow by up to 51 percent, which translated into potential capital benefits of up to 230 percent of first-year energy savings. On average, paybacks were cut in half, meaning that the *average return on investment exceeded 300 percent.*

The upgrades also provided other, nonquantified benefits. Equipment life was extended because loads were reduced and operating time was cut (by turning compressors off when they were not needed). System reliability increased as equipment was run closer to design specifications. And environmental impact was reduced, including air pollution and greenhouse gas emissions from the power plants that provide system electricity. Other air compressor upgrades at companies such as glass manufacturers and foundries have reduced defects and increased productivity.

The largest sources of savings in compressed air came just from reducing leaks or using the compressed air efficiently. *Fixing leaks saved more energy than all other measures combined, providing 35 percent of the 49 percent savings.* Every plant audited benefited from fixing leaks, which often allowed a compressor to be turned off entirely, improving savings even more.

Systematic Energy Savings: The Case of Southwire

What happens when a company applies a systems approach to making its motor systems and buildings more energy efficient? It becomes a cool company like Southwire. The Southwire Company, a large manufacturer of copper rod, cable, and wire headquartered in Carrollton, Georgia, had soaring energy costs in the early 1980s. Energy bills had reached 20 percent of overhead, up from 10 percent a decade earlier, and were rising 15 to 20 percent annually. Southwire's profit margins were dropping, and the company had to lay off 1,000 workers.[14]

Top management decided to embrace a comprehensive approach to energy savings. They set a goal of 35 percent savings, where many in the industry thought 20 percent was the most that was possible. Ultimately, Southwire did far better than 35 percent—it saved 60 percent of its gas and 40 percent of its electricity per pound of rod, wire, and cable produced. To achieve these remarkable results, the energy management team used a combination of efficiency measures: new motors, efficient HVAC, and improved lighting, including new skylights in all of its plants.

Southwire's motor efficiency program is an excellent case study in how to approach any problem systematically. Every standard motor under 125 hp that fails is replaced with a high-efficiency motor rather than being rewound (which involves stripping out the old windings and replacing the wire). For larger motors, Southwire compares the costs and savings of rewinding versus new motors, and it buys a new motor if its five-year life-cycle cost is lower than that of rewinding.

Southwire favors new motors because rewound ones are not always reliable, and there are efficiency losses from the rewind process. The key to their success is their careful survey of equipment. Engineers check and tag every motor that is clearly oversized; when these burn out they are replaced with the designated correctly sized, efficient motors. The company stocks some new replacement motors on site. It buys large numbers of high-efficiency motors, primarily from one supplier. Southwire expects that supplier to have their motors in stock at all times.

Thus, Southwire's motor replacement policy is best described as proactive—a systems approach. Waiting for a motor to burn out before deciding what to do is disastrous policy. Like most manufacturers, Southwire operates continuously. Employees are paid on a piece rate (with profit-sharing) and don't want to shut equipment down—then they lose money. When a motor burns out, they want it replaced immediately with whatever is available. If the company had not determined *in advance* what to do, and if it did not have high-efficiency motors readily available, people would inevitably use whatever motor they could get the fastest. The proactive policy has ensured the company that its motor supplier stocks high-efficiency motors. And more— Southwire's volume purchases have dropped the price for high-efficiency motors to only 5 percent above the cost of standard-efficiency motors.

What did Southwire's systems approach to energy mean for the company? From 1981 to 1988, Southwire estimates that it saved $40 million in energy costs, a decrease from 20 percent of overhead to under 13 percent. *During a rough financial period, the savings from Southwire's systematic approach to motors were almost equal to all of the company's profits.* Energy efficiency turned around its profit margin and may well have saved the company, which now has $1.7 billion in sales and provides 5,000 jobs.

Today, Southwire has other reasons for deserving the label *cool company.* It makes specially designed cables that can improve the performance of variable-speed drives for large motors. And, coolest of all, it is developing superconducting cable, which is cooled to very low temperatures by liquid nitrogen flowing through it. Such cable will soon allow some power lines to carry far more electricity with lower losses to resistance, bringing large potential electricity and carbon dioxide savings. Today, up to 8 percent of electricity generated by power plants is wasted just due to losses and inefficiencies in power transmission and distribution (on top of the inefficiencies in electricity generation discussed in the previous chapter). Widespread use of superconducting cable and other power equipment could cut those losses *in half,* eliminating significant quantities of fossil fuel combustion and greenhouse gases. As Roy Richards, Jr., Southwire's CEO, said in 1995, "This is one of the most exciting and challenging projects ever undertaken by Southwire. The efficient use of energy is critical to our country's future competitiveness, and we are confident we can make a major contribution to that goal."

CONCLUSION

Any company that wants to dramatically reduce its greenhouse gas emissions will need a comprehensive or systematic approach to improving the efficiency of its motor systems. A systems approach avoids a "one-size-fits-all" approach to motors.

One manager of a major U.S. company proudly reported to Ron Perkins, of the consulting firm Supersymmetry, how the company had "solved its motor efficiency problem" using adjustable-speed drives. The company saved half of its motor energy by putting drives on its motors, most of which had been running at partial load. Perkins did not want to burst the manager's bubble by explaining that if the company had first surveyed its motor systems and then bought smaller, correctly sized motors (and put drives on some of them), it could have saved three-fourths of motor energy. Again, the end-use approach—finding out what is needed before acting—is invariably the least-cost approach.

Because production is so crucially dependent on motors, the kind of proactive approach that Southwire has is crucial. Even if a change reduces energy use and operating cost, no company *likes* to disrupt its operations. For a change as disruptive as a motor upgrade, it's particularly important to get it right the first time. There are a number of resources available to your company.

MOTOR EFFICIENCY RESOURCES

Companies can find help in improving the efficiency of their motor systems:

- The Energy Department's Motor Challenge program provides technical assistance and free software for motors. Call their clearinghouse at 1-800-862-2086.
- The Compressed Air Challenge provides similar assistance for compressed air improvements. They can be reached at 1-800-559-4776.
- Many utilities offer rebates and technical assistance for motor upgrades.
- If you are a small or medium-sized manufacturer, you may be able to get a free energy, waste, and productivity audit if you are near one of the nation's many university-based Industrial Assessment Centers. To find out if you qualify, call 1-800-363-3732.

The best way for your company to identify where and how to improve every process is to tap the expertise of your employees. How to do this systematically is a key focus of the next chapter.

Chapter

FACTORIES—PART II: STEAM AND INDUSTRIAL PROCESSES

For the vast majority of companies seeking to reduce greenhouse gas emissions, the previous chapters covered most of the strategies they will need to pursue. The process industries—chemicals, pulp and paper products, petroleum refining, steel, aluminum, glass, and metal casting—will also be able to achieve significant reductions with these strategies. These industries, however, have a number of energy- and waste-intensive processes specific to them that need special attention.

While most of the *growth* in carbon dioxide emissions from the manufacturing sector is expected to come from the nonprocess manufacturers, these seven industries currently account for about 80 percent of the energy consumed in the sector and for more than 90 percent of the hazardous waste. Large energy use, however, also means large opportunities for savings, as a number of companies have found:

- From 1993 to 1997, DuPont's 1,450-acre Chambers Works in New Jersey reduced energy use per pound of product by one-third and *carbon dioxide emissions per pound of product by nearly one-half.* Even as production rose 9 percent, the total energy bill fell by more than $17 million a year.

- Simply by insulating its steam lines, Georgia-Pacific reduced fuel costs by one-third with a six-month payback at its Madison, Georgia, plywood plant. The project saved 18 tons of fuel per day, lowered emissions, made the workplace safer, and improved process efficiency.
- By modifying one steam turbine and making other steam system improvements at its large Burns Harbor plant, Bethlehem Steel generated annual savings of 40 million kilowatt-hours of electricity with a simple payback of just over one year.
- At a multi-factory complex in Flint, Michigan, General Motors combined efficiency with cool power *to cut carbon dioxide emissions from steam use by more than 60 percent*. Annual savings came to $4 million with a two-year payback.
- After ten years of running one of the industry's most successful programs for capturing energy savings, Dow Chemical's Louisiana Division was still able to identify more than one hundred projects from 1991 through 1993 with an average return on investment of 300 percent and savings exceeding $75 million a year.

In this chapter, we will examine how companies have achieved these results, exploring some of the approaches that are applicable across many industries, such as the more efficient use of steam and process heat. Steam is a particularly large opportunity as it accounts for $20 billion a year of U.S. manufacturing energy costs and over one-third of U.S. industrial carbon dioxide emissions.[1]

Steam is crucial for production in industries such as chemicals, food products, plastics, primary metals, pulp and paper, textiles, and petroleum refining. It is widely used to heat raw materials and treat semi-finished products at constant temperature. It is also used as a source of power for equipment and for heating buildings. Just as motors consume most industrial electricity, steam production consumes most of the fossil fuel burned directly by industry. And as with motor energy consumption, we will see large opportunities to save energy use by steam systems. Indeed, companies from DuPont to General Motors have reduced greenhouse gas emissions from the generation and use of steam by 30 to 60 percent. Clearly, any cool industrial company will need to improve the efficiency with which it generates and uses steam.

Finally, great opportunities exist to reduce process energy, in some cases by as much as 80 percent. Because so many processes are specific to a given industry, one of the best approaches for reducing carbon dioxide emissions is to develop a strategy that systematically taps the skill and expertise of your line employees and engineers. The benchmark here is what Ken Nelson was able to achieve when he was energy manager for the Louisiana Division of Dow Chemical and then a consultant to the Department of Energy.

Here are the key points to remember:

(1) You can cut the carbon dioxide emissions from the generation and use of steam by 30 to 60 percent with a rapid payback.

(2) To capture the large energy savings available from improving your processes, you will need a system for harnessing the ideas and creativity of your employees.

Before examining how to set up a suggestion system like Dow's, let's first examine how two of America's largest companies, DuPont and General Motors, systematically reduced the carbon dioxide emissions from steam.

DuPONT

DuPont is one of the world's largest chemical manufacturers, with energy expenditures exceeding $1 billion a year. It also has one of the most ambitious programs to reduce greenhouse gas emissions. While strongly supporting efforts "to better define the science and develop responsible policy," the company has "chosen to focus on steps we can take now to reduce greenhouse gas emissions," said John A. Krol, who retired in 1998 as chairman and chief executive officer and chief safety, health and environmental officer. In 1997, he noted that "Our current projections show that we will achieve a 40 percent reduction in these emissions in the United States and 50 percent globally by the year 2000 from a 1990 base year."[2]

From 1991 through 1996, the company has reduced greenhouse gas emissions by 16 percent, the equivalent of 25 million metric tons of carbon dioxide. The company emits a number of different greenhouse gases, including nitrous oxide, chlorofluorocarbons, hydrofluorocarbons, and perfluorocarbons. As part of the Climate Wise program begun by the EPA and the Department of Energy, DuPont has pledged to eliminate nitrous oxide emissions by implementing projects that will destroy or recapture it for beneficial use.

Emissions of carbon dioxide have dropped 10 percent during that time, in large part because DuPont adopted an aggressive corporate energy policy in 1992, which focused on three areas: maximizing energy efficiency, lowering the environmental impact of energy consumption, and renewing the power infrastructure. They set up a Corporate Energy Leadership Team composed of a cross-functional team from DuPont's businesses, functions, and energy-related disciplines worldwide to gain insights beyond what individual disciplines or experts could achieve. They committed to reduce energy consumption per unit product by 15 percent by 2000.

By 1996, the company had achieved an 8.4 percent reduction. Some sites have done much better, such as the 1,450-acre Chambers Works in New Jersey, home of manufacturing operations for thirteen different businesses together with a major research and development laboratory. From 1993 to 1997, it reduced energy use per pound of product by one-third, and, with the help of improved cogeneration, cut carbon dioxide emissions per pound of product by nearly one-half. Even as production rose 9 percent, the total energy bill fell by more than $17 million a year.

The Chambers Works has used a broad spectrum of approaches to achieve these results, including more efficient lighting, heating, cooling, and compressed air, as well as better use of cogeneration. One key opportunity has been steam systems, a principal source of energy in chemical plants. The process industries as a whole spend a remarkable $20 billion a year to boil water, much of which is generated in inefficient, aging boilers or wasted through leaks. A particularly large opportunity is to fix steam traps, which are designed to drain off condensed water in the steam lines without losing any steam and to help remove air from the steam system. Many steam traps malfunction, however, venting steam or allowing the water to pass through, which can harm the manufacturing process. In the winter, condensed water might cause a steam line to freeze over.

DuPont has 150,000 steam traps at its U.S. chemical operations. The Chambers Works has 5,000 of them. When the company first started looking at steam traps in the early 1990s, it found that as many as 35 percent had failed; it vowed to slash that figure. To identify traps requiring maintenance, it has used a portable steam-monitoring device called a Trapman, manufactured by TLV America Corporation in Charlotte, North Carolina. By touching the Trapman's sensor to the trap for fifteen seconds, and later loading that information into a computer, a maintenance technician can determine the state of repair of each trap. Using this system for finding and fixing malfunctioning traps, together with fixing leaks and replacing worn pipe insulation, has saved more than $1.5 million a year, or 12 percent of total steam use at Chambers Works. It has cut the failure rate of steam traps to 5 percent—an improvement of a factor of seven. DuPont has identified the elements of effective steam trap programs at its sites:

- An individual in the power area, manufacturing area, or a predictive maintenance group who is responsible for ensuring that steam trap testing and maintenance are performed in a timely manner.
- Personnel who perform area/site-specific steam trap testing and timely maintenance. The number of people involved in this process (from two to five people at a site with 4,000 steam traps) is a function of the actual number of steam traps, population size, system condition, and degree of program automation.
- Training for personnel responsible for trap testing and maintenance.
- Steam trap testing equipment and computer hardware/software (linked

with the site procurement system) to analyze test results, compute costs and savings, and report trap maintenance results.
• Standardized site steam trap models and installations.

Chambers Works also introduced energy-efficient improvements in wastewater treatment that are saving some $2 million a year. It optimized air distribution for aeration in the treatment plant, which allowed it to eliminate the use of a 1,000-hp motor entirely. Improved monitoring of the wastewater temperature allowed a reduction in steam used in the treatment process.

In another case, Praxair Company was providing on-site conversion of natural gas to hydrogen and carbon monoxide, both of which are used in DuPont's chemical manufacturing. The conversion required a great deal of electricity, but a process change that eliminated one step in the manufacture of carbon monoxide cut electricity costs $400,000 a year.

The plant has three refrigerated lines of brine (salt water) that go all over the plant to provide process cooling. Insulating the lines cut 55 tons from the cooling load and allowed the company to use smaller, more efficient refrigeration units.

"The reason that we were able to accomplish so much in energy savings at Chambers Works is because we had involvement in the various areas," according to Ernie O'Rourke, energy manager for Chambers Works. "It is not just something driven from a service organization. We had active members in the production groups. When you have those people willing to make changes in the production areas, that's when you can really see some results in energy savings."

The energy team calculates detailed metrics for energy used per pound of product every month—steam and electricity usage for every building at Chambers Works. "When you report things like that," says O'Rourke, "things tend to improve."

Interestingly, for all of the remarkable energy savings Chambers Works achieved from 1993 to 1997, O'Rourke told me in mid-1998, "We're only really getting into motors right now." In one case, a 1,000-hp motor failed and the company was going to rewind it. But then the energy team realized it was an inefficient motor and that they could replace it with an efficient motor with a one-year payback. That one change is saving $20,000 a year. To find the other such large opportunities, the facility recently signed up for the Department of Energy's Motor Challenge Program, so the energy savings will continue to grow.

The energy-efficiency measures, as noted, reduced energy use—the BTUs in their steam and electricity—per pound of product by one-third from 1993 to 1997; this reduced the carbon dioxide emitted per pound of product by 27 percent. During the same time period, DuPont also increased the efficiency of the generation of that electricity and steam by some 25 percent. The local utility had been running a cogeneration plant near Chambers Works that had been in operation since 1929. DuPont finally abandoned that plant in the early 1990s and contracted with U.S. Generating Company to purchase steam and electricity from a modern, cleaner, more efficient on-site plant. The previous plant had provided energy with relatively fixed costs and constant steam output, creating little incentive for efficiency. If Chambers Works had used less steam, the cogeneration facility would have merely vented it into the atmosphere. The new cogeneration facility allowed DuPont to purchase and pay for only the electricity and steam it needed, which motivated it to become more efficient. The combination of the more efficient use of steam and electricity coupled with the more efficient combined generation of heat and power have together allowed the Chambers Works to become a cool chemical manufacturing plant in a five-year period.

Krol, summing up DuPont's success as well as its continued commitment, stated in 1997, "DuPont had another year of significant progress toward our goal of zero waste [and] emissions."

GENERAL MOTORS

"Despite uncertainty about global climate science, General Motors has concluded that there is enough evidence linking global climate change to manmade greenhouse gases, to have cause for concern, and having said so, we accept certain responsibilities with respect to our products and manufacturing processes." So said Harry Pearce, GM vice chairman, in his keynote speech to the 1998 Automotive News World Congress.[3] GM is pursuing a variety of cool strategies.

GM's Delphi E, Flint East site, for instance, has achieved remarkable reductions in greenhouse gas emissions from steam use.[4] This 4.5-million-square-foot site comprises one administrative building and six operating plants that manufacture everything from spark plugs and air filters to cruise control systems and the instrument cluster on the dashboard panel for GM cars. The site originally had annual energy costs of some $16 million. After signing a ten-year contract with the local Michigan utility in the early 1990s, several utility engineers were assigned to work with GM to find energy savings.

As one of those engineers, Thomas Mort, told me, "We started with steam because that was the biggest bang for the buck. We knew it would provide the largest amount of savings in the shortest amount of time." First, they reduced the steam load, by taking such measures as insulating 700 feet of high-pressure steam piping, repairing broken condensate return line, eliminating the use of steam to melt snow, and reducing steam heating in unused building areas. By spending $128,000, GM saved $808,000 a year, a payback of under two months.

During the 1990s, GM also made a series of improvements in its steam generation. Originally, like many companies, GM generated the steam for this site with several centralized coal-fired boilers. These boilers were only about 64 percent efficient in converting the energy in coal to steam. Another 10 percent was lost in piping the steam to all the buildings in this site, which measured some two miles by three-quarters of a mile. Worse still, the site had large swings in the steam load, using six to eight times as much steam in the winter as in the summer. When steam use was at a minimum, however, it still had to be generated in a large central boiler and go through the site's entire distribution system, which is incredibly inefficient. GM decided to switch over to gas-fired boilers and to decentralize steam production by putting in smaller boilers around the site. As Mort explained, though, "smaller" still means "bigger than a school bus."

Switching from coal to gas for boilers of the same efficiency would by itself cut carbon dioxide emissions by more than 40 percent. These gas-fired boilers average 75 percent efficiency (rather than 64 percent), however, so there is even more savings. Finally, the large losses in distribution have been dramatically cut. The combination of fuel switching, increased efficiency, and elimination of distribution losses deserves the label "cool steam."

The efficiency and cool steam measures combined cost $8.6 million and resulted in annual savings of $4.0 million, a payback of slightly more than two years. At the same time, these improvements cut carbon dioxide emissions from steam generation and use by more than 60 percent.

So far, by focusing first on steam, the Flint site has cut overall energy use by about 25 percent. Many other savings opportunities have already been identified. For example, on Sundays and holidays the site still uses 40 percent of the energy it uses when it is producing product. That can probably be reduced to at least 25 percent. Potential savings in HVAC and compressed air are also large. All together, these improvements will ultimately reduce energy use at the site by more than one-third and carbon dioxide savings by more than that, which will make these plants particularly cool.

While these results are remarkable, the Flint site turns out to be fairly typical. In 1997, GM conducted energy audits at ten manufacturing plants as part of an internal benchmarking exercise. It found that opportunities for savings in steam and compressed air averaged 30 to 60 percent. It also found plants whose energy consumption when not producing product was as much as 50 percent of the levels of energy used when it was manufacturing.

So, many, if not most, GM plants will have the opportunity to become cool. Indeed, company-wide, GM has been shifting away from the more carbon-intensive primary fuels (coal and oil) toward natural gas. In 1993, coal, coke, and oil comprised almost 40 percent of all the primary (nonelectric) energy used in its facilities. By 1996, that had dropped to under 27 percent. As part of its strategy to reduce carbon dioxide emissions, the company is also expanding its use of cogeneration. For instance, GM's Linden, New Jersey, small-truck plant is installing a 20-MW cogeneration plant.

Just by converting boilers from coal to natural gas at five facilities, General Motors cut its carbon dioxide emissions by 415,000 tons per year.

DOW'S CONTINUOUS ENVIRONMENTAL IMPROVEMENT

Because so many processes are specific to a given industry or even a given company, one of the best approaches for reducing carbon dioxide emissions is to develop a strategy that systematically taps the skill and expertise of your line employees and engineers to take advantage of the large opportunities that exist. The benchmark here is what Ken Nelson was able to achieve when he was energy manager for the Louisiana Division of Dow Chemical and then a consultant to the Department of Energy.

Rather than repeating the full story from the Introduction, I will just highlight the key points. In 1982, Dow's Louisiana Division began a contest to find energy-saving projects with a high return on investment.[5] The first year's results—twenty-seven winners requiring a capital investment of $1.7 million providing an average return on investment of 173 percent—were somewhat surprising. What was astonishing to everyone was that year after year, Dow's engineers kept finding such projects.

Even as fuel prices declined, the savings kept growing. Contest winners increasingly achieved their economic gains through process redesign to improve production yield and capacity. *By 1988, these productivity gains exceeded the energy and environmental gains.*

One might think that after ten years, and nearly 700 projects, the 2,000 employees would be tapped out of ideas. Yet the contests in 1991, 1992, and 1993 each had in excess of one hundred winners with an average return on investment of 300 percent. Total savings to Dow from the projects of those three years exceed $75 million a year.

If Dow, with all its well-trained engineers and a systematic process for identifying opportunities, hadn't finished capturing all its energy-savings opportunities, how likely is it that your company has? The only question is whether or not Ken Nelson's approach can be transferred to other enterprises in completely different lines of business.

I was able to answer that question in 1993 when I became special assistant to the Department of Energy's chief operating officer, the deputy secretary. I brought Nelson on as a consultant to train several of our facilities around the country on Dow's approach.

We held a "return-on-investment" contest. The eighteen winning projects *cost $4.6 million and saved the Department $10.0 million every year,* while avoiding more than 100 tons of low-level radioactive pollution and other kinds of waste. Because of the success of this headquarters-based program, many of the regional operating offices of the Department decided to replicate it. *They funded 260 projects at a cost of $20 million that have been estimated to achieve savings of $90 million a year.*[6]

➡️ **If an organization as diverse and bureaucratic as the U.S. Department of Energy can adopt Dow's approach, any company can.**

For this reason, it's worth examining key features of Dow's contest, which match those of many continuous improvement programs.[7]

Sustained Management Support

Long-term support by management was perhaps the most important reason for the success at Dow, according to Nelson. He notes that while virtually all managers are in favor of reducing waste, saving energy, and increasing productivity, the key is to develop a program that is easy for them to support.

The contest was designed to be easy to run. It did not require a new department, redeployment of people, or a multi-million-dollar budget. All that was required was a committee and a contest. Rather than setting up separate functions, the goal became to use people in their existing positions and have project development and evaluation be a natural part of their jobs.

Similarly, at DOE, the support of the chief operating officer was crucial to our success. At DOE, it is rare that one division manager (assistant secretary) will spend money to reduce the operating costs of another division manager. Our Waste Minimization and Pollution Prevention Executive Board had been languishing since it was chaired by the assistant secretary for environmental management. Reorganizing the board with the Department's COO as the chair and myself as the executive director solved that problem. But once the COO left the Department and I took a job managing one of the Department's divisions, the headquarters-based program slowed dramatically.

Use Objective Evaluation Criteria and Measure Results

The return-on-investment (ROI) calculation is simple and objective. Projects that exceed a certain ROI are funded, those that don't are not.

At Dow, they kept close track of energy and waste costs, as well as yield and other productivity measures. Most winning projects were audited: What gets measured gets improved. The audit occurred after a project has been installed and running for a while. The purpose of the audit was to compare each project's actual cost and performance with the contest values used to justify the project. On the average, projects do perform as expected. Total *audited* savings for 575 projects were over $110 million a year.

At DOE, the ROI approach avoided many problems. One of our divisions had a well-respected pollution prevention program. At one early meeting of the board, the program manager tried to dismiss the ROI contest, saying he had been doing pollution prevention for years and didn't need "head-quarters" trying to improve it. I pointed out that the ROI methodology is very objective: If his program was identifying the projects with the biggest bang for the buck—that is, the highest ROI—then the contest would simply be a way for him to get more money and more recognition. If, on the other hand, his program was not, then the ROI contest would allow him to identify the best projects, saving him more money for less investment. *The ROI contest is profit-maximizing by design*, which is why it is ultimately so successful.

Multifunctional Evaluation Committee

Every program needs a focal point, and the Energy Evaluation Committee was the focal point for the contest at Dow. The committee included representatives from process engineering, economic evaluation, and various production areas. Including a representative from economic evaluation is important because the committee needs someone who knows the procedures for getting projects authorized, a person who works with managers in allocating the division's capital resources. Having a committee avoids creating new levels of hierarchy or bureaucracy. The aim is to work *within* the system, taking advantage of the existing procedures and framework.

The DOE also used a multifunctional team. Having participation from the chief financial officer's staff was critical. They were the most skeptical at the beginning that such large, untapped savings opportunities existed. But once they saw the numbers, the CFO's office became one of the contest's biggest supporters.

Train People

At Dow, a key reason that the results endured—and even improved—was that the contest helped workers get smarter. The contest has intrinsic training benefits. In addition to learning the technical design aspects of a project, many engineers were able to follow their project from the idea stage through preliminary evaluation, formal evaluation, authorization, engineering, construction, and start-up. While developing and implementing projects, they learn how to get through the "system." Along the way, they gain valuable experience in dealing with a variety of departments, disciplines, vendors, other engineers, supervisors, and operators. This develops technical ability, people skills, and self-confidence.

Dow also developed three highly effective means of training its workers to identify high-ROI projects. First, every year the company published a complete list of all projects, with the name of the plant, the people submitting the project, a brief description of the project, and the cost, savings, ROI, and waste reduced.

Second, Dow published a *Waste Elimination Idea Book*. It contains improvement ideas organized by subject (such as pumps, heat exchangers, and distillation). Project ideas were taken from past contests and from work done at other Dow locations.

Third, a Continuous Improvement Workshop was held every year or two starting in the late 1980s. This intensive two-day course gives people practical ideas for improving plant processes. It included analytical, creative, and pragmatic approaches to finding cost-saving projects as well as specific information about various unit operations. One session, "How Winners Think," was based on interviews with Dow's top twelve project generators.

The workshop may be a key reason why the contest was so successful even after ten years. The reason Dow never exhausted the so-called "low-hanging fruit" is that those who were good at finding high return-on-investment projects got better, and those that never knew such projects were possible learned how to identify them and get them funded.

At DOE, we already had dozens of experts in pollution prevention in sites around the country. What we lacked was a systematic approach to funding the best projects that they identified. We solved that problem by bringing in Ken Nelson to train our people in Dow's approach.

ENERGIZING EMPLOYEE SUGGESTIONS

A remarkable, yet disturbing, story on employee suggestions appeared in the July 15, 1998, edition of the *Washington Post*.[8] It began:

Sam, a forklift operator at a tape and adhesive distribution center in San Bernardino, Calif., thinks he was stonewalled by his manager when he suggested a "no-brainer idea": shutting off excess lights and computer systems to save money and energy.

"My foreman acknowledged it [the excess energy used] was a waste," he recalled, "but he said it was just the way the electrical system was set up. He stopped my idea right there."

So Sam, who did not want his full name used, contacted BrainBank Inc., a six-month-old company that serves as a sort of electronic suggestion box, sending unsolicited recommendations from employees back to their companies. BrainBank is part of a growing cluster of contractors that help companies cull feedback from their own workers. . . .

BrainBank solicits suggestions from workers through its website and "offers the ideas to company managers, if they agreed to pass along half of a year's savings to BrainBank." The story later explains, "within weeks of submitting his suggestion, Sam's concept was implemented and his firm was on its way to a little less than $20,000 in annual savings, according to BrainBank. Sam's idea yielded him $7,400. Representatives of the company he worked for declined to comment for this report." Needless to say, BrainBank ended up with some $10,000—half the first year's savings—that the company should have pocketed.

What a sad commentary this story is on the state of affairs in many American companies. The story ends with Alan G. Robinson, a professor at the University of Massachusetts at Amherst, saying that BrainBank "is taking advantage of the shameful tendency of management not to believe employees have anything to tell them." He notes that "employees fear retribution and don't feel comfortable talking to their boss. Most companies don't have a system for listening to employees."

The Labor Department estimates that fewer than 10 percent of U.S. companies have formal suggestion systems. In Japan, however, they are commonplace.[9]

According to the Japan Human Relations Association, the two main subjects for suggestions in Japan are (in order):

- Improvements in one's own work
- Savings in energy, material, and other resources[10]

So, as Dow found out, a suggestion system can be an important part of becoming cool. A typical Japanese employee suggestion involved compressed air used for cleaning a crankshaft. The cleaner blows air for twenty-five seconds to remove cutting waste from oil holes in the crankshaft. The distance between the crankshaft and the tip of the air-blower nozzle was 8 millimeters. The oil holes were just barely being cleaned to their tolerance limit. An employee suggested lengthening the nozzle so that the distance to the oil holes was reduced to 2.5 millimeters. The air blower could now be run for fifteen seconds, and cleanliness was at the middle of the tolerance range. This one suggestion saved 40 percent of the cleaning time and energy, improved the quality of the cleaning process, and cut energy costs by $642 a month.[11] This energy-saving suggestion could have been thought of only by the person working on the machine day in and day out and asking, "How can I improve this?"

Ironically, while the modern suggestion system was taken to a high art in Japan, like many U.S. management practices it was born in America. The Japan Human Relations Association traces the origin of the modern suggestion system to America in 1898. In that year, records show than an Eastman Kodak worker received a prize of $2 "for suggesting that windows be washed to keep the workplaces brighter." A fitting omen—*the first known modern industrial suggestion was how to improve lighting at low cost.*[12]

An employee suggestion system requires tremendous effort and commitment from the supervisors. Managers must see suggestions not as implying poor management by them but rather as strong evidence of their ability to lead. Supervisors have to be trained in the art of stimulating, managing, and evaluating ideas. Line workers, stunted from long years of being ignored, need to be taught a variety of problem-solving skills, including statistical analysis.

Employees should know the cost of the raw material as well as the cost of parts, tools, energy, and office supplies. *Training* magazine reported that at GM's Saturn plant, "one person checks scrap and receives weekly reports on the amount of waste. If the line on the chart is rising, she reminds everyone during a team meeting that they need to be more careful. Since team members know the cost of each part, they know how much money their scrap costs the company."[13]

As a cool manufacturer, you will want your employees to understand every aspect of their job that affects greenhouse gas emissions. Depending on the specific job, this will involve lighting, HVAC, motors, compressed air, steam, fuel choices, cogeneration, and process and product design. Special awards could be given to the employees whose suggestions avoid the greatest emissions of greenhouse gases.

As discussed in Chapter 2, your employees must do more than improve their own operations. If your company is to capture the biggest energy savings and productivity gains, you must improve processes. You don't just want to replace an inefficient motor with an efficient one, you want to know if the motor is oversized or in need of a control system or perhaps entirely superfluous if the process were redesigned.

Seeing such deeper "anomalies" can be much more difficult, according to a 1991 study, "When Do Anomalies Begin?"

> An anomaly in science is an observed fact that is difficult to explain in terms of the existing conceptual framework. Anomalies often point to the inadequacy of the current theory and herald a new one. It is argued here that certain scientific anomalies are recognized only after they are given compelling explanations within a conceptual framework. Before this recognition, the peculiar facts are taken as givens or are ignored in the old conceptual framework.[14]

If the scientific community, which is dedicated to observing the world and explaining it, can ignore observations that undermine its world view, isn't it likely to be common in the business community also?

For many businesses, energy and resource use, scrap, and pollution may be largely neglected. They may feel that high levels of pollution and greenhouse gas emissions are inevitable by-products of industrial activity. For the company to see these deeper *process* flaws, it needs an entirely new conceptual framework, a new orientation. A key goal of this book has been to provide one such world view, cool and lean production, continuous process improvement aimed at reducing greenhouse gas emissions.

One important source of ideas for managers, engineers, and line employees on how to reduce emissions is the success stories from other industries. The following cases touch on some of the key opportunities for process industries.

FOREST PRODUCTS

The forest products industry, which includes paper manufacturing and wood products, is one of the most energy intensive in the manufacturing sector, consuming some 12 percent of total U.S. manufacturing energy. Yet, as a 1996 evaluation of several electric efficiency measures implemented in three paper mills concluded, "Much of the potential for cost-effective efficiency improvement in paper mills remains untapped. . . . Annual energy savings for VSDs [variable-speed drives] ranged from 26 percent to 70 percent; savings for process measures were 50 percent to 60 percent."[15]

For instance, the paper mill's steam boiler has a number of motors, including the feedwater pump and the fans that help regulate the required combustion airflow. Installing VSDs on the feedwater pump reduced energy consumption by 26 percent (142,000 kWh), while installing them on the two fans saved 65 and 70 percent, respectively (a total of 203,000 kWh). An improved refiner for modifying the pulp fiber during the papermaking process cut electricity use by 62 percent (1,280,000 kWh).

Finally, a retrofit was made on an egg carton manufacturing process. Three production lines were consolidated into two by moving the location where color is added to the pulp, which allowed the stock circulation and transfer pumps to be eliminated. Also, a control system was added to turn the remaining pumps on and off, thereby reducing runtime. Energy use was cut by 50 percent (1,123,000 kWh).

This type of energy-saving project is a particularly effective way for forest products companies to reduce their greenhouse gas emissions because they self-generate so much of their power from wood and pulp waste by-products of the manufacturing process. Through steady increases in both the energy efficiency of manufacturing as well as in cogeneration, the paper industry increased its level of self-generation from 36 percent in 1972 to 57 percent in the mid-1990s. The key point is that the industry self-generates with a biomass feedstock that is a zero-carbon or renewable source of energy when derived from a sustainably harvested forest. The self-generation is doubly cool power—renewable and cogeneration combined.

Consider, then, a plant that self-generates 60 percent of its energy and obtains the remaining 40 percent of its energy from grid electricity and combusting natural gas. If it can cut its overall energy use by 20 percent, it will be cutting its purchased power—and hence its greenhouse gas emissions—in half. Since most power boilers and recovery furnaces in U.S. pulp and paper industry plants are twenty to thirty years old, more than half of them will need to be replaced or upgraded over the next five to fifteen years.[16] Chapter 6 already discussed the improvements in cogeneration now available in the marketplace, as well as one that will be introduced soon, biomass gasification that drives an advanced turbine. Coupling this improved cogeneration technology with the energy-efficiency opportunities described throughout the book hold the prospect of seeing a paper mill in a few years that has no net greenhouse gas emissions at all. To achieve that goal, companies should aggressively pursue a number of approaches to reduce electricity, steam, and process energy, as many manufacturers already have.

Georgia-Pacific

Like many manufacturers, Georgia-Pacific had uninsulated steam lines at its plywood plant in Madison, Georgia.[17] This wasted energy and thus occasionally forced the company to buy extra fuel. Normally the plant used wood bark and wood by-products for fuel. Also, the lower temperatures in the steam lines made the drying process less efficient. During the manufacturing process, water-softened pine logs pass through dryers set at 405°F. The uninsulated steam lines to the dryers caused heat loss, resulting in reduced temperature.

Using a software tool called 3E Plus, Georgia-Pacific determined the optimal insulation thickness. It installed two inches of fiberglass insulation on 1,500 feet of steam lines. *This one measure reduced fuel costs by one-third with a six-month payback.* Not only has the project eliminated the plant's dependence on outside fuel, the company now sells excess fuel to a local paper company. "The insulation has allowed us to cut our steam usage by approximately 6,000 pounds per hour," noted Boiler Superintendent Darryl Jackson. "This is equivalent to saving about 18 tons of fuel per day."

The project had a number of other benefits. It increased operating temperatures by 15 percent and maintained the process temperature along the length of the line, resulting in a faster and more efficient plywood veneer process. Yet it required no downtime to install. The upgrade lowered emissions and reduced ash generation. Finally, the insulation makes working around the steam lines much safer for employees by lowering the surface temperature of the pipes from 400°F to 85°F.

> Insulate your steam lines.

Blandin Paper Company

Blandin Paper Company employs some 1,100 workers making paper at its Grand Rapids, Minnesota, plant.[18] The company, which has been making paper at this location since 1902, had annual sales in 1994 of about $300 million. A 1994 energy audit uncovered significant heat losses in gaseous stack emissions from paper drying and other processes. With the help of Minnesota

Power's Industrial Conservation Pilot Program, the company installed a heat recovery system that reclaims the heat from effluent water and other liquids for a variety of uses throughout the plant.

The system eliminated the use of 654 million pounds of steam a year, which in turn eliminated more than 740 million cubic feet of natural gas, providing $1,638,000 in fuel savings and $77,000 in reduced costs for boiler feedwater makeup treatment. The project also produced a net annual electric savings of $91,000 (2.3 million kWh) resulting from lower electrical use in steam production. Total savings exceeded $1.8 million per year, compared to a total project cost of $2,168,000. Minnesota Power covered $833,000 of the project cost, which brought the payback to under one year.

This project won Blandin the 1994 award for energy management and innovation from the American Forest and Paper Association. It cut annual carbon dioxide emissions by 37,000 tons, NOx emissions by 200 tons, and carbon monoxide emissions by 14 tons. Blandin's product costs dropped by $4.20 a ton.

Bowater Incorporated

Bowater Inc. manufactures pulp, newsprint, and coated magazine paper.[19] The company realized that it was venting low-pressure steam into the atmosphere from its seven thermomechanical pumping (TMP) refiner lines at its mill in Columbia, South Carolina. The refiners have large counter-rotating disks driven by huge motors to macerate wood chips that are injected through the center of the disks. These green wood chips are half water and half fiber, and the water flashes to steam as the fibers are separated, processed, and pumped to the machines that convert it to newsprint and coated magazine stock.

To convert its low-pressure steam to useful power, the company installed a mechanical vapor recompression heat pump, which converts the low-pressure, 250°F steam to a higher pressure, 470°F steam that can be used in the paper-drying operations. The $1.5 million heat pump system generates annual energy savings of $1 million, for a 1.5-year payback. The system generates 60 to 90 percent of the steam used by the dryers of the company's largest papermaking machine.

The system has many other benefits. It eliminates the noise of the venting steam. Some 200 gallons of turpentine are recovered daily, reducing atmospheric emissions and providing an extra source of revenue. Also, Bowater now saves 100 gallons of water per minute that had been escaping to the air as steam, saving another $144 a day.

METAL PROCESSING

The companies that produce metals such as steel and aluminum, and those that forge those metals into useful products, consume a great quantity of energy. They too have a large opportunity for reducing energy use and carbon dioxide emissions through process improvement, heat recovery, cogeneration, new technologies, and upgrades to motors and steam systems. Indeed, when the Alliance to Save Energy, leading corporations, and the Department of Energy launched their public-private initiative "Steam Challenge" in 1998 to help save steam energy, they chose as a site one of the largest steel mills in the country, Bethlehem Steel's Burns Harbor facility in Indiana.

Burns Harbor Steel Mill

The Burns Harbor facility is located on 1,700 acres on the shores of Lake Michigan. Built in 1962, the plant is Bethlehem Steel's largest and most efficient plant. Some 6,000 workers produce more than 5 million tons of steel sheet and plate products for manufacturers of automotive products, machinery, and appliances. The facility has a *daily* electricity, natural gas, and potable water bill of $300,000. Naturally, reducing energy costs has always been a priority.[20]

Because its electricity use is so high, the plant makes much of its electricity on site with steam turbines. The steam that drives the turbines is generated in boilers that are primarily fueled with coke oven and blast furnace gases, which are by-products of the steelmaking process. When the by-product gases are not available, the boilers are also fueled with natural gas. The system heats lake water for feedwater, using low-pressure steam. The plant lacked sufficient generating capacity to consume all of the blast furnace gases during an outage of one of the turbines, which caused by-product gases and their energy to be released into the atmosphere and forced the plant to purchase extra power, incurring large demand and energy charges.

Since Turbine #5 was due for a maintenance overhaul and already had an oversized generator, Bethlehem Steel targeted the 42-MW turbine for an upgrade. The company rebuilt the turbine to take advantage of the latest steam-path technology to control steam flow losses and optimize capture of the steam's available energy. The redesign also used some of the warm condenser cooling-water exhaust stream as boiler feedwater in place of the lake water (which is 20°F cooler). This in turn made it possible to take the low-pressure steam previously used to heat the lake water and inject it instead into the redesigned turbine, significantly increasing the capacity and efficiency of the system.

The upgraded turbine now has a capacity of 48 MW under normal operating conditions. If another turbine has an outage, some of the excess steam is piped to the modified turbine, which can now generate up to 57 MW.

The modifications to the turbine and other system improvements generate *annual savings of 40 million kWh of electricity and 85,000 million BTUs of natural gas with a simple payback of just over one year.* The increase in turbine efficiency saves $1.3 million, while the increase in turbine capacity saves $1.45

million from reduced demand charges. Avoiding temporary power costs when other turbines are down saves $270,000. Finally, switching to condenser water reduced natural gas costs $280,000. Total energy savings come to about $3.4 million annually, and yet the cost of the upgrade was only $3.3 million more than a standard maintenance overhaul. Beyond the energy and cost savings, the improvements reduced high-temperature water discharges and decreased emissions of coke oven and blast furnace gases.

The technology used in this steel plant could be used in almost any industrial application where steam turbines are used to generate power on site. A key lesson is that when a turbine is scheduled for an overhaul, opportunities to improve system performance should be examined, as should opportunities to use waste-heat streams. This strategy of matching heat sources and heat sinks through heat exchangers is called *pinch technology*. It can lead to substantial energy savings.

Burns Harbor also implemented a motor upgrade that proves even the largest of process industries have huge energy saving opportunities in motor systems. A key part of the plant's steelmaking process is blowing oxygen into the basic oxygen furnace (BOF), creating high temperatures and chemical reactions that oxidize impurities in the metal and convert the iron to steel. Burns Harbor has three BOFs, each of which can make some 300 tons of molten steel in thirty minutes. Bethlehem worked with General Conservation Corporation (GCC), an energy conservation project specialist, to identify a large energy savings opportunity at BOF #3.

A 7,000-hp fan removes the gases generated when oxygen is blown into BOF #3. The furnace's heat cycle takes about forty-five minutes, and it has idle periods of varying length. The fan was operated continuously at 1,200 rpm, with variations in ventilation requirements achieved by modulating inlet dampers—a classic waste of energy. A study in the late 1980s by GCC revealed that the fan could operate in the range of 960 to 1075 rpm during operation and 560 rpm during idling. GCC concluded that replacing the oversized, inefficient fan motor run at constant speed with a correctly sized, efficient one run by a variable-frequency drive (VFD) would cut energy use in half.

Bethlehem was reluctant to make the upgrade for several reasons. The existing system, though inefficient, did run smoothly; VFDs were then new to the market and this fan was a critical piece of hardware; and the company lacked the needed funds to complete the project. For those reasons, GCC agreed to fund the project entirely and receive payment from half of the energy savings. Also, GCC would assume all the risk: GCC would maintain ownership of the equipment (with Bethlehem having the option to purchase it after seven years, have it removed, or extend the contract) and provide an override capability that would enable Bethlehem to bypass the VFD and almost instantly return the system to its previous operating mode. Monthly energy readings would determine GCC's payment.

As projected, the upgrade cut the energy consumption for the system in half, saving 15.5 million kWh a year or $620,000. The project's total capital cost came to $1,225,000. Since Burns Harbor put up no money, they started saving $310,000 a year with an instant payback. GCC made its money back in four years. Besides the energy and costs savings, "the modifications significantly decreased noise levels in the furnace area; many system components, such as the bearings and fan wheel, achieved longer lifetimes; and the system's tolerance to slight imbalances was improved because fan speed was reduced, thus reducing maintenance and downtime and increasing production flexibility. Finally, with the VFD's soft-start capability, the effect of motor start-up on the Burns Harbor Facility's power grid has been considerably reduced." Bethlehem was very pleased with the outcome and ultimately extended GCC's contract. The steam turbine and fan motor upgrades together reduced carbon dioxide emissions at Burns Harbor by 68,000 tons a year.

Decatur Foundry

Decatur Foundry in Decatur, Illinois, employed seventy-five people to produce 1,000 tons of iron castings per month in 1993. The foundry specializes in castings for electric-motor frames and parts as well as pump components. In response to environmental regulatory constraints and pollution prevention initiatives, foundries are moving away from quick-drying coatings based on organic solvents to environmentally safer but slower drying water-based coatings. This change has created a bottleneck in the production process of many firms.[21]

For Decatur, the problem was particularly acute because its customers, such as utilities and manufacturers of products containing its castings, were moving to just-in-time inventory systems and expected their suppliers to provide short-cycle responses to orders. Decatur had an average run of only ten to twenty-five parts on any particular mold and sometimes had orders for individual items, so it was crucial that molds be formed and made ready for casting as quickly as possible. The company needed a faster drying process.

Working with the Electric Power Research Institute and the local utility, Decatur decided to replace its electric-resistance ovens with an infrared/forced-air unit manufactured by BKG Finishing Systems in Minneapolis, Minnesota. The old ovens warmed the coatings indirectly by warming the air in contact with the mold's surface; the new infrared system radiates heat directly to the surface of the mold. Also, the infrared system needs no warm-up time, so it can be powered up only when needed.

The annual energy costs for mold drying dropped by a factor of four, from $12,000 to $3,000, a savings of 120,000 kWh per year (and of the 27 tons of carbon dioxide associated with the production of that electricity). The payback for the $12,000 system was a little over a year. It was installed in three working days without interrupting production.

Like many energy-efficiency improvements, the system has numerous nonenergy benefits. Less heat is emitted to the surrounding area, creating a more comfortable work environment, and with fewer hot surfaces, workers are less likely to be burned. Also, the infrared drying unit is considerably smaller than the previous dryer, freeing up valuable floor space.

The new system has precision instrumentation that allows a greater degree of control throughout the drying process. The net result has been a reduction in mold failure rates, an increase in product quality, and a dramatic decrease in drying time of 85 percent. The old drying process had been a bottleneck that forced extensive idle time for workers waiting for the mold to dry, which created large amounts of overtime wages. The new process has improved product flow, reducing wage costs, and enabling Decatur Foundry to offer a very competitive turnaround time from initial bid to delivery of finished product. Decatur has added two new lines, increased sales 40 percent from 1993 to 1997, and added ten employees during that time.

REFRIGERATION

As with steam, many process industries use a considerable amount of refrigeration. And as with steam, large opportunities exist for cost-effective savings. Probably the best example of that is the Sealtest ice cream plant in Framingham, Massachusetts, which was on the brink of extinction in 1989. The Chicago-based conglomerate Kraft General Foods had been closing its oldest and least profitable plants. The Framingham plant, which makes six types of frozen desserts (20 million gallons a year), had been built in the early 1960s, making it one of the oldest—and least efficient—of Kraft's plants. To cuts costs, the plant had already gone to a four-day work week, but more cuts were necessary. If the plant had closed, 200 jobs would have been lost.[22]

The plant manager, Joseph Crowley, got help financing a sixteen-day on-site audit of the plant's energy needs from the state's Office of Energy Resources. The audit identified $3.6 million in cost-effective efficiency improvements. A senior Kraft executive later told then Governor William Weld and former U.S. Secretary of Energy James Watkins that many senior Kraft executives thought the project was impossible. Like many corporate executives, they were unaware of the amazing opportunities afforded by energy-efficient technology and design. Kraft went forward with the energy upgrades only after the local utility, Boston Edison, offered to pay for most of the $3.6 million project. The upgrade was expected to reduce energy use $350,000 in the first year of operation and cut energy costs from 7.5 cents to 5.5 cents per gallon, "a major competitive edge," in the words of a company spokesman.

Workers from all the plant's divisions were included in implementation. The original audit had had very little input from the plant's workers. As a result, the plant's engineers were resistant to the proposed changes, which included replacing the entire refrigeration system. In response, Crowley put together an implementation team that included the plant engineer, the refrigeration engineer, the chief electrician, operating personnel, plant management, and utility representatives. The team decided to modify the existing system, rather than replace it.

The project had a "phenomenal effect on our employees," according to Crowley. It created a feeling that every plant employee had a personal stake in its success. After learning that the efficiency upgrades would include a computerized refrigeration control system, one foreman quietly signed up for a night-school computer course to help him prepare to operate the new system. While some of the improvements were specialized to the needs of an ice cream manufacturer, others—such as using waste heat from the compressors to provide hot water for the plant's daily washdowns—could be used in a variety of industries. The upgrade also saved a million gallons of water a year.

The heat recovery system cost $250,000 a year and was not part of the original utility-supported project, since it saves fossil fuels rather than electricity. Kraft covered its cost. The full project, which included a motor and lighting upgrade, greatly exceeded expectations and won the Association of Energy Engineers Project of the Year Award for 1992. It ultimately saved 6 million kWh a year and lowered the company's energy bill by one-third. Even if Boston Edison had not put up a penny, the energy savings alone would have paid for the system in eight years, but the system had much bigger nonenergy benefits.

The productivity gains were enormous. The improved refrigeration and air handling system were much more efficient. The system blew more air and colder air, and it defrosted the air handler faster. As a result, the time required to harden the ice cream was cut in half. *The overall result was a 10 percent across-the-board increase in productivity,* which in the long term will be worth more to the company than the energy savings, says Crowley. In other words, the system really paid for itself in just a few years. In some sense, the productivity gains are far greater, considering that the alternative might have been a shutdown of the entire plant. In 1993, Kraft sold the plant to Good Humor, which is part of Unilever. Subsequently, the plant expanded production and added manufacturing jobs, employing as many as 250 people during peak times.

The project turned an aging plant into a highly competitive state-of-the-art facility. A team effort—management, workers, the state government, and the local utility—led to process improvement that increased productivity, raised competitiveness, and sustained and increased jobs, while saving electricity and water, reducing air pollution, and even eliminating the use of chlorofluorocarbons in the refrigeration process. This was truly a cool process improvement.

SAVINGS FROM "PINCH" ANALYSIS

As a number of the previous examples show, the process industries tend to have large opportunities to recapture or cascade waste heat throughout their operations. One common opportunity for energy savings occurs in any industrial process that requires both heating and cooling of the process stream. This straightforward change, called "pinch" analysis, can track the heat flow, find the best configuration for process equipment and heat exchangers, and cut energy costs (and emissions) dramatically with rapid payback.

Pinch analysis should be considered for chemical plants, food processing plants, pulp and paper mills, or textile plants. Case studies of such process redesign in those industries have found savings from $31,000 to over $4 million, with an average payback of 1.5 years.[23]

Oil refineries are a particularly good opportunity for a pinch analysis because they use many types of heating and cooling throughout the operation. The Department of Energy partnered with Planetec Utility Services Company and Energy Concepts Company to develop a unique waste heat–powered fuel-recovery system, Waste Heat Ammonia Absorption Refrigeration Plant (WHAARP). In mid-1997, WHAARP began operation at the 30,000 barrel per day refinery in Denver, Colorado, run by Ultramar Diamond Shamrock.[24]

WHAARP operates on the same principle as the absorption chillers described in Chapter 6 that take waste heat (such as from a cogeneration unit) and use it to run an air conditioning system. WHAARP incorporates a number of advanced heat exchangers. At the Denver plant, pinch analysis had revealed the opportunity to use low temperature waste heat (at +295°F) to achieve subzero refrigeration temperatures (–30°F). WHAARP also provides +26°F cooling for intermediate applications such as precooling air and fluids at key points in the refining process.

The WHAARP's ammonia absorption sub-zero cooling is applied to the refinery's fuel-gas system to condense some 200 barrels per day of liquid hydrocarbon products, such as gasoline, for subsequent sale. The refinery uses fuel gas in process equipment such as heaters and boilers. A plant-wide energy audit had determined that excess fuel gas containing some salable petroleum products was being produced in the summer months and flared.

The system saves almost 2 million kWh a year, worth $80,000. The 73,000 barrels per year of recovered liquid increases annual refinery profits by almost $900,000. As we have seen again and again, the productivity gains—here a higher yield—exceed the energy savings by a factor of ten. In addition, the project reduced plant NOx emissions by some 200 tons. WHAARP costs $2.3 million, a two-year payback, though for this demonstration a Department of Energy grant of $760,000 reduced the simple payback to about one and a half years. The WHAARP unit uses less crude oil to produce the same amount of product and uses one-tenth the energy of conventional refrigeration units. It can be used in any industry that has simultaneous heating and cooling or to generate district cooling for space conditioning of nearby buildings.

The WHAARP unit was actually the second phase of a four-phase "Master

Efficiency Plan" for Ultramar Diamond Shamrock that was developed in partnership with the DOE and Planetec Utility Services Company. The first phase involved more than a dozen low-cost or no-cost measures including upgrades to steam traps, the use of premium efficiency motors, and improvements to selected heat exchangers. The third and fourth phases, which have not been completed, include an 8-MW cogeneration system, a comprehensive steam system upgrade, the use of variable speed drives, and increased waste heat recovery.

These upgrades, when completed, will cut the plant's $9.6 million utility bill in half and increase yield by $5.17 million a year, for a total annual energy and productivity benefit of $10 million. The Master Efficiency Plan will cost $23.4 million, resulting in a 2.3-year payback. Carbon dioxide emissions per unit product will drop by one-third to one-half. So even an oil refinery, if it adopts a comprehensive approach, can become cool.

Chapter

BEYOND BENCHMARKING

Although we gave a boost to the benchmarking industry with our previous book . . . we now feel that benchmarking is a waste of time for managers that understand lean thinking. . . .

Our earnest advice to lean firms today is simple: To hell with your competitors; compete against *perfection* by identifying all activities that are *muda* [waste] and eliminating them.

—James Womack and Daniel Jones, *Lean Thinking*[1]

Most firms today do not qualify as completely cool. The majority of the case studies in this book are about companies that have performed one task in a cool way, such as designing a cool building or making a cool factory. Rare is the company that has combined all of these cool strategies sufficiently to reduce greenhouse emissions continuously throughout all of their operations (though 3M, Toyota, and DuPont are well on their way).

Moreover, to be truly cool requires looking at more than merely the carbon dioxide released by your company's energy use or the energy consumed by your products (as Toyota has). It also requires looking at the carbon dioxide released in producing the materials consumed by your company—the "embodied carbon dioxide." Just as you can "decarbonize" the electricity you purchase—by choosing cogeneration or renewable energy that generates little or no carbon emissions—so too can you decarbonize the materials and other goods your company purchases. *For many companies, the embodied carbon dioxide exceeds the carbon dioxide released by the energy they consume.*

Since so many strategies to reduce greenhouse gas emissions also save money, once you have gained expertise in becoming cool, you should help your employees, suppliers, and community become cool. This chapter examines some of the decarbonizing strategies used by the coolest companies and communities.

The key lessons in this chapter are:

(1) Cool companies need to reduce the carbon dioxide emissions generated in the production of the materials they purchase—the "embodied carbon"—by, for example, reducing virgin material consumption.

(2) Once you have gained expertise in reducing the greenhouse gas emissions in your buildings and factories, use your expertise to help reduce the emissions of your employees, suppliers, and communities.

COOL CARPETS FROM INTERFACE

For many manufacturers, the energy used to create and transport the raw materials they buy (the so-called "embodied energy") exceeds the energy they purchase. One of the corporate benchmarks in understanding and reducing embodied energy is Interface, Inc., a leading manufacturer of carpet and carpet fiber. Interface, which has seen its sales grow from $600 million in 1993 to $1.1 billion in 1997, is committed to some innovative goals. In the words of their chairman, Ray Anderson, who is co-chair of the President's Council on Sustainable Development:

> At Interface, we seek to become the first sustainable corporation in the world, and, following that, the first restorative company. It means creating the technologies of the future—kinder, gentler technologies that emulate nature's systems. I believe that's where we will find the right model. . . .
>
> We look forward to the day when our factories have no smokestacks and no effluents. If successful, we'll spend the rest of our days harvesting yesteryear's carpets, recycling old petrochemicals into new materials, and converting sunlight into energy. There will be zero scrap going into landfills and zero emissions into the biosphere. Literally, our company will grow by cleaning up the world, not by polluting or degrading it.[2]

This is an ambitious dream, but those who are skeptical should first read the company's singular *Sustainability Report.* Published in 1997, it is one of the most detailed analyses by any company on its inputs and outputs, as well as its strategies for minimizing both. For instance, we learn that *the embodied energy in the raw material that Interface uses to make 25 million square meters of carpet tile a year exceeds the process energy needed to manufacture that carpet tile by a factor of twelve.* So when Interface Flooring Systems made waste-minimizing process improvements that saved 2.5 million pounds of nylon from being purchased in the first place, the embodied energy of the unconsumed nylon equaled the energy used by all their manufacturing and administrative facilities. Waste minimization is cool, which is the main reason Interface has pursued it so diligently.

Interface's goal is to be a "zero waste company." That includes scrap, one of the traditional meanings of waste, "but it also includes what we don't do right the first time—a misdirected shipment, an incorrect invoice, a defective product." In other words, Interface defines waste the same way as Toyota (see Chapter 2).

Anderson realized that he could not achieve his ambitious goals alone. So he began to assemble a team of the top experts in energy, environment, and sustainability, starting in the summer of 1994 with John Picard, president of Environmental Enterprises in Los Angeles. Picard is an expert in green design and electronic commerce who was helping Southern California Gas Company build the Energy Resource Center. The center, which makes extensive use of daylighting, including sun-tracking skylights, beats California's strict Title 24 building code by 45 percent.[3] It also showcases advanced technologies from companies such as Carrier Corporation and features one of Interface's first Evergreen carpet leases (discussed below).

At the same time, Anderson understood that becoming a sustainable corporation would require harnessing the skills and experience of his 6,300 employees. So he launched QUEST (Quality Utilizing Employee Suggestions and Teamwork). QUEST teams operate in every Interface plant and division. From 1994 through 1998, they have cut costs by $76 million. Those savings are paying for early investments in cool power and other sustainable technologies, such as solar energy.

For instance, Interface Architectural Resources recycled enough concrete waste to cut their total waste 54 percent by weight. Interface Flooring Systems in the United States and Canada cut the weight of standard tile backing by up to 15 percent, saving materials and energy while improving quality. This was achieved by "a systems approach to material and energy efficiency," as Interface's Mike Bennett told me. The company used an integrated design where "everything was on the table" and the goal was to simultaneously minimize cost and environmental impact.

The company is also "redesigning its processes and products into cyclical material flows where 'waste equals food.'" Guilford of Maine, an Interface company that manufactures most of the fabric used by U.S. office systems furniture, is completing a transition from virgin polyester to 100 percent recycled fiber made from PET (polyethylene terephthalate), which comes from post-consumer soda bottles. This cuts the consumption of nonrenewable materials, reducing the energy needed to process oil into polyester (the embodied energy) and reducing landfill waste. Recycling a million pounds of polyester provides an energy savings equivalent to 4,000 barrels of oil.

Interface has taken the ultimate step in waste minimization, which is to redesign commerce itself. The company notes that "the key to resource efficiency is a shift from thinking of products as things to understanding products as a means to deliver a service to the customer." The services that customers want from flooring systems include "color, texture, warmth, beauty, acoustics, flexibility, comfort under foot, cleanliness, safety and healthier indoor air." In order to "transform a durable commercial product (carpet tiles) into a service," Interface introduced the remarkable Evergreen Lease:

> Whereas carpet tiles are usually sold and installed, Interface has implemented a program to lease the services of the carpets to the building owner. As carpet tiles wear out and are replaced, the old ones would be broken down and remanufactured into new tiles as part of the lease fee. The customer would not pay an installation cost, only a monthly fee for constantly fresh-looking and functional carpeting. Over time, the amount of raw materials used would drop, but employment would increase while saving the customer money and providing a superior product. As in nature, the product becomes part of a cycle, either decomposing or breaking down into parts or molecules to become "food" in an organic cycle, or being synthetically broken down into a technical nutrient for a new product.

This, in turn, means the company must design and create its products with components that will retain their value when they return rather than just when they leave the factory. That is one of the goals of Interface Research Center. Amory Lovins, Hunter Lovins, and Paul Hawken identify this strategy of turning a product into a service as a key part of the transition to "Natural Capitalism," in their book of the same name.[4] A number of other companies are pursuing this strategy, including Carrier (see the accompanying boxed text).

In their effort to be a leading cool company, Interface has launched a new initiative in which they are "treating all fossil fuel energy as waste that is to be eliminated through efficiencies and shifts to renewable energy sources." We have already seen how one of their divisions, Prince Street Technologies in Georgia, used daylighting to cut energy use and saw worker's compensation cases drop *by more than a factor of twenty* (Chapter 4). Their Bentley Mills plant in California is installing a 109-kW photovoltaic system, one of the largest commercial PV systems in the world (Chapter 6).

Interface Europe/Asia-Pacific found huge savings through smarter layout of their new Shanghai facility. By reducing friction through the use of large

Cool Carrier

Carrier Corporation is the world's largest air conditioning company. As Carrier's Rick Fedrizzi told me, the company is "experimenting on ways to redesign commerce." Carrier would maintain ownership of an air conditioning system and lease back to the customer the service: "cool, clean, comfortable, conditioned air."[5]

The entertainment company DreamWorks SKG became one of the first to lease comfort rather than buy air-conditioners for its 350,000-square-foot, five-building animation campus in Glendale, California. John Picard helped arrange this deal, and Sempra Energy Solutions, an energy management company, financed, built, owns, and manages the entire energy system, including an on-site central plant for heating and air conditioning that uses Carrier equipment.

DreamWorks pays a monthly lease fee for conditioned air that meets its specifications. This financial arrangement takes the cost of the energy system out of the capital budget, saving DreamWorks a good deal of money that it can use for making movies.

Also, Sempra will make investments that minimize costs over the entire lifetime of the lease, as opposed to the two-year payback companies like DreamWorks normally make. As Sempra's Michael Dochterman told me, "My goal is to provide highly reliable energy services that enhance my customers' productivity at the lowest price per square foot." Sempra will make money through energy-efficiency investments with paybacks as long as fifteen years, which allows them to truly minimize energy use and costs at DreamWorks.

Carrier is part of United Technologies, a $25 billion company that also makes fuel cells (as well as Pratt & Whitney engines and Otis elevators). United Technologies has learned from the energy-saving efforts of its smaller divisions and has begun to make commitments to constrain carbon dioxide emissions company-wide. In an October 1998 speech, Chairman and CEO George David cited examples from his company's divisions and said, "I recite them for the straightforward purpose of being persuasive that we can be efficient, much, much more efficient in both our energy production and in the operation of equipment consuming that energy."

pipes and small motors, as opposed to the standard practice of small pipes and large motors, *they slashed pumping horsepower from 95 to 7.* The slightly higher first cost paid for itself in energy savings *in under a month.* This stunning drop of more than 90 percent in pumping energy is possible only with a

very proactive design strategy in which energy and environmental considerations are integrated into the design of an entire factory from the very
beginning.

Interface Flooring Systems of Canada, with only some seventy employees,
has achieved some of the company's most astonishing results. In 1995, it used
3.6 kWh of electricity and 0.6 cubic meters of natural gas to produce a square
yard of carpet. By the end of 1998, those numbers had dropped to 1.7 kWh
and 0.18 cubic meters. And 25 percent of that electricity was from certified
100 percent renewable power from Ontario Hydro. In other words, *within a
three-year period, IFS of Canada had cut carbon dioxide emissions per unit of
product by more than 50 percent.*

I asked Rahumathulla Marikkar, the company's technical manager, how
they had achieved such a remarkable result. His answer provides crucial
lessons for every company seeking to become cool. First, he explained how
valuable Ray Anderson's leadership has been. He "gave us tough emissions
targets" and a "structure for action."

Second, Marikkar noted that a key reason the company achieved such
big savings is that as technical manager for the company, he is in charge
of *both* manufacturing process and the environment. As a result, there aren't
two different divisions fighting each other every time a decision must
be made. The company could take an integrated approach to process redesign.

Third, Marikkar explained that his company pursued *all* of the standard
energy-saving measures. They upgraded lighting, improved HVAC, made
extensive use of waste heat recovery, increased the efficiency of compressed
air, and improved motor systems. In other words, they used every cool strategy in the book, and they were rewarded with the expected productivity gains.
For instance, installing motor controls on their tufting machine allowed them
to cut energy use while increasing output.

Fourth, they redesigned processes. By incorporating printing into the tufting process (so that in some sense they were embroidering their carpets), the
company eliminated a number of energy- and waste-intensive steps: dye
printing, using steam to fix the dyes on the fabric, spraying high-pressure
water to wash away the gum that held the dye, vacuuming to suck out most
of the water from the fabric, and heating the fabric in a gas-fired oven to
remove the rest of the water. Not only did this process redesign save a tremendous amount of energy, it helped the company *reduce its water use from
120,000 gallons a month to about 10,000—within one year.* The local water
utility was so surprised by the rapid reduction it sent someone out to see if
the meter was broken.

Fifth, the company began keeping a variety of energy-related measurements. They tracked total energy use per month; peak load per month; gas
and electricity use per unit product; total BTUs per unit product; and "sustainable energy cost" per unit product, which is essentially a measure of envi-

ronmental impact (including carbon dioxide emissions). *As always, what gets measured gets improved.*

Sixth, Marikkar noted that when the company started its energy-saving efforts, employees were skeptical. He began to believe that "if employees do not see the benefits of energy conservation for themselves, we will not be suc- cessful at the company." So they began a program to educate employees about energy use and to help them reduce energy use in their own homes. The company circulated a memo offering to provide free audits and subsidized retrofits to employees interested in reducing their home energy bills. Interface hired experts to check homes for heating loss, fix leaks, do caulking, and provide cost-benefit calculations for retrofits that required buying new materials, such as windows or lighting. The company also subsidized specific retrofits, such as insulation for ducting and hot water heaters. Some employees saved as much as 20 percent of their energy bill, which was worth hundreds of dollars a year. (More on how your company can help your employees reduce their home energy bills later in this chapter.)

As remarkable as its achievements are, Interface Flooring Systems of Canada is committed to continuous improvement. *They have committed to 100 percent sustainable energy—zero carbon dioxide emissions—by 2002.*

Interface's goals may seem extremely ambitious, but because of them Interface is well on its way to becoming one of the coolest companies in the world. By designing efficiency into its products and processes, Interface has gone beyond benchmarking in its ability to eliminate waste.

Until you are a leader, you will need benchmarks (such as the case studies in this book) to know what is possible. After you become the leader, everyone will follow you.

COOL XEROX COPIERS

The coolest companies, like Interface, do not merely think "cradle to grave" when designing their products and services. They think cradle to cradle, or cradle to reincarnation: remanufacturing a product rather than having the consumer just toss it away. According to a 1984 *Technology Review* article:

> Remanufacturing is an industrial process in which worn-out products are restored to like-new condition. . . . In a factory environment, a discarded product is completely disassembled. Usable parts are cleaned, refurbished, and put into inventory. Then the new product is reassembled from both old and, where necessary, new parts to produce a unit fully equivalent—and sometimes superior—in performance and expected lifetime to the original new product. In contrast, a repaired or rebuilt product normally retains its identity, and only those parts that have failed or are badly worn are replaced or serviced.[6]

The idea itself is decades old. Remanufacturing of automobiles on a significant scale dates back at least to 1929, when watchmaker Albert S. Holzwasser formed Arrow Automotive Industries Inc. to remanufacture automobile parts.

The typical remanufactured product keeps about 85 percent of the original components (by weight), creating significant environmental advantages: Remanufacturing is estimated to use one-fifth the energy and one-tenth the raw materials needed to make a product from scratch. Remanufacturing has another advantage common to many clean production measures: It is labor-intensive. Junking a product and manufacturing a new one from scratch is capital-, resource-, and energy-intensive. With remanufacturing, workers are needed to disassemble a product; inspect it; repair, replace, or upgrade parts; and then reassemble it. Human brainpower and labor replace resource use.

Designing products to be returned by the customer for remanufacturing has a competitive advantage:[7]

Manufacturers can see first hand the types of failures that are actually occurring, and incorporate this information in future products, thereby improving quality.

—E. Thomas Morehouse, Jr., "Design for Maintainability," 1992

The feedback of seeing products at the end of their life cycle will help the designers at the start of the next product life cycle.

Xerox is a leader in remanufacturing, offering the service for many parts in its copiers: electric motors, power supplies, photoreceptors, and aluminum drums.[8] The company now recycles more than 1 million parts a year, for replacement components and new equipment. Xerox's Copy and Print Cartridge Return Program, launched in 1991, achieved a return rate of 65 percent in 1996, diverting some 1,200 tons of material from landfill to useful product. In 1995, the company launched its Toner Container Return Program. The percentage of containers returned for reuse rose from 15 percent at the start of 1996 to more than 35 percent by the end of the year, saving more than 1,000 tons. Xerox's leadership role was driven in part by customers, as the company explained in a case history:

> Recognizing customer concerns about disposable products, Xerox has developed procedures for retrieving and recycling customer-replaceable copy cartridges. The company has now established design standards for its future products, including copy cartridges and toner containers, that provide an integrated approach to extended life, reduced cost, recycling, and

remanufacturing compatibility. Customers participate in partnership with Xerox, returning copy cartridges.[9]

Xerox's actions were also driven by a desire to improve the bottom line.
As Paul Allaire, Xerox's chairman and CEO, has said, "There are good reasons
to protect the Earth. . . . It's the safest and surest way to long-term profitability." In 1995, Xerox's recycling and remanufacturing efforts created savings in
raw materials, labor, and waste disposal of $300 million to $400 million. The
company recognizes that "significant financial opportunities exist which outweigh the environmental aspects of this business." As part of its overall Total
Quality Environmental Management plan, Xerox has developed a strategy it
calls "asset management—the management of products and inventory to
minimize their environmental impact at all stages of the product life-cycle,
particularly end-of-life." Because asset management is a complex process
requiring "the integration of design, engineering, and re-manufacturing,"
Xerox created a cross-functional Asset Management Quality Improvement
Team.

The team set up a program that has trained over 1,000 design engineers in
remanufacturing. Those engineers can now work up front with the design
teams so that the remanufacturing capability is built into the product delivery process more explicitly and is ready at product launch. Xerox engineers
are taking a variety of steps in the design process to facilitate and improve
remanufacturing. They are standardizing designs so more parts can be used
in a wider variety of products. Remanufacturing lines were put in parallel
with new product lines to match their level of quality. And Xerox has brought
its suppliers into the design process in order to maximize opportunities for
remanufacturing.

The company has learned to harvest the maximum amount of value in the
returned equipment. The best is when a piece of equipment (typically one
used for demonstration) needs only to be cleaned or refurbished. Next best is
a good quality return that can be remanufactured or made good as new with
some component replacement and repainting. Then comes a return that
needs to be disassembled and stripped down to reuse the individual components (often after some treatment). Finally, if equipment or components cannot be reused, the recyclable materials, such as aluminum and glass, can be
recovered.

Rank Xerox, the company's European affiliate, has found that over 60,000
of its customers have been willing to buy a remanufactured copier. Indeed,
demand for these recycled copiers outstrips supply by about 50 percent. Rank
Xerox's Asset Management Center at Venray, in the Netherlands (together
with its satellite operations), employs 400 people and has an annual turnover
of nearly $200 million. It takes back 80,000 copiers a year (two-thirds of the
number that reach the end of their useful lives). Three-quarters are remanu-

factured and the rest are taken apart for reuse or recycling. In 1995, asset recovery allowed Rank Xerox to avoid $80 million of raw material and component purchases. Given how energy-intensive it is to process raw materials into components, this represents a considerable reduction in embodied energy.

Allaire asserts, "The environment is a business issue of strategic importance and Xerox must take the lead." In turn, Jim MacKenzie, Director of Corporate Environmental Health and Safety, has noted that while the company's primary driving force is responding to customers and regulatory requirements, "we are not always creating designs to satisfy our customers now, but to anticipate the future customer requirements and business strategies." This has driven the company to take a very proactive approach, as explained in its 1996 Environment, Health & Safety Report:

> At Xerox, all waste is believed to result from an inefficient product, material or process with negative impacts on the environment, customers, employees and surrounding communities. Often, non-hazardous waste is not controlled by law; regardless, Xerox has targeted all waste with its corporate goal of producing "Waste-Free Products from Waste-Free Factories." Waste-Free initiatives worldwide have resulted in products and processes being retooled and designed to eliminate inefficiencies.

We have seen the beginnings of waste-free products: remanufactured toners, cartridges, and copiers. Xerox initiated its Waste-Free Factory program in 1993. Each factory is to achieve the following goals (compared to its individual baseline):

- Decrease municipal, hazardous, and chemical waste by 90 percent.
- Decrease air emissions by 90 percent.
- Decrease water discharges by 50 percent.
- Increase the utilization of post-consumer materials to 25 percent of material purchases
- Increase energy efficiency to within 10 percent of each facility's theoretical optimum.

Xerox's factories have been performing annual self-assessments against nine specific target areas to provide an overall Waste-Free Factory Score, including energy conservation, strategic planning, use of post-consumer materials, air emissions, solid waste, hazardous waste, and water emissions. Plants are designated "Waste Free" when they have achieved an overall score of 450 out of a possible 500. In 1993, the average score throughout Xerox Supplies, Manufacturing, and Development was 250. In 1996, it was 459.

Worldwide, all of Xerox's manufacturing operations are planning to achieve Waste-Free Factory status by the year 2000.

In 1995, the Waste-Free Office program was started at selected sites across Europe and North America, including forty-five Xerox buildings in Monroe County, New York. Each office is to achieve the following goals (compared to its baseline):

- Decrease waste to landfill by 90 percent through recycling efforts.
- Decrease overall waste generation by 50 percent through source reduction and reuse initiatives.
- Increase the utilization of post-consumer materials to 60 percent of material purchases.
- *Reduce energy consumption by 50 percent.*

In other words, Xerox expects its offices to be cool. In 1995, Xerox cut energy consumption in its Monroe County buildings—some 9 million square feet—by 4 percent. In 1996, HVAC and lighting controls and other improvements cut energy consumption by 10 percent, saving 32 million kWh. Xerox projected another 7 percent cut in 1997.

Xerox's famous Palo Alto Research Center (PARC) in California already cut energy use in half in the early 1990s. Using advanced lighting, window films, and an energy management control system, *PARC cut energy use from 13.2 million kWh in 1988 to 6.5 million kWh in 1995—a 50 percent savings.* Xerox is on its way to becoming one of the first completely cool companies in the world.

SUPERCOOL COMPANIES: CARBON NEUTRAL

Another very cool company is A. Finkl & Sons Company. One of the country's largest and most innovative custom steel forgers, the Chicago-based company employs more than 400 people and has some $100 million in revenues. A fully integrated steel production facility makes die blocks for the closed die forging industry, custom open die forgings, and forge shop and steel mill repair parts.[10]

The company has pursued continuous improvements in energy efficiency, many of which stem from the company's more than one hundred worldwide patents for a variety of steels, steelmaking processes, techniques, and equipment. Using improved computer-controlled process equipment, advanced heat treat and heating furnaces, including a Vacuum Arc Remelt furnace, Finkl has reduced energy consumption per ton of steel shipped by more than 36 percent in the past decade.

To become carbon neutral, Finkl calculated it would need to plant some 2 million trees to absorb the carbon dioxide generated by the remaining energy used to produce its products. In 1989, Finkl launched its Forging a Fresher America program, which has already planted more than 1.6 million trees. About half the trees are planted in a Wisconsin forest managed by the state of Wisconsin, and most of the rest are in Illinois state parks and managed by the Illinois Department of Conservation. Each year, Finkl also distributes saplings to any of its employees or retirees who desire them. Finkl works with the city of Chicago to plant trees at schools, parks, and parkways. The company has also planted hundreds of trees, bushes, and flowers around its plant. As the company notes, "It's not all about carbon dioxide—trees do much more than simply absorb CO_2. They shade, filter, cool, reduce noise, reduce energy consumption, stabilize soil, minimize erosion, shelter wildlife, and impart psychological, economic, and aesthetic values to the human condition." The direct and indirect cooling benefits of trees will be examined later in this chapter.

Finkl has also worked to reduce the energy embodied in its steel. To start with, all of the steel Finkl manufactures is made from scrap metal. In addition, Finkl has extended the life of a melt-shop furnace and ladle brick by 400 percent, and when it does have to reline the furnace, the company returns the brick for recycling rather than throwing it away. Instead of discarding the used shot and dust from its shot blaster, Finkl sends it to its own melt furnaces, so it eventually leaves the factory as steel. And instead of discarding used wooden pallets, it reuses them, and, when they are no longer usable, delivers them to a pallet-rebuilding company. Each individual measure may not seem like much, but *the company now reuses or recycles 99.7 percent of the solid waste it generates.*

Finkl's energy efficiency and pollution prevention efforts have not merely made it carbon neutral. They have also helped the company partner with the city of Chicago to create an urban manufacturing campus in the heart of the city's exclusive Lincoln Park–Clybourn Corridor community. More than 10,000 manufacturing jobs provided by Finkl and other nearby industrial companies have been preserved, through an effort that allows the steelmaker to be adjacent to single-family homes valued at more than $500,000. Cool manufacturers make good neighbors.

Another supercool company is Stonyfield Farm. The company has pursued energy efficiency aggressively, through actions such as lighting retrofits and waste heat recovery. The company then took some of the savings from energy efficiency efforts in its New Hampshire yogurt-manufacturing plant and invested it in forestry projects. As a result, like Finkl, Stonyfield Farm's net manufacturing emissions of greenhouse gases are zero.

At the same time, the company has been achieving a leading market share position in a number of product categories and its bottom line has been growing by 30 percent annually. "Through a program of measurement and continuous improvement, Stonyfield Farm is rapidly growing while dramatically decreasing its impact on global climate change," says CEO Gary Hirshberg. "It's a classic win-win-win situation—good for business, good for our children, and good for America."

COOL SUPPLIERS

As you master all of the cool strategies, you should share your experience with your suppliers. That way, they will be able to keep costs low while boosting profits, too. Equally important, by helping your suppliers become cool, you will be making your goal of lowering your company's embodied carbon dioxide emissions a snap.

One company that has started to help its suppliers become cool and lean is General Motors. Since 1992, GM has provided teams of engineers to help its thousands of suppliers become leaner—reduce cost and product cycle time. They call this process PICOS, a Spanish word meaning "mountain peaks."[11]

In 1996, PICOS added energy efficiency and pollution prevention to the tools it offers its suppliers. PICOS engineers, working with EPA's Climate Wise program, the Business for Social Responsibility Education Fund, and the Industrial Assessment Center at Rutgers University, have begun to provide information and assistance in the areas of steam use, compressed air, and motors.

GM understands the intimate connection between becoming lean and becoming cool. In 1998, GM held a workshop at a supplier that had an off-site warehouse, primarily because of inefficient operating practices. "We changed their methods in order to 'lean out' their system," explained James P. Olson, GM's Manager of Supplier Development. "We anticipate that in a very short period of time they won't be needing that extra warehouse." That, notes Olson, eliminates the energy consumed by the warehouse as well as the energy and emissions from the trucks that had been traveling back and forth continuously between the supplier's plant and the warehouse. Given the success GM is having in making its own operations cooler, it seems likely that through PICOS, many of its suppliers will soon also become cool.

COOL HOMES

Just as you have large opportunities to reduce greenhouse gas emissions and save money, so too do your employees. A cool company will work to help its employees to become cool. The biggest producers of employees' carbon dioxide emissions are their cars and homes. Interestingly, *the average home generates more than twice as much carbon dioxide as the family car, about eleven tons a year versus five tons.*[12] So, let's start with homes.

The typical American home energy bill is about $1,300 a year. About three-fifths of home energy use is from electricity, and the rest is from natural gas and oil. Just as companies can reduce the energy bill in their buildings by one-quarter to one-half with rapid payback (see Chapter 3 and 4), employees can do the same in their homes.

Results from the Massachusetts Electric Company's Advanced Retrofit pilot program "indicate that reductions in [home] energy consumption of 25 percent can be achieved." The Department of Energy's low-income Home Weatherization Assistance Program routinely achieves even larger savings on home heating.

For instance, the Barnwell Family of Cleveland, Ohio, had an old furnace replaced with a new efficient gas furnace and their home extensively caulked and insulated. The winter natural gas bill was cut *37 percent* (a $40 monthly savings). "The drafts are gone," says James Barnwell, "the house is more comfortable and I have more money to spend on other bills." PG&E demonstrated savings slightly *in excess of 50 percent* in two California retrofitted homes. Most of the energy-saving techniques for homes are the same as for commercial buildings: energy-efficient lighting, windows, insulation, and heating and cooling equipment.[13]

Take action in the following 10 areas and you can reduce home energy use and associated greenhouse gas emissions *by more than one-third*:

1. *Heating and cooling systems.* They account for 44 percent of the home energy bill. Purchase energy-efficient equipment (such as is identified with the Energy Star label), use a programmable thermostat, and have equipment maintained with regular tune-ups.

2. *Hot water systems.* Heating water accounts for 14 percent of typical energy usage in the home. Buy high-efficiency water heaters, heat pump water heaters, and solar water heaters. Proper maintenance, insulation (wrapping the hot-water heater), and water-saving features like high-efficiency showerheads and aerators in faucets can significantly reduce energy consumption.

3. *Insulation.* Insulating attics, walls, ducts, and basements is very cost-effective.

4. *Windows.* Inefficient windows can account for 10 to 25 percent of your bills. Look for windows with the Energy Star label to help decrease your heating and cooling bills.

5. *Air leaks.* Poorly sealed ducts and air leaks in the home waste dollars and can cause health and safety problems. The average U.S. home has five square feet of leaks—that's like having a window wide open all the time. Sealing cracks, penetrations, and heating and cooling ducts can provide savings of 10 percent or more.

6. *Refrigerators.* New refrigerators can save $35 to $70 a year over the models available fifteen years ago. This can mean $500 to $1,000 in savings over the life of the refrigerator. If you have an old model in the basement

or garage, it may be consuming even more electricity. It should be replaced or, if hardly being used, disposed of.

7. *Clothes washers.* New high-efficiency washing machines clean clothes better while saving more than half of the energy used for washing. They also use 40 percent less water and save on the energy needed for drying your clothes.

8. *Lighting.* Lighting accounts for 5 to 10 percent of household energy usage. Compact fluorescent bulbs, together with installed timers and motion sensors, can significantly reduce lighting costs. If you have a halogen floor (torchiere) lamp, buying a compact fluorescent one instead will not only save most of the energy, it will also eliminate a dangerous fire hazard.

9. *Consumer electronics.* Home electronics equipment is responsible for the fastest energy growth in the home in recent years. Again, look for the Energy Star label when buying computers, VCRs, and TVs.

10. *The systems approach.* Treating the whole house as a system saves even more energy and money. For example, when you install better insulation, energy-efficient windows, and air sealing, you need a far smaller and less expensive HVAC system.[14]

Taking these actions will save a typical homeowner more than $500 a year in energy bills with a payback of three to five years (a return on investment of 20 to 33 percent), while reducing annual carbon dioxide emissions by more than 3 tons. Yet, homeowners tend not to pursue these benefits. They lack the necessary information and the financing to pay for the efficient equipment. Here is the role for a cool company.

Every company should, at the minimum, provide its employees access to the very best information on how to achieve low-cost home energy savings. Many local utilities have good residential efficiency programs. Other useful sources include *Homemade Money,* by Rocky Mountain Institute in Snowmass, Colorado (970-927-3851); *Consumer Guide to Home Energy Savings,* by the American Council for an Energy-Efficient Economy in Washington, D.C. (202-429-0063); and *Energy Savers,* by the U.S. Department of Energy (1-800-363-3732).

Cool companies will want to do far more. Employees should be given free energy audits. Your company could do this in partnership with a local utility or energy service company. You might consider training some of your employees to perform such an audit.

Perhaps most important, a company should help its employees finance the implementation of the audit recommendations. A good model is the Home Energy Loan Program begun in 1983 by the Environmental and Conservation Services Department (ECSD) of Austin, Texas.[15] The program permits qualifying homeowners to borrow from $500 to $6,000 ($9,000 for a duplex).

Borrowers choose between a three- to five-year loan with zero percent interest or a seven-year loan with a 2 percent rate. When a house is sold, the buyer may assume the loan.

Homeowners are eligible for a loan only if they have a certified energy audit. Loans can be used to finance only those energy-saving measures identified by the audit, which include attic insulation and ventilation, duct repair and insulation, water-heater wraps, air-conditioning and furnace replacement, heat-pump replacement, heat-recovery water-heating units, heat-pump or solar water heaters, and air-conditioner servicing.

The ECSD formed a partnership with a local lending institution to provide financial services. For thousands of Austin homeowners, the program has removed the initial information and cost barriers to energy-efficient upgrades. The post-upgrade monthly electric bill and loan payment *combined* add up to *less* than the monthly pre-upgrade electricity bill in 80 to 85 percent of homes. Once the loan is paid off, the homeowner keeps all the savings. Some homeowners have cut energy bills in half. These improvements also increase the market value of the homes. Because the loan is transferable to the next owner, it allows flexibility in home sales: Sellers do not have to increase their asking price to pay off the loans at the time of the sale, so that potential buyers get both an efficient and a low-price home. With one stroke a key barrier to energy-efficient home improvements is gone—concern that a homeowner will not stay in a house long enough to recoup the investment or that the next buyer will not value the energy-efficiency features.

What can a cool company do to help its employees? Partner with a local lending institution to buy down the interest-rate on the loan. Perhaps the lending institution will also want to be seen as cool and will help defray the costs. A cool bank may well want to become a leader in such lending instruments. In any case, efficiency loans are typically piggybacked on other home-improvement loans, and the company is paying only to buy down the interest rate on the incremental cost of the efficiency measures.

Beyond energy efficiency, there are new cool power choices for even deeper emissions reductions. Local utilities are beginning to offer green power options that allow consumers to buy their electricity from renewable sources, just as Toyota did in Southern California (as discussed in Chapter 6). A company could help its employees form an energy-buying cooperative to purchase green power at a discount. Better still, it could actually offer a financial incentive to employees who choose green power. Toyota, for instance, is offering its employees a 10 percent discount on the extra cost of green power. As utility markets fully deregulate, you might consider contracting to build a wind turbine or other renewable power plant and sell the electricity to your employees, even as you buy it for the company.

Another approach: Encourage installation of a photovoltaic system on site at everyone's house. A 3-kilowatt rooftop PV unit could provide about *one-third of a typical home's energy* (and a higher fraction of an efficient home's energy), saving more than 3 tons of carbon dioxide a year. General Motors Acceptance Corporation (GMAC) Mortgage has not only expanded its line of mortgage financing for energy-efficient housing, but the company in June 1998 also agreed to provide regular mortgage financing for rooftop solar units at commercial rates. At the time of the announcement, the rate was 7 percent with no points for a thirty-year loan. The company will also offer equity lines of credit for homeowners who want to add photovoltaic systems. You could offer to buy down the interest rate for your employees.

Here's a technology to watch: Small proton exchange membrane (PEM) fuel cells powered by natural gas will soon be available for the home, as discussed in Chapter 6. In June 1998, for the first time, Plug Power of Latham, New York, powered a home with a fuel cell. By 2000, General Electric Fuel Cell Systems will be selling, installing, and servicing them. These fuel cells will provide not only the electricity for a home but also much of the heating for space and water. Carbon emissions will drop sharply.

A homeowner who combines energy efficiency with cool power (either rooftop photovoltaics or a cogenerating fuel cell), will cut home carbon dioxide emissions *by one-half to three-fourths.* Your cool company will be taking another giant step in reducing the nation's greenhouse gas emissions while at the same time increasing the morale and disposable income of your own work force. You are giving employees a hefty raise without affecting payroll.

COOL TRANSPORTATION

The fossil fuels burned by cars, trucks, and planes account for more than one-third of all U.S. greenhouse gas emissions. As a cool company, you can reduce your transportation carbon dioxide emissions; this is part of reducing your embodied carbon dioxide emissions. For instance, if your company has a transportation fleet, you can ensure that the vehicles are fuel efficient, or— even better—that they run on fuels that reduce greenhouse gas emissions, "cool fuels" such as ethanol from renewable biofuels.

Like Interface or A. Finkl and Sons, you can reduce resource inputs and/or waste outputs that otherwise need to be transported. Procter & Gamble took a different approach when they introduced compact powdered detergents in 1989. Consumers typically use half the volume or less of these detergents versus traditional ones; they are a denser product and use 30 percent fewer product raw materials. The smaller volume uses less energy to ship and distribute. P&G calculates that trucking needs have decreased by 40 percent globally for compact detergents compared to traditional ones.[16]

This section focuses on how your company can help your employees reduce the carbon dioxide emissions from commuting to and from work. AT&T has been a pioneer in telecommuting and providing office space for workers who spend a lot of time outside the office with customers. For instance, AT&T's global systems division in Morristown, New Jersey, makes use of computing and networking technology to consolidate office space. Employees can work at home, and if they need meeting or office space, they can log into a company computer and reserve it, allowing them to go to the office only when they need to. AT&T calculates that Morristown will save $460,000 a year from this strategy.[17]

Company-wide, AT&T's telework program now includes some 36,000 workers (or more than half of AT&T's U.S.-based managers) who work at home part of the time. AT&T studies have found that employees see telework as a way to have more control over their personal lives, enhancing productivity and work satisfaction. It estimates its program saves 80,000 tons of carbon dioxide a year in reduced transportation-related emissions each year.

Quad/Graphics, the largest privately held printing company in North America, adopted a different strategy for reducing commuting energy use. The billion-dollar company replaced three 8-hour shifts with two 12-hour shifts, resulting in one-third fewer trips to work. It also located a new facility in an existing urban structure in West Allis, Wisconsin (rather than building a new facility outside of town), which decreased averaged commuting distance for each of the facility's 700 workers by about 20 miles.[18]

One city that has done outstanding work promoting alternative transportation for businesses is Portland, Oregon.[19] Nike, for example, has its corporate headquarters in the Portland area, with a downtown retail outlet called Nike Town. Nike offers workers a $1 voucher (a "Nike Buck") each day they bike, run, walk, skate, or carpool to work. Nike Bucks can be redeemed at the employee store, the cafeteria, and the company's childcare center. The company also provides reduced-cost transit passes for workers of as much as 75 percent off the regular price. Before these efforts, only a few of the seventy-five Nike Town employees used transit alternatives. Now they have two carpools, twenty-seven bus riders, and twenty employees who bike, run, walk, or skate to work. This adds up to more than 6,700 avoided single-occupancy vehicle trips per year, reducing annual vehicle miles traveled by 135,000 miles per year. From such a small effort, total carbon dioxide savings come to about 70 tons per year.

A vast array of different kinds of workers are telecommuting in Oregon and around the country, including health care administrators, insurance claims processors, nurse executives, secretaries, administrative assistants, personnel staff, information systems staff, public relations representatives, scheduling staff, social workers, therapists, attorneys, accountants, computer programmers, and software engineers. Some might spend most of their time at home. Others might telecommute only one day a week, devoting that time to computer work and phone calls that otherwise suffer from constant office interruptions.

The key point is: Your company needs to explore all opportunities to reduce the greenhouse gas emissions generated by the commutes of all your employees, including yourself.

COOL COMMUNITIES

Companies can partner with their communities to reduce greenhouse gas emissions. In many cases, the company will already be in a community that is interested in pursuing greenhouse gas reductions. The U.S. office of the International Council for Local Environmental Initiatives (ICLEI) is working with dozens of communities as part of ICLEI's "Cities for Climate Protection—U.S." program. Your first step is to contact ICLEI in Berkeley, California (510-540-8843) to see who in the community is taking an active role in greenhouse gas mitigation. If no one is, then your company will have to be the leader.

You can help your community in a variety of ways. For instance, as state deregulation efforts continue, a company that cogenerates will be able to sell its excess low-carbon electricity to its neighbors. Even now, a company can partner with its local utility to do so, something that Trigen has facilitated in a number of cities (see Chapter 6). Companies can partner with local municipal utilities, or work with local governments to create virtual utilities, which distribute not only cogenerated electricity but also district heating and cooling and energy-efficiency services.

Another useful role a company can play in the community is providing technical expertise and financial resources to help local schools reduce greenhouse gas emissions. Schools have large energy bills, often exceeding the budget for supplies and books combined. Yet we have seen that, like all buildings, schools have large opportunities for cost-effective energy savings. For instance, as Texas A&M found (Chapter 3), virtually all the schools they examined in one district had disabled energy management and control systems. And as Waverly Junior-Senior High School found out (Chapter 6), schools can save money and reduce emissions by cogenerating. Moreover, most schools in this country are quite old, with aging lighting and HVAC equipment that undermine students' ability to learn. As seen in Chapter 4, North Carolina found out that daylighting in schools significantly increased test scores. Other studies have found a correlation between the physical condition of a school and student performance.

A cool school could pay for the upgrade to its facility with the stream of energy savings, if it had access to both the technical expertise and financing, which few schools do today. A local cool company that has gained knowledge in making its buildings energy-efficient and that has rigorously documented that there are large, enduring energy savings to be found, should be able to assist in both areas. If it cannot provide financing itself, it could at least provide assistance in auditing the schools and perhaps work with a local financial institution to set up a revolving loan fund. The state of Iowa has had such a fund for years and has saved many school districts enough money to hire extra teachers.

Philadelphia schools have achieved measured savings in excess of $85 million since 1983 with a revolving fund as part of their Save Energy Campaign. Consider the remarkable case of the Franklin Learning Center, a high school housed in a building constructed in 1910.[20] The center was awarded $80,000 in the mid-1980s, and the whole school pitched in to find savings. The vice principal crawled under the building to look for steam trap leaks. A student patrol turned off lights in empty rooms and closed windows when the heat was on. Students could spend a weekend weatherizing the school if their schoolwork assignment included public service. Energy efficiency was incorporated into the curriculum. Energy savings came to $200,000—a 52 percent savings in their energy bill. In the second year, *savings rose to 64 percent.* Given how old and run down most school buildings are in this country, comparable savings could probably be found around the country.

Another benefit of such a program is that it can be used to teach students theoretical concepts, having to do with both the production and use of energy, and practical skills, such as how to conduct an energy audit and how to retrofit a building and monitor savings. If, as seems likely, concern over global warming continues to grow, these will be increasingly valuable and marketable skills.

COOLING A COMMUNITY

Probably the single most cost-effective and environmentally beneficial action a company can help a community take to become cool will actually directly cool the community down (which in turn will lower the air conditioning use by the company). This remarkable strategy deserves to be examined in some detail, since it provides so many other benefits to a community, including very low-cost smog reduction.

On a summer afternoon, central Los Angeles registers temperatures typically 5°F higher than the surrounding suburban and rural areas. Hot roofs and pavements, baked by the sun, warm the air blowing over them. The resulting urban "heat island" causes discomfort, raises air-conditioning bills, and accelerates the formation of smog.[21]

Heat islands are found in many large cities, including Chicago, Washington, D.C., and Atlanta. The effect is particularly well recognized in cities that quote two airport temperatures on the weather report. Thus Chicago-Midway airport is typically a few degrees hotter than suburban O'Hare, and the same difference applies between Washington's Reagan National Airport and Dulles International Airport.

Heat islands do not arise mainly from heat leaking out of cars, buildings, and factories. Rather, dark horizontal surfaces absorb most of the sunlight falling on them. Consequently, dark surfaces run hotter than light ones. The choice of dark colors has caused the problem; wiser choices can reverse it.[22]

The country is now paying dearly for this extra heat. One-sixth of the electricity consumed in the United States goes to cool buildings, at an annual power cost of $40 billion. Moreover, a 5°F heat island greatly raises the rate at which pollutants—nitrogen oxides and volatile organic compounds emanating from cars and smokestacks—"cook" into ozone, a highly oxidizing and irritating gas that is the main ingredient of smog. In Los Angeles, for example, ozone rises from an acceptable concentration at 70°F to unacceptable at 90°F. The Los Angeles heat island raises ozone levels 10 to 15 percent and contributes to hundreds of millions of dollars in annual health-related expenses. (In winter, we have plenty of smog precursors but, because it is cool, little smog.)

Fortunately, we can go a long way toward dissipating urban heat islands with modest measures. One solution is to use lighter colors for roofs and pavement. The other is to plant many trees, which have a twofold benefit. First, they provide cooling shade. Second, trees, like most plants, soak up groundwater. The water then "evapotranspires" from the leaves, thus cooling the leaves and, indirectly, the surrounding air. A single properly watered tree can evapotranspirate 40 gallons of water in a day—offsetting the heat equivalent to that produced by one hundred 100-watt lamps burning eight hours per day.

Increases in temperature do not have to follow from an influx of population. The Los Angeles basin in 1880 was still relatively barren, and yearly highs ran about 102°F. Then settlers introduced irrigation, the fruit trees cooled the air, and, within fifty years, summer temperatures dropped 5°F. But as Los Angeles began to urbanize in the 1940s, cool orchards gave way to hot roofs and asphalt pavements. Over the next fifty years, summer highs climbed back to their 1880 values and are still rising at 1°F per decade, with no end in sight.

But with white roofs, concrete-colored pavements, and about 10 million new shade trees, Los Angeles could be cooler than the semi-desert that surrounds it, instead of hotter. Such measures would be in keeping with approaches that have been taken for centuries. As civilization developed in warm climates, humans learned to whitewash their dwellings. Even today, building owners in hot cities like Haifa and Tel Aviv are required to whitewash their roofs each spring, after the rains stop.

In the United States, dwellings tended to be built with white roofs through the 1960s. Then, as air conditioning became widespread, cheap, and taken for granted, priorities shifted. It became popular to use darker roofing shingles, which more resembled wooden shingles and better concealed dirt and mold.

The colored granules on typical "white" shingles made today are coated with only one-sixth as much white pigment as in the 1960s. Under the summer sun, modern shingles become 20°F hotter than the old-style ones.

In discussing a "cool communities" strategy, the focus will be Los Angeles—the smog capital of the United States—though its elements could be applied in most other cities as well.

SIMULATING A COOLER LOS ANGELES

Urbanized Los Angeles covers 10,000 square kilometers and includes about 1,250 square kilometers of roof and another 1,250 square kilometers of pavement. Obviously, we cannot instantly replace these with cooler-colored materials. Nor can we quickly plant the 10 million shade trees that would make a difference. We can, however, simulate these actions using computer models. A simulation performed by Lawrence Berkeley National Laboratory raised the city's albedo (the reflected fraction of incident solar heat) by a modest 7.5 percent and covered 5 percent of its area with 10 million trees.

The models indicate that such a "cool community" strategy could lower the average summer temperature in the Los Angeles heat island by 5°F with a lucrative benefit/cost ratio. The use of white roofs and shade trees in Los Angeles would lower the need for air conditioning by 18 percent, or 1 billion kilowatt-hours, for the buildings directly affected by the roofs and shaded by the trees. If we assume a price of peak electricity of 10 cents per kilowatt-hour—not uncommon—this translates into savings of $100 million per year.

For a 1,000-square-foot roof, the cost premium of cooler shingles is less than $25. If lighter shingles or tiles raise the albedo 35 percentage points, the additional investment pays for itself in less than one summer's worth of lowered air-conditioning bills.

There is also a large indirect benefit. If an entire community drops a degree or so in temperature, thanks to lighter roofs and pavement and to the evapotranspiration from trees, then everyone's air-conditioning load goes down, even those buildings that are not directly shaded or that still have dark roofs. These indirect annual savings would total an additional 12 percent—0.7 billion kilowatt-hours, or $70 million. Overall, implementing these cool community measures would lower the need for peak electrical generating capacity by about 1,500 MW, which is equivalent to two or three large power plants.

The cooler temperature would lower smog, too. Smog "exceedance"—the amount by which ozone levels top the California standard of 90 parts per billion—would drop 12 percent. Ozone can irritate the eyes, inflame the lungs, trigger asthma attacks, and lower the respiratory system's ability to fight off infection. While other components of air pollution also exact a toll on health—especially particulates and sulfur dioxide—ozone is figured to be responsible for about $3 billion in health-related costs every year in the Los Angeles basin. Thus a 12 percent reduction in ozone exceedance could save $360 million.

The benefits of light surfaces and shade trees extend beyond Los Angeles. The 18 percent direct savings of air conditioning attained by shading and lightening individual buildings do not depend on the size of the city, only on its climate; Atlanta, for example, would enjoy the same percentage reduction as Los Angeles. The indirect savings, on the other hand, will be significant only in large cities with significant heat islands. Since about half the U.S. population lives in heat islands, the annual direct plus indirect U.S. air-conditioning energy savings, after twenty years, might be 10 percent. Peak air-conditioning demand would probably drop by 5 percent.

THE BENEFITS OF URBAN TREES

One of the remedies for urban heat islands has an even greater benefit. Carbon dioxide mitigation strategies focus on two strategies: cutting the use of fossil fuels and planting trees, which sequester carbon dioxide in their wood. The planting of trees in cities does both of these and is far more effective than planting trees in forests.

Any tree—whether in the forest or the city—removes carbon dioxide from the air through photosynthesis. Typically, a tree sequesters a few kilograms of carbon per year in its wood. For a forest tree, that is the total benefit of the tree's existence, from the standpoint of cutting carbon dioxide levels. But a tree planted in a city also lowers fossil-fuel usage, by cooling the city and thus reducing the amount of electricity consumed in air conditioning. A tree in Los Angeles, for example, will save an additional 3 kilograms of carbon per year by lowering the city's overall need for air conditioning, plus 15 kilograms more if it directly shades a building.

Thus, any company concerned enough with greenhouse warming to plant trees in forests ought to consider working with utilities in cities with growing air-conditioning demand to start shade-tree/cool-surfaces programs. Such programs would not only save more carbon dioxide per tree than would forest trees, but they would mitigate smog problems as well.

Not all trees are equally beneficial. It is better to plant deciduous trees, for example, which give shade in summer but do not block the warmth in winter. Also, some types of trees emit large amounts of the volatile organic hydrocarbons (VOCs) that combine with oxides of nitrogen to form smog. Ash and maple are among the more VOC-free trees, emitting only about one VOC unit (defined as 1 microgram per hour per gram of dry leaf). Eucalyptus trees, on the other hand, are a problem. They were introduced a century ago, are thriving, and emit thirty-two units; perhaps they should be replaced with more suitable native trees. Weeping willows top the emissions list, releasing a whopping 230 VOC units.

WHAT SHOULD A COOL COMPANY DO?

Measures to reduce L.A.'s heat island could reduce air-conditioning bills by $175 million per year and alleviate $360 million per year of smog-related expenses. Similar measures can achieve benefits nearly as remarkable in many of the major cities in this country.

How will we get to this point? To start with, a company will want to make sure that it is not contributing to the local heat island. That means planting plenty of trees, especially for shade. Also, buildings will need light-colored roofs.[23]

Another contributor to the heat island effect is pavement. Asphalt pavement is, by volume, about seven-eighths rock aggregate, cemented together with one-eighth sticky black asphalt. Over a few months, asphalt wears close to the color of the aggregate. By choosing lighter aggregate for parking lots and any roads maintained by your company, you can triple the solar reflectivity of worn asphalt pavement. Better yet would be to switch the binder from asphalt to lighter-colored Portland cement. Although its first cost is higher than asphalt, cement is stronger and lasts longer, so its life-cycle cost is lower. Iowa already requires cement roads as a long-term cost-savings policy.

Once the company has gained experience in making its facilities cool, it should work with the local government and civic groups to make the entire community cool. Utilities can be important partners. In 1990, the Sacramento Municipal Utility District (SMUD) initiated the Sacramento Shade Program, whose goal is to plant 500,000 trees by the year 2000 in collaboration with the Sacramento Tree Foundation.[24] The utility provides free deciduous trees to its customers (including stakes and fertilizer) with the only requirement being that the trees are planted on the western, eastern, or southern exposure to provide shade. A "Community Forester" from the Tree Foundation supervises the siting and provides growing instruction. The program provides seasonal tree care tips as well as a toll-free telephone advice line. Foresters also visit sites as needed. When fully mature, the half million trees are projected to reduce home cooling costs by up to 40 percent, saving 7 million kWh and more than $1 million in avoided cost annually. The ten-year program is projected to cost about $20 million and provide savings exceeding $40 million over a thirty-year period.

Urban trees do require more effort to maintain and that is why they fall into neglect in many, many cities. Nonetheless, the benefits of city trees so outweigh the costs that it is incumbent on all members of a community to work together to maintain and expand their number. Not only will this ultimately lower everyone's energy bill, including that of your company, but also if global climate change is occurring, it will help mitigate the local effect of warming.

The task of reducing greenhouse gas emissions is large. So if your company wants to go beyond benchmarking in helping to reduce greenhouse gas emissions, you will need to look at your products and your embodied carbon, and you will need to help your employees, suppliers, and communities reduce their greenhouse gas emissions.

Chapter

10

WHAT PRICE CARBON DIOXIDE?

This chapter explores a key issue for your company's planning: What is the future price of carbon dioxide likely to be as the world's nations move to restrict greenhouse gas emissions?

The principal greenhouse gas emitted by businesses is carbon dioxide, which is released in the combustion of fossil fuels such as coal, oil, and natural gas. The industrialized nations of the world agreed in December 1997 at Kyoto, Japan, to reduce greenhouse gas emissions below 1990 levels by 2008 to 2012. That means that within a decade, carbon dioxide is likely to have a price, which would either be in the form of a tax on emissions, or, more likely, the cost of a permit to emit carbon dioxide.

If the price is very high, as some economic models suggest, $30 to $60 or more per ton emitted, it could raise average energy prices 20 to 40 percent or more. This in turn would have a dramatic impact on a number of key investment decisions for your company. For the vast majority of companies, however, the main effect of such a price rise would be to make the cool strategies described in this book a necessity, rather than just a very good idea for boosting profits and productivity. For a few of the most energy-intensive companies (such as are discussed in Chapter 8), a price near $60 a ton could impact fundamental decisions, such as which country to base production in.

If, as I believe, the price will be low, $5 to $15 a ton, the impact on your company would be slight. Investments in cool power would be a little more attractive, but the fundamental reason for becoming cool would not change—it is immensely profitable. The bottom line for managers:

If a significant number of companies adopt the cool strategies discussed in this book, the price of carbon dioxide emissions will be low. If not, it will be especially important for you to become cool, so as to minimize the impact of any price hike. However, becoming cool is so straightforward that it is unlikely the price of carbon dioxide would stay high for any extended period of time.

This chapter looks at the price question through the experiences of an oil company, British Petroleum, and an energy services company, SYCOM.

CLIMATE LEADERSHIP AT BRITISH PETROLEUM

British Petroleum is the third largest oil company in the world, and hence it is one of the largest sources of greenhouse gas emissions. In 1990, it emitted 40 million tons of carbon dioxide. And, of course, its fossil fuel products are a leading source of greenhouse gases. The carbon dioxide generated by the combustion of BP's products exceeds 300 million tons.[1] Nonetheless, the company has been among the leaders in the world on the climate issue. In a remarkable May 1997 speech at Stanford University, BP's CEO, John Browne, said:

> There is now an effective consensus among the world's leading scientists and serious and well informed people outside the scientific community that there is a discernible human influence on the climate, and a link between the concentration of carbon dioxide and the increase in temperature. . . .
>
> The time to consider the policy dimension of climate change is not when the link between greenhouse gases and climate change is conclusively proven but when the possibility cannot be discounted and is taken seriously by the society of which we are part.
>
> We in BP have reached that point.

In September 1998, Browne announced that BP would voluntarily reduce its emissions to 10 percent below 1990 levels by 2010—to 36 million tons. This exceeds the 5 percent reduction the industrialized nations agreed to at Kyoto (and the 7 percent reduction the United States agreed to). BP estimates that without its reduction plan, its emissions would have soared from 40 million tons in 1990 to 58 million tons in 2010.

Instead of growing 45 percent, BP's carbon dioxide emissions will drop 10 percent. BP has made a very cool commitment indeed.

In making this commitment, the company is relying on two key strategies: "market-based incentives and the creative talent of our employees to seek innovative and cost-effective solutions." First, let's look at how the company is tapping the expertise of its employees.

Using Employee Creativity

Browne noted in a February 1998 speech that immediately after the Kyoto conference, he wrote to all 350 leaders within the BP group, the people who run BP's business units, to get their ideas on how BP could reduce carbon emissions. Browne said, "Two weeks ago I got the response and I was stunned by it. It consisted of 200 pages of the most detailed and serious proposals. . . . Every single one reflected the view that we were doing the right thing in trying to tackle our own emissions and to make a positive constructive contribution to the public debate."

He said that as a high-technology company, it is easy to get carried away with high-tech solutions, but that "the responses are impressively full of straightforward common sense." He quoted the response of one of the company's most senior technologists:

> There is a lot to be done through employee awareness. I suspect that we can make significant gains in fuel efficiency and emission control by getting the message home to the people with their hands on the valves.

That is one of the primary messages of this book. Indeed, Browne has learned that "it is clear how frequently environmental logic and commercial logic coincide. This is not surprising: Cutting down emissions is often a matter of cutting down energy consumption, and energy is a cost." He cited the "remarkable story" of BP's refinery at Kwinana, south of Perth in Australia. Kwinana's *unit carbon dioxide emissions have been cut by 19 percent since 1995:*

- The refinery commissioned a cogeneration plant in late 1996, supplying all its needs and dramatically cutting emissions.
- The refinery has worked hard to reduce flaring. Since the beginning of 1997, it has reduced emissions from flaring by 55 percent.
- Renewed effort is being put into energy efficiency. Even as the refinery's production expands, the initiatives are expected to *cut emissions by an additional 27 percent* through reduced consumption of fuel gas, electricity, and steam.
- The refinery, with the assistance of the Western Australia Department of Agriculture, has a unique opportunity *to achieve a net zero greenhouse gas emissions* by changing land use and forestry sequestration. And that will also be of great benefit to the rural community, because it will help mitigate soil salinization, which is a significant environmental issue in the area.

Thus, Kwinana will soon be the home of one of the coolest refineries in the world, combining efficiency and cool power to reduce emissions some 45 percent. And, ultimately, its emissions may be offset entirely.

A very different emissions reduction approach being examined by BP and other companies is to reinject carbon dioxide into existing wells to improve oil recovery. That would simultaneously cut emissions and improve yield—an ideal approach. In the long term, sequestration of carbon dioxide in wells and in deep underground aquifers may be a key element of the world's response to climate change. It is, for instance, possible to take oil (or natural gas, coal, or biomass) and split it into carbon dioxide and hydrogen. If the carbon dioxide can be safely and permanently sequestered, the hydrogen could run proton-exchange membrane fuel cells, providing energy for transportation, buildings, and electricity.

The company is also using a technology to reduce the drag in transporting oil on the Trans-Alaska pipeline. That has allowed to it to cut out a number of pumping stations, reducing carbon dioxide emissions by more than 200,000 tons.

Emissions Trading

BP's second strategy is the development of an internal emissions trading system in collaboration with the Environmental Defense Fund. This market-based incentive is similar to the international trading system included in the Kyoto Treaty and to the domestic system already used to trade emissions of sulfur dioxide under the Clean Air Act administered by the EPA. Browne notes, "The aim is to set a value on emissions and to encourage cooperation between our different business units to achieve targets at the lowest practical cost."

The company is giving its various business units (such as refineries and chemical plants) an allocation of emission rights—permits to emit a certain level of carbon dioxide. A chemical plant can then decide whether it is cheaper to reduce its own emissions to its targeted level, or, if it turns out to be cheaper, to pay a refinery to reduce its emissions *below its target* to achieve the same overall level of reductions.

That is, suppose the chemical plant and the refinery both have to reduce emissions by 1 million tons of carbon dioxide, and that the refinery figures out it can cut 2 million tons through energy efficiency and cogeneration for very little money (indeed, a net savings), but the chemical plant thinks that reducing its emissions by 1 million tons will cost $10 million dollars. Then the refinery could cut its emissions by the 2 million tons and sell half of the reductions to the chemical plant.

As always, the very act of setting targets and an internal price on carbon dioxide savings is likely to spur the identification of the many low-cost options discussed in this book. As Browne says, "It will build into our systems a new consciousness about our own emissions. Reducing our CO_2 emissions will become part of our business plan. It will give full rein to the creative flair of all our people to develop innovative solutions. As the scheme develops, we will learn and disseminate lessons internally."

Renewables

Finally, British Petroleum has another strategic response to climate change. Just as Royal Dutch/Shell is expanding its renewable energy business (Chapter 1), BP is aggressively pursuing efforts to expand its photovoltaics company, BP Solar. Established in the mid-1980s, BP Solar has become one of the largest solar companies in the world, with about 10 percent of the international photovoltaic market. BP believes as Shell does that renewable energy, including solar, could comprise 5 percent of the world's energy by 2020 and half the world's energy by 2050. They have invested more than $150 million in expanding BP Solar, including $20 million in its first U.S. manufacturing plant in Fairfield, California. The company projects that its worldwide sales of solar technology will increase tenfold to $1 billion in the next decade. And as John Browne, the CEO of BP, puts it:

> So what have we learned? Within the company, we're learning the extraordinary motivating power of a constructive environmental stance. We're learning that there is no trade-off between profits and pollution.

A NEGATIVE PRICE FOR CARBON DIOXIDE AT SYCOM

British Petroleum's emissions trading strategy is based in part on the experience that states and businesses have had meeting the Clean Air Act's targets, particularly for reductions in sulfur dioxide and oxides of nitrogen (NOx).

SYCOM is one of the nation's leading energy services companies. Based in New Jersey, it helps commercial and industrial companies reduce their emissions of sulfur dioxide and NOx, which at the same time reduces their carbon dioxide emissions. SYCOM's work is relevant to understanding the future price of carbon for three reasons.[2]

1. SYCOM uses all of the cool strategies described in this book to reduce the NOx emissions of its customers—efficient lighting, improved HVAC (heating, ventilation, and air conditioning), heat pumps, variable frequency drives for motors, and cool power (including fuel switching to gas and cogeneration).

2. In New Jersey, permits to emit NOx are valuable, and the state allows companies to get credit for emissions reductions if they reduce their energy use.

3. New Jersey has a Measurement and Verification Protocol that served as one of the models for the International Performance Measurement and

Verification Protocol (IPMVP) discussed in Chapter 3. The protocol ensures reliable monitoring and verification of energy savings and hence emissions reductions, since energy savings directly reduce the air pollution created by electric power plants.

SYCOM has helped a number of businesses and public enterprises in New Jersey earn emissions reduction credits with energy efficiency. For instance, SYCOM installed high-efficiency lighting in five buildings of the United Jersey Bank, which in turn received a block of credits for emissions reductions. SYCOM is now working with the government of Mercer County, New Jersey, to upgrade all county facilities to cut energy costs and capture emissions credits.

Overall, SYCOM's cool upgrades have reduced energy consumption by more than 300 million kilowatt-hours, generating creditable NOx emissions savings of 221 tons. *These upgrades have also reduced carbon dioxide use by 223,000 tons.*

In an important analysis, SYCOM selected forty energy-efficiency upgrades at random from the hundreds it has performed. It included commercial, industrial, and governmental sectors, and a cross-section of energy-efficiency strategies.

➡️   **SYCOM calculated a cost per ton of NOx reduced that came to negative $9,000 and a cost per ton of carbon dioxide reduced of negative $30.**

In other words, because the building and factory upgrades made money, the effective cost of reducing NOx and carbon dioxide was negative.

As astonishing as these results are, they are not unique to SYCOM. The energy wizards of Texas A&M, discussed in Chapter 3, analyzed the environmental impact of the upgrades they performed on 290 buildings since 1989, as part of the Texas LoanSTAR revolving fund. They found that their building retrofits resulted in similarly large negative costs per ton for NOx and carbon dioxide.[3]

Two recent analyses reveal that some of the key efficient technologies used by SYCOM and Texas A&M in their retrofits have reached only a small fraction of the potential nationwide market. One study found that as of 1996, roughly 80 percent of commercial and industrial fluorescent lighting stock was still made up of inefficient lamps and ballasts. A 1998 survey of factories for the Department of Energy found that energy-efficient motors account for under 11 percent of all motors in use and that only about 20 percent of all the motors that could cost-effectively be equipped with adjustable-speed drives had such controls installed.[4]

And beyond just the installation of key energy-efficient technologies, there can be little doubt that far fewer than 10 percent of companies have taken the kind of systematic approach to buildings and factories described throughout this book, such as Texas A&M's strategy of continuous commissioning. While there are many reasons why energy efficiency has lagged, I think the primary one is that since the mid-1980s most companies simply have not focused much brainpower or many resources on their energy use. That was when we entered an era of flat or declining energy prices and the memory of the energy crises of the 1970s had begun to fade. Many companies think they did energy conservation two decades ago, as if it were a vaccination that you get once and forget about. Yet in the past decade there have been remarkable advances in efficient technologies and control systems, and as we have seen, the cool companies that *have* focused on energy have achieved significant cuts in energy use while boosting profits and productivity.

The bottom line is that if a significant number of companies adopted the cool strategies discussed in this book, the price of carbon dioxide needed to achieve the targets set at Kyoto will be very low indeed. Certainly, if companies follow BP's lead and voluntarily agree to reduce emissions at a faster pace than Kyoto requires, that will keep the price low.

THE LIST OF CLIMATE WISE COMPANIES GROWS

Many companies are beginning to take action. More than 500 companies have joined EPA's Climate Wise program, a voluntary program in which companies first agree to develop comprehensive greenhouse gas mitigation plans and then to start reducing emissions. A number of the companies profiled in this book are Climate Wise partners, such as DuPont, General Motors, Interface, Malden Mills, Anheuser-Busch, 3M, and Bethlehem Steel.[5]

Many other Climate Wise partners have also begun to achieve impressive results, such as Fabe-Litho, a family-owned and operated commercial printing business in Tucson, Arizona. Improved motors, HVAC, and lighting in its 48,000-square-foot facility cut carbon dioxide emissions by 42 percent per square foot, while saving the company over $30,000 per year in reduced energy costs.

In some cases, whole industrial sectors are doing the kind of strategic planning done by BP and Royal Dutch/Shell. For example, the energy-intensive industries discussed in Chapter 8, such as pulp and paper, and steel, have partnered with the Department of Energy to develop long-term visions, strategies, and roadmaps for increasing productivity while decreasing energy use and pollution.

The American Iron and Steel Institute (AISI) and the Steel Manufacturers Association (SMA), which represent nearly all of U.S. steel manufacturing companies, developed a vision, *Steel: A National Resource for the Future*, in May 1995 in partnership with the DOE's Industry of the Future Program. The vision calls for achieving industry goals of zero waste and increasing the percentage of steel manufactured from recycled scrap from over 50 percent today to nearly 70 percent over the next two decades.[6] To achieve these goals, the AISI and SMA signed a research and development compact with the DOE to develop, demonstrate, evaluate, and accelerate new clean technologies into the marketplace.

One project that will aid in achieving the recycling goal is a demonstration of a two-step process for the continuous dezincing (removing the galvanized coating) of steel scrap. Applying this technology to process 4.5 million tons of galvanized scrap would save 50 trillion BTUs of energy per year. It would also lower raw materials costs to the industry by $150 million a year, reduce the need to import at least 75,000 tons of zinc per year, and eliminate zinc from the steelmaking fume and effluent water. This is but one of many new technologies now being demonstrated that will aid in reducing carbon emissions in steelmaking.

The value of having a strategic plan is that it allows a company or industrial sector to prioritize its investments and to find innovative partners to achieve its long-term goals. In the case of the steel industry, the broad understanding of what energy and environmental goals are achievable has also allowed them to make a major climate commitment: On October 1, 1997, AISI announced that *the steel industry would voluntarily reduce greenhouse gas emissions by at least 10 percent by the year 2010.*[7] This exceeds the U.S. national target agreed to at Kyoto, a 7 percent reduction by 2010. The plan would achieve "gradual but steady reductions through more effective utilization of materials, improving the efficiency of existing energy producing processes, introducing new in-plant reduction efforts, and developing and installing new technology," according to senior AISI officials.

❖

Some industry trade associations, such as the American Petroleum Institute, have taken a different approach to planning for global warming. They have commissioned economic models to examine the impact of taking action on global warming. These models suggest that reducing greenhouse gases will harm the U.S. economy and cost jobs, and that carbon would cost as much as $60 a ton or more, which would raise energy prices by as much as 40 percent.

Some studies support the view that the price of carbon dioxide will be high, while others come to a different conclusion. One of the most comprehensive studies that considers in detail the kind of technologies discussed in this book is "Scenarios of U.S. Carbon Reductions: Potential Impacts of Energy Technologies by 2010 and Beyond," a study performed in 1997 by five U.S. national laboratories.[8] The survey, which I initiated and supervised, suggests that significant emissions reductions are possible for the country with no net increase in the nation's energy bill and a much lower price for carbon dioxide permits, a price between $7 and $14 per ton.

CARBON VERSUS CARBON DIOXIDE

Some people use carbon rather than carbon dioxide as a metric. The fraction of carbon in carbon dioxide is the ratio of their weights. The atomic weight of carbon is 12, while the weight of carbon dioxide is 44, because it includes two oxygen atoms that each weigh 16. So, to switch from one to the other, use the following formula:

One ton of carbon equals 44/12 = 11/3 = 3.67 tons of carbon dioxide.

Thus 11 tons of carbon dioxide equals 3 tons of carbon, and a price of $30 per ton of carbon dioxide equals a price of $110 per ton of carbon.

Indeed, the case studies in this book suggest that almost any company that wants to can reduce its emissions significantly while increasing profits and productivity. This would suggest that if a national trading system for carbon were ultimately put in place, similar to the Clean Air Act's sulfur trading system, the price for carbon dioxide would be very low. If the entire steel industry believes that it can beat the Kyoto target voluntarily and if two of the world's largest oil companies are committed to take action, then I suspect the price will be at the lower range.

Moreover, any company that wants to reduce greenhouse gas emissions outside of its buildings and factories can do so at low cost. My colleagues and I at the Center for Energy and Climate Solutions have been working with a number of the people, businesses, and organizations profiled in this book to develop a least-cost strategy for reducing greenhouse gas emissions using energy efficiency and cool power. We believe a variety of approaches can achieve significant reductions at well under $15 per ton of carbon dioxide, and with innovative financing strategies that take advantage of the savings from lowered energy bills, the net costs are likely to come in under $5 per ton.

For instance, your company (or any individual or organization) could set up a revolving loan fund, similar to the Texas LoanSTAR program, to finance the upgrade of schools and other buildings in your community. The upgrades would be performed using the International Performance Measurement and Verification Protocol, discussed in Chapter 3, to maximize emissions reductions and ensure persistence of results while minimizing both risk and financing costs.

Also, your company could establish for your suppliers something analogous to the DOE's Industrial Assessment Centers (IACs), which perform energy, waste, and productivity assessments for small and medium-size businesses. This "supplier IAC" would perform free assessments for any interested supplier, identifying all cost-effective greenhouse gas mitigation improvements and then *providing low-cost financing for those upgrades.* This would simultaneously lower the costs and increase the productivity of your suppliers while reducing the embodied carbon dioxide in their products (see Chapter 9).

These and other strategies will be increasingly commonplace in the coming years, which will help to keep the price of carbon dioxide low when the country starts trading carbon dioxide.

YOUR COMPANY'S STRATEGIC PLANNING

A company doing strategic planning about climate change will want to consider the impact of different prices for carbon dioxide. If climate change is occurring, then it is almost inevitable that carbon will have a price and very likely that a domestic trading system will be put in place. This will improve the cost-effectiveness of all carbon-mitigating actions and at the same time presumably make carbon-mitigating products more attractive to would-be buyers.

The Minnesota Public Utilities Commission established an economic value for carbon emissions from power plants and other sources that contribute to global warming of $0.30 to $3.10 per ton. In May 1998, the Minnesota Court of Appeals affirmed that "the commission's determination that [carbon dioxide] negatively affects the environment was proper." The Burlington Electric Department in Vermont incorporated into its 1994 Integrated Resource Plan an externality "adder" of $16.50 per ton.[9]

For the basic purposes of strategic planning, I would suggest developing scenarios for $0, $10, and $30 per ton. For operational planning—for instance, determining the cost-effectiveness of long-term investments, such as an on-site cogeneration plant—a small, nonzero value for carbon is probably the best to use for now. A $10 per ton figure will have little impact on most decisions (since applied nationwide it would only raise electricity prices about 5 percent). Nonetheless, it is probably enough to accelerate your company's transition away from having any on-site coal combustion, a policy companies like General Motors and 3M are already putting into place.

The key to turning your strategic plan for reducing carbon dioxide into an operational plan is to see carbon-mitigating investments as "strategic" investments that merit a low capital hurdle rate.

 Rather than a two-year payback (a 50 percent return on investment), as is now typical for energy-saving investments, your company should use a rate more typical of strategic investments—15 percent, close to a seven-year payback.

As shown in many of the earlier chapters, taking such an approach will stimulate the kind of systems approach to workplace and process redesign that can achieve productivity gains that paradoxically achieve a much faster payback.

And what could be more strategic than simultaneously mitigating global warming and capturing unique productivity gains?

Conclusion

CARBON DIOXIDE AND PRODUCTIVITY

This book has been about carbon dioxide and productivity, about cool and lean thinking, about the future and the present. It's about what you can do to be part of the global solution while you generate more profits.

Today, as we have seen over and over again, your company can use energy-efficient technologies to cut in half the energy costs—and greenhouse gas emissions—of your buildings and factories with rapid paybacks. These technologies not only earn a high return on investment but also are very low risk, having been used successfully by innumerable companies. At the same time, when they are applied in a systematic fashion—through cool design of workplaces or cool design of motor systems and manufacturing processes—these technologies can achieve huge productivity gains that can bring paybacks to under a year—*better than a 100 percent return on investment.*

With the wave of new cool power technologies, such as advanced cogeneration and solar energy, your company can continue lowering its emissions of carbon dioxide while saving money.

Some of our best companies—DuPont, 3M, Compaq, Toyota, Interface, Xerox—continue to pursue these huge opportunities, refuting the notion that the low-hanging fruit of energy savings and pollution prevention ever become exhausted. Most companies never start down this lucrative road, in the mistaken belief that, after the oil shocks, they "did energy conservation" in the late 1970s and early 1980s. Indeed, because of that very misconception, many companies cut back on their energy staffs during the corporate down-sizings of the 1990s. Most companies still believe their energy consumption is simply a source of costs, rather than a source of profit opportunities, so that their energy usage gets neither the necessary capital nor management attention.

I believe the strategies described in this book represent the near future for American companies. In part that is because of the 1997 Kyoto agreement among the industrialized nations to reduce greenhouse gas emissions to below 1990 levels by the years 2008–2012. Yet even if the United States does not ratify the agreement quickly (because of a mistaken belief by many in Congress that it would harm U.S. companies), every multinational corporation will need a carbon-mitigation strategy as Europe and Japan move forward to limit emissions. Moreover, the Kyoto agreement itself is merely a manifestation of something of far greater long-term importance to business planning—the growing consensus among the vast majority of the world's governments and their climate scientists, as represented in the UN's Intergovernmental Panel on Climate Change, that global warming is occurring.

As that consensus grows, climate change will increasingly become a driver for business decision making. Your company's greenhouse gas emissions will become both a strategic risk and a strategic opportunity. Further, as more and more of the world's best companies demonstrate that reducing emissions is both straightforward and profitable, governments, environmental groups, and consumers—your stakeholders and customers—will increasingly demand that you take action.

Sustained annual reductions of 5 percent or more in carbon emissions per unit of product sold, now achieved by only the best buildings, factories, and companies, will become commonplace in the 2008 to 2012 timeframe. That is, within only ten years, the benchmark of best practices described here will be standard practice for most companies because of their desire to help the environment, to avoid being seen as hurting the environment, or—above all—to remain competitive.

Simply put, *global climate change is making carbon mitigation a strategic corporate investment.* Already, large international companies, like Toyota, British Petroleum, and Royal Dutch/Shell, see climate change as a major driver for strategic and operational planning.

Shell's scenarios (Chapter 1) are of special importance, not merely because Shell is the benchmark for strategic planning in the corporate world or because the company itself is betting so heavily on them. Shell's scenarios are important because *they show a plausible path to stabilizing global emissions and avoiding the worst of global warming while maintaining the historical rates of growth needed to continue to broaden and deepen economic prosperity around the globe.*

These scenarios are not merely *possible* futures, they are *necessary* futures. Achieving them will require that we greatly expand the use of energy efficiency, cogeneration, and renewable energy. Your company—indeed each company, each community, and each nation—can affect the outcome.

If these scenarios are to prevail, if we are to have a livable future, all companies, not just the best, will have to become cool, as will a host of other organizations—the financial and investment community; the international lending institutions; the scientific, engineering, and architectural communities; and local, state, and national governments.

The national implications of such a transition are staggering. SYCOM, one of the nation's leading energy service companies, selected forty energy-saving projects at random out of the hundreds they have worked on (see Chapter 10). The projects covered the full range of energy-efficiency strategies discussed in this book: lighting, motor controls, heating, ventilation, and cooling. SYCOM then calculated a cost per ton of NOx (oxides of nitrogen) reduced that came to *negative $9,000* and *a cost per ton of carbon dioxide reduced of negative $30.* In other words, a profit was made at the same time emissions were cut. The energy wizards of Texas A&M (Chapters 3 and 10) found that their building upgrades achieved similarly large negative costs per ton of NOx and carbon dioxide reduced.

What would happen if any significant fraction of U.S. companies became cool? The country as a whole would be able to meet the Kyoto targets while lowering the nation's annual energy bill by tens of billions of dollars and accelerating economic growth through productivity gains. At the same time, emissions of harmful urban air pollutants—NOx, sulfur dioxide, and particulates—would drop sharply, immediately improving human health and local environments.

We must all work to create this cool and livable future.

Appendix

THERE IS NO SUCH THING AS THE "HAWTHORNE EFFECT"

Managers continue to dismiss data that links quality work environments to productivity. The higher the percentage of correlation found (5, 10, 15, 20% improved productivity), the greater their disbelief. *Executives consistently cite the Hawthorne effect as clear disproof of any real linkage of productivity to the physical workplace—all that matters is management method.*

This allows workers to be put into increasingly poorer work environments—smaller workstations, cheaper furniture, less work surface, less storage, no daylight or view, no control of air, temperature, or light. It is time to put the Hawthorne study away, and to teach business students the mountain of international evidence that links physical and environmental quality to great gains in individual and organizational productivity.[1]

—Vivian Loftness, Head of Carnegie-Mellon's School
  of Architecture, August 1998

You have already seen a portion of the mountain of productivity cases in Chapter 4. Here I want to focus on the Hawthorne study itself and put it away once and for all, as Loftness asks.

The original experiments failed miserably at demonstrating the "Hawthorne Effect." In fact, as we will see, they demonstrated the reverse—that work conditions greatly impact worker productivity. Yet, the myth continues to have a detrimental effect on the beliefs and actions of managers. Virtually every published reference to the experiment and its results is wildly inaccurate—including most management textbooks. They all should be changed. Typically wrong is this description from the classic, *In Search of Excellence,* which purports to describe the work of Harvard researcher Elton Mayo:

> On the shop floors of Western Electric's Hawthorne plant, [Mayo] tried to demonstrate that better work place hygiene would have a direct and positive effect on worker productivity. So he turned up the lights. Productivity went up, as predicted. Then, as he prepared to turn his attention to another factor, he routinely turned the lights back down. Productivity went up again! For us, the very important message of the research that these actions spawned, and a theme we shall return to continually in the book, is that it is *attention to employees,* not work conditions per se, that has the dominant impact on productivity. (Many of our best companies, one friend observed, seem to reduce management to merely creating "an endless stream of Hawthorne Effects.")[2]

This description is entirely in error. First, Mayo had nothing to do with the lighting experiments: He didn't even show up at the plant until *a year after* they were completed (this mistake is so common, even *Encyclopedia Britannica* makes it). Second, the experiment wasn't about hygiene, it was about determining optimal light levels for industrial workers, and so the lights weren't "routinely" turned back down—that was a key part of the experiment. Third, far from being a surprise, the productivity rise that (only sometimes) followed when the lights were turned down had in fact been predicted by the researchers. Fourth, a 1991 study—the only statistical analysis ever published of one of the lighting experiments—concluded that productivity and lighting were, in fact, correlated.

Finally, and most importantly, "the research that these actions spawned" did *not* prove that it was "attention to employees, not work conditions per se, that has the dominant impact on productivity," but that quickly became the most commonly held view of the Hawthorne Effect.

The heart of the research that the lighting experiments spawned was a 270-week study of women producing electrical relays, which involved two dozen experimental periods of varying length during which working conditions were changed, usually to learn the impact on productivity. The stunner was that in this Relay Assembly Test Room study, productivity rose about 34 percent over the first two years, and 46 percent over the whole period— a truly remarkable gain, and all the more so because the plant's managers and ultimately the Harvard researchers called in for help could offer no simple explanation. This became probably the single most analyzed and influential study of workers ever performed, helping to spawn a revolution in management philosophy and to launch the entire field of industrial social psychology.

The Relay Assembly experiment itself involved *only five women* assembling relays, too tiny a number to prove anything. There was no control group. Productivity actually *dropped* in the first five-week period when the workers were moved to the test room.

Productivity did not begin rising until *a special pay system was set up* that for the first time in their jobs essentially rewarded the women directly for their level of output. The women were also given *constant feedback on their output* and dramatically fewer types of relays to assemble, making it much easier for them to learn how to pace themselves. Nine months into the experiment two of the women who were apparently restricting output intentionally *were replaced;* one of the replacements was "the fastest assembler in the department's history."[3] Halfway through the experiment, the Great Depression began.

Those were the main reasons productivity shot up so quickly and then kept rising. Management style had little to do with it.

Nevertheless, even such fatal flaws in methodology and perception rarely convince true believers. Typically, what ultimately disproves the results of a scientific experiment are

- an inability to reproduce the results;
- identification of significant flaws in the methodology; and
- an alternative explanation that fits the data better and has been reproduced in subsequent experiments.

Until now, these three requirements have never been gathered together to analyze the complete Hawthorne Effect, an exercise that must examine both the lighting experiments and the relay assembly test room experiments.

The term "Hawthorne Effect" is, as we will see, *meaningless.* The Hawthorne researchers own follow-up experiments—as well as decades of subsequent research—failed to substantiate the results or even to reproduce them. No comprehensive statistical analyses of the original relay assembly data were performed until the late 1970s. Those that have been done in the last quarter century do not support a Hawthorne Effect. In fact, every single one of these analyses are consistent with the view that the work conditions—particularly the special pay and feedback—can explain 80 to 90 percent of the productivity rise.

My interest in the Hawthorne Effect arose from my work documenting how specific workplace changes, particularly higher quality lighting, had improved productivity. I was often asked if the wonderful results were not simply due to the Hawthorne Effect—by which people meant that they believed *any* change in lighting would increase production, not just higher quality lighting. The myth, after all, says that any change in lighting signals special attention to employees by management. Only a deep understanding could help me answer those who raised the issue.

The initial area I examined, the literature of workplace design, was the first surprise. It is filled with studies that refute the Hawthorne Effect. For instance, a major 1984 study of 6,000 workers in some seventy organizations on the effect of office design on productivity found a direct correlation between specific changes in the physical environment and worker productivity. The authors did "*not find the across-the-board increase in productivity the Hawthorne Effect should confer.*"[4]

Far more surprising, the deeper I looked in the technical literature, the more I found that the "Hawthorne Effect" had largely been debunked in many places but that this information was not all in one place. Thus, it has failed to seep into the popular literature or into textbooks.

One reason is that many subsequent critiques were too brief and took on only one aspect of the Hawthorne Effect—such as proving one element of the experiment had flawed methodology. To push so entrenched a notion out of the minds of managers and the authors of textbooks and encyclopedias requires a far more comprehensive analysis.

So the Hawthorne Effect retains an unjustified hold on both popular and technical thinking. Two standard literature searches found some one hundred references *per year* to the Hawthorne Effect in popular and trade publications over the past several years, ranging from *The Washington Post* and the *Financial Times* to myriad management publications and dozens of articles in the world's most respected medical journals. The vast majority of the references are as wrong as Tom Peters was in *In Search of Excellence*. Yet, as a 1998 article by the *Financial Times* notes: "The name of Elton Mayo must be near the top of any list of influences on management in the twentieth century."[5]

The experiments remain harmfully influential. Yet we will see just how confused and ultimately how perverse the entire notion of the Hawthorne Effect is. And bear in mind that to be *for* throwing it out is not to be *against* people-centered or humanistic management—it is only to realize that the Hawthorne experiments provide no evidence whatsoever in support of such an approach.

THE LIGHTING EXPERIMENTS

I begin with the Hawthorne lighting tests, not only because they later launched the paradigm-shifting relay assembly experiments but also because they are a key part of the myth that says improved work conditions such as lighting have no significant impact on productivity. The enduring mythology of the Hawthorne Effect comes partly because the original researchers *never published* either a detailed discussion of the lighting tests or an analysis of the results. "Knowledge" about them exists primarily as often-repeated anecdotes, which the archival records, as well as a few recent technical studies, completely undercut. The original records are the basis for much of the analysis below. They tell a fascinating tale.

The experiments were motivated by two factors. First and perhaps foremost, electric utilities and equipment manufacturers wanted industry to increase its use of artificial light. Second, industry, the U.S. National Research Council (NRC), and Western Electric's management wanted to increase labor productivity. A group of power companies and manufacturers, led by General Electric, funded the NRC's newly created Committee on Industrial Lighting to coordinate the research, which included an exhaustive literature review and trials at several factories, including Hawthorne. The chair of the Committee was Dugald C. Jackson, an electrical engineering professor at MIT.[6]

Professor Jackson chose Charles E. Snow, a recent MIT graduate in electrical engineering, to supervise the tests. Snow was assisted by Homer Hibarger, an analyst at Hawthorne. From 1924 to 1927, they ran three series of lighting tests, where workers' output was measured as light levels were varied. In these series of tests, unlike the relay assembly tests that came after, control groups were often used.

The experimenters found it exceedingly difficult to separate the effects of lighting from other factors. For instance, in one case, a control group increased output every time the test group did, "the reason being," in Snow's words, "*a determination not to let the Test Group beat them out!*" Indeed, in many of the lighting experiments, the control group paralleled the test group, even when they were separated.[7] Snow also reported that one of the groups in the first series of tests had a big jump in output not because of anything to do with lighting but because a new foreman "told them what would happen if they raised their percentage and if this did not attract them told them what would happen if they didn't."[8]

The first two series of tests seemed to show no correlation between lighting levels and productivity. The researchers leaped to the conclusion that supervision and psychological factors were more important than lighting. But methodological flaws undercut that conclusion, although they did not know it then. Their tests mainly combined changing artificial light levels with the background level of daylight in the plant, which itself changed during the course of the day and the season. Yet the light meters used by the researchers to determine the total level of illumination (artificial light plus natural light) were out of calibration for as much as 30 percent of the days. A 1991 recalculation of the actual level of daylight using weather data and statistical analysis for one of the experiments found "*substantial and significant effects of illumination upon worker productivity.*"[9]

The experimenters noticed with the very first series what came to be the most well-known result of the lighting experiments, namely that while productivity seemed at first to rise with illumination, it did not drop to its original level when lighting levels were reduced. As noted, some of this may be due to flaws in the light meters. In an unpublished report, Professor Jackson noted another key factor:

> The failure of the groups to return to their original working efficiency after having increased their production rate may be due to a certain amount of inertia and to *unwillingness on the part of the operatives to let their pay fall after it was once raised to a higher level. Some of the comments of the operatives indicated this point.*[10]

Light levels for the first two tests were between 10 and 60 foot-candles nearly all of the time. The researchers concluded that light levels above 10 foot-candles would not boost productivity.[11]

The third series of tests is the most well known of the lighting experiments. Since the researchers were now convinced that "high" levels of lighting would not boost productivity, they wanted to see how *low* the lighting levels could go. They covered the windows with paper or burlap bags to eliminate all daylight but let air in. "Good ventilation was ensured" by using electric fans. As for the artificial light, "elaborate precautions were taken to maintain uniformity of distribution of the light over the entire working plane," including diffusing units. Indeed, Jackson noted "the complete absence of objectionable glare from the lighting arrangements."[12]

This test started the coil winders at 11 foot-candles, which was ratcheted down slowly every three weeks, to 9, 7, 6, 5, 4, and then 2.7. Output rose slowly but fairly steadily, a 6 percent increase after four months. When light levels were dropped to 1.4 foot-candles, the coil winders protested bitterly, but production dropped back only 3 percent (though this test ran only a day). When light levels were returned to 11 foot-candles, output rose 2 percent the first three weeks and then another 3 percent over the next three weeks at the same light level. When one last test was run at 4 foot-candles, output remained constant.

These results, together with the first two series of tests, famously become part of the Hawthorne myth, supposedly proving that output goes up whether you turn the lights up or turn the lights down—hence light levels don't matter. Another part of the myth is that all these results came as a surprise to the researchers. Yet by the third series, not only weren't they a surprise, the researchers had predicted the outcome before the test began.

THE REAL EXPLANATION

Jackson expected "the production level to be maintained until the illumination intensity arrives at a point where it becomes impossible for the group to produce at the previous rate." He gave two reasons, neither of which supports the "Hawthorne Effect" explanation. First, "Operatives having become accustomed to a good illumination will have established themselves in a definite *rhythm of work*," which they will tend to maintain even as the illumination is lowered. Second, "The productivity of the workers at the higher illumination intensities having resulted in certain *wage earnings,* the workers will attempt to maintain those earnings as long as possible, and with each succeeding decrease in illumination the tendency will be to work harder and harder."[13]

In the case of the final lighting test, Jackson's prediction was all the more likely because the subjects were coil winders. These workers, who wound the coils used in telephones, were paid on an individual piece rate—the more you produced, the more you were paid. The fact that they kept producing more as light levels dropped to 2.7 foot-candles is not too surprising (especially since they were used to working in light levels as low as 3 foot-candles).

Some of the researchers were concerned about this very possibility—that the workers were driven by money—"that the employees were putting additional effort into their work in order to maintain their wage scale even though the illumination intensity made working conditions more difficult." So they extended the 2.7-foot-candle test for another three weeks but switched the workers to an "individual day rate which was based on each individual's production rate for the previous eight weeks." Output of the test group *dropped* 1.3 percent—30 percent of the increase so far—which the researchers dismissed as "not enough to indicate any pointed influence" but which seems significant for two reasons.[14] First, the researchers knew that the workers tended to maintain their "rhythm of work" over a period of a few weeks even as test conditions changed. Second, historian Richard Gillespie noted in 1991 that "it is not clear how this [pay change] was explained to the workers, or whether the workers seriously believed that if they slowed production they would not be penalized."[15] If only some of the workers understood the change, that would mean the wage effect was even bigger.

As for the overall results of the experiments, Snow noted one confounding factor: "Some piece rate workers perhaps intentionally limit their production in the fear of having the rate cut."[16] This is a typical response for piece rate workers; it even had a name—"soldiering." We will see the importance of this factor in the later Hawthorne experiments. In particular, Gillespie pointed out that the "workers in the relay assembly test room came to realize that no matter how high their output and pay, the company would not reduce the piece rates, something it would do as a matter of course in regular departments."[17] If even only a few of the coil winders in the final lighting test came to the same conclusion, that would more than explain why they continued to work a few percentage points harder as the weeks wore on with little regard to light levels.

It is unwarranted to draw the conclusion, as so many have, that these tests meant that lighting didn't matter, given the problematic experimental design and the wage effect. Many things further undermine this faulty conclusion. For instance, it is not clear how important lighting was for some of the tasks being tested, especially when performed by a worker who had been doing the same thing for years. Skilled relay assembly workers could work in the dark by memory and feel. *Before the tests began, the coil winders had been working in light levels as low as 3 foot-candles.*

Another crucial point made in Chapters 3 and 4 is that it is not *quantity* of light that matters so much as *quality*. The relay assembly test room workers complained of glare and overlighting at 7 foot-candles and asked for light levels to be *reduced*. Bad lighting quality trumps adequate lighting quantity. *Yet, the final lighting test was done in a special room with improved ventilation and a lighting system with "the complete absence of objectionable glare."* So 2.7 foot-candles of light of higher quality than they normally had may not have had a major impact on workers.

The issue, then, is not so much whether higher lighting levels increase productivity (which some of the data did show). The issue is whether the workers' desire to maintain work rhythm and increase wages overwhelms the effect of lower lighting (which some of the data also showed).

What is also surprising to me is that while, as we have seen, Jackson and the other researchers had a theory that predicted that workers would maintain their rhythm of work and wage rate, at least until light levels were extremely inadequate, they apparently never bothered to test the theory statistically. They seem to have just eyeballed the data and leaped to the conclusion that output and lighting were not particularly correlated. But they should not have looked simply for a correlation between output and *one* factor—light level. They should have looked at the relationship between output and *two* factors—light level together with a factor to take into account the tendency of workers to maintain (or increase) their previously achieved level of output and wages.

When such an analysis was performed five decades later in 1979 using modern statistical techniques, it revealed that indeed *these two factors alone did explain much of the data.* As the authors of a subsequent analysis in 1991 wrote:

> The initial work by Wiljanen (1979) and the current analysis of illumination experiments show that *lighting can contribute to worker productivity.* In one of the experiments, *most* of the performance differences across experimental treatments is

explained by differences in total illumination. While these results are sixty years late in responding to electrical industry interests in expanding their markets, they do suggest to those of us primarily interested in productivity that *conditions of work can influence performance.*[18]

This was not the conclusion of the original researchers. Though Jackson completed a draft final report, it was never published. Ironically, part of the reason appears to be that the sponsors of the research, the electrical industry representatives, did not like the researchers' conclusion, namely that light level didn't correlate with worker performance. Without a final report, our understanding of the lighting experiments has come mainly from second-hand reports and anecdotes.

In sum, for the lighting experiments, instead of finding a Hawthorne Effect, we find the following conclusions: (1) The results have not been reproduced—there are many modern instances in which better lighting improved productivity while worse lighting hurt it; (2) the original experiments had a flawed methodology; and (3) an alternative explanation fits the data better and has been reproduced in subsequent experiments.

We will see that the essential explanation—workers want to maintain their rhythm of work and their level of wages—was proven in the very next experiment, the relay assembly tests.

As for Homer Hibarger of Western Electric, his conclusion at the time was essentially that since lighting didn't seem to have much of an effect on worker output, supervision and psychological factors must have an important, yet unknown, effect. Since workers increased output under low lighting, he wondered, why hadn't they increased output under regular shop conditions? He told George Pennock, superintendent of the Technical Branch at Hawthorne and the person responsible for production methods, that he, Homer, could answer that question, determine the causes for increased/decreased output, and perhaps learn how to boost worker output. All he would need to do was to put a small group of relay assembly operators in a test room and track output as experimental conditions were changed (with himself supervising).[19]

THE BIGGEST CONFUSION: THE RELAY EXPERIMENTS

Of all the famous paradigm-shifting experiments in history, few have been as poorly understood as the one that took place in the Relay Assembly Test Room of the Hawthorne Works from 1927 to 1932. The single biggest confusion is the mistaken belief that productivity increased every time an experimental change was made. For instance, a statement from the 1982 book, *Introduction to Social Research:* "Each time a change was made, worker productivity increased, leaving the impression that each change had a progressive effect." The 1985 book, *Research Methods in Psychology:* "With few exceptions, no matter what changes were made—whether there were more or few rest periods, whether the work day was made shorter or longer, et cetera—the women tended to produce more and more telephone relays. . . . The workers knew that the experimenters expected the changes in working conditions to affect them, so they did."[20]

Summing up these all-too-typical erroneous descriptions in a 1992 article in the *American Journal of Sociology,* Stephen Jones writes, "As these sources reveal, the received wisdom is that there were Hawthorne Effects at the Hawthorne Plant."[21] That is, the received wisdom said that no matter what action the experimenters took, productivity went up. Hence the increase in productivity must have been caused by the simple fact that actions of any kind were taken, or that the experimenters were demonstrating special attention to the workers. In this interpretation, two points are key. First, work conditions were said to be irrelevant. Second, *the irrelevancy of the work conditions was supposedly demonstrated over and over again* since, each time they changed, productivity rose.

In fact, go back to the original data and there we will find that *productivity dipped immediately following an experimental change almost as often as it jumped.* It dropped the first time the five workers were put in the special test room. More important, the general rise in productivity over the 270-week period was not correlated with the experimental changes. Jones reanalyzed the data to see if there was a correlation between productivity and either the explicit changes made at the start of each new experimental period or to *any* changes in experimental conditions at all. He found none: "Contrary to the conventional wisdom in much research and teaching, I found essentially no evidence of Hawthorne Effects. . . ." He concludes:

> The one remaining interpretation of the Hawthorne Effect that could survive my investigation is . . . that the whole 270-week period of study was but one experiment, and that all of the various changes introduced at the start of the study and maintained throughout were one experimental change. Since we have no data on a control group, this interpretation means that *there is, in essence, only one data point.*[22]

In other words, while productivity did rise, it did *not* do so repeatedly in response to the experimental changes, which would have provided *many instances* of the Hawthorne Effect. In fact, the remarkable rise in productivity was independent of the experimental changes; it was a rise that provides at most one instance of the Hawthorne Effect (or, as I will argue below, of something else entirely). Jones finishes by saying:

> In this context, I must conclude that there is slender or no evidence of a Hawthorne Effect in the Hawthorne Relay Assembly Test Room. Finally, in light of these results, I must also con-

clude that the Hawthorne Effect is largely a construction of subsequent interpreters of the Hawthorne experiments.[23]

Elton Mayo himself had written, "This steady increase [in production] as represented by all the contemporary records seemed to ignore the experimental changes in its upward development."[24] As Thomas North Whitehead, the MIT professor in charge of analyzing the Hawthorne data, had explained in his meticulous 1938 study of the tests: "The following facts stand out: . . . Changes in output rate do not correspond in time with changes in experimental periods for the most part." (The one exception is Period XII, when rest pauses were eliminated and group output for the period dropped about 4 percent.)[25]

So Whitehead back in 1938, like Jones in 1992, pretty much reduces the entire 270-week experiment to one data point: the remarkable increase in productivity of 46 percent. The *repeated* instances of the Hawthorne Effect are a myth.[26]

At this point, then, we are trying to explain that one remaining data point, the general rise in productivity in the first relay assembly room, which was not linked to the changes in the experimental periods, or at least not directly. The explanation offered by Elton Mayo and his colleagues came to be called the Hawthorne Effect.

THE MANY "HAWTHORNE EFFECTS"

What exactly is the Hawthorne Effect in the eyes of those responsible for the term? In a 1966 book, two of the key interpreters, William J. Dickson of Western Electric and F. J. Roethlisberger of Harvard (who had together written the definitive *first* Hawthorne interpretation *Management and the Worker* in 1939) offer their explanation after having more than three decades to think about the subject: "A number of different explanations can be given of the positive Hawthorne Effects. Let us mention some in connection with the Relay Assembly Test Room where we have more data":

a. the "special" attention and treatment by the workers from the experimenters, inadvertently produced by

b. the artificial conditions set up for measurement in a controlled experiment, which can be stated as

c. changes in the methods of supervision, the significance of which might be seen better as

d. changes in the methods of customary supervision which can be stated more operationally as

e. changes in the behavior of the experimenters in order to secure the cooperation and participation of the workers to the experimental conditions imposed, the significance of which might be better seen as

 f. more "openness" of relationship of a more permissive, participatory, and transactional kind between experimenters and workers than customarily obtained between supervisors and workers, all of which (a, b, c, d, e, and f) might have been perceived by the workers as

 g. "special" social treatment (social rewards), that is, in terms of the language of the workers

 h. being treated as "human beings," as "persons" and as "members of the human race," that is, speaking more psychologically,

 i. having their feelings, needs, and ideas recognized, particularly their needs to belong, to be wanted, to be heard, and to be respected, which resulted in

 j. a "special" social position which they reciprocated by

 k. changes in their personal attitudes, which also might have affected

 l. changes in their relations to each other (a change in their informal social organization) which might be seen more clearly as

 m. changes in the norms of behavior of the group, particularly their norms about output, which might have facilitated

 n. changes in their relations to supervision and management; these changes—k, l, m, and n—being in the direction of

 o. more cooperative relationships with each other at work (more team work),

 p. an identification of themselves with the aims of the experimenters, i.e., as cooperative subjects in the experiment performing in accord with what they saw as the requirements of this role, which they might have perceived as

 q. an identification with the aims of management, resulting in sustained high output.[27]

Little wonder everyone is confused as to what the Hawthorne Effect is. Dickson and Roethlisberger immediately go on to say:

> We have kept these different explanations purposely interrelated in order to make a point. To select one or the other as the explanation, as many commentators of the Hawthorne studies have done, is often a misleading oversimplification. What does it mean to say that the positive Hawthorne Effect resulted from the *special attention or treatment* the workers received? For many this statement becomes a premature closure, that is a kind of final buttoning up to the effect, "Well, we see now how silly the experimenters were in not seeing clearly what they were up to; they were, of course, giving the workers the special treatment; *ergo* output went up. Now we have settled this, let's think about something else." But what made this special treatment so special? In what way was it special? To whom and for whom was it special? Was it special to everyone? etc.[28]

Thus, the authors give one possible explanation for the one remarkable data point of rising output as some combination or interrelationship of these seventeen aspects; either individually or collectively, to Dickson and Roethlisberger they are the Hawthorne Effect. This posited seventeen-part explanation is so nebulous as to be almost undisprovable. Therefore, it will always remain possible to stick to the story of the "Hawthorne Effect," even if those closest to the experiment could not explain it in one breath.

In sharp contrast, there are very compelling reasons for not believing this explanation. First, subsequent experiments have failed to demonstrate the existence of a Hawthorne Effect.

SUBSEQUENT EXPERIMENTS DO NOT FIND A HAWTHORNE EFFECT

Consider a major 1967 study by the U.S. Office of Education that involved both new field research aimed at reproducing the Hawthorne Effect and a review of published educational studies. The new field research failed to reproduce the effect, and the review failed to find any evidence of it either.[29]

Two decades later, a group of researchers attempted an even more comprehensive review of educational studies, examining every journal article, unpublished paper, or dissertation included in three major databases and previous Hawthorne reviews. They found thirty-eight studies with (1) an experimental group (subjects who received some specific treatment or intervention, such as physical training); (2) a traditional control group (subjects that had no intervention or treatment); and (3) a "Hawthorne" control group (subjects that received no real treatment but received special attention or knowledge they were in an experiment or "an activity to equate them with the experimental group in terms of time, effort, interest, or novelty.")[30] The purpose was to see if the Hawthorne control group had a different (i.e., more positive) outcome than the pure control group. The results were "discouraging":

> First, there was no evidence of an overall Hawthorne Effect. The mean effect associated with Hawthorne manipulations was nonsignificant, and hence such groups essentially could be regarded as no different from a no-treatment control. . . .
>
> [T]he conclusion we derive from an exhaustive survey of all available studies employing Hawthorne controls seems clear. There is no artifact that should be labeled the Hawthorne Effect. . . .[31]

Once again, the term "Hawthorne Effect" was shown to have little meaning and little scientific validity.

THE REAL EXPLANATION

The second compelling reason for not believing the "Hawthorne Effect" explanation is that there is a better explanation with the following virtues that the Hawthorne Effect lacks: It actually explains the data, and it is consistent with the methodology.

The explanation for the rise in productivity among the small group of relay assembly room workers over the 270 weeks is, I believe, best phrased as follows: *For the first time in their jobs, the five relay assembly room workers were put in unique circumstances that gave them the ability to make more money—or, equally important—to avoid making less money and over time they learned how to do so.* It was, in other words, the reverse of the Hawthorne Effect: Work conditions, not attention to employees, were responsible for the productivity rise. A number of unique factors contributed.

In Period I of the experiment, a base production rate was established when the workers were observed in the regular department without their knowledge. Relay assembly was chosen because it was the kind of highly repetitive work where fatigue was common. It required "the simultaneous use of both hands to place pins, bushings, springs, terminals and insulators between plates, insert a coil and armature, then screw the assembly together."[32] Assembly required about one minute.

The workers on the shop floor were paid by a group-piece rate system. Each unit produced had a piecework value. The workers received a guaranteed hourly wage, and, if the group as a whole produced a total number of units with a piecework value greater than the sum of the guaranteed wages of the work-group members, then each worker was paid a larger sum.

In Period II, which began in mid-May of 1927, five workers (and a layout operator) were relocated to a test room. The workers were all young women. Four were still teenagers. Across from the work bench was supervisor and experimenter Homer Hibarger. In this second work period, which lasted five weeks, the first in the new test room, productivity (output per hour) dropped.

Period III, which started in mid-June, introduced what I believe to be the key change of the entire five-year experiment. On the regular shop floor, there were a hundred women in the group that determined the group piece rate. Starting with the third period, the group piece rate in the test room was based on just the work of the five relay assemblers, not the larger group of a hundred. George Pennock later explained, "This meant that each [woman in the test room] would earn an amount more nearly in proportion to her individual effort since she was paid with a group of five instead of a group of 100."[33] Even more, as Gary Gottfredson wrote in 1996, "The use of group contingencies with groups of about five persons should influence individual performance because it combines the influence of contingent reinforcement with the influence of peer pressure to perform well because all members of the groups have a stake in the improved performance of each."[34]

In addition to the pay incentive, the test room had another key change from the shop floor—*a specially designed workbench that provided a running record of an assembler's output.* Every day, Hibarger gave each of the assemblers a report of her output. Thus each worker had accurate feedback of her performance, usually given as a percentage of the rate at which piece-rate engineers believed the assemblers could theoretically work. This had a strong impact. For instance, after receiving the figures confirming that production had hit a new high, one worker said, "80.6 percent! No? Hurrah for our side! And on Monday too, isn't that nice?" to which another replied, "Gee! We made 80 percent yesterday, today we ought to make 90 percent."[35] Even two years later, the feedback continued to have impact. One of the assemblers said, "I'm about 15 relays behind yesterday." Another one said, "I made 421 yesterday, and I'm going to make better today." The observer-supervisor at the time wrote that the assemblers were "trying to beat their former output records. . . . Each girl was conscious of how much work she was doing. Frequent attempts were made by certain operators to break the record for a day's work."[36]

So the workers had a very strong incentive to increase output as well as feedback on their performance. They had, for the first time ever, the power and the information needed to give them direct personal control over their income. It didn't take them long to learn how to make more money.

LEARNING TO MAKE MORE MONEY

H. M. Parsons proposed the above idea in 1974, arguing that the women learned to work faster through operant conditioning.[37] In 1981, Brian Pitcher did a comprehensive statistical analysis showing that the production figures did in fact *fit a learning curve.*

Considerable research exists on the relationship between output (or performance) versus time whenever learning of any kind, such as skill acquisition, is going on. Pitcher applied a typical learning model to the relay assembly room: The relative improvement in output is modeled as proportional to the relative increment in hours worked. This means most of the improvement occurs early on, and then it slows over time. For the three operators who were in the test room from the beginning, *the learning trend accounts for a remarkable 83 to 89 percent of the variance in the Hawthorne data over the five-year period.* This is all the more astonishing since the model "assumes that the work conditions relevant to learning were constant throughout the experiment and to the degree that this assumption is not true—i.e., the experimental manipulations and other changes interfered with motivation and the normal learning process—then the level of fit should be lowered." So factoring in the 4 percent drop in productivity in Period XII when rest pauses were temporarily eliminated would improve the fit to the learning curve even more.[38]

The learning curve explanation accounts for why productivity kept rising over time and why the increase was never correlated with the various experimental changes. A 1980 analysis showed that a curve designed to model the effect of the pay incentive over time, very similar to a learning curve, accounted for an extraordinary *86.5 percent of the variance* in the weekly group productivity numbers for the *entire* five-year period.[39] Gottfredson's 1996 analysis came to the same conclusion and cited a number of studies showing how goals, feedback, and rewards increase performance. He bemoaned the fact that Parsons' interpretation "has largely been ignored."[40] Pitcher's 1981 learning curve work, which proved statistically that Parsons' view is valid, has also been largely ignored.

Over half a century ago, Professor Whitehead, the official analyst of the experiments, dismissed the idea of learning: "The long upward trend of working rate . . . could have nothing to do with practice or learning, as these terms are usually understood, for all the operators were experienced at this work and had long ago reached a steady state in these respects."[41] But this is too narrow a view of learning. Gillespie noted in 1991, "As they became more confident, the women would stroll across to the junior clerk's desk during the rest period in order to inspect the output figures." This is exactly the kind of learning that occurred. One of the longtime observers in the test room noted that "any individual who believed her output for a given period was exceptional or below par would check the records to verify this belief."[42]

Perhaps the assemblers did not learn how to make each individual relay faster. What they did learn was how to increase their overall rate—they learned how to pace themselves to make more money. Here is Shigeo Shingo, one of the creators of the remarkable Toyota lean production system (Chapter 2), describing the work of Frederick Taylor, the father of scientific management:

> In 1898, Taylor conducted his famous pig-iron hauling experiment at Bethlehem Steel following a detailed study of human fatigue and rest. In these experiments, a trial method was adopted in which hauling work was performed only 42% of the time. A worker would haul fifteen bars of pig-iron for seven minutes and then rest for ten. While previously even the best haulers could move no more than 12.5 tons per day, they could haul 47.5 tons with the new method. This made it possible to increase workers' wages by 60%—a perfect example of high efficiency, high wages, and low cost.[43]

Rest periods were introduced in Period IV of the relay assembly test and, with one exception, were continued throughout. The rest periods provided the workers two benefits: the chance to optimize their performance (as Taylor taught) and as much feedback as they ever wanted on just how well they were optimizing. Simply put, *the workers learned how to pace themselves,* which was always a key part of Taylorism, even if it has been subsequently forgotten, ignored, or abused.

> I would go further than Frederick Taylor and argue that Hawthorne
> proved something that Taylor did not understand but that the
> Japanese and many U.S. companies proved many years later. Taylor
> believed that one of management's key tasks was to figure out the
> "one best way" of doing a job to maximize productivity and then dic-
> tate to workers exactly how they should perform their tasks. In fact,
> under the right circumstances, workers can figure out how best to do
> their own jobs. I have argued throughout this book that they are usu-
> ally in a superior position to do so.

As for the rest pauses, Pitcher's analysis showed further that their main impact "was simply to eliminate much of the nonproductive or lost time taken as voluntary rest time." That is, the data show that workers learned to pace themselves. The original Hawthorne researchers themselves noted that the workers' performance was far more uniform during the times when there were rest periods than during the times without rest periods.[44]

One very special, rarely mentioned, condition in the test room helped productivity and made it easier to optimize pace and output: The variety of relays the women worked on was reduced, making work easier and faster. Gillespie notes that "as a result of the reduction in the variety of relays (to simplify standardization of the output data), [the workers] could become proficient on a few relays; in the regular department they might be required to work on as many as twenty-five different relays in a day."[45] Yet for most of the time in the test room, workers 1, 2, 3, and 4 had fewer than two changes *a week.* During the key two-year stretch from November 1927 to August 1929, those four workers spent most weeks, including stretches lasting over a month, assembling a *single* relay type.[46]

Other than the rest periods, virtually all of the other so-called experimental manipulations in the five-year period were largely irrelevant (how long or how often the rest periods occurred, stopping work at 4:00 or 4:30, and so on). The data makes that clear. Indeed, the rest periods themselves were important, since, as noted earlier, experimental Period XII (the lone instance in which they were eliminated) was the only one in which a change in working conditions was clearly correlated to a change (in this case a drop) in output. Perversely, when Period XII ends, Whitehead, who said he did not believe in the "learning" hypothesis, wrote that the effect of bringing back the rest pauses is "clearly seen" in the graphical data "*where rate of work rises almost with the vigor of a 'learning curve'.*"[47]

We now have the explanation for the one data point of rising productivity—as well as the statistically far more significant explanation for the shape of the entire productivity curve over the five-year test period. *The essential conditions of the experiment were established in Period II with the basic daily feedback (and fewer changes in relays). Five weeks later the pay incentive was introduced and eight weeks after that, the rest periods began.* The workers were put in an ideal situation to learn how to optimize their output and earnings. They did so, and productivity rose exactly as it should have.

THE TWO REPLACEMENTS AND MORE LEARNING

But there were more economic incentives—and more learning—to come. Two days into Period VIII, which began in January 1928, two of the women, Bogatowicz and Rybacki, were replaced. The two workers were restricting output. As the woman who sat closest to them explained a few years later when asked why the two were removed, "They were cutting down on their work and they said they couldn't do any more." Indeed, the pair were vocal about it. When two of the other workers were racing each other, Rybacki asked rhetorically, "Do you think I've got holes in my head to work like Theresa and Wanda do?" When one of the workers was overhead bragging how many relays she could make in a day, Bogatowicz was replied, "Don't do it, don't be a fool." Pennock of Western Electric decided both women should be replaced.[48]

The effect on output was remarkable. In the first thirty-seven weeks (Periods II to VII) productivity rose 12 percent. Over the seven weeks of Period VIII, it jumped another 12 percent. No big mystery here. The replacement workers Volanga and Sirchio were about 20 percent faster than the women they replaced. In fact, "Jennie Sirchio held the record as fastest relay assembler in the regular department." Fully 8 of the 25 percentage point gain in group productivity between Periods II and VIII can be attributed to these two workers.

Equally important, as Gillespie writes, "the removal of the two workers constituted an explicit threat to the remaining workers of their own removal from the privileged conditions of the test room if they did not perform adequately."[49] While hard to quantify this impact, it could serve only to reinforce the operant conditioning. Whereas before the women had only positive incentives and positive feedback to produce more, now they could also see the negative impact of restricting output and producing less. Perhaps not surprisingly, two of the remaining three workers had their greatest increase in output during Period VIII.

Sirchio "had a reputation for breaking the rates in the regular department." And a series of family layoffs and deaths was making her the family's "major breadwinner." She therefore "did everything she could to increase group production in the test room," taking on the role of leader, pushing the other women to perform, and chastising the slowest worker if daily output fell.[50]

Such replacements of two-fifths of the test subjects in the middle of a modern experiment would be enough to invalidate it utterly. Throwing out two subjects who were starting to slow down, apparently intentionally, and then inserting the speed queen of the whole plant should certainly be considered fatal to the experiment's value.

Although the 25 percent productivity increase through Period VIII does not seem particularly startling as I've explained it, it was a baffling puzzle to Hawthorne's management. In part that was because the Hawthorne researchers' progress reports downplayed key parts of the experiment, such as the effect of the removal of the two workers. They ignored the reduction in variety of relay types. They assumed wrongly that most of the production increase stemming from the new pay incentive would have occurred during the eight weeks of the first period that it was introduced. They were blind to the idea that workers, especially working class "girls," as they were always referred to, might be consciously controlling production or learning. Gillespie, probably the best chronicler of the methodological flaws in the experiment and the biases of Mayo and his colleagues, says it well: "As managers they could not accept that they might not be in complete control of production, and that included workers' behavior."[51]

Unable to explain the 25 percent productivity gain, Western Electric sought help in early 1928 from two academic consultants, Clair Turner from MIT and Elton Mayo from Harvard. Meanwhile, the relay assembly experiment continued, with some twists: The experimenters occasionally tried returning to previous conditions. In particular, Period XII, a three-month period beginning September 12, eliminated all rest pauses (the same as in Period III) and *while productivity did drop, as noted earlier, it remained 19 percent above the level for Period III.* Roethlisberger later made much of this in a 1941 book:

> After Period XII in the Relay Assembly Test Room, the investigators decided to change their ideas radically. What all their experiments had dramatically and conclusively demonstrated was the importance of employee attitudes and sentiments. It was clear that the responses of workers to what was happening about them were dependent on the significance these events had for them. . . . This was the great *eclaircissement*, the new illumination, that came from the research.[52]

Ultimately, as we have seen, this led to his and Dickson's formulating those seventeen elements to explain the Hawthorne Effect.

Mayo said he believed the relay assembly test results could be explained by the workers' psychological adjustment to a "novel industrial milieu," a more cohesive environment that had come about from the creation of the test room and the experimenter's efforts to ensure the cooperation of the workers. To Mayo, this cohesion was so strong that even the elimination of rest pauses had little effect: "By strengthening the 'temperamental' inner equilibrium of the workers, the Company enabled them to achieve a mental 'steady state' which offered a high degree of resistance to a variety of external conditions."[53]

The first thing to be said is that the original data shows that the 19 percent is actually only 13 percent for the three workers who were there in both

Period XII and Period III. Comparing the two new fast workers in Period XII with the two slower workers in Period III is meaningless analysis, if not deceptive.

In any case, since the workers had spent the months prior to Period XII learning how to pace themselves to make more money, and since they were still getting feedback on their performance every morning, we would certainly expect them to maintain much of their gains and drop off only a little in productivity. Moreover, without the rest pauses, they were working more hours, and if they could maintain their output rate, their paychecks would increase. Certainly, this explanation seems more straightforward and consistent than "novel industrial milieu" or the seventeen Hawthorne Effects.

This explanation has another advantage. It is almost identical to one cited previously, by the MIT Professor, Dugald Jackson, in charge of the earlier lighting tests: "The failure of the groups to return to their original working efficiency after having increased their production rate may be due to a certain amount of inertia and to unwillingness on the part of the operatives to let their pay fall after it was once raised to a higher level." Maintaining work rhythm and wages would have been even easier for the relay assembly workers since they were getting daily feedback on their output. The Hawthorne researchers, however, were not looking for such simple answers.

The design of the relay assembly room test, a 270-week time series, was so sloppy that the experimenters are not entitled to draw any conclusions. As H. M. Parsons put it, "In time series designs, it is advisable to make sure that a response rate is steady before changing experimental conditions; such designs are often called steady state designs (and are inappropriate in studying a process of change itself, such as acquisition of a skill)." The point is, in the absence of a control group, when output is rising or falling in a period, if you introduce a new change in the next period, you have no way of knowing if a subsequent rise or fall in output is due to that new change or is merely a continuation of whatever was happening in the previous period. That confusion, of course, describes the Hawthorne experiment to a T. It is exactly the within-period changes, mainly increases (which are suggestive of learning), that result in graphical and statistical analyses showing for the most part no correlation between experimental changes and output.[54]

I was struck by one aspect of the "novel industrial milieu." The workers had a lot of influence over the test room conditions. For instance, when the workers complained in May 1927 about working in direct sunlight, a request to the plant department was made to rush the installation of window shades. When the workers complained in November about the artificial lighting being too bright—"They reflect from the springs and make your eyes hurt" and "These lights hurt my eyes"—the light intensity was reduced.[55] *The relay assembly test room workers were given the kind of control over their workplace environment that recent research has found can lead to huge productivity gains* (see Chapter 4).

OTHER EXPERIMENTS AT HAWTHORNE
FAIL TO SHOW THE "EFFECT"

A second relay assembly test was run toward the end of 1928 with a different group of workers. Baseline output data was taken on five assemblers in the regular department paid on the large-group piece rate. They were then moved to a common bench in the department (not a test room) and given the small-group payment incentive that paid them much more according to their own collective effort. Their output jumped 13.8 percent in the first week and remained 10 to 15 percent above the base for all nine weeks of the test. When they were returned to being paid as part of the larger group, their output dropped back below the baseline.[56]

This seems like strong support for the view that the pay incentive was a decisive factor. Hibarger, Western Electric's own analyst, concluded, "*The basis of pay has been an important item in increasing output in the [relay assembly] test room.*" Gillespie goes on to note that "the effect may have been even greater in the initial test room, where the workers came to realize that no matter how high their output and pay, the company would not reduce the piece rates, something it would do as a matter of course in regular departments."[57] The point is that when Western Electric workers increased their productivity too much, they were usually punished for it, leaving them working faster, but little to show for it (which was exactly why Taylor had always urged that piece rates not be raised following a gain in productivity). In the first relay test room, however, the workers came to learn that no such punishment was in store.

Roethlisberger and Dickson wrote in 1939 that this experiment "*tended to substantiate the hypothesis that the formation of a small group for the purpose of determining piecework earnings was an important factor in the Relay Assembly Test Room performance.*"[58] They had it right then but neglected to include it as one of their seventeen elements of the Hawthorne Effect in their 1966 book, and it largely disappeared from accounts of the Hawthorne experiments.

While the second relay test was designed to learn the impact of the pay incentive alone, a study of mica splitters was designed to look at just the effect of rests, working conditions, and test room. Mica splitting, one of the highest paid jobs at the plant, required splitting mica to a thickness of about a thousandth of an inch, then trimming it for use as an insulator.

Five mica splitters were put in a test room in October 1928. Their pay system—an individual piece rate—was *not* changed, but the experimenters imposed all the other test conditions from the relay assembly test, to separate out their effect from that of the pay incentive. Output fell at first, then began to rise above the baseline *after the rest pauses* were introduced. By fall of 1929, output had risen to 15.6 percent above baseline. Then output started *declining* and by March 1930, it was only 4.4 percent above the base.[59]

What lessons can be drawn from the mica test? It confirmed that rest pauses were important. The reasons that productivity fell back were not clear to the experimenters, and the test received little attention in their reports. This may not be surprising since, as historian Gillespie notes, "the results of the mica splitting test seemed to undermine the argument that the test room conditions, in particular the change in supervision, were a major factor in increasing output in the relay test."[60]

Also, the Hawthorne works management decided to have all the employees interviewed. They conducted some 10,000 interviews. The major topic of discussion by the workers was pay, both wage levels and piece rates. While the workers liked the higher pay available to them at the Western Electric, Gillespie noted:

> But they overwhelmingly disliked the predominant system of paying workers a piecework rate based on the earnings of the "gang," many workers feeling they could earn more on individual piecework. Many complained that the current piecework rates were set too low by the rating engineers, who tended to base the rates on the fastest workers and did not allow for slowdown in production due to a delay in receiving parts or the time required to reset machines. Some reported that *piece rates were lowered when the job had not changed,* requiring the workers to produce more to earn the same wage. Others complained that *the bogey*—a production quota set for each job by engineers, which served as a basis for calculating bonuses—was set too high or too low or *was raised if workers consistently achieved it.*[61]

Again, Mayo and his colleagues ignored the pay issue and much of the content of the interviewing and focused on the process of interviewing and its impact on workers.

Finally, there was the Bank Wiring Observation study from 1931 to 1932. Three solderers, two inspectors, and nine wirers put together large terminal banks for telephone exchanges, each consisting of 100 to 200 terminals and thousands of wires. The workers were put in a special room but not given a special group rate. Instead, they shared in the group earnings of a department of 175 workers. No elaborate system of measuring output was introduced. The only changes were a test room, an observer, and the interviewing. Not surprisingly, given the results discussed above, the workers *restricted* output since they had little incentive to increase output (as it would be spread over all the workers in the department), and they worked under the constant fear that if they did increase productivity, piece rates would be lowered and they would be working harder for the same money. (This was called "soldiering" and it was what Taylor designed his scientific management to avoid. Subsequent misusers of Taylorism borrowed his name but did not implement all of its features.)[62]

Once again an experiment at Hawthorne did not support the "Hawthorne Effect," since special treatment without a pay incentive led to no productivity gain.[63] Indeed, none of the experiments at Hawthorne supported the "Hawthorne Effect." Most provided evidence to the contrary.

THE GREAT DEPRESSION

Meanwhile, back in the first relay test room, the long experiment continued during all those other, shorter ones. Productivity kept rising albeit more slowly (as predicted by a learning curve). Then one more important economic incentive came along in the middle of the five-year test to continue to motivate the workers—the Great Depression.

The Depression had a number of effects. The October 1929 crash might well have given most employees an incentive to work harder, since about three-fourths of the workers owned stock in Western Electric's parent company, AT&T.[64]

Perhaps more important, in the spring of 1930, hours were reduced for all Hawthorne workers, including the test workers. Since the workers could see that the group piece rate was not going to be changed no matter how productive they were, the test room workers had an incentive to "ameliorate the effect of steadily declining hours by working harder."[65] Finally, in mid-1932, the test room workers themselves started to be laid off and the test ended.

THE GENUINE HAWTHORNE EFFECT

The explanation for the productivity gain of five women in the relay assembly test room over the 270-week period is, as we have seen, not much of a mystery. The test room conditions were quite different than the shop floor and though the supervision was not as benign as has been suggested by some, both the supervision and the work conditions were ideal for learning. The small group incentive and the feedback were probably the most critical, with the rest periods and fewer relay types of next importance. These factors alone would induce learning, which can account for the vast majority of the variance in the data. Second-order factors include: The effect of the replacement of the two slower workers with faster, more motivated workers, the Depression, and the fact that piece rates were never changed. Finally, the general special social conditions of being in the test room with special supervision had an effect, though not because of any "Hawthorne Effect." The test room encouraged the kind of bonding and teamwork that the small-group pay-system made very profitable for the workers. It also allowed the workers considerable control over their work environment, such as the lighting.

Why didn't Mayo and the other Harvard researchers see these factors as critical? It seems like a much better explanation than the seventeen-part Hawthorne Effect. Every single subsequent experiment in the Hawthorne plant—the second relay test, the mica splitting, the interviewing, and the bank wiring—are consistent with it. The answer to that question involves the experiences and biases the researchers brought with them to Hawthorne as well as what they were trying to get out of Hawthorne. Gillespie's entire book, *Manufacturing Knowledge,* was written to explain those biases and motivations. He charges that Mayo and his colleagues essentially manufactured the results that they ultimately popularized. Fundamentally, Mayo was trying to humanize a workplace that Taylorism—or, more accurately, the misapplication of Taylorism—had dehumanized.

Certainly the workers themselves felt that the better work conditions and small-group wage incentive were important. So did many of the supervisors at the plant. So did two researchers, Imogen Rousseau and D. D. Davisson, who interviewed the test room workers extensively over a period of many months in 1931 and 1932. Rousseau concluded "explanations of test group behavior may not lie in as obscure causes as is generally supposed," and that increased earnings were the primary motivation. Davisson believed that not enough attention was given to "such factors as the excellent supply of parts to the test room, the limited number of relay types, and in particular the pay incentive, observing that *the women had a keen interest in their daily percentages and a much clearer understanding of the piecework system than other workers.*"[66]

Mayo, in contrast, later insisted that the entire plant had excellent working conditions and that the workers' view that the test room conditions were superior should not be viewed as objective: "This is simply a type of statement almost inevitably made when a not very articulate group of workers tries to express an indefinable feeling of relief from constraint.[67] He similarly waved away the views of the interviewers. Mayo was looking for a different answer. When Whitehead was in the early part of his analysis and thought (mistakenly, it turned out) that physiological factors were correlated with production, Roethlisberger wrote that Mayo was ecstatic because "it looked as if the organization of the girls in the test room was more conditioned by biological factors rather than *anything so naive as economic incentive.*"[68]

CONCLUSION: WORK CONDITIONS MATTER

The Hawthorne story is a cautionary tale. It has taken many pages to demonstrate the following statement: Far from proving that work conditions matter little when compared with social conditions, as virtually every textbook and popular reference would have one believe, the Hawthorne experiments proved the exact opposite. This is not to say that special attention to employees has no value or that the humanist view of management is flawed. It is only to say that the Hawthorne experiments provided no evidence, statistical or otherwise, on behalf of that view. If anything, the tests proved that Frederick Taylor was correct: The right wage incentive and rest pauses are the key to increased productivity.

Equally important from the perspective of my own work is the fact that the Hawthorne lighting experiments have unexpectedly joined the large body of work that demonstrates that lighting can improve worker productivity.

There is no such thing as the "Hawthorne Effect." There never was. It never existed. At best the term is meaningless, at worst completely wrong. It should be edited out of textbooks and dropped from popular and technical use. Managers who, as Vivian Loftness says, "*consistently cite the Hawthorne effect as clear disproof of any real linkage of productivity to quality work environments*" are deceiving themselves, hurting their employees, and losing a great deal of money—altogether undermining their competitiveness.

May I suggest a way to test the conclusions presented here: Rather than assuming that improved lighting and workplace design cannot improve your worker's productivity, pick a workspace in your company and test it for yourself.

May I also suggest that, rather than assuming that reducing greenhouse gas emissions will be costly for your company, pick a building or a factory and test it out. Then enjoy watching your bottom line grow.

Notes

INTRODUCTION

1. *Fortune,* December 8, 1997.
2. *Fortune,* May 11, 1998.
3. *Business Week,* July 7, 1997.
4. The Dow Chemical case is based on Kenneth E. Nelson, "Dow's Energy/WRAP Contest," paper prepared for the 1993 Industrial Energy Technology Conference, March 24 and 25, 1993, Houston, Texas; and personal communications with Ken Nelson.
5. The discussion of the DOE's savings is based on information and analysis provided by Kent Hancock, U.S. DOE, Washington, D.C.

CHAPTER 1

1. John S. Jennings, "Sustainable Development," Shell International, London, April 17, 1997. If the merger between Exxon and Mobil is approved, Shell will no longer be the world's largest, publicly traded oil company.
2. Shell's projected greenhouse gas emissions reductions are derived from *Health, Safety, and Environment Report '98,* Shell International, London, 1998; *People and the Environment,* the 1997 Shell International Exploration and Production Health, Safety, and Environment Report, Shell International Exploration and Production, The Hague, Netherlands, 1998; and information available on their website (www.shell.com).
3. *Economist,* September 28, 1991. See also Peter Senge, *The Fifth Discipline* (New York: Doubleday, 1990), p. 181.
4. Pierre Wack's quotes come from two articles, "Scenarios: Uncharted Waters Ahead," *Harvard Business Review,* September/October 1985, pp. 73–89, and "Scenarios: Shooting the Rapids," *Harvard Business Review,* November/December 1985, pp. 139–150.
5. Both Wohlstetter and Fuchida are quoted in Wack, "Scenarios: Shooting the Rapids," pp. 148–149.
6. The discussion of Shell and its two scenarios is based on meetings with Shell staff, including Ged Davis, Kurt Hoffman, Peter Langcake, Douglas McKay, Gerry Matthews, and Jan Smeele during an October 1998 visit to Shell's London headquarters; Ged David, "Global Warming: The Role of Energy Efficient Technologies," Shell International (SI), London, October 1989; Peter Kassler, "Energy for Development," SI, London, November 1994; E. J. Grunwald, "Energy in the Long Term," SI, London, 1994; Chris Fay, "Fossil Fuels and Beyond—Meeting the Energy Needs of the 21st Century," SI,

London, 1995; "The Evolution of the World's Energy Systems," SI, London, 1996; John Jennings, "Sustainable Development"; "Shell Invests US\$0.5 Billion in Renewables," press release, SI, London, October 16, 1997; Mark Moody-Stuart, "A Force for Progress—The Royal Dutch/Shell Group in the 21st Century," SI, London, February 10, 1998; "Connecting You to the Sun," SI, London, 1997; *Profits and Principles—Does There Have to be a Choice?* SI, London, July 1998; Jeroen van der Veer, "The Greenhouse Challenge," SI, London, August 31, 1998; information available on various websites (www.shell.com, www.shell-pro.brentstar.com, and www.foe.org/orgs/ga/niger.html); *Financial Times,* October 17, 1997; and *The Washington Post,* August 2, 1998, pp. H1, H5.

7. Shell's scenario does not anticipate significant increases in nuclear energy. "Future societal attitudes towards nuclear power, which are currently largely negative, are hard to foresee, but it is possible to say that, for many years into the future, the world's energy demand could be met without significant additional nuclear capacity." E. J. Grunwald, "Energy in the Long Term," p. 6.

8. *New York Times,* February 13, 1996, p. A1.

9. *Oil & Gas Journal,* November 24, 1997, pp. 29–36.

10. *Washington Post,* p. C13, April 22, 1998.

CHAPTER 2

1. The TABC case is based on *Energy User News,* October 1994, p. 9; *Energy User News,* December 1994, pp. 24, 65; and personal communications with Petar Reskusic.

2. David Halberstam, *The Reckoning* (New York: Avon, 1986), pp. 59–82.

3. Henry Ford, *Today and Tomorrow,* reprint (Cambridge, Mass.: Productivity Press, 1988), pp. 124–126. All Henry Ford quotes are from this book (pp. 6, 16, 53, 92–100, 112–121, 132–133, 136). See also Joseph Romm, *Lean and Clean Management* (New York: Kodansha, 1994), pp. 16–30.

4. The discussion of interchangeable parts and the moving assembly line, as well as the cycle time numbers, come from James Womack et al., *The Machine That Changed the World* (New York: Rawson Associates, 1990).

5. Shigeo Shingo, *Study of the Toyota Production System* (Tokyo: Japanese Management Association, 1981), pp. 138–145, as cited in Robert Hayes, Steven Wheelwright, and Kim Clark, *Dynamic Manufacturing* (New York: The Free Press, 1988), p. 45.

6. Spender quoted in Halberstam, *The Reckoning,* p. 80.

7. Halberstam, *The Reckoning,* p. 84.

8. Ibid., p. 81.

9. David Garvin, *Managing Quality* (New York: The Free Press, 1988), pp. 182–183.

10. Alex Taylor III, "How Toyota Defies Gravity," *Fortune,* December 8, 1997, pp. 100–108.

11. Shigeo Shingo, *Modern Approaches to Manufacturing Improvement: The Shingo System,* Alan Robinson, ed. (Cambridge, Mass.: Productivity Press, 1990), pp. 43–44.

12. Ibid., pp. 35, 44.

13. Hayes, Wheelwright, and Clark, *Dynamic Manufacturing,* p. 58.

14. Shingo's discussion of the Industrial Revolution comes from Shigeo Shingo,

The Shingo Production Management System (Cambridge, Mass.: Productivity Press, 1992), pp. 7–8.

15. Ibid., p. 54.
16. Shingo (1990), p. 23.
17. Ibid., p. 23, and Shingo (1992), p. 55. For a further discussion, see Joseph Romm, *Lean and Clean Management* (New York: Kodansha, 1994), pp. 22–27.
18. The examples are cited in Shingo (1990), p. 9.
19. Robert Hayes and Kim Clark, *Interfaces*, 15 (1985), p. 13, as cited in Shingo (1990), p. 9.
20. Shingo (1992), p. 55.
21. Taiichi Ohno, *Toyota Production System,* translated (Cambridge, Mass.: Productivity Press, 1988), pp. 97–109. The book was originally published in Japan by Diamond Inc., 1978. All subsequent Ohno quotes are from this book, pp. 17–20, 54–59.
22. James P. Womack and Daniel T. Jones, *Lean Thinking: Banish Waste and Create Wealth in Your Corporation* (New York: Simon & Schuster, 1996), p. 15.
23. The numbers for the Toyota suggestion system come from Tom Peters, *Thriving on Chaos* (New York: Harper & Row, 1988), p. 88.
24. Mark Dorfman, "Source Reduction," *Pollution Prevention Review,* Autumn 1992, pp. 403–414. See also Mark Dorfman et al., *Environmental Dividends: Cutting More Chemical Wastes,* a report published by INFORM, Inc., in New York, 1992.
25. Hayes, Wheelwright, and Clark, *Dynamic Manufacturing,* pp. 176–177.
26. Michael E. Porter and Claas van der Linde, "Green and Competitive," *Harvard Business Review,* September–October 1995, pp. 120–134.
27. Stuart L. Hart and Gautam Ahuja, "Does It Pay to be Green?" Working Paper #9550-09, University of Michigan, School of Business Administration, Ann Arbor, Mich., September 1994. Hart chose 1988 as the base year because it was "the first year that firms in the U.S. were required by law to disclose their emission levels of some 300 pollutants under the 'Toxic Release Inventory.'"
28. Gavin Wright, "The Origins of American Industrial Success, 1879–1940," *The American Economic Review,* September 1990, pp. 651, 662.
29. "Some Companies Cut Pollution by Altering Production Methods," *Wall Street Journal,* December 24, 1990, pp. 1, 21.
30. U.S. Congress, Office of Technology Assessment, *Industry, Technology, and the Environment: Competitive Challenges and Business Opportunities,* OTA-ITE-58 (Washington, D.C.: U.S. Government Printing Office, January 1994), pp. 244–250.
31. Alex Taylor III, "How Toyota Defies Gravity," *Fortune,* December 8, 1997, p. 104.
32. "Our Precious Planet," *Time* Special Issue, November 1997, p. 4.
33. These quotes come from Ford Motor's website (www.ford.com) and "A Different Sort of Scion," Business Section, *New York Times,* September 20, 1998.
34. Porter and van der Linde, "Green and Competitive," pp. 127, 130–131.

CHAPTER 3

1. The source information is available from the Energy Cost Savings Council, Washington, D.C. (www.plug-in.org).
2. The Centerplex case is based on "Centerplex," U.S. EPA, December 1997; information on their website (centerplex.net/office); and personal communications with Jonathan Pool.

3. Air-Conditioning and Refrigeration Institute (www.ari.org).
4. This case study is based on *Ridgehaven: Green Building Demonstration Project,* Gottfried Technology, Inc., San Francisco, December 1996; David A. Gottfried, Ellis A. Shoichet, and Mitch Hart, "Green Building Environmental Control: A Case Study," *HPAC,* February 1997, pp. 71–78; Lynn Froeschle "Renovating Ridgehaven into a Successful Green Office Building," *Environmental Design & Construction,* January/February 1998 (www.edcmag.com); and personal communications with David Gottfried.
5. The 100 Market Building case is based on "1995 National Awards Program for Energy Efficiency and Renewable Energy," U.S. DOE, Office of Energy Efficiency and Renewable Energy, Washington, D.C., 1995, pp. 5–6; *Energy User News,* December 1994, pp. 30, 65; and personal communications with MicroGrid, 1998.
6. See "Introducing . . . The Energy Star Buildings Program," U.S. EPA, Washington, D.C., March 1997; and "Building on Our Success," U.S. EPA, May 1997 (phone: 1-888-782-7937; www.epa.gov/appdstar/buildings.html).
7. The Lausche case is based on Kenneth J. Walker, *Ohio Power Boosters,* Safe Energy Communication Council (SECC), Washington, D.C., July 1995, p. 30, as well as information and analysis provided by Chris Moser, SECC, March 1998.
8. The Community Towers case is based on Jessica S. Lefevre, *The Energy Services Industry: Revolutionizing Energy Use in the United States,* National Association of Energy Service Companies, Washington, D.C. (202-371-7816), May 1996, pp. 28–30.
9. Scott Rickard et al., "The Investment Risk in Whole Building Energy-Efficiency Upgrade Projects," *ACEEE 1998 Summer Study on Energy Efficiency in Buildings Proceedings,* American Council for an Energy Efficient Economy, Washington, D.C., 1998, pp. 4.307–4.318.
10. Aspen Systems calculated IRR in a standard fashion, as "the interest rate percentage that produces a net present value of zero when calculated for the expected stream of future costs and revenues."
11. The discussion of the IPMVP is based on personal communications with Greg Kats and information available on the website (www.ipmvp.org).
12. The Texas A&M case is based on Claridge et al., "Can You Achieve 150 Percent of Predicted Retrofit Savings: Is It Time for Recommissioning?" *ACEEE 1994 Summer Study on Energy Efficiency in Buildings Proceedings,* American Council for an Energy Efficient Economy, Washington, D.C., 1994, pp. 5.73-5.87; Liu et al., "Identifying and Implementing Improved Operation and Maintenance Measures in Texas LoanSTAR Buildings," *ACEEE 1994 Summer Study on Energy Efficiency in Buildings Proceedings,* American Council for an Energy Efficient Economy, Washington, D.C., 1994, pp. 5.153–5.165; Claridge et al., "Implementation of Continuous Commissioning in the Texas LoanSTAR Program: 'Can You Achieve 150 percent of Estimated Retrofit Savings' Revisited," *ACEEE 1996 Summer Study on Energy Efficiency in Buildings Proceedings,* American Council for an Energy Efficient Economy, Washington, D.C., 1996, pp. 4.59–4.67; Claridge et al., "Energy and Comfort Benefits of Continuous Commissioning in Buildings," Energy Systems Laboratory, Texas A&M, College Station, Texas, 1998; and personal communications with David Claridge.
13. *Office Access* (San Francisco: Harper Perennial, 1992), p. 53.
14. *Energy User News,* December 1995, p. 41; and *Green Lights* (Washington, D.C.: EPA, July 1993).

15. The discussion of Boeing is based on a visit to some of their Washington State buildings, personal conversations with Larry Friedman and Steve Cassens, articles in *Boeing News* from May 10, 1991, and January 15, 1993, and information provided by Boeing and EPA.

16. Arnold Fickett, Clark Gellings, and Amory Lovins, "Efficient Use of Electricity," *Scientific American,* September 1990, pp. 11–23.

17. There is some labor cost in removing the unneeded overhead lamps, but that is probably more than covered by the salvage cost of those lamps and the reduced maintenance required by fewer lamps.

18. Paul Scanlon, "Effective Management Cuts Costs and Helps Environment," *AS&U,* September 1991, pp. 40–42.

19. *Energy User News,* April 1996, pp. 1, 10.

20. These numbers are from Amory Lovins and Rick Heede, *Energy-Efficient Appliances,* Competitek report, 1990. For a discussion of recent energy-saving advances in computers and office equipment, see John B. Horrigan, Frances H. Irwin, and Elizabeth Cook, "Taking a Byte Out of Carbon," World Resources Institute, Washington, D.C., 1998.

21. The Verifone case is based on "ACT² Verifone Commercial Site Impact Evaluation Report," prepared by Eley Associates, PG&E, San Ramone, Calif., July 1997.

22. Bruce Nordman et al., "Measured Energy Savings and Performance of Power-Managed Personal Computers and Monitors," ACEEE 1996 *Summer Study on Energy Efficiency in Buildings Proceedings,* American Council for an Energy-Efficient Economy, Washington, D.C., 1996, pp. 4.267–4.278.

23. "The Challenge: Improving Ventilation System Performance at a Metal Plating Facility," Showcase Demonstration Case Study, Motor Challenge Program, U.S. DOE, Office of Energy Efficiency and Renewable Energy, Washington, D.C., August 1996.

24. Margaret Suozzo et al., "Guide to Energy-Efficient Commercial Equipment," American Council for an Energy-Efficient Economy, Washington, D.C., 1997, pp. 3–14.

25. *Energy User News,* December 1997, p. 78.

26. *Energy User News,* May 1997, pp. 1, 12, 13, 64, and personal communications with Norm Thornton, March 1998.

27. *Energy User News,* December 1997, p. 30.

28. Chris Robertson and Jay Stein, "How to Manage Chiller Plants Through the CFC Refrigerant Phase Out," February 15, 1994, available from Chris Robertson and Associates, Portland, Oregon.

29. The Way Station case is based on Alex Wilson et al., *Green Development* (New York: John Wiley & Sons, 1998), pp. 156–158 and 436–437, and information provided by Greg Franta.

30. This case study can be found on the home page of the Energy Office of the City of Portland (www.ci.portland.or.us/energy/web/besthenning.html).

31. Jim Wingerden, *DOE 1998 Energy Efficient Award Application,* Utah Department of Natural Resources, Salt Lake City, 1998; "Daylighting on the Cutting Edge in Utah," *Solar Today,* July/August 1997, pp. 24–27; and *Energy User News,* December 1996, p. 26.

32. *DOE This Month,* U.S. DOE, Washington, D.C., November 1996, and Will Zachmann, " 'Whole Building' Approach to Sustainable Design," *Environmental Design & Construction,* July/August 1998 (www.edcmag.com).

33. "ACT² CSAA Commercial Site Impact Evaluation Report," prepared by Eley Associates, PG&E, San Ramone, Calif., August 1997. PG&E calculated that the present value of the energy savings exceeded the cost of the upgrade by almost a factor of two.

34. The Comstock case study is based on U.S. Congress, Office of Technology Assessment, *Building Energy Efficiency*, OTA-E-518 (Washington, D.C.: U.S. Government Printing Office, May 1992), p. 51, and personal communications with Paul Scanlon.

35. Amory Lovins, "Energy-Efficient Buildings: Institutional Barriers and Opportunities," a strategic issue paper published by E Source, Inc., Boulder, Colo., 1992, p. 11.

36. Ibid., and personal communications with Scanlon.

CHAPTER 4

1. Michael D. Shanus et al., "Going Beyond the Perimeter with Daylight," *Lighting Design & Application*, March 1984, p. 39.

2. This discussion is based on information and analysis provided by Carnegie Mellon University's "Intelligent Workplace," Center for Building Performance and Diagnostics, School of Architecture, Pittsburgh, 1998 (412-268-2350), plus a June 1998 visit and personal communications with Vivian Loftness and other staff members.

3. The Verifone case is based on personal communications with Randolph Croxton in August 1998; William R. Pape, "Healthy, Wealthy, and Wise," *Inc. Technology #2* (www.inc.com/issue/tech298/), June 15, 1998; William R. Pape, "At What Cost Health? Low Cost, as it Turns Out," *Inc. Extra Special* (www.inc.com/extra/special/), August 5, 1998; Alex Wilson et al., *Green Development* (New York: John Wiley & Sons, 1998), pp. 46, 360, 433–434; and personal communication with Bill Browning.

4. Thomas J. Peters and Robert H. Waterman, Jr., *In Search of Excellence* (New York: Harper & Row, 1982), pp. 5–6.

5. Personal communications with Vivian Loftness, August 1998 (emphasis added).

6. The Prince Street case is based on Daniel McQuillen, "The Art of Daylighting," *Environmental Design & Construction*, January/February 1998, p. 23 (www.edc-mag.com), and personal communications with Frank Boardman, March 1998.

7. The North Carolina case is based on Michael Nicklas and Gary Bailey, "Analysis of the Performance of Students in Daylit Schools," Raleigh, N.C., 1996; Michael Nicklas and Gary Bailey, "Energy Performance of Daylit Schools in North Carolina," Raleigh, N.C., 1996; and McQuillen, "The Art of Daylighting," p. 25.

8. Nicklas and Bailey, "Analysis of the Performance of Students in Daylit Schools," p. 5.

9. "A Study into the Effects of Light on Children of Elementary School Age: A Case of Daylight Robbery," Policy and Planning Branch of Alberta Education, Alberta, Canada, 1992.

10. The California Wal-Mart and Target cases are based on *Energy User News*, February 1997, pp. 30–35; *Energy User News*, May 1996, pp. 1, 22; "Demonstrating Profitable Energy Savings in Retail Establishments," U.S. EPA, Washington, D.C., September 1996; and personal communication with Gregg Ander.

11. This EcoMart case is based on Rocky Mountain Institute's design consulting for and analysis of the EcoMart, and personal communications between Bill Browning and Tom Seay, Wal-Mart's Vice President for Real Estate.

12. The California Steel Industries case is based on analysis conducted by Lutron, and personal communications with Energy Controls and Concepts.

13. Wright is quoted in Michael Shanus et al., "Going Beyond the Perimeter with Daylight," *Lighting Design & Application,* March 1984, pp. 30–40.

14. The Reno case study is based on interviews of Robert McLean and Lee Windheim and U.S. Postal Service data developed by McLean.

15. The sorter is grueling to use. Once every second, it drops a letter in front of the operator, who must punch in the correct zip code before the next letter appears a second later. If the operator keys in a zip code that doesn't exist, or no zip code at all, the letter will immediately be sent through the machine for repunching. If the wrong zip code is keyed in, the letter will be sent to the wrong bin and it will take even longer to track down the mistake. The job is so intense that an operator can work only a maximum of thirty minutes on the machine at one time before being replaced.

16. One reason this story was not replicated is that shortly after the events described took place, the post office was reorganized and individuals moved to other jobs or retired.

17. This case is based on Russell Allen, "Pennsylvania Power and Light: A Lighting Case Study," *Buildings,* March 1982, pp. 49–56; "Office Lighting Retrofit Will Pay Back in 69 Days," *Facilities Design & Management,* p. 13.

18. Ibid.

19. This Wisconsin case study is from the National Lighting Bureau, *Office Lighting and Productivity,* 2101 L Street, NW, Suite 300, Washington, D.C. 20037, 1988.

20. This case study is from the National Lighting Bureau, *Office Lighting and Productivity,* 2101 L Street, NW, Suite 300, Washington, D.C. 20037, 1988, as well as the Bureau's press release on the lighting upgrade, January 31, 1985.

21. The Hyde Tools story is based on a report in the *TPM Newsletter,* January 1993, p. 7; personal communications with DeVries; and Joseph E. Paluzzi and Timothy J. Greiner, "Finding Green in Clean: Progressive Pollution Prevention at Hyde Tools," *Total Quality Environmental Management,* Spring 1993, pp. 283–290.

22. The Lockheed case study is based on Charles C. Benton and Marc Fountain, "Successfully Daylighting a Large Commercial Building: A Case Study of Lockheed Building 157," *Progressive Architecture,* November 1990, pp. 119–121; "Employees Respond to Lockheed Building 157," *The Professional Energy Manager,* July 1984, p. 5; "Lockheed's No. 157: Ex Post Facto," *Facilities Planning News,* October 1984; and personal communications with Lee Windheim and Don Aitken.

23. The discussion of West Bend Mutual is based on Paul Beck, "Intelligent Design Passes IQ Test," *Consulting-Specifying Engineer,* January 1993, pp. 34–38; and Walter Kroner et al., "Using Advanced Office Technology to Increase Productivity" (Troy, N.Y.: The Center for Architectural Research, 1992).

24. The Carnegie Mellon case is based on information and analysis provided by Carnegie Mellon University's "Intelligent Workplace"; a June 1998 visit and personal communications with Vivian Loftness and other members of CMU's staff; *Energy User News,* April 1998, pp. 1, 6, 8; and "Academic Initiative," *Architecture,* May 1998, pp. 203–206.

25. Vivian Loftness et al., "The Intelligent Workplace Retrofit: Investing in the Hidden Infrastructures for Workplace Flexibility and Performance," Center for Building Performance and Diagnostics, School of Architecture, Carnegie Mellon University, Pittsburgh, 1997.

26. A CD with the latest analytical results is available from the Intelligent Workplace.

27. Roger S. Ulrich, "Biophilia, Biophobia, and Natural Landscapes," in Stephen R. Kellert and Edward O. Wilson, eds., *The Biophilia Hypothesis* (Washington, D.C.: Island Press, 1993), pp. 73–137.

CHAPTER 5

1. The information here updates the material in my 1994 book, *Lean and Clean Management*, with information provided by Compaq; information available from Compaq's website (www.compaq.com); and personal communications with Ron Perkins and Lee Eng Lock.

2. Ernst von Weizsacker, Amory B. Lovins, and L. Hunter Lovins, *Factor Four: Doubling Wealth, Halving Resource Use* (London: Earthscan Publications Ltd, 1997), p. 55.

3. The semiconductor discussion is based on Robertson, Stein, Harris, and Cherniack, "Energy Efficiency/Semiconductor Manufacturing," *Oregon Insider,* July 15, 1997, Eugene, Ore. (541-343-8504); Chris Robertson et al., *Opportunities for Efficiency,* Northwest Power Planning Council, Portland, Ore., 1997; Philip Siekman, "Turn Down the Energy," *Fortune,* May 11, 1998, p. 132J; "Energy Efficient Renovation of Western Digital Disk Drive Factory," application for the Association of Energy Engineers 1996 Energy Project of the Year Award, AEE, Atlanta, Ga. (770-447-5083); and information and analysis provided by Chris Robertson, Chris Robertson & Associates, Portland, Ore.

4. The STMicroelectronic case is based on information and analysis provided by the company; personal communications with Murray Duffin, Vlatko Zagar, Chris Robertson, and Lee Eng Lock; and information available from the company's website (www.st.com).

CHAPTER 6

1. The Malden case is based on a May 1998 visit to the plant and personal communication, information, and analysis provided by the plant; Tina Kaarsberg and R. Neal Elliott, "Combined Heat and Power: Saving Energy and the Environment," *NE-MW Economic Review,* March/April 1998, pp. 5–6; information from Massachusetts Electric Company (www.nees.com/news/073197a. htm); Kalwall Corporation of Manchester, N.H. (www.kalwall.com/1.htm); and Amoco Chemicals (www.amoco.com).

2. The Waverly case is based on information and analysis provided by Walt Robbins, Superintendent of Buildings and Grounds, Waverly Central School District, 15 Frederick Street, Waverly, N.Y., and analysis performed by Tina Kaarsberg, Art Rosenfeld, and myself for Kaarsberg, Fiskum, Romm, Rosenfeld, Koomey, and Teagen "Combined Heat and Power for Saving Energy and Carbon in Buildings" *Proceedings of 1998 ACEEE Summer Study,* Washington, D.C., 1998, pp. 9.77–9.92.

3. See Morris A. Pierce, "A History of Cogeneration before PURPA," *ASHRAE Journal*, May 1995, pp. 53–60.

4. Thomas Casten, *Turning Off the Heat* (Amherst, N.Y.: Prometheus Books, 1998), p. 5.

5. Henry Ford, *Today and Tomorrow*, reprint (Cambridge, Mass.: Productivity Press, 1988), pp. 132–133, originally published by Doubleday, 1926.

6. Thomas R. Casten, *Turning Off the Heat.*

7. The Trigen case study is based on information and analysis provided by Trigen; visits to the Trigen facilities in Philadelphia and Oklahoma City; personal communications with Tom Casten and other Trigen staff; *Energy User News*, December 1995, p. 40; Kevin E. Brown and Herman A. Schopman, "Meeting Philadelphia's Future Heat and Power Needs: The Grays Ferry Cogeneration Project," *District Energy*, Second Quarter, 1997; and *Philadelphia Inquirer*, December 16, 1997, pp. C1–C2.

8. The Coors case is based on Susan Odiseos and Peter Laliberte, "Trigen Helps Brewers Get Back to Basics," *District Energy*, Second Quarter, 1996, pp. 21–24; information and analysis provided by Trigen; and personal communications with Trigen staff.

9. The Superior Fibers case is based on Sanjay Agrawal and Richard Jensen, "Cogeneration for a Small Company: A Case Study," Industrial Assessment Center, Department of Engineering, Hofstra University, Hempstead, N.Y., 1998; and an April 1998 visit to Superior Fibers, and personal communications with the staff and management of the company and with Sanjay Agrawal.

10. The discussion of emerging cogeneration technologies, including microturbines and fuel cells, is based on, Tina Kaarsberg et al., "Combined Heat and Power for Saving Energy and Carbon in Buildings," *Proceedings of 1998 ACEEE Summer Study*, Washington, D.C., (1998); Kaarsberg, Bluestein, Romm, and Rosenfeld, "The Outlook for Small-Scale CHP in the USA," *CADDET Newsletter*, June 1998, pp. 15–17; and "Natural Gas Fuel Cells," *Federal Technology Alert*, Federal Energy Management Program, U.S. DOE, Office of Energy Efficiency and Renewable Energy, Washington, D.C., November 1995.

11. The Mercury 50 discussion is based on personal communications with Solar Turbines and information on their website (www.cat.com).

12. The fuel cell discussion is based on Thomas Ditoro, "Banking on Fuel Cells to Supply Critical Loads," *Pure Power*, Supplement to *Consulting-Specifying Engineer*, Fall 1998, pp. 18–21; personal communications with Arthur Mannion of Sure Power and information available from their website (www.hi-availability.com); personal communications with Scott Weiner of Ballard Power Systems; and "Natural Gas Fuel Cells," U.S. DOE, pp. 8–9.

13. The Toyota case is based on information provided by Toyota Motor Sales, U.S.A.; personal communications with Jeremy Barnes of Toyota; and *Business Wire*, July 29, 1998.

14. Cavallo, Hock, and Smith, "Wind Energy: Technology and Economics," in Johansson et al., eds., *Renewable Energy* (Washington, D.C.: Island Press, 1993), pp. 122–124.

15. The historical discussion of geothermal power is based on Civis G. Palmerini, "Geothermal Energy," in Johansson et al., eds., *Renewable Energy*, pp. 554–555.

16. The discussion of modern geothermal technology is based on "Ground-Source Heat Pumps Applied to Commercial Facilities," *Federal Technology Alert*,

Federal Energy Management Program, U.S. DOE, Office of Energy Efficiency and Renewable Energy, Washington, D.C., September 1995, and "Space Conditioning: The Next Frontier," U.S. EPA, Washington, D.C., April 1993.

17. The Phillips case is based on information from the web page of the International Ground Source Heat Pump Association (IGSHPA), Oklahoma State University, Stillwater, Okla. (www.igshpa.okstate.edu/Publications/CaseStudy/Phillips_66/Phillips_66.html).

18. The McDonald's case is based on information and analysis provided by McDonald's and Detroit Edison, Westland, Mich., and personal communications with Detroit Edison.

19. The Galt House case is based on information from the IGSHPA's web page (www.igshpa.okstate.edu/Publications/CaseStudy/Galt_House/Galt.html), and Paul Liepe, "GeoExchange Systems Heat and Cool Commercial Buildings," *Environmental Design & Construction*, January/February 1998, p. 72 (www.edc-mag.com).

20. The sun's energy, stored in plant biomass, provides an energy source with no net increase in greenhouse gases, since the carbon dioxide that plants give off when burned had previously been captured from the atmosphere. There will be no net carbon emissions as long as the plants had been harvested sustainably and regrown each time—that is, as long as there had been no net decrease in plant matter as occurs when a forest is cut down or burned down and not replaced.

21. The Anheuser-Busch case is based on Bill Sugar, *DOE 1998 Energy Efficient Award Application*, Anheuser-Busch Company, St. Louis, Mo., and "Anheuser-Busch Is Brewing Solutions," *California Manufacturer*, Summer 1997, pp. 28–36.

22. Both wind and biomass energy are indirect solar energy in the sense that the Earth's winds are generated by solar heating of the planet, and plant life derives its energy from photosynthesis of sunlight.

23. *New York Times*, May 19, 1997, p. A14; "California Utility Solar Energy Purchase Builds on DOE Partnerships," DOE Press Release, May 14, 1997; "EPV Wins Go-Ahead Recommendation from SMUD Staff for Up to 10 MW of PV," *The Solar Letter*, April 11, 1997, p. 138.

24. The Interface case is from *Sustainability Report*, Interface, Inc., Atlanta, Ga., 1997. The Austin, Queens, and Berlin cases are from *Solar Electric Buildings*, Office of Utility Technologies, U.S. DOE, Office of Energy Efficiency and Renewable Energy, Washington, D.C., February 1996, pp. 9, 11, 14. The Riker's Island and Charlotte cases are from Daniel McQuillen, "Harnessing the Sun," *Environmental Design & Construction*, July/August 1998 (www.edcmag.com).

25. The Amtrak case is based on "Nation's First Solar-Powered Rail Station Opens in Normal," *Illinois Resources*, July/August 1990, p. 7; and *Solar Electric Buildings*, U.S. DOE, p. 19.

26. "Solar Shines Brighter," *Industry Week*, April 28, 1998, pp. 24–29.

27. The Four Times Square case is based on *Lessons Learned: Four Times Square*, Earth Day New York, New York City, 1997; information provided by the Durst organization (www.DurstNY.com); *New York Times*, March 30, 1997, p. R7; *Wall Street Journal*, July 16, 1997, p. B7; and Murray S. Liebman and Nancy J. Zacha, "What's So Green About the New Building at 4 Times Square?" *American Gas*, October 1997, pp. 26–28.

CHAPTER 7

1. Philip Siekman, "Turn Down the Energy/Tune Up the Profits," *Fortune,* May 11, 1998, p. 132C.
2. Ibid., p. 132F. See also DOE's Motor Challenge website (www.motor.doe.gov).
3. Livio D. DeSimone and Frank Popoff with the World Business Council for Sustainable Development, *Eco-efficiency: The Business Link to Sustainable Development* (Cambridge, Mass.: The MIT Press, 1997), p. 9.
4. The 3M case is based on "The Challenge: Optimizing Electric Motor Systems at a Corporate Campus Facility," Office of Industrial Technologies, U.S. DOE, Office of Energy Efficiency and Renewable Energy, Washington, D.C., September 1996; "Energy Management and Clean Air," 3M Energy Management, St. Paul, Minn.; information from their website (www.3m.com), and personal communications with Robert Renz and other 3M engineers.
5. The MotorMaster software is available free by calling 1-800-862-2086.
6. The Perkin-Elmer case is based on Philip Siekman, "Turn Down the Energy," pp. 132C–132J; information from Perkin-Elmer's website (www.perkin-elmer.com); and personal communications with Jim Oberndorfer in 1998.
7. The energy numbers throughout this section on motors come from Steven Nadel et al., *Energy-Efficient Motor Systems* (Washington, D.C.: American Council for an Energy-Efficient Economy, 1991); Fickett, Gellings, and Lovins, "Efficient Use of Electricity"; Mitchell Rosenberg, "The US Motor Systems Market Assessment," *Proceedings of 1997 ACEEE Summer Study on Energy Efficiency in Industry,* American Council for an Energy-Efficient Economy, Washington, D.C., 1997; and Mitchell Rosenberg, "The U.S. Industrial Motor Systems Market Opportunities and Assessment: Overview and Key Findings," presentation to Office of Industrial Technologies, U.S. DOE, Office of Energy Efficiency and Renewable Energy, Washington, D.C., May 27, 1998.
8. The Greenville case is based on "The Challenge: Improving the Efficiency of a Tube Drawing Bench," Office of Industrial Technologies, U.S. DOE, Office of Energy Efficiency and Renewable Energy, Washington, D.C., February 1997.
9. This Regal Fruit case is based on Todd Campbell, "From Megawatts to Nega-Watts," *Horizon Air Magazine,* November 1991, pp. 17–37, and personal communications with Ron Gonsalves.
10. The Alumax case is based on "The Challenge: Improving Dust Collection Systems at an Aluminum Refiner," Office of Industrial Technologies, U.S. DOE, Office of Energy Efficiency and Renewable Energy, Washington, D.C., May 1997.
11. The Nisshinbo case is based on "The Challenge: Improving Ventilation System Energy Efficiency in a Textile Plant," Office of Industrial Technologies, U.S. DOE, Office of Energy Efficiency and Renewable Energy, Washington, D.C., July 1997.
12. Philip A. Jallouk and Charles D. Liles, *Industrial Electric Motor Drive Systems* (Sittard, the Netherlands: Centre for the Analysis and Dissemination of Demonstrated Energy Technologies [CADDET], 1998), pp. 73–74, 80–81, 81–85, and 102–107.
13. The compressed air discussion is based on Wheeler et al., "Airmaster: Compressed Air System Audit Software," *Proceedings of 1997 ACEEE Summer Study on Energy Efficiency in Industry,* American Council for an Energy-Efficient Economy, Washington, D.C., 1997, pp. 281–286; and information

available from the City of Portland Energy Office's homepage (www.ci.port-land.or.us/energy/bestboeing.html).

14. The Southwire case is based on William D. Browning and L. Hunter Lovins, *The Energy Casebook* (Snowmass, Colo.: Rocky Mountain Institute, 1989), pp. 18-19; and Steven Nadel et al., *Energy-Efficient Motor Systems*, pp. 10, 80, 186, and 247; and Southwire's homepage (www.southwire.com).

CHAPTER 8

1. "Steam Partnership," Office of Industrial Technologies, U.S. DOE, Office of Energy Efficiency and Renewable Energy, Washington, D.C., April 1997.

2. The DuPont case is based on Philip Siekman, "Turn Down the Energy/Tune Up the Profits," *Fortune*, May 11, 1998, p. 132H; Loretta Clevenger and Jerry Hassell, "Case Study: From Jump Start to High Gear—How DuPont is Cutting Costs by Boosting Energy Efficiency," *Pollution Prevention Review*, Summer 1994, pp. 301–312; *Climate Wise: Case Study Compendium, Report I*, Office of Industrial Technologies, U.S. DOE, Office of Energy Efficiency and Renewable Energy, Washington, D.C., 1996, pp. 6, 36–37; information available on DuPont's website (www.dupont.com); and personal communications in 1998 with Michael Jones of U.S. Generating Company and Ernie O'Rourke.

3. As cited in U.S. EPA, "Supply Side Economics," *Climate Wisdom*, Spring 1998, Washington, D.C., p. 3 (the newsletter of EPA's Climate Wise program, 1-800-459-WISE).

4. The GM case is based on information and analysis provided by General Motors, information available from their website (www.gm.com), personal communications with Thomas Mort, and *Climate Wisdom*, Spring 1998.

5. The Dow case is based on Kenneth E. Nelson, "Dow's Energy/WRAP Contest," paper prepared for the 1993 Industrial Energy Technology Conference, March 24 and 25, 1993, Houston, Tex., and personal communications with Ken Nelson.

6. The discussion of the DOE's savings is based on information and analysis provided by Kent Hancock, U.S. DOE, Washington, D.C.

7. The discussion of Dow's Continuous Improvement program is based on Nelson, "Dow's Energy/WRAP Contest," and personal communications with Ken Nelson.

8. *Washington Post*, July 15, 1998, pp. C9, C12.

9. Ibid., and Shigeo Shingo, *Modern Approaches to Manufacturing Improvement: The Shingo System*, Alan Robinson, ed. (Cambridge, Mass.: Productivity Press, 1990), p. 13.

10. Masaaki Imai, *Kaizen* (New York: McGraw-Hill, 1986), p. 112.

11. Japan Human Relations Association, *The Idea Book* (Cambridge, Mass.: Productivity Press, 1988), p. 190.

12. Ibid., pp. 201–202.

13. Beverly Geber, "Saturn's Grand Experiment," *Training*, June 1992, p. 32.

14. Alan Lightman and Owen Gingerich, "When Do Anomalies Begin?" *Science*, February 7, 1991, pp. 690–695.

15. Englander et al., "Saving Electricity in Paper Manufacture: Measured Results for a Variety of Measures," *Proceedings 1996 ACEEE Summer Study on Energy Efficiency in the Buildings*, ACEEE, Washington, D.C., 1996.

16. "Combined Cycle Biomass Gasification," Fact Sheet, Office of Industrial Technologies, U.S. DOE, Office of Energy Efficiency and Renewable Energy, Washington, D.C., 1997.

17. The Georgia-Pacific case is based on "Steam Partnership," U.S. DOE; and information provided by the Steam Partnership, Office of Industrial Technologies, U.S. DOE, Office of Energy Efficiency and Renewable Energy, Washington, D.C., 1998.

18. *Climate Wise,* U.S. DOE, 1996, pp. 30–31.

19. Ibid., pp. 32–33.

20. The Burns Harbor case is based on "The Challenge: Improving Steam Turbine Performance at a Steel Mill," Office of Industrial Technologies, U.S. DOE, Office of Energy Efficiency and Renewable Energy, Washington, D.C., April 1998, and "The Challenge: Reducing BOF Hood Scrubber Energy Costs at a Steel Mill," Office of Industrial Technologies, U.S. DOE, Office of Energy Efficiency and Renewable Energy, Washington, D.C., April 1998.

21. The Decatur case is based on *Climate Wise,* U.S. DOE, 1996, pp. 48–49; and *Toolbook for Financing Energy Efficiency and Pollution Prevention Technologies,* U.S. DOE, Office of Energy Efficiency and Renewable Energy, Washington, D.C., 1997.

22. The Sealtest case is based on conversations with Joseph Crowley, the plant's manager, and John Donoghue, of Boston Edison; a paper by written Crowley and Donoghue, "The Energy Efficiency Partnership," presented to the American Council for an Energy-Efficient Economy workshop on partnerships for industrial productivity through energy efficiency, September 20, 1993; Ross Gelbspan, "At Sealtest, Sweet Smell of Success with Energy," *Boston Globe,* October 9, 1991, p. 37; and "The Energy Efficiency Industry and the Massachusetts Economy," a report from the Massachusetts Energy Efficiency Council, Concord, Mass., December 1992.

23. Peter Jaret, "Putting the Pinch on Energy Costs," *EPRI Journal,* July/August 1991, pp. 24–31.

24. The Ultramar Diamond Shamrock case is based on Benjamin Brant et al., "New waste-heat refrigeration unit cuts flaring, reduces pollution," *Oil & Gas Journal,* May 18, 1998, pp. 61–65; personal communications with Benjamin Brant; information and analysis provided by Planetec Utility Services, Evergreen, Colo.; and information provided by the Office of Industrial Technologies, U.S. DOE, Office of Energy Efficiency and Renewable Energy, Washington, D.C.

CHAPTER 9

1. James P. Womack and Daniel T. Jones, *Lean Thinking: Banish Waste and Create Wealth in Your Corporation* (New York: Simon & Schuster, 1996), pp. 48–49.

2. *Sustainability Report,* Interface, Inc., Atlanta, Ga., 1997. The Interface case is based on this report and personal communications with Ray Anderson, Mike Bennett, and Rahumathulla Marikkar. Unless otherwise specified, all quotes and facts are from the report.

3. Alex Wilson et al., *Green Development* (New York: Wiley, 1998), pp. 342–343 and 440–441.

4. Amory B. Lovins, L. Hunter Lovins, and Paul Hawken, *Natural Capitalism* (New York: Little Brown, 1999).

5. The Carrier case is based on personal communications with Rick Fedrizzi and

Sempra Energy Solutions as well as information available from various websites (www.utc.com and www.pacent.com).

6. Robert T. Lund, "Remanufacturing," *Technology Review,* February/March 1984, pp. 19–29. The discussion of remanufacturing draws material from the Lund article as well as "A Growing Love Affair with the Scrap Heap," *Business Week,* April 29, 1985, pp. 60–61.

7. E. Thomas Morehouse, Jr., "Design for Maintainability," American Electronics Association Design for the Environment White Paper, 1992.

8. The discussion of Xerox is based on "Xerox: Design for the Environment," Harvard Business School Case Study, N9-794-022, January 7, 1994; Claude Fussler with Peter James, *Driving Eco-Innovation* (London: Pitman Publishing, 1996), pp. 238–246; Livio D. DeSimone and Frank Popoff with the World Business Council for Sustainable Development, *Eco-efficiency: The Business Link to Sustainable Development* (Cambridge, Mass.: The MIT Press, 1997), pp. 59, 74–75; Stuart L. Hart, "Beyond Greening: Strategies for a Sustainable World," *Harvard Business Review,* January/February 1997, pp. 66–76; personal communications with former PARC facilities engineer, Richard Constanza; and information available on Xerox's website (www.Xerox.com).

9. As cited in Bruce Smart, ed., *Beyond Compliance: A New Industry View of the Environment* (Washington, D.C.: World Resources Institute, 1992), p. 35

10. The discussion here is based on *Toolbook for Financing Energy Efficiency and Pollution Prevention Technologies,* U.S. DOE, Office of Energy Efficiency and Renewable Energy, Washington, D.C., 1997, pp. 29–32 and the website of A. Finkl & Sons (www.finkl.com).

11. The GM case is from U.S. EPA, "Supply Side Economics," *Climate Wisdom,* Spring 1998, Washington, D.C., pp. 1, 3, 7.

12. *Power Smarts,* Alliance to Save Energy, Washington, D.C., 1998.

13. Elizabeth Titus, "Advanced Retrofit: A Pilot Study in Maximum Residential Energy Efficiency," *Proceedings of 1996 ACEEE Summer Study on Energy Efficiency in Buildings,* American Council for an Energy-Efficient Economy, Washington, D.C., 1996; Ken Walker, "Ohio's Home Power Boosters," Safe Energy Communication Council, Washington, D.C., 1996, p. 8; Grant Brohard et al., "Advanced Customer Technology Test for Maximum Energy Efficiency (ACT^2) Project: The Final Report," *ACEEE 1998 Summer Study on Energy Efficiency in Buildings Proceedings,* Washington, D.C., American Council for an Energy Efficient Economy, Washington, D.C., 1998.

14. These ten steps are based on a list put out by U.S. DOE, Office of Energy Efficiency and Renewable Energy, Washington, D.C., 1997.

15. The discussion of the Austin home energy loan program is based on *Cities and Countries: Thinking Globally, Acting Locally,* Public Technology, Inc., Washington, D.C., 1996, pp. 12–16; and personal communications with Mike Myers, U.S. DOE.

16. DeSimone and Popoff, *Eco-efficiency,* p. 61.

17. John B. Horrigan, Frances H. Irwin, and Elizabeth Cook, "Taking a Byte Out of Carbon," pp. 25–27.

18. As cited in U.S. EPA, "Quad/Graphics: Promoting Efficiency in the Energy-Intensive Printing Industry," *Climate Wisdom,* Winter 1997, Washington, D.C., pp. 1, 3, 4.

19. The telecommuting case studies discussed here can be found at www.ci.portland.or.us and www.cbs.state.or.us.

20. "School District of Philadelphia: Save Energy Campaign," IRT Environment (The Results Center), Aspen, Colo., 1995.
21. The discussion of urban heat island mitigation is based on an article by Akbari, Rosenfeld, Lloyd and Romm, "Paint the Town White and Green," *Technology Review,* February/March 1997, and personal communications with Art Rosenfeld.
22. The same steps that make buildings easier to cool in the summer can also make them more difficult (and expensive) to heat in winter. It turns out, however, that in hot climates the summertime benefit greatly outweighs the wintertime penalty. That's because in summer the sun is high overhead and shines mainly on the roof of a home; in winter the low sun shines on the walls and through the windows.
23. Cooler shingles and tiles will most likely contain a coating of titanium dioxide (TiO_2) to provide an attractive light color. The coolness of a material cannot always be discerned from its apparent lightness of color. Tests have found that terra-cotta tiles run 6°F cooler than white asphalt-fiberglass shingles. The reason: Half the heat from the sun arrives as invisible radiation in the near-infrared part of the spectrum, to which architects and roofers have paid little attention. Fortunately, TiO_2 reflects well in the infrared. So one can make a cool pastel shingle by adding a little light color to a modern cool white TiO_2 shingle.
24. The SMUD shade-tree case study comes from "1995 National Awards Program for Energy Efficiency and Renewable Energy," U.S. DOE, Office of Energy Efficiency and Renewable Energy, Washington, D.C., 1995, pp. 44–45. See also, Eric W. Hildebrandt et al., "Maximizing the Energy Benefits of Urban Forestration," *Proceedings of 1996 ACEEE Summer Study on Energy Efficiency in Buildings,* American Council for an Energy-Efficient Economy, Washington, D.C., 1996, pp. 9.123–9.131.

CHAPTER 10

1. The BP case is derived from speeches and information available on their website (www.bp.com) and personal communications with Kenneth E. Blower, Director, Health, Safety, Environment, BP America.
2. The SYCOM case is based on information and analysis provided by SYCOM, personal communication with Cris Cooley of SYCOM, and case histories of SYCOM retrofits from Jessica S. Lefevre, *The Energy Services Industry: Revolutionizing Energy Use in the United States,* National Association of Energy Service Companies, Washington, D.C. (202-371-7816), May 1996, pp. 45–52.
3. Aamer Athar et al., "Environmental Impact of the Texas LoanSTAR Program," Texas A&M University, College Station, Tex., 1998.
4. Chris Calwell, Danielle Dowers, and Doug Johnson, "How Far Have We Come?" E Source Strategic Memo, Boulder, Colo., May 1998, and Draft Final Report of the U.S. Industrial Electric Motor System Market Assessment, performed by Xenergy Inc. for the Office of Industrial Technologies, U.S. DOE, Office of Energy Efficiency, Washington, D.C., 1998.
5. The discussion of Climate Wise is based on conversations with Pamela Herman Milmoe of EPA and information provided by the Climate Wise program, 1-800-459-WISE.
6. *Steel: A National Resource for the Future,* American Iron and Steel Institute and

the Steel Manufacturers Association, May 1995 (available through the Office of Energy Efficiency and Renewable Energy, U.S. DOE, Washington, D.C.).

7. "Steel Industry Plan Would Cut Greenhouse Gas Emissions 10 Percent by 2010," press release, American Iron and Steel Institute, October 1, 1997.

8. *Scenarios of U.S. Carbon Reductions: Potential Impacts of Energy Technologies by 2010 and Beyond,* Interlaboratory Working Group (Berkeley, Calif.: Lawrence Berkeley National Laboratory, and Oak Ridge, Tenn.: Oak Ridge National Laboratory, September 1997).

9. *Minneapolis Star Tribune,* May 21, 1998, p. 3b; and *Global Warming Network Online Today,* Environmental Information Networks, Inc., October 13, 1995.

APPENDIX

1. Personal communications with Vivian Loftness, August 1998.

2. Thomas J. Peters and Robert H. Waterman, Jr., *In Search of Excellence* (New York: Harper & Row, 1982), pp. 5–6.

3. Richard Gillespie, *Manufacturing Knowledge: A History of the Hawthorne Experiments* (New York: Cambridge University Press, 1993), p. 92

4. Michael Brill et al., *Using Office Design to Increase Productivity,* Volume I (Buffalo: Workplace Design and Productivity, Inc., 1984), pp. 224–25.

5. The searches performed were Lexis-Nexis and Proquest. *Financial Times,* February 16, 1998, p. 17.

6. Gillespie, *Manufacturing Knowledge,* pp. 38–48,

7. Charles D. Wrege, "Solving Mayo's Mystery: The First Complete Account of the Origins of the Hawthorne Studies—The Forgotten Contributions of C. E. Snow and H. Hibarger," in Taylor et al., eds., *Proceedings,* Academy of Management Conference, Kansas City, Mo., August 1976, p. 14. The use of the term "control group" by the researchers deserves elaboration, as it does not fit most modern definitions of the term. In most of the tests, the researchers did want some sort of control group where the lighting did not vary as it did in the tests. But because the researchers quickly came to the view that factors such as increased supervision were responsible for some of the changes in output, the control groups were often subjected to special test conditions, such as increased supervision. Moreover, in the first two series of tests, the control groups often experienced changing lighting conditions even though the artificial lighting wasn't changed; the daylight did vary by day and by season (indeed, those two series began in late fall and winter, respectively, and ended in the spring, thereby ensuring the control groups tended to see increasing light levels). Finally, in at least the one case cited in the text, and probably more, the control group seemed to be competing with the test group.

8. Charles D. Wrege, "Solving Mayo's Mystery: The First Complete Account of the Origins of the Hawthorne Studies: The Forgotten Contributions of Charles E. Snow and Homer Hibarger," paper delivered to Academy of Management Conference, History Division, Kansas City, Mo., August 1976, p. 13, as cited in Gillespie, *Manufacturing Knowledge,* pp. 45–46.

9. Richard H. Franke and Richard P. Urian, "Illumination and Productivity at Hawthorne," paper presented to the Academy of Management Conference, History Division, Miami Beach, Fla., August 12, 1991, p. 2.

10. Appendix H, "Factory Illumination—Production Tests at Hawthorne Works of the Western Electric Co.," Box 5, Folder 330, Dugald Caleb Jackson Papers

(D.C.J/5/330), Institute Archives and Special Collections, Hayden Library, M.I.T., Cambridge, Mass., p. 6.

11. While 10 foot-candles may seem low to us today, it was consistent with the literature review done at the time by Harvard psychologist Leonard Troland. He examined some 9,000 sources and concluded, "The vast majority of industrial operations can be carried out at maximum efficiency with an illumination intensity in the neighborhhod of 10 foot-candles, and many of these operations can be done equally well at 1 foot-candle." L. T. Troland, "An Analysis of the Literature Concerning the Dependency of Visual Functions upon Illumination Intensity, p. 2, DCJ/5/329.

12. Appendix H, "Factory Illumination," (D.C.J/5/330), pp. 13–14, Dugald C. Jackson, "Progress Report of the Illumination Test at the Western Electric Company, Hawthorne Works, Chicago," Committee on Industrial Lighting, National Research Council, September 11, 1926, p. 3 in Thomas Alva Edison Papers, Edison National Historic Site, West Orange, N.J., 1924.

13. Jackson, "Progress Report," p. 3.

14. Appendix H, "Factory Illumination," p. 16.

15. Gillespie, *Manufacturing Knowledge,* p. 44.

16. C. E. Snow, "Research on Industrial Illumination," *The Tech Engineering News,* Vol. 8, November 1927, pp. 257–282.

17. Gillespie, p. 83.

18. Richard H. Franke and Richard P. Urian, "Illumination and Productivity at Hawthorne," paper presented to the Academy of Management Conference, History Division, Miami Beach, August 12, 1991, p. 9. See also Laurel Wiljanen Neece, *Lighting the Way: First Quantitative Analysis of the Hawthorne Illumination Experiments of 1924 to 1927,* unpublished undergraduate dissertation, Department of Management, Worcester Polytechnic Institute, 1979.

19. Wrege, "Solving Mayo's Mystery," in Taylor et al., eds., p. 15.

20. As cited in Stephen R. G. Jones, "Was There a Hawthorne Effect?" *American Journal of Sociology,* Vol. 98, No. 3 (November 1992), pp. 451–468.

21. Ibid, p. 453.

22. Ibid, p. 467. Jones notes that "my result appears to be robust across a wide variety of specifications, alternative samples, and two definitions of experimental change."

23. Ibid, p. 467. This is the same position that Gillespie argues at length in *Manufacturing Knowledge,* that Mayo and his colleagues essentially "manufactured" their conclusions.

24. Elton Mayo, *The Human Problems of an Industrial Civilization,* 2nd ed. (Boston: Division of Research, Harvard University Graduate School of Business Administration, 1946), p. 65.

25. T. N. Whitehead, *The Industrial Worker,* Vol. I and II (New York: Arno Press, 1938, reprinted 1977), pp. 42–43.

26. Whitehead (ibid., p. 43) notes that "A negative finding is never very convincing; it is always possible that some phenomenon remains undiscovered through a defect in the investigation.... It is well known that the ultimate effects of changed conditions may not declare themselves at once." Whitehead believed the effect could be explained by what came to be called the Hawthorne Effect. Yet his words were more true than he realized, since it has taken several decades for these experiments to be understood.

27. William J. Dickson and F. J. Roethlisberger, *Counseling in an Organization: A Sequel to the Hawthorne Researches* (Boston: Division of Research, Harvard University Graduate School of Business Administration, 1966), pp. 31–33.

28. Ibid.

29. Desmond Cook, *The Impact of the Hawthorne Effect in Experimental Designs in Educational Research Final Report,* Report No. P1757, U.S. Office of Education, Washington, D.C., 1967. The report (p. 130) notes that, "Researchers have established the Hawthorne Effect as a variable contaminating study results when there is very little evidence that the effect has been operationally defined in a manner that its role in comparative educational studies can be firmly established. In essence, the Hawthorne Effect concept is being put in the position of being guilty (i.e., operational) with efforts then being directed to establish its innocence rather than being considered as innocent (i.e., nonoperational) until its guilt has been established."

30. John G. Adair, Donald Sharpe, and Cam-Loi Huynh, "Hawthorne Control Procedures in Educational Experiments: A Reconsideration of Their Use and Effectiveness," *Review of Educational Research,* Summer 1989, Vol. 59, No. 2, pp. 215–228. Examples of activity matching include "sedentary physical activities as a control for the physical training of experimental subjects" or "control group lessons of the same duration and from the same source as those for the treatment group." (p. 217)

31. Ibid., pp. 224–225. In particular, "There was also no evidence to support any of three distinctive subtypes of Hawthorne Effects as the source of the artifact." The three subtypes being special attention, knowledge they were in an experiment, or activity matching.

32. Gillespie, p. 51

33. George Pennock, "Industrial Research at Hawthorne: An Experimental Investigation of Rest Periods, Working Conditions, and Other Influences," *Personnel Journal,* 1929–1930, Vol. 8, pp. 296–313, as cited in Gary D. Gottfredson, "The Hawthorne Misunderstanding (And How to Get the Hawthorne Effect in Action Research)," *Journal of Research in Crime and Delinquency,* Vol. 33, No. 1, February 1996, pp. 28–38.

34. Gottfredson, "The Hawthorne Misunderstanding," p. 33. The relay assembly test workers understood this. See, for example, Relay Assembly Test Room (RATR) Daily History Record, September 26, 1927. (This is part of the *Records of the Industrial Relations Experiment Carried Out by the Western Electric Company at Hawthorne Works, Hawthorne, Illinois,* [1927–1932]—1961, available on microfilm at a number of libraries, including the University of Wisconsin, Milwaukee Library.)

35. RATR Daily History Record, September 13, 1927.

36. As cited in H. McIlvaine Parsons, "What Caused the Hawthorne Effect?" *Administration & Society,* Vol. 10, No. 3, November 1978, p. 269.

37. H. McIlvaine Parsons, "What Happened at Hawthorne?" *Science,* Vol. 183, March 8, 1974, pp. 922–932.

38. Brian L. Pitcher, "The Hawthorne Experiments: Statistical Evidence for a Learning Hypothesis," *Social Forces,* Vol. 60, September 1981, pp. 133–149. Even for operators one and two, who came in to the experiment late (after the other workers had been working in the room 2,000 hours and had experienced half of their learning) and, as we will see, under unusual circumstances, learning

accounted for 63 percent to 74 percent of the variance in their output. In a learning curve, output is linearly related to the logarithm of time.

39. Franke, "Worker Productivity at Hawthorne," *American Sociological Review,* Vol. 45 (1980), pp. 1006–1027.
40. Gottfredson, "The Hawthorne Misunderstanding," p. 34.
41. Whitehead, *The Industrial Worker,* p. 128.
42. Gillespie, pp. 92–93.
43. Shigeo Shingo, *Modern Approaches to Manufacturing Improvement: The Shingo System,* Alan Robinson, ed. (Cambridge, Mass.: Productivity Press, 1990), p. 34.
44. Pitcher, "The Hawthorne Experiments," p. 144. For the analysis by the Hawthorne researchers showing greater uniformity in worker performance during experimental runs with rest periods, see RATR Progress Report No. 3, Section VIII. See also RATR Daily History Record for Thursday, August 11, 1927.
45. Gillespie, pp. 60, 67.
46. Whitehead, The Industrial Worker, Vol. II, Figs. K-63 and K-66; Pitcher, "The Hawthorne Experiments," p. 139. Worker 5 experienced far more changes, ten to forty a week during the two years, but then after August 1929, she too dropped to zero, one, or two changes a week for the next three years. The greater variety in relays and then the sudden switch to reduced relay variety may well explain why the learning trend accounts for only 83 percent of the variance in her output over the five-year period but a remarkable 88 percent to 89 percent of the variance for workers 3 and 4.
47. Whitehead, *The Industrial Worker,* pp. 128–130.
48. Gillespie, p. 63. Some confusion has existed over why the replacements occurred, as some have tried to argue that the two were removed because they didn't get along with the other workers. Gillespie clears up the confusion by looking at the original reports closely, which suggest that the Hawthorne researchers themselves tried to obfuscate the issue. Whitehead, *Industrial Worker,* p. 122, notes "After the removal of [workers] 1a and 2a, the records contain no more allusions to lack of cooperation, and very few to excessive talking and noise." So whatever the stated reason for the removals, the effect was clear enough.
49. Gillespie, p. 63.
50. Ibid., pp. 63–64. Sirchio's sister had died shortly before she entered the test room, her mother died three months later, and then her father and a brother learned they were to be laid off the following month.
51. Gillespie, pp. 66–67. Gillespie adds, "Moreover, why wouldn't they downplay the effect of wages, since that factor was "out of their control . . . determined by a separate department in collaboration with the works manager and head office in New York?"
52. Roethlisberger, *Management and Morale,* as cited in Gillespie, pp. 77–78.
53. Mayo, *The Human Problems of an Industrial Civilization,* pp. 74–75. Whitehead (p. 130) says of Period XII, "The rest pauses were valued not so much for the absence of work or for the opportunity for eating, as for the positive change they provided and for their social opportunities."
54. Parsons (1974), p. 929. Parsons goes on to explain, "Experimenters must either wait until the rate levels off, or they must find and remove whatever is causing the rate to rise. The Hawthorne investigators were more remiss, technically, in doing neither than in using a time series design in the first place."

55. RATR Daily History Record for May 16, November 1, 8, and 10, 1927. Interestingly, not only did the workers have more control over the lighting, but it was higher quality to begin with: The test room had "more uniform distribution of day light, as the day light value is much higher since the building in which the test is being conducted is equipped with full sectional width sky lights." RATR *Progress Report No. 1,* December 3, 1927, Section No. 2, p. 3. (This report is also available on microfiche at a number of libraries around the country.)

56. Gillespie, pp. 129–133. Why didn't the group of workers in the second relay assembly test learn how to increase their output and wages over time as the five women did? First, the workers did not get the feedback their counterparts in the first test were getting; by design, they never got rest pauses, making it even harder for them to learn how to pace themselves; and it appears that they did not see the reduction in relay type that their counterparts did. Second, the second test was marred by an unexpected occurrence: "[D]uring the third week of the experimental period, it became necessary for the operators to work overtime: one extra hour on Mondays, Tuesdays, Thursdays, and Fridays, and three and one-half hours longer on Saturdays." This is a huge increase in hours (and pay) and yet in the main, the workers kept up their increased level of hourly output. In other words, even working a tremendous number of hours with no rest pauses, they were motivated (or learned how) to maintain a very high level of output for two months.

57. Gillespie, p. 83. Interestingly, this last observation "was never made by the company researchers, but was noted by Mayo's assistant, the economist R. S. Meriam."

58. *Management and the Worker,* p. 133.

59. Gillespie, pp. 82–84.

60. Ibid., p. 84. From my perspective, mica splitting is so different from relay assembling both in the work and the pay that one should be hesitant to draw too many other conclusions.

61. Gillespie, pp. 127–142.

62. Gillespie, pp. 158–168.

63. Parsons, "What Happened at Hawthorne?" p. 926 notes that "It was relatively easy for the Bank Wiring Observation Room operators to adjust their response rate in order to produce only two units a day. They could observe their own performance and slow down their work on the second unit in the afternoon if necessary." He sums up the main conclusion to be drawn: "In short, the Bank Wiring Observation Room study showed what could *prevent* a rise in response rates."

64. Gillespie, pp. 18–19. AT&T was a pioneer in employee stock purchase plans. Starting in 1915, employees could purchase AT&T stock on installment at below market price. Hawthorne works management applied "considerable pressure" to workers to purchase stock. Participation at Hawthorne reached 75 percent in 1929, when 18,000 workers at the factory subscribed to more than 100,000 shares.

65. Ibid., p. 95.

66. Ibid., pp. 86–88.

67. Mayo, *Human Problems,* pp. 81–82.

68. As cited in Gillespie, pp. 88.

Company Index

The following is a list of the companies whose experiences or expertise has been documented and presented at length or in brief in *Cool Companies.*

A. Finkl & Sons Company, 10, 190–92
ADI Control Techniques Drives, 151
Alumax, 150
Amkor/Anan Pilipinas, 109–10
Amtrak, 137
Anheuser-Busch, 114, 135–36
Applebee's, 137
Aspen Systems, 55
AT&T, 197

Ballard Power Systems, 25, 129–30
Bank of America, The, 73
Bethlehem Steel, 158, 173–75

BKG Finishing Systems, 175
Blandin Paper Company, 171–72
BlueCross BlueShield of Oregon, 5, 46, 52–53
Boccardo Properties, 54
Boeing, 47, 64–65, 153
Boston Edison, 176
Bowater, Inc., 172
British Petroleum (BP), 11, 206–9, 217
Burns Harbor steel mill (see *Bethlehem Steel*)
Burt Hill Kosar Rittelman Associates, 75

Carrier Corporation, 182, 184
Centerplex, 4, 46, 48–51
Compaq, 6, 101–8, 216
Con Edison, 124, 125
Coors Brewing Company, 113, 123
Croxton Collaborative, 80

DaimlerChrysler, 25
Decatur Foundry, 175–76
Dow Chemical, 12–13, 158, 164–67
DreamWorks, 184
DuPont, 2, 10, 157, 159–62, 216
Durst Organization, 138

ENSAR Group, 74
EUA Cogenex, 67

Fabe-Litho, 211
First National Bank of Omaha, 114, 128
Ford Motor Company, 25, 28, 30–35, 45, 138

General Conservation Corporation (GCC), 174–75
General Electric, 72
General Motors, 8, 153, 158, 162–64, 192, 196
Georgia-Pacific, 9–10, 158, 171
Greenville Tube Company, 147–48
Guilford of Maine (see *Interface, Inc.*), 182–83

Hartman Company, 52
Henningsen Cold Storage Company, 74
Hyde Tools, 91–92

IBM, 110
Interface, Inc., 5, 10, 77, 82–83, 137, 181–86, 216

Johnson Controls, 72

Kalwall Corporation, 116
Kraft General Foods, 176–77

Lockheed-Martin, 72, 78, 92–94
Lucent Technologies, 9, 110, 140

Malden Mills, 1, 115–17
Massachusetts Electric Company, 115, 116, 193
MicroGrid, Inc., 52
Musashino Brewery (see *Suntory*), 152

Natural Lighting Company, 84
New Energy Ventures, 125
Nisshinbo California, 150–51

Ontario Hydro, 185

Ortho-McNeil Pharmaceuticals, 64

Pacific Gas and Electric Company (PG&E), 70
Parker Chiropractic College, 72–73
Pennsylvania Power and Lighting Company, 89–91
Perkin-Elmer, 9, 145–46
Phillips 66, 134
Planetec Utility Services, 178, 179
Potomac Electric and Power Company, 67
Praxair Company, 161

Prince Street Technologies (see *Interface, Inc.*), 83, 183
Procter & Gamble, 196

Quad/Graphics, 197

Rank Xerox, 188–89
Regal Fruit Co-op, 149–50
Rochelle Municipal Utilities (IL), 125
Royal Darwin Hospital, 152
Royal Dutch/Shell, 3, 16–27, 130–31, 209, 217

Sacramento Municipal Utility District (SMUD), 136, 203
Scott Paper Company, 152
Sempra Energy Solutions, 184
Siemens Solar Industries, 112
Solarex, 137
Solar Turbines, 115, 125–26
Southern California Gas Company, 182
Southland Industries, 73
Southwire Company, 154–55
St. Francis Hotel, 64
STMicroelectronics, 6–7, 100–101, 110–12

Suntory, 152
Superior Die Set Corporation, 91
Supersymmetry, 6, 100–101, 108–10
Sure Power Corporation, 128–29
SYCOM, 11, 209–11, 218

Target, 84
3M, 2, 142–45, 216
Toyota, 3–4, 28–30, 44–45, 129–31, 216, 217
Trigen Energy Corporation, 121–23

Ultramar Diamond Shamrock, 178
United Jersey Bank, 210
United Technologies, 128, 184

VeriFone, 5, 70, 77, 79–81

Wal-Mart, 47, 84–85
Way Station, The, 47, 74
West Bend Mutual Insurance Company, 94–96
Western Digital, 7, 101, 109

Xenergy, 146, 151
Xerox, 15, 47, 186–90

General Index

A. Finkl & Sons Company, 10, 190–92
AC Battery, 137
Adhesive tapes, medical, 145
Advanced Turbine System, 125–26
Air compressor systems, 8, 29, 152–54. *See also*
    Motors and motor systems
Air conditioning, 184, 200. *See also* HVAC
    (heating/ventilation and air conditioning)
Air exchange/recirculation, 58, 80, 81, 193. *See
    also* HVAC (heating/ventilation and air
    conditioning)
Air quality, 51, 52, 200–202. *See also* Carbon
    dioxide; Emissions, polluting; Price of
    carbon dioxide
Aitken, Don, 94
Alcohol-based fluxes, 107
Allaire, Paul, 188
Alliance to Save Energy, 144, 173
Alumax, 150
Aluminum, 150
American Council for an Energy-Efficient
    Economy, 194
American Forest and Paper Association, 172
American Iron and Steel Institute (AISI), 211,
    212
American Journal of Sociology, 228
American Petroleum Institute, 212
American Society of Heating, Refrigeration and
    Air Conditioning Engineers (ASHRAE),
    58
Amkor/Anan Pilipinas, 109–10
Amtrak, 137
Anderson, Ray, 181, 185
Anheuser-Busch, 114, 135–36
Applebee's, 137
Archimedes, 137
Architects and their fees, 76
Ash trees, 202
Aspen Systems, 55
Assembly line, the moving, 32–33
Association of Energy Engineers, 177
AT&T, 197
Austin Convention Center, 137
Australia, 207–8
Automobiles:
    commuting to and from work, 196–98
    Ford and waste reduction, Henry, 30–35
    proton exchange membrane (PEM) fuel
        cell, 129
    remanufacturing, 187
    super-efficient cars, 22
    see also Toyota
Avedissian, Jacques, 93

Ballard Power Systems, 25, 129–30
Ballasts, electromagnetic/electronic, 66
Bank of America, The, 73
Banks, 73, 114, 128, 195, 210
Bank Wiring Observation Study (1931–1932),
    240
Barriers to cool design, 76, 78
Basic Research Building (Houston), 58, 60
Beer brewing, 113, 123, 135–36
Bell Laboratories, 136
Benchmarking, 13, 180
Best practices, 14
Bethlehem Steel, 158, 173–75, 234
Bidding process and building upgrades, 49
Biomass power (plant matter), 20–21, 24,
    135–36
Biophilia, 98
Biophilia Hypothesis, The, 98
Biotechnology, 22
BKG Finishing Systems, 175
Blandin Paper Company, 171–72
Blue Angel eco-label, Germany's, 101
BlueCross BlueShield of Oregon, 5, 46, 52–53
Boccardo Properties, 54
Boeing, 47, 64–65, 153
Boilers, coal and gas, 145, 163
Bonneville Power Administration, 149, 153
Boston Edison, 176
Bottom line, triple, 23–24
Bowater, Inc., 172
BrainBank, Inc., 167–68
Brent Spar (oil storage tank), 17, 22–23
Brew Moon Restaurant & Brewery, 123
British Petroleum (BP), 11, 206–9, 217
Browne, John, 206
Buildings:
    BlueCross BlueShield of Oregon, 52–53
    Boeing, 64–65
    Centerplex, 48–51
    costs, life-cycle, 78
    daylit, 5
    end user, focus on the, 67–69
    Energy Cost Savings Council, 47
    energy reductions, 46–47
    equipment, improved office, 69–72
    exit signs, 69
    financing, 57
    50 percent reduction goal, 47–48
    HVAC (heating/ventilation and air
        conditioning), 72–73
    International Performance Measurement
        and Verification Protocol (IPMVP),
        56–58

Buildings (*continued*)
  investment, a low-risk and high-return,
    54–56
  lighting, improved, 63–64, 66–67
  managers, building, 106–7
  new, designing, 73–75, 98–99
  Ridgehaven office building (San Diego),
    51–52
  Texas A&M, energy wizards of, 57–63
  see also Productivity-enhancing design
Burns Harbor steel mill, 173–75
Burt Hill Kosar Rittelman Associates, 75
Business Environment Trophy in Europe
    (1998), 110
Business Week, 11

Cable, superconducting, 155
Caldwell, Philip, 35
California State Automobile Association
    building, 75
California Steel Industries, 86–87
"Can You Achieve 150 Percent of Predicted
    Retrofit Savings" (Claridge & Haberl), 58
Capitol Square Building (Canada), 73
Carbon dioxide:
  automobiles, 192
  Blandin Paper Company, 172
  Boeing, 64
  British Petroleum (BP), 207
  carbon vs., 213
  Chicago Convention Center, 122
  cogeneration, 7, 50, 116, 120, 122
  commuting to and from work, 196–98
  Coors Brewing Company, 113
  DuPont, 157
  dust collection system, 141
  embodied, 180
  employees, tapping expertise of line, 158,
    164–70
  First National Bank of Omaha, 114
  fossil fuels, burning of, 3
  fuel cells, 129
  Galt House East Hotel (KY), 134
  General Motors, 158
  home energy use, 192, 196
  manufacturing, 14–15
  nonprocess manufacturers, 157
  price issue, 21
  reasons for having strategies for reducing, 2
  Royal Dutch/Shell, 26
  service sector companies, 14
  solar energy, 196
  STMicroelectronics, 111
  SYCOM, 11
  technology and reducing, 3
  3M, 145
  United Technologies, 184
  Waverly Junior-Senior High School (NY),
    117, 118
  zero-carbon energy sources, 114
  see also Decarbonization; Emissions,
    polluting; Price of carbon dioxide
Carbon monoxide, 161
Carnegie Mellon University, 6, 78, 82, 96–97
Carpets, *see* Interface, Inc.

Carrier Corporation, 182, 184
Cascading, 123
Castings for electric-motor frames, 175–76
Caterpillar, 126
Center for Architectural Research, 95
Center for Energy and Climate Solutions, 14
Center for Services Research and Education, 95
Centerplex, 4, 46, 48–51
Chambers Works, 160–62
Champions, energy, 49, 100
Chemical manufacturing, 10, 12–13, 41
Chicago, 191
Chicago Convention Center, 7, 113, 122
Chillers, 50, 134–35. *See also* HVAC
    (heating/ventilation and air conditioning)
Chlorofluorocarbons (CFCs):
  chillers, 50
  Compaq, 107
  cooling load, reducing the, 73
  DuPont, 159
  Royal Dutch/Shell, 26
  Sweden, 101
Ciba-Geigy, 41
Claridge, David, 57–61
Clark, Kim, 38
Clayton, Taylor, 54
Clean production, 31. *See also* Lean
    thinking/production system
Clemson University, 125
Climate change, global, 162, 217. *See also*
    Global warming
Climate Wise program, 159, 192, 211
Coal boilers, 145, 162
Coffee break areas, 104
Cogeneration, 1
  carbon dioxide, 7, 50
  Chambers Works, 162
  Chicago Convention Center, 113
  Coors Brewery and Trigen, 123
  cost-effective analysis, 113, 114, 119, 120
  defining, 113
  energy bills, lowering, 7
  environmental benefits of, 120
  Ford, Henry, 32
  fuel cells, 127–30
  General Motors, 163
  history of an old idea, 120–21
  Malden Mills, 115–17
  manufacturing, 15
  microturbines, 126–27
  natural gas, 145
  paper industry, 170–71
  regulations, 119
  semiconductor manufacturing, 112
  Superior Fibers, 124–25
  Trigen Energy Corporation, 121–23
  turbine system, advanced, 125–26
  Waverly Junior-Senior High School (NY),
    117–19
  see also Steam systems
Commissioning, continuous, 211
Commonwealth Brewery, 123
Communities, cool, 198–202
Commuting to and from work, 196–98
Compact fluorescents, 66

Compaq, 6, 216
  environmental strategy, 101
  Lee Eng Lock, 105–6
  life-cycle analysis, 103–4
  paybacks, allowing longer, 102–3
  production improved through energy
    reduction, 107–8
  success story, the great American, 102
  support staff, value and train, 106–7
Compressed air and steam systems, 8, 29,
  152–54. *See also* Motors and motor
  systems
Computers, 69–71. *See also* Compaq
Comstock building (Pittsburgh), 75–76
Con Edison, 124, 125
Congressional Office of Technology
  Assessment, 44
Conoco, 134
Conserval Systems, 138
Conservation, 49
Consumer Guide to Home Energy Savings, 194
Consumption, cutting down energy, 207
Continuous improvement, cool:
  Dow Chemical, 164–65
  Energy, Department of (DOE), 13
  Ford, Henry, 34
  obvious energy-saving investments, 11–12
  Royal Dutch/Shell's energy scenario, 16
Contractors and building upgrades, 49
Control Data, 91
Control over workplace conditions, 86–87, 98,
  151–52, 238
Cooling equipment, 50–51, 53, 193. *See also*
  HVAC (heating/ventilation and air
  conditioning)
Coors Brewing Company, 113, 123
Copiers, 69, 70, 186–90
Corporate Conservation Council, 144
Cost-effective analyses:
  cogeneration, 113, 114, 119, 120
  life-cycle analyses, 75, 78, 103–4, 129, 146
  renewable energy, 130
  submetering, 50
Creativity, 104
Crowley, Joseph, 176–77
Croxton, Randolph, 80–81, 100
Croxton Collaborative, 80
Crystal-growing capacity, 112
Cummins, 126
Cusumano, Michael, 36

DaimlerChrysler, 25, 129
David, George, 184
David, Paul, 53
Da Vinci, Leonardo, 120
Davis, Ged, 25
Davisson, D. D., 242
Daylit buildings, 5. *See also* Lighting, efficient
Decarbonization, 3, 180
  Interface, 181–86
  Royal Dutch/Shell, 25
  what should a cool company do?, 203–4
  Xerox, 186–90
Decatur Foundry, 175–76
Dematerialization, 16, 22, 26

Deming, W. Edwards, 35
Department of Natural Resources building (Salt
  Lake City), 74
Depression, The Great, 241
Deregulation, 119, 122
"Design for Maintainability" (Morehouse, Jr.),
  187
Design strategies, prevention-oriented, 4, 5. *See
  also* Energy efficiency; Productivity-
  enhancing design
DeSimone, Livio, 142
Detergents, 196
Detroit Edison, 129, 134
DeVries, Doug, 91, 92
Dickson, William J., 229–30, 239
Dochterman, Michael, 184
DOE, *see* Energy, Department of (DOE)
Dow Chemical:
  continuous improvement, cool, 12–13, 164–65
  evaluation committee, multifunctional, 166
  investments and returns, energy efficiency
    and, 158, 165–66
  management support, sustained, 165
  training people, 166–67
DreamWorks, 184
Drying process for castings of electric-motor
  frames, 175–76
Duffin, Murray, 111
DuPont, 2, 10, 157, 159–62, 216
Durst, Jonathan, 139
Durst Organization, 138
Dust collection system, 141, 150
Dye-making process, 41
Dynamic Manufacturing, 37, 41–42

Eastman Kodak, 168
*Eco-Efficiency: The Business Link to Sustainable
  Development* (DeSimone), 142
Economist, 18
Edison, Thomas, 120
Electricity use, submetering to track, 50. *See also*
  Buildings; Cogeneration; Lighting, efficient;
  Motors and motor systems; Productivity-
  enhancing design
Electric Power Research Institute, 66, 175
Electronics, consumer, 194
Elkhart General Hospital, 64
Embodied energy, 10, 180–82
Emissions, polluting, 1–2
  British Petroleum, 11
  cogeneration, 115–16, 118
  communities, cool, 198
  DuPont, 159–62
  50 percent reduction goal, 15, 26, 47–48, 50
  forest products industry, 170–72
  General Motors, 162–64
  profits, 42
  proton exchange membrane fuel cell, 130
  Royal Dutch/Shell, 3, 17, 26
  steam systems, 158, 159
  steel industry, 212
  Superior Fibers, 124
  trading, emissions, 208–9, 213
  see also Carbon dioxide; Decarbonization;
    Price of carbon dioxide

Employees:
carbon dioxide emissions and tapping
expertise of line, 158, 164–70
educating, 186, 207
suggestion systems, 167–69, 182
see also Hawthorne Effect
End-of-pipe approach to quality, 44
End user, focus on the, 67–69, 76, 85–86, 98
Energy, Department of (DOE):
Dow's approach, training people in, 12–13,
167
energy-intensive industries, 211
Energy Savers, 194
Home Weatherization Assistance Program,
193
Industrial Assessment Centers (IACs), 124,
153
Industry of the Future Program, 211–12
International Performance Measurement
and Verification Protocol (IPMVP), 56
lighting, efficient, 66–67
Lockheed-Martin, 72
management support, 165
motors and motor systems, 9, 140, 143, 156,
210
Office of Industrial Technologies (OIT),
115
productivity study, 139
solar energy, 136
Steam Challenge, 173
waste heat-powered fuel-recovery system,
178, 179
Energy Concepts Company, 178
Energy Controls and Concepts, 86
Energy Cost Savings Council, 47
Energy efficiency, 3
buildings, 46–48. *See also* Buildings
champions, energy, 49, 100
dematerialization, 22
Energy Star programs, 53–54, 64, 70–71, 84,
107
motors and motor systems, 140–42, 146–47
rebates for, 146
simple payback and return on investment, 5
see also Cogeneration; Decarbonization;
individual subject headings
Energy Management Control System (EMCS),
48, 57–58, 60–61, 105, 109
Energy Resource Center, 182
Energy Savers, 194
Energy Star programs, 53–54, 64, 70–71, 84,
107
Energy User, 47
Engineers, carbon dioxide emissions and
tapping expertise of, 158, 164–70
ENSAR Group, 74
Environmental and Conservation Services
Department of Austin, Texas, 194–95
Environmental Defense Fund, 208
Environmental Enterprises, 182
Environmentally responsive workstations
(ERWs), 94–95
Environmental Protection Agency (EPA):
Climate Wise program, 159, 192, 211

Compaq, 108
Energy Star programs, 53–54, 64, 70–71, 84,
107
Green Lights program, 63–64
halogen lamps, 49–50
heat pumps, 133
Equipment, improved office, 69–72
EUA Cogenex, 67
Eucalyptus trees, 202–3
Europe:
Eco-Audit and Management System, 110
emissions, polluting, 217
market and environmental performance,
the, 101
Quality Award for Business Excellence,
1977, 110
Evergreen Lease, 183
Exit signs, 69
Eyestrain, 63

Fabe-Litho, 211
*Factor Four: Doubling Wealth, Halving Resource
Use* (Lovins, Lovins & Weizsacker), 105
Fan systems, 52, 53. *See also* Motors and motor
systems
Fast-cycle manufacturing, 36
Fay, Chris, 20
Fedrizzi, Rick, 184
Feigenbaum, Armand, 35
Feuerstein, Aaron, 1, 115
50 percent reduction goal, 15, 26, 47–48, 50
Financial Times, 222
First National Bank of Omaha, 114, 128
Flat-panel monitors, 71
Fluorescents, compact, 66
Ford, Henry, 4, 30–35, 39, 121
Ford, William C., Jr., 45
Ford Motor Company, 25, 28, 30–35, 45, 129,
138
Forest products industry, 170–72
Forging a Fresher America program, 191
Forrestal Building (D.C.), 66
Fortune, 8, 36, 140
Fossil fuels, burning of, 3, 7, 20, 183, 196
Four Times Square building (NY), 114, 138–39
Fowle, Bruce, 139
Franklin, Benjamin, 120
Franta, Greg, 74
Friedman, Lawrence, 64
Fuchida, Mitsuo, 18
Fuel cells, 21, 127–30, 139, 196

Galt House East Hotel (KY), 134–35
Gas-fired boilers, 162
General Conservation Corporation (GCC),
174–75
General Electric, 72. *See also* Hawthorne Effect
General Motors:
compressed air, 8, 153
decarbonization, 192
General Motors Acceptance Corporation
Mortgage (GMAC), 196
proton exchange membrane fuel cell, 129
steam systems, 8, 158, 162–64

Georgia-Pacific, 9–10, 158, 171
Geothermal heat pumps, 132–35
Germany, 101
Gilbreth, E. B., 36, 105
Gilbreth, Lillian, 36, 105
Gillespie, Richard, 225, 235, 236, 240
Global Climate Coalition, 23, 26
Global warming, 20–23, 25–26, 44, 212, 217
"Global Warming: The Role of Energy-efficient
    Technologies," 25
Gottfredson, Gary, 232, 234
Gottfried, David A., 52
"Green *and* Competitive" (Porter), 42
Green buildings/designs, 74–75, 99
Greenhouse gas emissions, *see* Carbon dioxide;
    Emissions, polluting; Price of carbon
    dioxide
Green Lights program, 63–64
Greenville Tube Company, 147–48
Gribi, John, 102
Gross domestic product (GDP), 22
Gross national product (GNP), 19
Growth, sustainable, 20–21, 24–26
Guilford of Maine, 182–83
Guthrie, Stephen, 87

Haberl, Jeff, 57–58, 61
Halogen lamps, 49–50
Harbor Drive manufacturing plant (San
    Diego), 126
Hart, Stuart, 42
Hartkopf, Volker, 96
Hartman Company, 52
Harvard Business Review, 45
Hawken, Paul, 183
Hawthorne Effect:
    conclusions, 242–43
    Depression, The Great, 241
    flaws in methodology and perception,
        220–21
    genuine, the, 241–42
    lighting experiments, the, 222–27
    many Hawthorne effects, 229–31
    Mayo, Elton, 219
    money, learning to make more, 233–36
    other experiments at Hawthorne fail to
        show the effect, 239–41
    real explanation, the, 232–33
    Relay Assembly Test Room, 227–29
    replacements and more learning, the two,
        236–38
    skepticism about productivity-enhancing
        design, 81–82, 219
    subsequent experiments do not find a, 6,
        231
Hayes, Robert, 38
Heating:
    Environmental Protection Agency (EPA), 53
    geothermal heat pumps, 132–35
    home energy use, 193
    refrigeration, 176–77
    see also Cogeneration; HVAC
        (heating/ventilation and air
        conditioning)

Heat islands, urban, 199–202
Henningsen Cold Storage Company, 74
Herkstroter, Cor, 25–26
Hibarger, Homer, 223, 227, 232, 233, 239
Hirshberg, Gary, 192
Hofstra University, 124
Home Energy Loan Program, 194–95
Home energy use, 192–96
Homemade Money, 194
Home Weatherization Assistance Program, 193
Hot water systems, 193
HVAC (heating/ventilation and air
        conditioning), 8
    Basic Science Building (Houston), 60
    BlueCross BlueShield of Oregon, 52
    cogeneration, 127
    Compaq, 105–6
    Comstock building (Pittsburgh), 75
    General Motors, 163
    geothermal heat pumps, 132–35
    Intelligent Workplace, The, 96
    Lee Eng Lock, 105
    Perkin-Elmer, 145
    Ridgehaven office building (San Diego), 51
    schools, 198
    semiconductor manufacturing, 108–10
    solar heating, 137
    systematic approach to improving, 72–73
    Texas LoanSTAR program, 58, 60–61
    Wal-Mart, 84–85
    West Bend Mutual Insurance Company, 95
    Xerox, 190
Hyde Tools, 91–92
Hydrofluorocarbons, 159
Hydrogen, natural gas converted to, 161
Hydrogen fuel-cell powered cars, 25

IAC, *see* Industrial Assessment Centers
IBM, 110
Illinois, 191
Improvement, *see* Continuous improvement,
    cool
Indoor air quality, 51, 52
Industrial Assessment Centers (IACs), 124, 153,
    192, 213–14
Industrial Revolution, 37
Industry, Technology, and the Environment, 44
Industry of the Future Program, 211–12
Inefficiency, 4. *See also* Energy efficiency
Information technology, 16, 22
Infrared systems for mold drying, 175–76
Ink jet printers, 70
In Search of Excellence (Peters), 82, 219–20, 222
Instantaneous payback, 4
Insulation, 80, 193
Intelligent Workplace, The, 6, 78–79, 96–97
Interface, Inc., 216
    decarbonization, 181–86
    embodied energy, 10
    lighting, efficient, 5, 77
    productivity-enhancing design, 82–83
    solar energy, 137
Intergovernmental Panel on Climate Change,
    21

Internal rate of return (IRR), 55. *See also*
    Investments and returns, energy efficiency
    and
International Council for Local Environmental
    Initiatives (ICLEI), 198
International Energy Agency, 26
International Fuel Cells, 128
International Organization for Standards
    (ISO), 110
International Performance Measurement and
    Verification Protocol (IPMVP), 56–58, 60,
    210
Introduction to Social Research, 227
Investments and returns, energy efficiency and,
    5, 55, 216
    Anheuser-Busch, 136
    BlueCross BlueShield of Oregon, 52–53
    building upgrades, 73
    Burns Harbor steel mill, 175
    Centerplex, 48–51
    Compaq, 102–3
    cool companies, 47
    Dow Chemical, 158
    Energy Star programs, 54
    geothermal heat pumps, 134
    Intelligent Workplace, The, 97
    International Performance Measurement
        and Verification Protocol (IPMVP),
        56–58
    lighting, efficient, 64
    Lockheed-Martin, 94
    low-risk and high-return investments,
        54–56
    motors and motor systems, 140–41
    Pennsylvania Power and Lighting Company,
        90–91
    productivity gains dwarfing energy gains,
        99
    Reno (NV) post office, 88–89
    Ridgehaven office building (San Diego),
        51–52
    Superior Fibers, 124
    Texas LoanSTAR program, 58–63
    West Bend Mutual Insurance Company, 96
    Xerox, 188

Jackson, Darryl, 171
Jackson, Dugald C., 223–27, 238
Japan, 4, 18, 217
Jennings, John, 16
Johnson Controls, 72
Johnston County (NC), 60–61
Jones, Stephen, 228
Juran, Joseph, 35
Just-in-time (JIT) manufacturing systems, 85,
    175

Kalwall Corporation, 116
Kats, Gregory, 56
Kimura, Ben, 93
Kraft General Foods, 176–77
Krol, John A., 159
Kwinana (Australia), 207–8
Kyoto Conference on the Climate in 1997:

    future for American companies, 217
    lean thinking/production system, 44
    price of carbon dioxide, 11, 205
    Royal Dutch/Shell, 26
    trading system, international, 208
    warming, global, 21

Laptop computers, 71
Laser printers, 70
Lauret, Ronald W., 95
Lausche State Office Building (Cleveland), 54
Lawrence Berkeley National Laboratory, 201
Lean and Clean Management (Romm), 34
*Lean Thinking: Banish Waste and Create Wealth
    in Your Corporation,* 39
Lean thinking/production system, 4
    American companies, opportunity for,
        43–44
    Compaq, 103–4
    Comstock building (Pittsburgh), 75–76
    design, new building, 98–99
    Ford, Henry, 30–35
    Ford Motors, 45
    home energy use, 194
    Kyoto Conference on the Climate in 1997,
        44
    operations and process, 37–39
    process improvement and prevention-
        oriented design, 4
    productivity, clean production/cool design
        improving, 40–43
    Shingo and Taiichi Ohno, Shigeo, 35–37
    Toyota, 28–30, 44–45
    whys, Taiichi Ohno and the five, 39–40
    see also individual subject headings
Lean Thinking (Womack & Jones), 180
Learning curve and the Hawthorne experiment,
    233–36
"Learning From Waste" (Ford), 31–32
Leasing, 183, 184
Lee Eng Lock, 6, 100, 105–6, 108, 110
Legislation:
    Clean Air Act, 208, 209
    Public Utility Regulatory Policy Act of 1978
        (PURPA), 121
Leo J. Daly, 88
Life-cycle analysis, 75, 78, 103–4, 129, 146
Lighting, efficient, 6, 8
    basic hardware in upgrade, 66–67
    BlueCross BlueShield of Oregon, 52
    Boeing, 64–65
    Carnegie Mellon University, 78
    Compaq, 103, 104
    Comstock building (Pittsburgh), 75
    end user, focus on the, 67–69
    Energy Resource Center, 182
    Energy Star programs, 53
    halogen lamps, 49–50
    Hawthorne Effect, 222–27
    Henningsen Cold Storage Company, 74
    home energy use, 194
    Hyde Tools, 91–92
    individual control over lighting levels,
        86–87, 98

Intelligent Workplace, The, 97
Interface, Inc., 5, 77, 83
Lockheed-Martin, 92–93
Malden Mills, 116–17
M.D. Anderson Cancer Center, 58
occupancy sensors, 49, 50, 66, 117
Pennsylvania Power and Lighting Company, 89–91
Prince Street Technologies, 183
productivity, 63, 82
Reno (NV) post office, 88
schools, North Carolina, 78, 83–84
semiconductor manufacturing, 112
Texas LoanSTAR program, 60
VeriFone, 77, 80
Wal-Mart and Target, 84–85
West Bend Mutual Insurance Company, 95
Light surfaces and urban heat islands, 200–202
Lincoln Park-Clybourn Corridor community (IL), 191
Literature and the Hawthorne experiment, 222, 227–28
Loans for energy improvements, 58–63, 194–95, 213
Lockheed-Martin, 72, 78, 92–94
Loftness, Vivian, 82, 219, 243
Long Beach (CA), 73
Los Angeles (CA), 200–202
Lovins, Amory, 66, 111, 183
Lovins, Hunter, 183
Lucent Technologies, 9, 110, 140

MacKenzie, Jim, 189
Magnetic Metals Corp., 73
Maintenance, equipment, 53, 57
Malaysia, 7, 101, 109
Malden Mills, 1, 115–17
Management and the Worker (Roethlisberger & Dickson), 229
Managers, building, 106–7
Manila, 7, 101
Manufacturing:
　carbon dioxide, 14–15
　chemical, 10, 12–13, 41. *See also* Dow Chemical
　energy efficiency, 8
　fast-cycle, 36
　remanufacturing, 183, 186–90
　see also individual subject headings
Manufacturing Knowledge (Gillespie), 242
Maple trees, 202
Marikkar, Rahumathulla, 185
Massachusetts Electric Company, 115, 116, 193
Mayo, Elton, 219–20, 222, 229, 237, 240
McDonald's, 8, 134
McLean, Robert, 88
M.D. Anderson Cancer Center, 58
Measurements, energy-related, 185. *See also* Monitoring energy use
Mercer County (NJ), 210
Metal processing, *see* Automobiles; Steel industry
Methane, 26
Microcosm, corporate, 18–19

MicroGrid, Inc., 52
Microprocessors, 29, 151
Microturbines, 126–27
Minnesota Power's Industrial Conservation Pilot Program, 172
Model T, 30–35
Money and the Hawthorne experiment, 220, 233–36
Monitoring energy use:
　Energy Management Control System (EMCS), 48, 57–58, 60–61, 105, 109
　Interface, Inc., 185–86
　Perkins, Ron, 106
　Regal Fruit Co-op, 149
　Ridgehaven office building (San Diego), 51
　Student Recreation Center (TX), 61
　Texas LoanSTAR program, 59
　Trapman (steam monitoring device), 160
Monitors, computer, 71
Moody-Stuart, Mark, 26
Mort, Thomas, 162
Motors and motor systems, 8
　Alumax, 150
　Burns Harbor steel mill, 174–75
　case studies from around the world, 152
　compressed air, 152–54
　conclusions, 155–56
　control, the importance of, 151–52
　Decatur Foundry, 175–76
　Energy, Department of (DOE), 210
　Greenville Tube Company, 147–48
　inefficiency of most, 140
　investments and returns, energy efficiency and, 140–41
　maintenance and scrap, productivity increases/ decreases in, 9
　Nisshinbo California, 150–51
　oversized and undersized motors, 148–49
　Perkin-Elmer, 145–46
　planning for burnt-out motors, 141–42
　process improvement, 146
　Regal Fruit Co-op, 149–50
　replacing inefficient, 146
　resources for improving, 156
　Southwire Company, 154–55
　3M, 142–45
　variable-speed drives, 28–29, 151–52, 155, 170, 174–75, 210
Multi-year strategies, 14
Musashino Brewery, 152

National Aeronautics and Space Administration (NASA), 128, 136
National Renewable Energy Laboratory, 75
National Research Council (NRC), 223
National Science Foundation, 136
National Wildlife Federation, 144
Natural Capitalism (Lovins, Lovins & Hawken), 183
Natural gas technologies, 7, 21, 145, 161
Natural Lighting Company, 84
Nelson, Ken, 12, 13, 49, 158
New Energy Ventures, 125
New York City Department of Sanitation, 137

New York City Transit Authority, 137
New York Times, 23
Nigeria, 17, 23
Nisshinbo California, 150–51
Nitrogen, *see* Oxides of nitrogen (NOx)
North Carolina schools, 78, 83–84, 198
Northern States Power, 144

Oberndorfer, Jim, 145–46
Occupancy sensors, 49, 50, 66, 117
Office equipment, improved, 69–72
Office of Energy Efficiency and Renewable
    Energy, 1, 13–14
Office of Industrial Technologies (OIT), 115
Ogoni people, 23
O'Hearn, Tom, 135
Ohno, Taiichi, 33, 35–37, 39–40, 105
Oil & Gas Journal, 24
Oil refineries, 178. *See also* British Petroleum
    (BP); Royal Dutch/Shell
Okotec office building (Berlin), 137
Olson, James P., 192
Ontario Hydro, 185
Operations and maintenance (O&M), 57–63
Operations and process, distinction between,
    37–39
Oregon State University (OSU), 153
Organization for Economic Cooperation and
    Development (OECD), 22
Organization of Petroleum Exporting
    Countries (OPEC), 19
O'Rourke, Ernie, 161
Ortho-McNeil Pharmaceuticals, 64
Output vs. time, relationship between, 233
Oversized motors, 148–49
Oxides of nitrogen (NOx):
    Boeing, 64
    British Petroleum, 209
    DuPont, 159
    energy efficiency and decarbonization, 3
    Malden Mills, 115
    SYCOM, 11, 210
Ozone, 200, 202

Pacific Gas and Electric Co. (PG&E), 70
Paint booths, 28–29
Palo Alto Research Center, 15, 190
Pape, Louise, 79
Pape, William R., 79
Paper industry, 170–72
Parker Chiropractic College, 72–73
Particulates, 3, 202
Payback time, 5, 81. *See also* Investments and
    returns, energy efficiency and
Pearce, Harry, 162
Pearl Harbor, 18
Pennock, George, 227, 236
Pennsylvania Power and Lighting Company,
    89–91
Pentagon, the, 136
Perfluorocarbons, 159
Perkin-Elmer, 9, 145–46
Perkins, Ron, 6, 100, 102–6, 108, 156
Pfeiffer, Eckhard, 101, 108

Philadelphia (PA), 121–22, 199
Phillips 66, 134
Photovoltaics, *see* Solar energy
Picard, John, 182
PICOS, 192
Pig-iron hauling experiment, 234
Pinch analysis, 177–79
Pinckley, Marion, 135
Pistorio, Pasquale, 110
Pitcher, Brian, 233
Planetec Utility Services, 178, 179
Planning, strategic, 3, 14, 212–15. *See also* Royal
    Dutch/Shell
Plug Power, 129
Pollution, 4, 42. *See also* Carbon dioxide;
    Emissions, polluting; Price of carbon
    dioxide
Pollution Prevention Pays program, 144
Polyethylene terephthalate (PET), 183
Pool, Jonathan, 48–50
Porter, Michael, 42, 45
Post office, designing the Reno (NV), 87–89
Potomac Electric and Power Company, 67
Power, cool, 7
    emissions reductions and energy efficiency,
        8
    examples of companies using, 113–14
    Four Times Square building (NY), 138–39
    management controls, power, 70, 71
    Royal Dutch/Shell, 20–21
    strategy for, 139
    two types of, 113
    utilities, local, 195
    see also Cogeneration; Energy efficiency;
        Renewable energy
Power transmission/distribution, inefficiencies
    in, 155
Praxair Company, 161
President's Council on Sustainable
    Development, 144, 181
Prevention-oriented design strategies, 4. *See
    also* Energy efficiency; Productivity-
    enhancing design
Price of carbon dioxide:
    British Petroleum, 206–9
    Kyoto Conference on the Climate in 1997,
        11, 205
    loan fund, revolving, 213
    planning, strategic, 214–15
    range of potential prices, 205
    steel industry, 211–12
    studies on the, 212
    supplier IAC, 213–14
    SYCOM, 209–11
    trading system for carbon, national, 208–9,
        213
Prince Street Technologies, 83, 183
Printers, 70
Process and operations, distinction between,
    37–39
Process improvement:
    basic staple of lean thinking, 4
    Compaq, 107
    Interface, Inc., 185

motors and motor systems, 147, 149–50
Regal Fruit Co-op, 147–49
3M, 145
see also Energy efficiency; Productivity-
enhancing design
Process industries, 9, 15, 157. *See also* Dow
Chemical; *specific industry*
Procter & Gamble, 196
Production system, the workplace viewed as a,
87
Productivity:
building upgrades, 47, 53
clean production/cool design improving,
40–43
gains in, 5–6
lighting, efficient, 6, 63–65
waste reduction, 41–42
see also Hawthorne Effect
Productivity-enhancing design:
barriers to, 76, 78
California Steel Industries, 86–87
Compaq, 104
Comstock building (Pittsburgh), 75–76
conclusions, 98–99
end-user, designing for the, 85–86
examples of, 77–78
green buildings, 74–75
Hyde Tools, 91–92
Intelligent Workplace, The, 96–97
Interface, Inc., 82–83
Lockheed-Martin, 92–94
Pennsylvania Power and Lighting, 89–91
remanufacturing, 186–90
Reno (NV) post office, 87–89
schools, North Carolina, 83–84
service companies, 43
skepticism about, 81–82
thinking, shift in corporate, 6
VeriFone, 79–81
Wal-Mart and Target, 84–85
West Bend Mutual Insurance Company,
94–96
why isn't everyone doing it right?, 76
Profits, 1, 42, 44. *See also* Investments and
returns, energy efficiency and
Proton exchange membrane (PEM) fuel cell,
129–30, 196
Publications and the Hawthorne experiment,
222, 227–28

Quad/Graphics, 197
Quality:
end-of-pipe approach to, 44
Quality Utilizing Employee Suggestions and
Teamwork (QUEST), 182
systematic approach to, 35
see also Lean thinking/production system

Rank Xerox, 188–89
Rate of return, *see* Investments and returns,
energy efficiency and
Rebates for energy efficiency, 146
Recycling, 183
Reengineering, environmental, 149–50

Refrigeration, 176–77, 193–94
Regal Fruit Co-op, 149–50
Regulations, state-based utility, 119, 121
Rehm, Bill, 87
Remanufacturing, 183, 186–90
Renewable energy, 113
advances in, 8
biomass energy, 20–21, 24, 135–36
costs of, decreasing, 130
geothermal heat pumps, 132–35
hydrogen fuel-cell powered cars, 25
Royal Dutch/Shell, 17, 20–21, 24, 130–31, 209
Toyota, 8
wind power, 20, 21, 132
see also Solar energy
Reno (NV) post office, designing the, 87–89
Rensselaer Polytechnic Institute (RPI), 95
Research Methods in Psychology, 227–29
Reskusic, Petar, 49, 100
Resources, heavy reliance on, 43
Rest periods and the Hawthorne experiment,
234–35
Retrofits, systematic energy:
forest products industry, 170
heating/cooling loads, reducing, 51
Massachusetts Electric Company, 193
SYCOM, 210
Texas A&M, 210
Texas LoanSTAR program, 58
3M, 144
VeriFone, 70
see also Productivity-enhancing design
Return on investment (ROI), 5, 12–13, 165–66.
See also Investments and returns, energy
efficiency and
Richards, Roy, Jr., 155
Ridgehaven office building (San Diego), 4, 46,
51–52
River Market Brewing Company, 123
Robertson, Chris, 111
Robinson, Russell, 94
Rochelle Municipal Utilities (IL), 125
Rocky Mountain Institute, 85, 111, 194
Roethlisberger, F. J., 229–30, 237, 239
Roof insulation, 52
Roofs, use of white on, 200–202
Rosenfeld, Arthur, 56
Rousseau, Imogen, 242
Royal Darwin Hospital, 152
Royal Dutch/Shell:
benchmark for strategic planning, 16
Brent Spar (oil storage tank), 22–23
climate change, global, 217
dematerialization, 16, 22
emissions, polluting, 3
planners of, 17–20
purpose and long-term goals, rethinking,
23–27
renewable energy, 17, 130–31, 209
Shell Hydrogen, 25
Shell Solar, 24
sustained growth with cool power, 20–21
Russell, Allen, 89
Rutgers University, 192

Sacramento Municipal Utility District (SMUD), 136, 203
San Diego Environmental Services Department (ESD), 51
Savings, *see* Investments and returns, energy efficiency and
Scanlon, Paul, 75–76
Scenario planning, 18–20, 26–27. *See also* Royal Dutch/Shell
"Scenarios of the U.S. Carbon Reductions: Potential Impacts of Energy Technologies by 2010 and Beyond," 212
Schneider, Al, 134
Schools:
    communities, cool, 198
    HVAC (heating/ventilation and air conditioning), 198
    North Carolina, 78, 83–84, 198
    Philadelphia, 199
    Texas, north, 60–61, 198
    Waverly Junior-Senior High School (NY), 117–19, 198
Scott Paper Company, 152
Seay, Tom, 85
Semiconductor manufacturing, 6–7, 100–101, 108–12
Sempra Energy Solutions, 184
Service sector companies, 14, 43
Shingo, Shigeo, 35–37, 234
Short-term focus of facilities management, 102
Siemens Solar Industries, 112
Silicon Graphics workstations, 109
Silicon ingots, 112
Simple payback, 5
Sirchio, Jennie, 236
Skepticism about productivity-enhancing design, 81–82, 219. *See also* Hawthorne Effect
Skyscrapers, cool, 8, 114, 138–39
Smog, 200, 201
Smokejack, 120
Snow, Charles E., 223
Solar energy, 20
    British Petroleum, 209
    examples of buildings using, 137
    heating, solar thermal, 137–38
    home energy use, 195–96
    Interface, Inc., 137
    photovoltaics, 21, 24, 136–37, 195–96
    Shell Solar, 24
    Siemens Solar Industries, 112
    Sun Station, 24–25
Solarex, 137
Solar Turbines, 115, 125–26
Soldiering, 225, 240
Southern California Gas Company, 182
Southland Industries, 73
Southwire Company, 154–55
Speed controls for motors, electronic, 151–52, 155, 174, 175, 210
Spender, J. A., 34
St. Francis Hotel, 64
Steam systems:
    Alliance to Save Energy and DOE, 173

Bethlehem Steel, 173–75
    carbon dioxide, 158, 159
    crucial for production, 158
    DuPont, 159–62
    examples of companies efficient use of, 9–10
    forest products industry, 170–72
    General Motors, 162–64
    pinch analysis, 177–79
    Watt, James, 120
    see also Cogeneration
Steel: A National Resource for the Future, 211
Steel industry:
    decarbonization, 190–92
    future, vision for the, 211–12
    steam systems, 172–76
    variable-speed drives, 152
    voluntary plan to reduce emissions, 11
Steel Manufacturers Association (SMA), 211, 212
STMicroelectronics, 6–7, 100–101, 110–12
Stonyfield Farm, 191–92
Strategic planning, 3, 14, 212–15. *See also* Royal Dutch/Shell
Student Recreation Center (TX), 61
Submetering to track electricity use, 50
Suggestion system, employee, 167–69, 182
Sulfur dioxide, 3, 11, 64, 202, 208, 209
Sun Station, 24–25
Suntory, 152
Superconducting cable, 155
Superior Die Set Corporation, 91
Superior Fibers, 113–14, 124–25
Supersymmetry, 6, 100–101, 108–10
Suppliers, 192, 213–14
Support staff, valuing and training, 106–7
Sure Power Corporation, 128–29
Sustainability Report, 181–82
Sustainable development/growth, 20–21, 24–26
Sweden, 101
Switzerland, 133
SYCOM, 11, 209–11, 218
Systematic approach to solving problems, *see* Lean thinking/production system

Target, 84
Taylor, Frederick, 36, 234–35, 242
Technology:
    carbon dioxide reductions, 3
    dematerialization, 22
    energy efficiency, 16
    information, 16, 22
    power, cool, 7
    Toyota, 4
    see also Renewable energy; *individual subject headings*
Technology Review, 186
Telecommunications, 22
Telecommuting, 197
Temperature sensor calibration, 58
Texaco, 134
Texas A&M, 57–63, 198, 210, 211
Texas LoanSTAR program, 58–63
Texas schools, north, 60–61

Textile industry, 115–17, 150–51
Thermal Test Facility (Colorado), 75
Thermomechanical pumping (TMP), 172
Thinking disconnected from doing, 37
3M, 2, 142–45, 216
Time, reducing wasted, 32–34, 36
Time vs. output relationship, the, 233
Today and Tomorrow (Ford), 31
Total Factor Productivity (TFP), 41
Towers Complex (San Jose), 54
Toyoda, Eiji, 35
Toyota, 216
    California, Toyota Auto Body of, 28–30
    climate change, global, 217
    energy efficiency, 3–4
    proton exchange membrane (PEM) fuel
        cell, 129
    renewable energy, 8, 130, 131
    today and tomorrow, 44–45
Trading, emissions, 208–9, 213
Training magazine, 169
Training and valuing support staff, 106–7,
    166–67, 188
Transportation, 22, 196–98
Trapman (steam monitoring device), 160
Trees, planting, 10, 24, 191, 202–4
Trigen Energy Corporation, 121–23
Triple bottom line, 23–24
Turbines:
    Bethlehem Steel, 158
    Burns Harbor steel mill, 173
    Malden Mills, 115–16
    microturbines, 126–27
    Solar Turbines, 125–26
    see also Motors and motor systems
Turning Off the Heat (Casten), 121
Turnover of facilities/managers/building
    operators, 106

Ulrich, Roger, 98
Ultramar Diamond Shamrock, 178
Undersized motors, 148
Uninterruptible power supply system (UPS),
    128–29
United Illuminating, 133
United Jersey Bank, 210
United Technologies, 128, 184
University of Illinois, 69
Unnecessary operations, getting rid of, 38–39
UN's Intergovernmental Panel on Climate
    Change, 217
Utilities, local, 195

Vacuum Arc Remelt furnace, 190
van der Veer, Jeroen, 24, 26
Variable flow, 150
Variable-speed motor drives (VSDs):
    Bethlehem Steel, 174–75
    core of any motor upgrade, at the,
        151–52
    Energy, Department of (DOE), 210
    forest products industry, 170
    microprocessors, 151

Southwire Company, 155
Toyota, 28–29
Veiling reflections, 89, 90
Ventilation systems, 58, 72, 97, 141, 151. *See
    also* HVAC (heating/ventilation and air
    conditioning)
VeriFone, 5, 70, 77, 79–81
Volatile organic hydrocarbons (VOCs), 202–3

Wack, Pierre, 18
Wages and the Hawthorne experiment, 220,
    233–36
Walker, Karen, 102
Wal-Mart, 47, 84–85
Warming, global, 20–23, 25–26, 44, 212, 217
Washers, clothes, 194
Washington Post, 167, 222
Waste Elimination Idea Book, 166–67
Waste Heat Ammonia Absorption Refrigeration
    Plant (WHAARP), 178–79
Waste reduction:
    Dynamic Manufacturing, 41–42
    Ford, Henry, 30–35
    Interface, Inc., 182, 183
    Ohno, Taiichi, 39
    Xerox, 15, 47, 189–90
    zero waste company, 182
Wastewater treatment, 114, 161
Water systems, hot, 138, 193
Watkins, James, 176–77
Watt, James, 120
Waverly Junior-Senior High School (NY),
    117–19, 198
Way Station, The, 47, 74
Wealth of Nations (Smith), 37
Weeping willow trees, 203
Weld, William, 176
West Bend Mutual Insurance Company, 94–96
Western Australia Department of Agriculture,
    207
Western Digital, 7, 101, 109
Western Electric, 61, 223, 237. *See also*
    Hawthorne Effect
Whitehead, Thomas N., 229, 234
White roofs, the use of, 200–202
Whys, Taiichi Ohno and the five, 39–40
Wilson, Edward O., 98
Windheim, Lee, 87, 88
Windows, 72, 80, 193
Wind power, 20, 21, 132
Wisconsin, 191
Wohlstetter, Roberta, 18
Wood use, reducing, 31
World Environment Center, 144
Worldwide Office Environment Index Survey,
    63
Wright, Frank L., 87

Xenergy, 146, 151
Xerox, 15, 47, 186–90

Zero-carbon energy sources, 114
Zero waste company, 182